S0-BAL-222

THE EUROPEAN
CULTURE AREA

Harper & Row Series in Geography
Donald W. Meinig, Advisor

THE EUROPEAN CULTURE AREA
A Systematic Geography

TERRY G. JORDAN
North Texas State Universerty

HARPER & ROW, PUBLISHERS
New York   Evanston   San Francisco   London

THE EUROPEAN CULTURE AREA: A Systematic Geography

Copyright © 1973 by Terry G. Jordan

Printed in the United States of America. All rights reserved. No part of this book may be used or reproduced in any manner whatsoever without written permission except in the case of brief quotations embodied in critical articles and reviews. For information address Harper & Row, Publishers, Inc., 10 East 53rd Street, New York, N.Y. 10022

Standard Book Number: 06–043448–1

Library of Congress Catalog Card Number: 72–8264

Contents

List of Illustrations

Preface

One of the major recent trends in geography has been the reassessment of the traditional *regional* approach, coupled with a related rise of *systematic* or *topical* geography, both in research and in teaching. The principal difficulty with most traditional regional courses lies not in the fact that they deal with regions, but rather in the way the geographical material concerning those regions is subdivided. The general practice of both European and American geographers who teach or write textbooks for use in a course such as Europe has been to subdivide the subject matter further on a regional basis. Typically, Europe is fragmented into a series of subregions of varying rank and order. Most textbooks heretofore available display this approach, normally with political boundaries as the main borders. Now admittedly the political boundaries in Europe are very important, but it does not follow that they should serve as the structural basis for the entire geographical study of the area. Equally important distributions of languages, types of agriculture, population, climate, and the like have been obscured by the worship of these notoriously fluid political borders. Those textbook writers who have, at least to some degree, departed from the political framework usually have fallen back on *terrain* or landforms to provide regional borders. In view of the fact that the geographer's interest centers on the *people* of Europe, it is hardly justifiable to award the physical environment so much importance.

The crux of the problem, in my view, is the decision to subdivide the geographical subject matter of Europe along political or physical lines. One of the principal criticisms directed against traditional regional geography is that it tends to be purely descriptive, devoid of problem formulation and explanation of areal variations.

Seven years of experience in teaching European geography have convinced me that regional courses should be systematic or topical in organization. A glance at the chapter titles will reveal a topic-by-topic division of the subject matter rather than the traditional region-by-region and subregion-by-subregion treatment. I am convinced that this arrangement is superior because it facilitates observation and explanatory analysis of areal variations in Europe *as a whole,* variations which tend to be concealed in traditional regional studies. Viewing the various areal distributions topic by topic, the student is in a better position to understand the all-important geographical "why?".

The systematic and regional methods are by no means mutually exclusive, as many geographers have noted. Indeed, setting up a systematic outline of subject material leads logically to regional considerations on a secondary level. A chapter on the geography of agriculture is concerned in no small part with agricultural *regions,* a chapter on political geography with political *regions* (nations). Where the present book differs from other European geography texts is in the systematic chapter organization. It retains ties to regional geography both through specialization on the region of Europe and through consideration of the regional characteristics of the several geographical topics.

Systematic organization allows, even demands, much more attention to cause-and-effect relationships than has been true of traditional regional European geography texts. Rarely do considerations of central-place theory, Thünenian agricultural-location theory, factors of industrial location, or causal forces in political geography find their way into a geography textbook about Europe. I feel that such considerations are vital if we are to pass on to our students something more than an encyclopedia of geographical facts about Europe, if we are to escape the "places and products" syndrome in undergraduate "regional" geography courses. The present book, then, represents a systematic or topical treatment of a region.

Another unique feature of the present book is the use, insofar as is practical, of place names as spelled and pronounced in the individual countries. The long-accepted English modification of numerous names has been discarded, and the reader will find Roma, München, and Beograd in place of Rome, Munich, and Belgrade. The English versions only lead to unnecessary confusion, as is indicated by the perhaps apocryphal story of the American tourist bound for Florence, Italy, who refused to get off the train at the station bearing the placard "Firenze." Indeed, the English forms are generally much less attractive than the native versions. It is almost beyond comprehension how anyone could take melodic names such as Napoli and Livorno and render them into the sterile Naples and Leghorn. One can seek in vain the purpose of adding a final silent *e* to Bern. To aid in the place-name transition, cross-references are included in the index. In several instances the native names are not used. If a city, river, mountain range, or other feature extends across linguistic borders and is known by more than one native name, then the English version is given preference. For example "Danube" is used rather than "Donau," "Duna," or "Dunarea"; "Carpathians" rather than "Carpatii" or "Karpaty"; and "Brussels" in the place of "Bruxelles" or "Brussel." The English is also used if the native name conceals a meaning that would be evident in English. "Black Forest" thereby gains preference as the direct translation of the German "Schwarzwald." The native form of such names will be listed in parentheses after the English version. In addition, the English names for nations will be used rather than the native forms.

Throughout the book, measurements in the metric system and centigrade thermometer will be used, with English and Fahrenheit figures given in parentheses.

The area and peoples of the western part of the Soviet Union are deliberately not given detailed attention. Most colleges and universities in the English-speaking world provide a separate course in the geography of the Soviet Union, and lengthy consideration of that country in a textbook on European geography would be redundant. In the chapters on physical geography, languages, religions, and several other topics, brief mention is made of parts of the Soviet Union, mainly those parts included in peripheral western republics, such as the Baltic states Byelorussia, Moldavia, and the Ukraine. The undeniable European character of these areas warrants at least partial inclusion in the present text.

T. G. J.

THE EUROPEAN
CULTURE AREA

CHAPTER ONE

Europe: A culture rather than a continent

1.1 THE MISCONCEPTION OF EUROPE AS A CONTINENT

Defining Europe is by no means so simple as might be imagined. The most commonly encountered definition, and the one which first comes to mind, is "a continent." Many may recall from elementary school days being asked to recite the names of the family of continents, in which Europe held a place of full membership. Impressive support for the continental status of Europe can be found in various dictionaries and in the writings of numerous twentieth-century geographers. For example, *Webster's New Collegiate Dictionary* (1954) defined Europe as a "continent, Eastern Hemisphere," and the geographer Mark Jefferson described it as "one of the smaller continents." Numerous other examples of a similar nature could be cited in support of the traditional definition of Europe as a continent, as a *distinct physical entity*.

A continent is understood by geographers to be a sizable landmass which stands more or less separate from other landmasses. North and South America, connected by the narrow Isthmus of Panama, are continents, as are Africa, linked to Asia only by the severed land bridge at Suez, and Australia, which is isolated from other landmasses by surrounding seas.

Europe, however, cannot qualify as a continent in the sense of being a separate physical entity. To be sure, there is a clear separation from Africa to the south in the form of the Mediterranean Sea, and the western and northern limits are well defined by the Atlantic and Arctic oceans. It is in the east that the idea of continentality does not apply. Only the hint of a water separation is found in the southeastern fringe, where the sea reaches northward from the Mediterranean, through the Aegean, Dardanelles, and Bosporus to the Black Sea, and still beyond to the Sea of Azov. There the division ends, and to the north of Azov stretch the vast expanses of Russia. Instead of a narrow isthmus similar to Panama or Suez, the map reveals a wedge of land broadening steadily to the east, welding Europe and Asia into one large continent commonly called Eurasia. Europe lacks the clear-cut physical border, and as a result is not a continent. In fact, a glance at a map of the Eastern Hemisphere reveals that Europe is simply one rather small appendage of the continent Eurasia, merely a westward-reaching peninsula. At most, Europe forms only about one-fifth of the area of Eurasia.

1.2 EUROPE AS A CONTINENT: ORIGIN OF THE MYTH

The erroneous belief that Europe possesses the characteristics of a continent was passed down to the modern day from the civilizations of the classical Mediterranean, in particular from the Greeks and Romans. The Greco–Roman world-view in turn may have been shaped in part by other, older cultures. One theory concerning the origin of the words *Europe* and *Asia* relates them to the Semitic Assyrian–Phoenician *ereb* ("sunset") and *acu* ("sunrise"). Thus the "land of the sunset," Europe, may have first appeared as an entity among the peoples of the Fertile Crescent, meaning simply "the western land."

Figure 1.1 Hecataeus' world map, circa 500 B.C. Note that the Caspian Sea is linked to the open ocean and that Europe and Asia are tied together only by an isthmus. (After Parker.)

From their vantage point on the Aegean, the ancient Greeks perceived a world divided into three parts—Europe, Africa, and Asia—and the Romans, who were empire builders rather than map-makers, accepted the Greek outlook. Greece was always a nation of seafarers, and her sailors from the time of Ulysses and earlier had charted the marine separation of Europe and Africa. The "Land of the Lotus Eaters" described by Homer in the *Odyssey* was in all probability present-day Tunisia. In addition, the Greeks knew of a division of Africa and Asia, for the Phoenicians before them had circumnavigated the African continent. However, the Greeks and other classical peoples regarded the Nile River rather than the Red Sea as the border between Asia and Africa. The Argonauts and other Greek explorers had probed the Dardanelles, Bosporus, and into the Black Sea, founding trading colonies as far away as present-day Russia, and the real cause of the lengthy Trojan wars chronicled in the *Iliad* was probably a struggle for control over the strategic Dardanelles, the water gateway to Black Sea trade. Greek explorers and merchants had reached beyond the Black Sea to the shores of the landlocked, saltwater Caspian Sea. Certain Greek scholars evaluating the information brought by traders rather naturally assumed that the saline Caspian was part of the ocean. To them, the isthmus between the Black and Caspian seas was the only land bridge connecting Europe and Asia (Figure 1.1). Little did they know that the Caspian was an inland sea, with no opening to the ocean, similar to the Great Salt Lake of the western United States, and that north of the Caspian stretched a huge expanse of land. Certain other classical scholars, including Strabo, Pomponius Mela, and Ptolemy, mistakenly believed that only a narrow isthmus lay north of the Black Sea and the Sea of Azov, separating them from the northern (Arctic) ocean, and they placed the Europe–Asia border along the course of the Don (Tanais) River (Figure 1.2). Their lack of accurate information had led

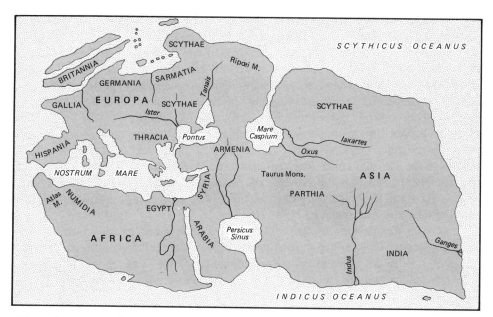

Figure 1.2 The world map of Pomponius Mela, A.D. 43. The Caspian is still shown as an embayment of the ocean, but the Tanais (Don) River is the eastern border of Europe. (After Parker.)

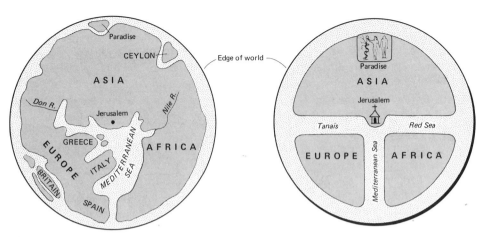

Figure 1.3   Two versions of the medieval "T in O" map, indicative of the low level of learning during the Dark Ages. Europe remains, as in classical Greek times, a separate continent.

them to whittle down the expansive Russian plains to a narrow land bridge. The classical Greeks and Romans, then, believed in a threefold division of the land-masses, and Europe was to them a separate physical entity.

From the Greeks and Romans, the concept of the three continents was passed intact to the monkish scholars of the medieval period. Perpetuation of the classical view was guaranteed when a Christian religious significance was attached to it in the Roman church. The result of churchly interpretation of cartography was the famous "T in O" map. It was believed that God, using the Latin alphabet, had fashioned the shape of the continents in such a way as to form the letters T, for *terrarum* ("earth"), and O, for *orbis* ("circle"). In this divine shorthand, the lower bar of the horizontal T was represented by the Mediterranean Sea, and the top bar was found in the Nile River (or Red Sea)–Aegean Sea–Black Sea–Don River line (Figure 1.3). In so doing, the medieval Christian scholars created a water separation of Europe and Asia by widening the Don River to marine propor-tions, discarding even the Greco–Roman isthmus connection. The letter O lay in the space between the outer perimeter of the three continents and the edge of the world, where imprudent mariners supposedly fell off into the void of space. The T- and O-shaped water areas surrounded Europe and Africa, both of which were quartercircles, and Asia, which had the shape of a semicircle. At the center of this ethnocentric Christian map was the holy city of Jerusalem, and far out in the inaccessible reaches of hinter Asia lay the abandoned Garden of Eden. The T-in-O map, which was still widely accepted in the 1300s, is a good indicator of the low level of scholarly learning in medieval times.

The Renaissance brought the revival of the more sophisticated, though still erroneous, Greco–Roman world map, with the isthmus concept restored (Figure 1.4). During the medieval period, much of the cartographic heritage of the classical period had been preserved by Arab scholars, and in the 1500s, when knowledge of Russia began to filter back to the west, men of learning first recognized that no isthmus existed north of the Black Sea and that the Don was a rather insignificant, short river whose headwaters did not even approach the great frozen ocean to the north. Instead of a relatively narrow land bridge, the

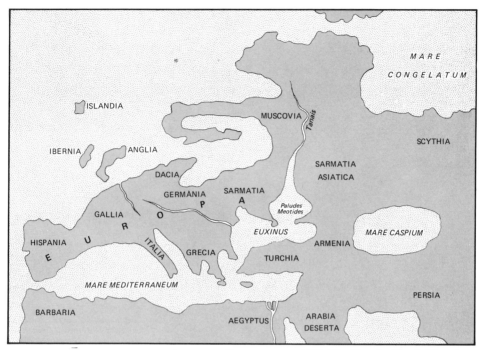

Figure 1.4 A portion of the world map by Grynaeus, A.D. 1532. The Tanais (Don) River has been magnified into a great waterway and its source incorrectly placed near the Arctic shore. The great width of Russia is reduced to a narrow isthmus. (After Parker.)

map-makers of Europe encountered a 2000-kilometer-wide wedge of land (about 1200 miles) between the White Sea in the north of Russia and the Sea of Azov in the south.

　　　Still the classical–medieval idea of European continentality persisted, and it has been passed down to the present day. Cartographers for the past 400 years or so resolved the problem rather unsatisfactorily by drawing an eastern border for Europe across the expanses of Russia approximately where the isthmus was formerly assumed to exist. Many different borders have been used through the years, and at one time or another just about every river and mountain range oriented in a north–south direction in Russia and western Siberia has served as some cartographer's boundary of Europe. Eventually one particular border gained widespread acceptance. It runs from the eastern end of the Black Sea along the crest of the Caucasus Mountains to the Caspian Sea, bends northward through the Caspian to the mouth of the Ural River, follows the Ural upstream to its head-waters in the Ural Mountains, and then extends north along the low, narrow Ural range to the shore of the Arctic Ocean (Figure 1.5). This utterly contrived border, which is still used by a surprising number of scholars, has no validity in either physical or human terms. It seeks out and elevates to a position of unwarranted importance an insignificant river and a low mountain ridge, the Urals, which is in no sense a barrier range or divider. It severs one of the most powerful nations in the world, the Soviet Union, leaving Russian-speaking people on either side of the border. The internal structure of the USSR is based on east–west contacts, with the directional flow of Soviet people and products at right angles to the

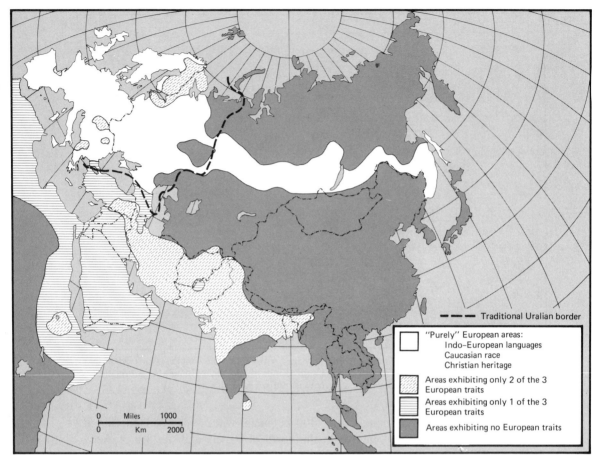

Figure 1.5   Europe defined areally on the basis of the three criteria.

Uralian "border" of Europe. In sum, the traditional eastern boundary of Europe is an unsatisfactory latter-day attempt to perpetuate the 2500-year-old idea of a Europe whose frontiers were physical in character. It has served only to preserve the myth that Europe is a continent in the geographical sense.

1.3 EUROPE AS A HUMAN ENTITY

Although Europe is not a continent and lacks physical geographical individuality, the idea that Europe is a separate entity persists, and courses in European geography and history are found in almost every university catalog. The explanation for this lies deeper than the mere perpetuation of a classical Greek misconception. In short, Europe is a human entity rather than a physical one, and its distinctiveness is to be sought in the character of the peoples who occupy it rather than in its physical environment. Europe is a *culture* which occupies a *culture area. Culture* may be defined briefly as a community of people who hold numerous features of belief, behavior, and overall way of life in common, including ideology, technology, social institutions, and material possessions. A "culture area" is any large area, usually contiguous, that is inhabited by people of a particular culture, a land upon which the visible imprint of that culture has been placed.

During the long period of belief in continental status, Europe was evolving and expanding as a culture area. Only gradually, and amid confusion which lingers still today, has Europe made the transition from physical to human entity. By the sixteenth century, when the isthmus concept was proven invalid, the human Europe was already well developed. This evolution of a culture area explains not only the numerous efforts to find a satisfactory eastern boundary for Europe since the 1500s, but also the remarkable survival of the myth of continentality in the face of contradictory evidence. The cartographers, aware that Europe was different from Asia, were simply trying to express this idea on their maps.

In a narrow sense, the European culture area can be defined as all Old World areas in which the people (1) have a religious tradition of *Christianity,* (2) speak one of the numerous related *Indo-European languages,* and (3) are of *Caucasian race.* Wherever in the Eastern Hemisphere these three basic human traits are combined, the result is "Europe." Beyond the Sahara Desert to the south lies the fundamentally different realm of the negroid peoples, where tribal religions (animism) or Islam and the languages belonging to the Bantu group dominate. Even North Africa, bordering the southern shore of the Mediterranean Sea, can claim only one "European" trait, a caucasoid population, for the inhabitants are predominantly Moslem and speak Semitic and Hamitic tongues. In southern and eastern Eurasia are found still other culture areas, including the Orient, whose population is dominantly mongoloid in race, Confucianist or Buddhist in religion, and Sino–Tibetan in speech. Only northern India, Iran, Pakistan, and Afghanistan can claim any large measure of European-ness, and they lack the very important Christian heritage. The areal extent of Europe is further confined by the presence of mongoloid Uralian and Altaic-speaking peoples in the interior of Eurasia and along the Arctic coast who are animistic, Moslem, or Buddhist.

Because Europe is a people and their culture, it has been subject to constant change. To present a detailed definition of Europe today requires the listing of additional traits, many of which were alien to it as recently as 300 years ago. To be sure, the three basic characteristics of race, language, and religion have persisted, though Christianity is in decline in much of Europe at present. But modern Europe is also distinguished by:

1. *A well-educated population.* The European culture, more than most others, places a high value on the written word as opposed to oral tradition. As a result, over 90 percent of all Europeans in most countries are literate, and in some nations it is illegal not to be. In West Germany, for example, about 99 percent of the population can read and write. As near as the southern shore of the Mediterranean, in Morocco, only about 15 percent of the people are literate, and in India to the east, only one person in five is able to read.

2. *A healthy population.* At birth most Europeans can expect to live between sixty and seventy-five years, as for example in the Netherlands, where the average male lives to age seventy-one. Across the Mediterranean in Algeria, the male life expectancy is only about *one-half* the Dutch average.

Another measure of the health conditions in a nation is the rate of infant mortality—the number of children per 1000 live births who do not survive to the age of one year. In European Sweden the infant mortality rate is only 13, while in African Tunisia it is 74, in African Ghana 113, and in Asian India 146 per 1000.

3. *A well-fed population.* The average daily calorie intake of the Europeans is far above the world average, and in no European nation is it less than the minimum total recommended for the development of healthy human beings. In contrast, the hunger and malnutrition of millions of Asians and Africans are among the great problems facing the world today.

4. *Birth and death rates far below world average.* Europe's educated population practices birth control, and the splendid medical facilities have caused a dramatic decline in the death rate. Some nations have stabilized or slightly declining populations. A greater contrast to the exploding population of the Orient and Middle East could hardly be imagined. Denmark and Greece, typical nations of northern and southern Europe, both have an annual rate of population increase of only 0.7 percent, less than one-half the rate of increase in Asiatic Saudi Arabia, and one-third the rate of Pakistan, the Congo, and Indonesia.

5. *An annual average national income per capita far above the world average.* The European receives enough not only for the necessities of life, but also for many luxuries. The net result is a very high standard of living, as judged by the precepts of Western Civilization. In areas adjacent to Europe, the large majority of Africans and Asians, less materialistic in their outlook, achieve a bare subsistence and live in what Europeans would call poverty. Per capita national income in Switzerland is over $2400, in Belgium over $1800, in Spain about $740, but in non-European Morocco only $186, in Nationalist China $270, and in Sudan $97.

6. *A population that is dominantly urban.* Most Europeans live in cities and towns. This is true of three-quarters of all West Germans, 82 percent of the British, and over 60 percent of the French. By way of comparison, only 13 percent of the Chinese, 14 percent of all Indians, and a quarter of the Turks and Algerians are urban-dwellers.

7. *An industrially oriented economy.* European industry is well developed and dominates the economy, while agriculture remains the livelihood of the majority of Asians and Africans. In western Europe, less than one-fifth of the people are farmers, while in both India and China the proportion of the population engaged in agriculture is over 70 percent.

8. *A market-oriented agriculture.* The Europeans who farm are commercial rather than subsistence agriculturists. The opposite is true in both Asia and Africa.

9. *An excellent transport system.* Europe is crisscrossed by a network of railroads, highways, inland waterways, pipelines, and airline routes, and few areas can be described as remote. The United Kingdom and France have between 370 and 430 kilometers (230 to 270 miles) of highway and 16 to

32 kilometers (10 to 20 miles) of railroad per 260 square kilometers (100 square miles) of territory. Other cultures do not place as high a value on movement from place to place. Communist China, for example, has only about 5 kilometers (3 miles) of highway and less than 1 kilometer (1 mile) of railroad per 260 square kilometers (100 square miles). In France and the United Kingdom, there are only 5 or 6 per automobile, but in India the figure is about 1,400 and in Communist China 22,000 per car.

10. *Nations that are old.* Most European states have long, distinguished, historical traditions reaching back many centuries, and the resultant stability is expressed in terms such as "there will always be an England." Beyond the Mediterranean in Africa, or to the east in Asia, on the other hand, relatively few nations are of any great age, and most gained their independence only since 1945. In many such Third World areas, allegiance to tribe or clan remains stronger than the tie to nation.

Many Europeans view their culture as a superior one and tend to judge other cultures by the standards of their own. This is a natural viewpoint for members of any culture to adopt. The feeling of superiority is quite evident in the work of the noted German writer, Thomas Mann. In his novel *The Magic Mountain,* Mann described two opposed principles in conflict for possession of the world—"force and justice, tyranny and freedom, superstition and knowledge, permanence and change. One may call the first Asiatic, the second European because Europe was a center of rebellion, the domain of intellectual . . . activity leading to change, while the Orient was characterized by quiescence and lack of change." One need not, indeed *should* not, accept the idea of European superiority, but it is important to recognize that Europe is distinctive, that it is a culture area unlike the others of the Old World.

Above all, Europe is the homeland of Western Civilization, a center of change and innovation. A "great" idea is one which, regardless of its merits or demerits, has wrought major changes in the world, and Europe is the source of just about every "great" idea that has, for better or worse, altered the human existence over the past millennium. To see the distinctiveness of Europe, to appreciate the degree to which this culture area has been a center of innovation, one need but plot on a map the place of origin of the "great ideas" which have revolutionized life since about A.D. 1000. Some of these innovations have proven to be boons to mankind. Others have brought great suffering and the threat of human extinction. Their common trait is that they all had a great impact on the world. It might be that the world would have been much better if Europe had never existed. But the overwhelming fact is that Europe has existed and changed the world.

Among the "great ideas" of Europeans is *democracy,* the child of classical Greece which reappeared in medieval Iceland and in the city-states of the Middle Ages and burst forth over much of Europe in the late 1700s and 1800s. Nowhere in Asia or Africa did this noble idea arise of its own accord, for, as Mann said, tyranny has been the rule there. Ironically, only a few years after Mann penned this sentiment, he was forced to flee his native country, Germany, to avoid being suppressed by one of the most totally tyrannical governments of all time, the nazism of the Third Reich. Even in Europe, its birthplace, democracy is often a rare and fleeting visitor. *Communism,* undeniably a "great" idea in terms of the numbers of people it has influenced, especially in China, is just as undeniably of European origin. *The Age of Discovery*, primarily the accomplishment of Italian and Iberian Europeans, allowed Europe to discover the remainder of the world, rather than the converse. The peoples of the great Asian civilizations did not choose to follow the stepping-stone islands to discover and colonize America or Australia. It was not the Chinese who sent traders and explorers to Europe, but rather the Italian Marco Polo who journeyed to China.

The *printing press,* a gift from the artisans of the German Rhine Valley, has had a tremendous impact in most parts of the world, revolutionizing man's means of communication. The concept of *the earth's rotundity,* developed by the classical Greeks, was revived by Italians and Iberians in the Age of Discovery, and the Polish astronomer Copernicus was the first to proclaim that the *earth revolves about the sun.* If Copernicus dealt a first great blow to human ego by removing the earth from the center of the universe, his fellow European Charles Darwin struck another in his *theory of evolution* by proposing that men were animals of humble biological ancestry rather than divine creatures made in the image of God. Perhaps the most far-reaching impact has resulted from the *Industrial Revolution,* the invention of machines and harnessing of inanimate power which arose in Britain and led to countless innovations, including the steam engine, railroad, internal-combustion engine, automobile, and radio, to mention but a few.

On the negative side, Europeans have given the world highly developed forms of *imperialism* or *colonialism,* with which they subjugated the unwilling inhabitants of most of the world's continents. From the time of ancient Greece to the present day, Europeans have founded overseas colonies and exploited the natural and human resources of those tributary areas. Still today, Europeans, together with their American offspring, consume the greater part of the world's natural resources, to the long-range detriment of the colonial areas which supply them. Also among the multitude of European "great ideas" is the concept of *genocide.* Only in Europe has a government ever undertaken the task of systematically murdering an entire ethnic group composed of many millions of people, a task well-nigh completed before opposing forces could intervene. The Turkish murder of Armenian Christians pales by comparison. European, too, is the obsession with *forced population movements* (see Chapter 3), the technique by which entire populations are uprooted and expelled from their ancestral homelands. Twentieth-century Europe has witnessed more of these forced movements than any other culture area at any time in history. While Europeans have recognized such fundamental natural truths as the *laws of motion and gravity,* discovered by the Englishman Isaac Newton, and the *theory of relativity,* conceived in the great mind of the German-born Albert Einstein, they

Figure 1.6   A measure of "European-ness." The twelve "European" traits (by national units) are as follows: (1) majority of population speaks an Indo-European language; (2) majority of population is Caucasian; (3) majority of population has Christian heritage; (4) 90 percent or more of population is literate; (5) infant mortality rate is twenty-five or less per thousand live births (fail to reach one year of age); (6) annual rate of population increase is ten or less per thousand population; (7) per capita annual income is $1000 or more; (8) 60 percent or more of population lives in towns and cities of 2000 or more inhabitants; (9) 35 percent or more of work force is employed in manufacturing, mining, and construction industries; (10) density of railroad network is 6 or more kilometers of rail per 100 square kilometers (10 or more miles per 100 square miles); (11) no violent or illegal overthrow of government since 1950; and (12) at least 100 kilograms of fertilizer applied to each hectare of arable land per year (90 pounds per acre).

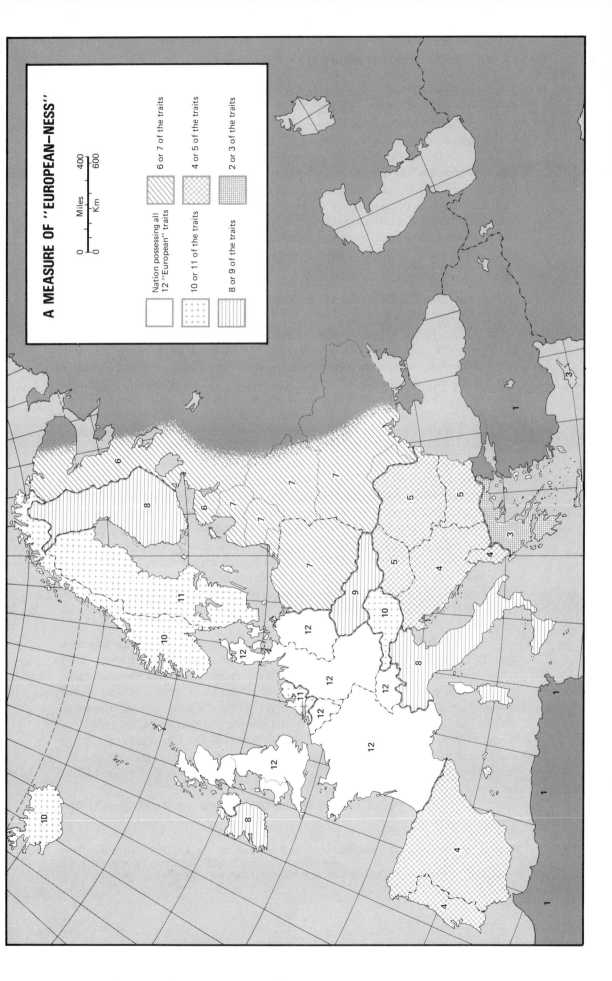

A MEASURE OF "EUROPEAN–NESS"

Miles
0   400

Km
0   600

Nation possessing all
12 "European" traits

6 or 7 of the traits

10 or 11 of the traits

4 or 5 of the traits

8 or 9 of the traits

2 or 3 of the traits

have used these for both good and ill. Had it not been for European innovations, the world would lack nuclear weapons.

Whether these various Europeans ideas have done more damage than good is not the question. As has been suggested, the Industrial Revolution may well lead to the destruction of the earth through environmental pollution, and European advances in medicine have contributed greatly to the overpopulation of the world. Indeed, European culture is drastically out of harmony with its physical environment and seems to be headed toward an unpleasant ecological judgment day. The point is, rather, that the inhabitants of the small piece of earth called Europe have had a far greater influence on the modern world as a whole than any other group, and it is this culture rather than physical features which makes Europe distinctive.

1.4 THE TERRITORIAL EXTENT OF EUROPE AS A CULTURE AREA

The rejection of both Europe's continentality and the equally unsatisfactory Uralian border necessitates the presentation of territorial limits more indicative of Europe's status as a culture area. In this respect, the major point to be made is that *Europe has no sharp borders*, and it is intellectually unprofitable to seek to draw a single line on a map to represent its outer limits. Rather, Europe blends gradually into other culture areas to the east, north, and south in broad transitional zones. This is true even if the defining characteristics are limited to the basic three: race, language, and religion (Figure 1.5). If the additional traits are mapped as well, a European core area appears in the northwestern and north-central parts, encompassing England, the Low Countries, northern France, Germany, northern Italy, and southern Scandinavia (Figure 1.6). This core exhibits *all* the various European characteristics. In any direction away from the core, the number of European traits gradually decreases, giving way to Asiatic cultures in the east and to African–Mid-Eastern peoples in the south. Italy is a splendid example of this transition. The northern part of that nation lies in the European core, but to journey south toward the heel and toe of the Italian boot is to witness a decline in literacy rate, a rise in birth rate, and a decrease in personal income, urbanism, and manufacturing. In the East, most of the gradual areal transition from Europe to Asia occurs within the Soviet Union.

The traits which define Europe and the areal extent of this culture area have changed considerably over the centuries. The territorial confines of Europe today are quite different from those of 1000 or 2000 years ago, for human phenomena rarely remain constant, and Europe is no exception. Both expansion and retreat have marked Europe's past. One thousand years before Christ, a small European nucleus had formed around the shores of the eastern Mediterranean, an embryo of Western Civilization (Figure 1.7). By the beginning of the Christian era, Europe was represented by the territorial extent of the Roman Empire, a considerable expansion from the nucleus of 1000 B.C., though the core still lay in the Mediterranean basin.

The passage of still another millennium, to about A.D. 1000, brought dra-

Figure 1.7 The territorial development of Europe, 1000 B.C. to A.D. 1000. (Adapted from *Environmental Foundations of European History*, by Derwent S. Whittlesey. Copyright 1949. By permission of Appleton-Century-Crofts, Educational Division, Meredith Corporation.)

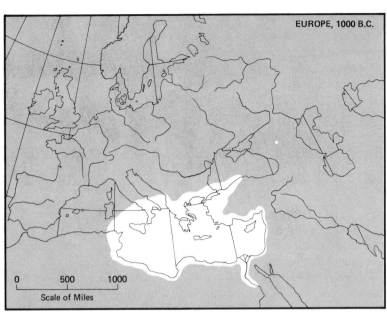

EUROPE, 1000 B.C.

0   500   1000
Scale of Miles

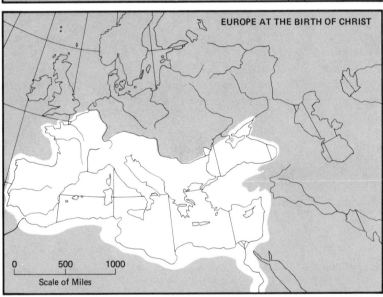

EUROPE AT THE BIRTH OF CHRIST

0   500   1000
Scale of Miles

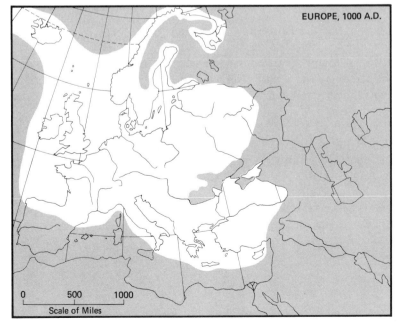

EUROPE, 1000 A.D.

0   500   1000
Scale of Miles

matic areal changes. The Arabs, driven by the evangelical spirit of a new religion, Islam, had wrested away all of North Africa, most of Iberia, and the larger islands in the Mediterranean Sea. The deepest intrusion of the Arabs reached into central western France, where they were finally turned back on the battlefield of Tours in 732 by the Frankish leader Charles Martel. Europe was also invaded by Asiatic horsemen from the east, in particular the Huns and Magyars. The latter group penetrated southern Germany, where a major battle was fought on the Lechfeld in 955. After long years of raiding, these fierce mounted warriors were eventually obliged to abandon all but a foothold in the grassland of Hungary, where their linguistic descendants are still found today. The first thousand years after Christ were not, however, entirely years of retreat. The loss of North Africa was paralleled by an expansion into heathen Germanic and Slavic realms, which Christian missionaries brought into the European community.

The territorial ebb and flow of Europe continued into the present millennium. Spaniards and Portuguese, gripped by a religious fervor reminiscent of the earlier Moslem expansion, drove the Arabic Moors from Iberia, a reconquest which was completed in 1492. In the east, however, two serious setbacks were suffered. The Tartars, or Golden Horde, followed the path of their earlier Asiatic kinsmen, sweeping across southern Russia to fall on Europe in the 1200s. Scarcely had they been beaten back when a new peril appeared in Asia Minor, where the Moslem Turks replaced the Arabs as the spreaders of Islam. The Turks overwhelmed the political power of the Greek Christian culture in Asia Minor and pressed on beyond the Dardanelles–Bosporus to seize permanently the center of Eastern Orthodox Christianity, Constantinople. From there the Turks spread northward to occupy most of the Balkan Peninsula. Three times, in 1529, 1532, and again in 1683, Europe's warriors gathered to turn the Turks back from the gates of Wien and preserve European culture. The Turkish tide gradually receded, leaving only Moslem relics in Albania and southern Yugoslavia and preserving a small Turkish bridgehead on the north shore of the Dardanelles and Bosporus around Istanbul. Even the most persistent efforts by Europeans, in particular Greeks and Russians, have failed to destroy this bridgehead, and it, along with Asia Minor, remains lost to Europe still today.

Another area of contest within the last thousand years has been Palestine. The Europeans seized a temporary foothold in the Holy Land during the Crusades, only to suffer eventual defeat. Renewed efforts to claim the area began with the Zionist movement, the British take-over after World War I, the flood of Jewish migration after the Nazi disaster, and the creation of Israel. To be sure, the Israelis are not Christian and they are abandoning their Indo-European Yiddish language in favor of the ancient Semitic Hebrew, but in standard of living and economic development their nation represents a transplanting of Europe to the eastern Mediterranean shores.

The truly spectacular European expansion, however, has been accomplished over the past 400 to 500 years by Germanic peoples, Slavs, and Iberian Latins. The Germanic-speaking peoples, in particular the English, have created overseas Europes in Anglo-America, Australia, New Zealand, and South Africa, while Spaniards and Portuguese transplanted much that is European in large parts of Latin America. The overseas activities of the Iberians and Germans coincided with a major Slavic expansion overland, accomplished by the European Russians, who have busily pushed Europe even deeper into the previously alien heartland of Eurasia and on beyond to the Pacific shore.

In addition to the middle- and upper-latitude areas, to which large European populations were transplanted bodily, destroying or subjugating the native peoples, great tropical colonial empires were established by the Spaniards, Portuguese, British, French, Dutch, Belgians, and Germans. While few people migrated to the inhospitable tropics, still an imprint of Europe was placed there. Consequently the Asian Indian rides on a railroad system founded by the British, the Haitian speaks a form of French, and the Filipino adheres to the Roman Catholic faith. In the words of the geographer Derwent Whittlesey, Europeans have carried their mode of life throughout the world, "transplanting it to unoccupied lands, or grafting it onto societies too firmly rooted to be dislodged."

The world is in the process of being Europeanized in numerous, fundamental ways. Japan has accepted the Industrial Revolution and experiences with some discomfort the resultant gradual destruction of its traditional culture, while Turkey has turned away from the Arabian source regions of its religion, discarding the Arabic alphabet to adopt the Latin characters. If the present trend continues, European culture may one day be world culture, as regional differences fade in an increasing acceptance of the European way of life. This text will focus on the European source area, shorn of its overseas and overland territorial expansion of the past 500 years, on the homeland of the peoples who are shaping the world in their own cultural image.

SOURCES AND SUGGESTED READINGS

Jan. O. M. Broek and John W. Webb. "Culture Realms," Chapter 8 in their *A Geography of Mankind*. New York: McGraw-Hill, 1968, pp. 183–207.

Eric Fischer. *The Passing of the European Age: A Study of the Transfer of Western Civilization and Its Renewal in Other Continents*. Cambridge, Mass.: Harvard University Press, 1943.

Denys Hay. *Europe: The Emergence of an Idea*. Edinburgh: University Press, 1957.

Mark S. W. Jefferson. *Man in Europe*. New York: Harcourt Brace Jovanovich, 1926.

Thomas Mann. *Der Zauberberg, Roman* (*The Magic Mountain, Novel*). Berlin, Germany: S. Fischer, 1924.

W. H. Parker. "Europe: How Far?" *Geographical Journal*. Vol. 126 (1960), pp. 278–297.

United Nations. *Demographic Yearbook. Annuaire Démographique*. New York: UN, various issues.

United Nations. *Statistical Yearbook. Annuaire Statistique*. New York: UN, various issues.

Philip L. Wagner and Marvin W. Mikesell. "The Themes of Cultural Geography." In their *Readings in Cultural Geography*. Chicago: University of Chicago Press, 1962, pp. 1–24.

Derwent Whittlesey. *Environmental Foundations of European History*. New York: Appleton, 1949.

CHAPTER TWO

The physical framework: Interaction of environment and culture

The peoples of Europe occupy a piece of the physical earth, a peninsula composed of many constituent peninsulas attached to the western extremity of Eurasia. To a degree the European environment has shaped the way of life of its inhabitants, and it is impossible to understand Europe thoroughly without knowing the nature of its physical framework. At the same time, Europeans have massively altered their environmental homeland, for both better and worse, to the extent that a "natural" environment no longer exists. It is to this interworking of culture and milieu that attention is now directed.

2.1 TERRAIN

The surface of the European land is quite varied, running the gamut from high, rugged mountains to almost totally flat plains. To simplify this complex pattern, a threefold division of terrain types is presented, involving mountains, plains, and hills (Figure 2.1).

MOUNTAINS

Rough terrain, in the form of mountains, is in large part confined to the southern half of Europe, with only one major outlier in Scandinavia as an exception.

Figure 2.1 Terrain regions.

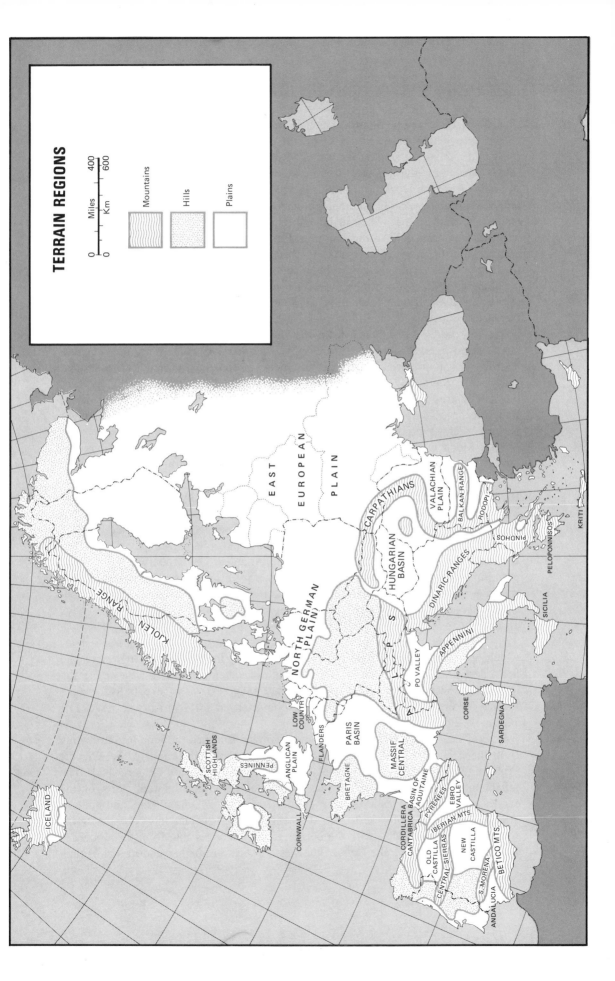

TERRAIN REGIONS

Miles
400
600
Km
0
0

Mountains

Hills

Plains

KJÖLEN RANGE

ICELAND

SCOTTISH HIGHLANDS

PENNINES

ANGLICAN PLAIN

CORNWALL

BRETAGNE

FLANDERS

LOW COUNTRY

PARIS BASIN

NORTH GERMAN PLAIN

EAST EUROPEAN PLAIN

CARPATHIANS

HUNGARIAN BASIN

VALACHIAN PLAIN

BALKAN RANGE

RODOPI

DINARIC RANGES

PINDHOS

PELOPONNISOS

KRITI

A L P S

PO VALLEY

APPENNINI

CORSE

SARDEGNA

SICILIA

MASSIF CENTRAL

BASIN OF AQUITAINE

CORDILLERA CANTABRICA

PYRENEES

EBRO VALLEY

IBERIAN MTS.

OLD CASTILLA

NEW CASTILLA

CENTRAL SIERRAS

S. MORENA

ANDALUCIA

BETICO MTS.

In marked contrast to the ranges of the Americas, most of the mountains of Europe are oriented generally in an east–west direction, a situation which has a major climatic effect, as will be discussed later in this chapter.

Progressing from west to east, the first ranges encountered are those of Iberia. Paralleling the southeast coast of Spain are the *Betico Mountains,* a series of ridges—including the famous Sierra Nevada—and several longitudinal valleys, stretching from the Rock of Gibraltar to the vicinity of Valencia. There the mountains disappear beneath the sea only to emerge again to the east as the Baleares Islands. The Betico area, which includes peaks of over 3350 meters (11,000 feet), was the final stronghold of the Moors in Europe, and their influence is seen in the architecture of the city of Granada, which lies in one of the longitudinal valleys at the foot of the Sierra Nevada. Arabic place names also survive as a Moorish relic, including Gibraltar, which is derived from *gebel-al-Tariq,* or the "rock of Tariq," who was a Moorish ruler. Generally, the southernmost ridge of the Betico fronts on the Mediterranean Sea, creating a rocky and picturesque coast, but in a number of places the ranges are set back from the shore, allowing small pockets of coastal plain, called *huertas,* literally "gardens," by the Spaniards. They are the scene of intensive irrigation agriculture as in the Huerta of Valencia, famous for its orange groves. The *Iberian Mountains,* an arc trending inland north and northwest from the general area of Valencia, might best be regarded as a lower continuation of the Betico Range. They do not exceed elevations of 2300 meters (7500 feet) and in general are not a major hindrance to transportation.

Much more impressive are the *Pyrenees,* a true barrier range along the border of Spain and France. The rivers which cut back into the single main ridge of the Pyrenees from the Spanish and French sides are not longitudinally aligned, and as a consequence no low passes have been carved out by adjacent headwaters. The resultant isolation has aided the survival of Andorra, a remote mountain nation whose people have often relied on smuggling as a livelihood. The barrier effect of the Pyrenees is partially nullified by the presence of wide "beach paths" at either end, adjacent to both the Mediterranean and Atlantic. The Moors used the beach path in invading France in the 700s, as have other armies moving both north and south. A lower westward mountain projection from the Pyrenees is the *Cordillera Cantabrica,* reaching only 2600 to 2750 meters (8500 to 9000 feet) at the highest, and paralleling the north coast of Spain.

Completing the list of major Iberian mountain areas are the *Central Sierras,* which bear several different names locally, such as the Sierra de Gredos, or the Serra da Estrêla, and the *Sierra Morena,* both of which trend east–west across the interior of the peninsula. Parts of the former range served as one base for anti-Franco forces in the Spanish Civil War, immortalized in Hemingway's novel *For Whom the Bell Tolls.*

The *Alps* are the highest and most famous European mountains, stretching from the French Riviera in an arc eastward through Switzerland to the Wiener-Wald, or Vienna Woods, on the bank of the Austrian Danube (Figure 2.2). The inhabitants use almost countless local names to designate different parts of the ranges, such as the Alpes Maritimes, Berner Alpen, Alpi Dolomitiche, and Julijske Alpe. For purposes of description, the range is best divided into two parts, the western and eastern Alps, with the border roughly along a line from the Bodensee (Lake Constance) to Lake Como. The western Alps are higher and narrower than

Figure 2.2   The Wiener-Wald (Vienna woods), easternmost projection of the Alps. Here, near the banks of the Danube, the Alps are little more than wooded hills, but the mountain range increases greatly in height to the west. As is typical in central and western Europe, the slopes have been left in forest while the adjacent valley was cleared and used for farming. (Courtesy Austrian National Tourist Office.)

those to the east, with deeply incised valleys and large remnant glaciers. Mont Blanc, towering 4813 meters (15,781 feet) above sea level, is the highest in Europe. Deep, sheer-sided U-shaped valleys, hollowed out by glaciers during the Ice Age, sometimes have floors 2750 meters (9000 feet) lower than the adjacent peaks. The narrowness is suggested by the Alpes-Maritimes, near the Mediterranean shore, where the entire width is only one ridge some 50 kilometers (30 miles) wide. In Switzerland, two alpine ridges are present, separated by a long east–west valley which is occupied by the headwaters of both the Rhine and Rhône rivers. The eastern Alps, in contrast, are broader from north to south, reaching a width of 240 kilometers (150 miles) along a line from Verona to München. Instead of one longitudinal valley, two, three, or even four are found, guiding the courses of rivers such as the Inn, Adige, Mur, and Drau. The peaks of the eastern Alps rarely exceed 3000 meters (10,000 feet).

While impressive in appearance, the Alps have never served as a barrier. There are so many low passes through which invaders may easily move that the Italians, who live south of the mountains and look to them as a "natural" border, refer to the Alps as the "magnificent traitor." The lack of a barrier is well illustrated by the exploits of the Carthaginian general Hannibal, who successfully moved a cavalry of elephants and 30,000 men through the Alps to attack northern Italy. He was followed centuries later by various German tribes from the north, who slipped through to deal a death blow to the Roman Empire. In the western Alps of Switzerland, the northern of the two ridges is completely severed by the Rhône,

Rhine, and Reuss rivers, which break through to enter the plains beyond. These river gaps allow easy access from the north into the central longitudinal valley. Also, the small tributary streams which flow into these three rivers from the south have cut back into the southern ridge directly across from the tributaries of the Po River on the other side of the ridge, producing a whole series of low passes. The most famous of these are St. Bernard (2470 meters, 8100 feet) and Simplon (2010 meters, 6600 feet) passes, which lie on ancient routes from Italy to France, and St. Gotthard and Splügen passes (both 2100 meters, 6900 feet), which link German-speaking lands with Italy. In the eastern Alps the great north–south route is Brenner Pass (1375 meters, 4500 feet), carved by tributaries of the Inn and Adige rivers through the middle of three ridges which are found in this part of the Alps. In northern and southern ridges are water gaps created by these same rivers and others.

The *Appennini Mountains,* which form the backbone of the Italian peninsula, branch out from the Alpes-Maritimes in the Riviera district, parallel the coast of the Gulf of Genova, and then arc gently to the southeast to approach Italy's Adriatic shore and south and west to return to the western coast at the toe of the Italian boot. Structurally they reappear bearing different names in the island of Sicilia, beyond the narrow Strait of Messina, the Scylla and Charybdis of Homer. The southern Appennini and Sicilian mountains are notorious as centers of volcanic activity. The eruption of Vesùvio near Nàpoli in A.D. 79 destroyed the Roman city of Pompeii, while on Sicilia some 500 recorded eruptions of Mount Etna over the past 2400 years have claimed an estimated one million lives. The perpetually active Stromboli occupies a small island north of Sicilia.

The *Dinaric Ranges* begin at the Alps near the point where Italy, Yugoslavia, and Austria meet, and stretch southeastward along the Adriatic coast through Yugoslavia, continuing as the Pindhos Mountains and others through Albania and Greece to the tip of the Pelopónnisos. The Dinaric area is extremely rugged and difficult to traverse, especially in areas of *karst* topography, where permeable limestones have been dissolved by water filtering down from the surface, forming numerous sinks or depressions called *dolines* and *polje,* which are used for farming activity. The Dinaric Range served as the base for Yugoslav guerrilla forces in World War II. One of the few easy passages through the Dinaric Ranges is in the extreme north, near the juncture with the Alps, where the so-called Pear Tree Pass near Postojna, Yugoslavia, and other routes allow access from the plains of Hungary into the lowlands of Italy, another "betrayal" by the magnificent, traitorous mountains which rim the northern edge of the Italian peninsula. While the Pear Tree Pass is of little significance today, both Hunnish and Gothic warriors poured through it to attack the Roman Empire in its period of decline.

Earthquakes also plague the Dinaric region and have taken many lives. In the 1960s Yugoslavia was particularly hard hit, with major disasters at the cities of Skopje and Banja Luka. The fatalities in Balkan earthquakes are often very numerous because many houses are tile-roofed stone structures, which allow little chance for survival when they collapse. The Greek islands of the Aegean, which belong in this same general mountain complex, were apparently the scene of one of the most violent volcanic eruptions ever to occur. It is now believed by many scholars, including Rhys Carpenter, that the small Aegean island of Thíra, or Santorini, which consists of a volcanic crater, erupted and collapsed with incredible force in about

1400 B.C. The noise was likely heard as far away as Scandinavia and central Africa. Huge tidal waves, perhaps 30 meters (100 feet) tall, crashed against the northern shore of nearby Kriti, the homeland of the great Minoan civilization, and the Kritian sky was likely soon blackened with falling volcanic debris. Parts of Kriti may have become temporarily uninhabitable, as volcanic ash killed vegetation, and with the flight of many survivors, the Minoan culture declined. Thíra itself, which had been populated by Minoans, partially disappeared from the map, perhaps giving rise to the legend of the lost continent Atlantis. Recently the remains of dwellings were found beneath 30 meters (100 feet) of ash cover on the insular remnant of Thíra.

Just east of Wien (Vienna), across the Danube River in Czechoslovakia, the *Carpathian Mountains* begin, almost as a continuation of the Alps. Their directional course inscribes a huge mirror-image C through Slovensko, southern Poland, a corner of the Ukraine, and Romania, ending as it began on the shores of the Danube at the Iron Gate. The southern part of the Carpathians in Romania is sometimes referred to in English as the Transylvanian Alps, though known locally as the Carpatii Meridionali. High elevations are rare in the Carpathians, with few peaks over 2500 meters (8000 feet). Furthermore, it is a very narrow range with numerous low passes, though the Soviet Union took the precaution after World War II to seize a territorial foothold on the plains west of the Carpathians to ensure control of adjacent Hungary.

South of the Iron Gate on the Danube, the Carpathian structure continues as the *Balkan Range* (Stara Planina) and *Rodopi Mountains* of Bulgaria and eastern Yugoslavia. These ranges turn back eastward in two prongs across central and southern Bulgaria.

The final major mountain area of Europe is the *Kjölen Range,* which forms the spine of the Scandinavian Peninsula in Norway and Sweden. It was heavily glaciated in the Ice Age, and remnant glaciers are still present. As a result, the soil cover is extremely thin or absent altogether, and the coastline is deeply indented by ice-carved fjords, U-shaped glacial valleys later flooded by the ocean. One of the most spectacular is the long, narrow Hardangerfjord (Hair-string Fjord). The Kjölen Range contains very few inhabitants but has served as a refuge for some Lappish people.

PLAINS

At the opposite extreme of terrain types are the plains areas of Europe. To a much greater extent than the mountains, the plains and lowlands have been the scene of human activity, and for this reason they are of greater importance to the European culture area. The plains are concentrated in the north and east, in contrast to the southern dominance of mountains (Figure 2.1).

The largest contiguous lowland plains region stretches from the foot of the Pyrenees in the south of France in a gentle curve north and east along the Atlantic and North Sea shores into Germany, widening rapidly through Poland and into Russia to span the entire breadth of the European peninsula from the Arctic Ocean to the Black Sea. The general names applied to these lowlands are the *North* and *East European plains*. Many constituent parts can be recognized, some of which deserve mention because of their great importance to the peoples of Europe.

Moving from west to east, the first segment of the North European Plain to be encountered is the *Basin of Aquitaine* in southwestern France. It is drained principally by the Garonne River, which flows through the two principal cities Bordeaux and Toulouse. Most of the basin has fertile limestone soil, but the area adjacent to the Atlantic shore, the Landes, is a region of poor sandy soil and small population. In both the east and north, there are narrow gateways providing access through bordering hill areas to the Basin of Aquitaine. The Gap or Gateway of Carcassonne opens eastward to the Mediterranean shore and was long guarded by the heavily fortified town of Carcassonne, which retains much of its medieval splendor today. To the north lies the Gate of Poitou, a plains pathway about sixty-five kilometers (forty miles) wide, which leads into the interior of France toward Paris. The Moorish invaders of the 700s entered the Basin of Aquitaine by way of Carcassonne and turned northward to the Gate of Poitou, where they were met and defeated by Frankish forces. Later, the basin provided a natural core area for the development of the medieval feudal states of Aquitaine and Gascogne. The orientation of the basin, facing outward toward the Atlantic, contributed to its long dominance by English kings.

Beyond the Gate of Poitou lies a second major part of the North European Plain, the *Paris Basin,* occupying the larger part of northern France. In surface configurations this basin is shaped in the fashion of a series of concentric, progressively larger saucers, with the city of Paris and the surrounding district, known as the Île de France, occupying the smallest, central saucer. In every direction from Paris, the land rises very gently until a sharp drop-off is reached, formed by outward-facing *cuestas.* From the foot of the cuesta the countryside again gradually increases in elevation until another cuesta is reached. To the east, seven such cuestas are present in at least fragmentary form. These escarpments have proven extremely valuable as natural defense walls for the French nation in wars with Germany. Invaders from the east and north have had to fight their way up the steep cuesta slopes in the face of French fortifications in order to reach the capital city. The city of Verdun, which lies at the foot of one of the east-facing cuestas, was the scene of bitter fighting in World War I, and 600,000 Germans and French died fighting for command of the slope during a six-month period in 1916. The series of natural defense lines made the Île de France an ideal birthplace for the French state.

Across the English Channel in the southeastern part of the island of Great Britain lies a third segment of the lowlands of northern Europe, the *Anglican Plain,* also referred to as Lowland England. It is in many respects simply a continuation of the Paris Basin, including a series of west-facing cuestas. The Cotswolds and Chilterns are hilly areas along the cuesta lines, with considerable land still forested, a rarity in Britain. At the eastern foot of the hilly escarpments are long valleys, oriented roughly southwest to northeast, including the Vale of Oxford and the once-marshy Fens. Just as the Paris Basin was the nucleus of the French state, so the Anglican Plain was the scene of initial nation-building by the Germanic invaders of Britain.

North from the Paris Basin, the European Plain once again narrows to form a broad gateway, the *Flanders Plain,* centered in western Belgium. As was true of Carcassonne and Poitou, Flanders has strategic value, for it was in these narrows at Waterloo that Napoleon suffered his final defeat. The very existence of Belgium as an independent nation is in part the result of the unwillingness of Germany and France to allow each other to control this strategic area.

Bordering Flanders on the north and east is an almost totally flat plain, the *Low Country,* a communal delta of the Rhine, Maas, Schelde, Ems, and several lesser rivers. The greater part of the Low Country lies in the Netherlands (Nederland), whose very name describes the terrain. Some of the area lies below the level of the sea, and the continuing sinking of this delta bodes ill for the long-range future. Much of the land which the Dutch struggle to keep is quite fertile, but the Low Country also contains sizable sandy districts, including the Kempenland on the Belgium–Netherlands border, as well as areas of moor and peat bog.

The Low Country blends gradually and imperceptibly into the *North German Plain,* which as traditionally defined includes not only most of northern Germany, but also the entirety of Denmark and much of Poland. The plain widens rapidly to the east, from about 160 kilometers (100 miles) in width where it joins the Low Country to over 480 kilometers (300 miles) in Poland. It differs from the Low Country in that there is considerably more surface irregularity, a great part of which can be attributed to the effects of the Ice Age, in particular the last southward advance of the glaciers from their Scandinavian source. Parallel chains of *moraine* hills, glacial deposits formed wherever the icemass paused in its retreat to leave behind a greater thickness of debris, extend east–west across the North German Plain, from the Jylland Peninsula of Denmark on into northern Poland, parallel to the Baltic shore. Between the hill chains are extensive zones covered with a layer of *ground moraine,* or *till,* where the glaciers deposited less material. The till surface is quite irregular, with many enclosed depressions containing lakes. These are so numerous that the coastal part of the North German Plain is called the Baltic Lake Plain. The glaciers did not entirely cover the North German Plain, but even the areas south of the icemass were altered by its proximity. Beyond the terminal moraine, the southernmost line of glacially deposited hills, meltwater streams from the icemass washed down finer sand and gravel, forming what are known as *outwash plains.* These remain today as infertile heath areas, sometimes called *geest,* of which the Lüneburger Heath south of Hamburg is a fine example.

If the Ice Age produced much inferior land, it also helped to form some of the most fertile districts of Germany. Winds sweeping down from the icemass picked up extremely small particles of earth, carried them to the southern edge of the North German Plain where the lowlands give way to a zone of hilly terrain, and deposited them at the foot of the hills. The forced ascent blunted the velocity of the winds, causing them to drop much of their load of dust. These wind-deposited, fine-textured soils, known as *loess,* are quite fertile and easy to work. The greatest depths of loess accumulated in numerous "embayments" of the North German Plain, called *Börde,* which reach south into the hills. Since the dawn of agriculture among the Germans, the loessial belt has been the most thickly populated part of the North German Plain, while the outwash geest areas supported only scattered inhabitants engaged mainly in sheepherding. Politically, this plain gave birth to the powerful state of Prussia, the eventual unifier of Germany. The militarism of the Prussians, which was the key to their success, can perhaps in part be attributed to the need for defense in a plains area not endowed with natural protection. To survive and expand, the Prussians had to be militarily proficient.

Most of southern Sweden and part of Finland can also be classified as plains, though it is impossible to find a single name to apply to these areas of level terrain. Like the northern German area, these plains of the trans-Baltic region show the effects of the Ice Age. Two great glacial ridges, called the Salpausselkä, parallel the south shore of Finland, beyond which is a remarkable concentration of lakes. *Eskers,* long snakelike hill ribbons laid down as beds by ice-flanked meltwater rivers, are very common in central Finland and are often used as routes of transportation, since the disappearance of their ice banks left them standing above the poorly drained, lake-studded countryside.

East of Poland and Finland, the plains broaden to span the impressive north–south dimensions of Russia. The entire area is for convenience lumped together as the *East European Plain* (Figure 2.1), though individual parts are known by local names, such as the Ilmen Basin and Dnepr Lowland. Relief from the monotony of this vast lowland is found only in scattered belts of low hills. Three major east-facing escarpments in the southern half of the East European Plain are faintly reminiscent of the cuestas of the Paris Basin, though on a much grander scale. The Dnepr, Don, and Volga rivers each flow at the eastern foot of one of the escarpments. The plateaux west of the cuesta heights have been dissected through erosion to form rolling plains and low hills. In the northern sector, surface irregularity is generally tied to the same glacial forces which shaped the North German Plain.

The East European lowlands are the ancient homeland of the Slavic peoples, in which they have defeated successive waves of invaders and built a most powerful nation, the Soviet Union. The soldiers of Hitler and Napoleon entered these extensive plains as proud conquerors, but only a relative few, numbed by cold and overwhelmed by distance, managed to escape. The western invaders never adjusted to the un-European vastness of the eastern plains, a vastness which dwarfed the myriad of miniature terrain units found in Germany, France, and other lands of the European core. Intruders from the east and south have fared little better, and the once-fierce Turks and Tartars survive today in Russia only as docile, defeated ethnic minorities.

The *Valachian Plain* is a fingerlike projection west of the main body of the East European Plain, along the lower course of the Danube River in southern Romania. These plains, a route of minimal terrain resistance, have witnessed the comings and goings of a great variety of invaders and migrating peoples, including the Huns, Slavs, Magyars, and Mongols. Today, the Valachian Plain is the heartland of the Romanians, who have somehow managed to preserve a language derived from the legions of the caesars, perpetuating an isolated eastern bastion of Romance speech.

All of the plains areas mentioned have been constituent parts of the great North and East European plains. Strewn elsewhere among the mountain ranges of southern Europe are other smaller, but still important, regions of level terrain. The *Hungarian Basin,* straddling the middle segment of the Danube River and extending from Hungary into border areas of Yugoslavia, Romania, Austria, Czechoslovakia, and the Soviet Union, is the largest of these scattered plains. It is enclosed on the north and east by the Carpathian Mountains, by the Dinaric Range in the south, and by the Alps of Austria in the west.

In no sense, however, is the Hungarian Basin isolated by its mountain rim, for there are numerous access routes. The Italian lands are easily reached through the previously mentioned Pear Tree Pass, while the Valachian Plain and south Russia lie beyond the Iron Gate on the Danube, where the river severs the

Carpathians from the Balkan Ranges. In the northwestern corner of the Basin, the Moravian Gate provides egress north to the plains of Poland, and the valley of the upper Danube leads on beyond Wien into southern Germany. Greece and the Aegean are accessible southward through the long, narrow Morava–Vardar Depression, a rift valley wedged between the Dinaric and Balkan ranges. Furthermore, there are numerous low passes in the Carpathian Mountains which lead into Russia. Through one or another of these numerous leaks and seams in the mountain wall, representatives of just about every major linguistic group in Europe and adjacent parts of Asia have passed as conquerors or refugees, and the recorded history of the basin is one of continued turbulence. It has been a zone of conflict between Roman and barbarian, Turk and Christian, Hun and German, Magyar and Slav. Warpaths have also been trade routes, from the time of the amber trade through the Moravian Gate several thousand years ago and earlier. The diverse ethnic makeup of the basin today, including German, Hungarian, Slav, and Romanian, is the heritage of a long history of warfare, trade, and migration.

The *Po Valley* of northern Italy, rimmed by the Alps and Appennini, is the only sizable plains area in that country. It represents a continuation of the structural depression containing the Adriatic Sea, filled to above the level of the sea with materials brought down from the surrounding mountains by streams and ice. Glaciers moving down into the fringe of the Po Valley from the north deposited moraines which dammed up the mouths of tributary Alpine valleys, creating a chain of natural lakes, including Como, Maggiore, Lugano, Iseo, and Garda. South of the moraine dams is an infertile outwash plain similar to that found in northern Germany. Beyond the outwash plain lies the greater part of the Po Valley, an area of fertile river-deposited soils. At the juncture of alluvium and outwash, the groundwater table reaches the surface, resulting in an east–west line of springs called *fontanili*. From ancient times the fontanili attracted human settlement, and today a row of cities, including Torino and Milano, traces the course of the spring sites. Still another line of cities, including Parma, Modena, and Bologna, lies along the southern edge of the Po Valley, at the foot of the Appennini. The western, uppermost part of the Po Valley served as the political nucleus of Italian unification in the nineteenth century, and today the same area contains the industrial heart of the nation.

France's gateway to the Mediterranean is the *Plain of Languedoc,* a narrow coastal lowland reaching from the Pyrenees to the Riviera. Two strategic routes connect the plain to the heart of France. To the west there is access through the previously mentioned Gate of Carcassonne to the Basin of Aquitaine, and the Rhône–Saône Corridor leads due north into the Paris Basin.

The mountain ranges of Iberia divide that peninsula into a series of separate plains, each of which is home to people of a distinct subculture. The *Lowland of Andalucia* is wedged in between the Betico Mountains and the Sierra Morena in far southern Spain, a land of olive groves dotted with place names which recall the Moorish occupation. The main river draining the lowland is the Rio Guadalquivir, a name derived from *Wadi-al-Kabir,* Arabic for "the great river." The *Portuguese Lowland,* fronting the Atlantic coast of Iberia, serves as the core area of the distinctive language of the nation of Portugal. Similarly, the *Ebro Valley* and coastal plain adjacent to the Mediterranean in northeastern Spain are the stronghold of the Cataloinan peoples, who also preserve a unique Romance language. The interior plains of Iberia, home of the Castillians, rather than those of the periphery, have been the seat of political power. A great tableland, called the *Meseta,* covers the larger part of interior Spain and is divided into two areas by the Central Sierras. In the northern part of the Meseta is the *Basin of Old Castilla,* an early center of state building activity. To the south, the *Basin of New Castilla,* including the *La Mancha* plains, was freed from Moorish control later than Old Castilla, hence the adjective "new." It contains the city of Madrid, the capital of Castillian-dominated Spain.

Smaller plains areas are scattered throughout southern Europe, too numerous to mention. They are, however, of great importance agriculturally, particularly in mountain-dominated countries such as Greece. These small plains have accumulated much of the soil eroded away from adjacent slopes, and thus offer the best opportunities for crop farming.

HILL LANDS AND LOW MOUNTAINS

The third, and final, terrain category includes the major hilly areas of Europe. The hills dominate the European midsection, just as the mountains are found mainly in the south and the plains in the north (Figure 2.1). From the coast of Normandie and Bretagne in western France, a broad, fragmented belt of hills and low mountains extends eastward through France, central Germany, and on into western Czechoslovakia. The entire region is composed of numerous small hill districts, each bearing its own distinctive name, interspersed with equally small valleys, basins, and lowland corridors.

Among the more important hill districts are the *Massif Central* of southern France; the *Ardennes* of Belgium and Luxembourg; the *Vosges* and *Black Forest* (Schwarzwald) which flank the Rhine River along the German–French border; the *Jura,* which extend from Switzerland and France into interior southern Germany; the *Harz, Erzgebirge,* and *Thüringer Forest* of East Germany; and the *Sudetes* and *Bohemian Forest* (Böhmerwald) on the borders of Czechoslovakia. Important lowlands scattered among these hills include the *Rhône–Saône* Corridor, east of the Massif Central, one branch of which leads through the Belfort or Burgundian Gate between the Vosges and Jura into the *Upper Rhine Plain.* An elevated plains area is found between the Jura and Alps in the *Swiss* and *Bavarian plateaux,* while the core of western Czechoslovakia is the *Bohemian Basin.*

The network of small plains and lowlands has long been important as routes of trade and invasion, while the hills have provided refuge and protection. The hills of Bretagne in France are still today the stronghold of a Celtic-speaking minority, and the hill rim of western Czechoslovakia helped the Czech people resist linguistic assimilation in the eastward push of German settlers in the Middle Ages.

Some major hill lands lie outside the main belt in central Europe, including the highlands of the British Isles. In Great Britain the hills dominate the west and north, confining the Anglican Plain to the southeastern part of the island. *Cornwall* is the hilly peninsula reaching southwest to Land's End, and the *Cambrian Mountains* occupy the larger part of the province of Wales. The *Pennine Chain* and hilly *Lake District* of northern England blend into the famous *Scottish Highlands.* On the island of Ireland, a hill rim parallels the coast except in the east, including among others the mountains of Knockmealdown, Mourne, Connemara, and Kerry. The interior of Ireland and the narrow core of Scotland are lowlands. The hills of Great

Britain have been the refuges of the Celtic people, where they were, for a time at least, able to resist the numerically superior Germanic invaders and preserve their customs and language. Gaelic, Erse, and Welsh are still spoken today as mother tongues in parts of the hills. In contrast, the lowlands and plains were invariably the scene of early Celtic defeat and assimilation. In Roman times the pattern was identical, for while the legions of Rome were able to secure the Anglican Plain, they rarely ventured out against fierce hill tribes such as the Picts. Hadrian's Wall, built across the waist of Great Britain to restrain the Picts, still stands as a monument to Roman failure in the hilly North. The lesson of British terrain is that a hill area can be held by its inhabitants against the repeated thrusts of a militarily and numerically superior enemy based in the adjacent plains. Part of the reason for the success of hill refuges is that such regions are less valuable than fertile lowlands, not worth the effort of conquest.

MAN'S APPRAISAL OF THE TERRAIN

Man, and in particular technological European man, is by no means a passive product of his environment. Still, many decisions made within the framework of cultural heritage are influenced by the physical surroundings; in choosing where to live, what form of livelihood to pursue, and like matters, man often does consider the character of the terrain.

Mention has already been made of the guiding influence of lowland corridors and mountain passes on routes of invasion and trade, as well as the political and linguistic refuge sometimes provided by rugged terrain. To these must be added the relationship between terrain and population density, for the large majority of Europeans have chosen to dwell in the lowland plains. In part this choice rests on a still earlier one—the decision to become sedentary farmers rather than wandering hunters and gatherers. The huntsman might well find rough terrain his most advantageous habitat, but agricultural peoples understandably chose regions of gentle terrain. Most of the plains of Europe stand out on a map of population distribution as regions of dense settlement, while the mountain ranges are discernible as lines of sparse population. The Po Valley, for example, contains over 100 persons per square kilometer (over 250 persons per square mile), while large areas in the adjacent Alps and Appennini Mountains have less than one-tenth as many. The trend in modern Europe is for the hills and mountains to be still further depopulated as the inhabitants migrate to the cities of the lowlands. The factories of Torino and Milano, for example, are drawing away the population of the highland rim of the Po Valley, leaving behind mainly a residue of the elderly. The original agricultural attraction of the plains is suggested by the greater deforestation in areas of level terrain.

2.2 MAN AS A MODIFIER OF TERRAIN

If terrain influences man in certain ways, then he has most assuredly responded in kind. It is true that the "everlasting hills" have not been as drastically altered as some other facets of the European physical environment, but the work of the ever-active human hand is definitely visible.

One modest example, admittedly confined to limited areas, is *terracing*. This ancient technology, probably derived from the mountain fringe of the Fertile

Figure 2.3 Terraced vineyard landscape of the German Rhine gorge. Man's imprint on the terrain is strikingly visible on the Rhine, one of the best wine districts of Europe. The terraces and vineyards date from Roman times, and both represent northward diffusion from the Mediterranean lands. Viticulture in this area is a traditional form of specialized market-gardening which dates back well over a thousand years. (Courtesy German Information Center.)

Crescent in the Middle East, has enabled man to "level" mountains for agricultural use. A river journey on the Rhine from Bonn to Mainz reveals one of the most thorough jobs of terracing in all of Europe, huge vine-covered stairsteps rising from the riverbank to the adjacent heights (Figure 2.3). In the Mediterranean lands, where level land is in short supply, terraced hillsides are also very common.

Man has even gone so far as to build "mountains." Huge slag piles rise from the green valleys of Wales, and on the North German Plain near Berlin stands the Teufelsberg, or "Devil's Mountain." The building material for the Teufelsberg was obtained from the rubble of the war-destroyed German capital, and the peak has now reached sufficient height to allow use as a ski slope in winter. In eastern Ireland there are numerous small hills called *motes* which were erected as fortifications by invading Normans in the Middle Ages. Similar man-made hills or mounds dot the delta plains on the approach to the ruins of Pella, the capital of Macedonia in northern Greece at the time of Alexander the Great.

Certainly the most impressive anthropogeomorphic development in Europe has been the modification of the Dutch coastline, preserving and expanding the Low Country in the face of the hostile North Sea. So remarkable is the Dutch effort that it warrants detailed attention.

DUTCH COASTLINE ALTERATION

The Dutch, through no fault of their own, live on the wrong end of a huge geomorphological seesaw. Their deltaic homeland is gradually sinking, at the rate of about twenty centimeters (eight inches) per century, coincident with an increase in elevation along the Swedish shore of the Baltic Sea. Since the end of the period of Pleistocene glaciation about 10,000 years before the Christian Era, the coastal fringe of the Netherlands has sunk some twenty meters (sixty-five feet). Silt brought in and deposited by the Rhine, Maas, and Schelde rivers has partially off-set the sinking of the land, but without the active efforts of men, the coastline would have drastically deteriorated.

ENVIRONMENTAL DETERIORATION.   Before the encroachment by the sea began, the ancient Dutch coast was apparently quite straight and paralleled by a protective wall of sand dunes (Figure 2.4). The only major breaks in the dunes occurred where the many distributaries of the Rhine, Maas, and Schelde cut through the dunes to reach the North Sea. As thousands of years passed and the level of some lands on the inland side of the dunes fell below sea level, parts of the Low Country were flooded. Driven by storms, the North Sea broke through the sand-

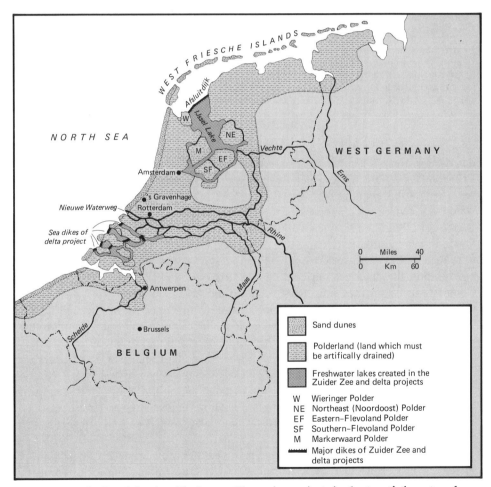

Figure 2.4   The Dutch battle with the sea. The major projects in the twentieth century have been the partial reclamation of the Zuider Zee and the protection of the Rhine–Maas–Schelde Delta area.

Figure 2.5 One of the many *terpen* which dot the Dutch coastal province of Friesland. This *terp,* or artificial mound, dates from the earliest period of the Dutch battle against the sea, and today contains the church and cemetery of the village of Jelsum. Before the era of dike-building, the countryside all around the *terp* was subject to periodic inundation by the waters of the sea. (Copyright Marianne Dommisse, from Netherlands Information Service, used with permission.)

dune barrier in the northern and southwestern Netherlands and permanently inundated large areas. This damage can still be seen today, especially in the north. The Friesche (Frisian) Islands, which lie in an east–west string along the northern coast, represent all that remains of the sand-dune wall in that sector, and the shallow saltwater Waddenzee which separates the islands from the coast was once dry land. Besides the Waddenzee, the other major marine incursion helped create a huge flooded river mouth, or estuary, where the Rhine, Maas, and Schelde rivers came to the sea on the southwestern coast (Figure 2.4).

Still the deterioration continued. Parts of the coastal margin of the Low Country was fragmented into marshy tidal islands, and numerous freshwater lakes were formed in depressions. From time to time storm tides broke through to join some of these lakes to the sea. When the Romans came to rule the Low Country, they found a large lake just south of the Waddenzee, fed and drained by a distributary of the Rhine, and called it the Flevo Lacus. Modern man was a witness when the Roman lake eventually became a saltwater embayment of the North Sea. A series of storms from A.D. 693 to 1237 cut through the ribbon of dry land separating the lake from the Waddenzee, creating the shallow Zuider Zee, or "southern sea," to replace Flevo Lacus. The other freshwater lakes in the coastal fringe awaited their turn to be joined to the sea.

Another type of deterioration involved the slow eastward migration of what remained of the sand-dune barrier. The westerlies, prevailing winds from the west, gradually moved the dunes inland, and the sea followed close behind. A fortress built during the Roman occupation on the landward side of the dunes was covered by drifting sands, disappeared, and was soon forgotten after the legions left, only to reappear during the Christmas season in the year 1520 on the *seaward* side of the dune wall. Soon thereafter the ruins were flooded by the advancing North Sea. This involved an eastward migration of about three kilometers (two miles) in 1500 years, and it is estimated that in the vicinity of the city of s'Graven-hage the dunes have moved at least five to eight kilometers (three to five miles).

EARLY HUMAN REACTION. Human action to resist the environmental deterioration has gained momentum over the last 1500 to 2000 years. At first the early Dutch inhabitants did nothing more than to pile up mounds of earth upon which to build their homes. These mounds, called *terpen,* can be seen today in parts of the Netherlands and are generally still inhabited (Figure 2.5). During periods of high water, the terpen temporarily became little islands protecting the people in clustered dwellings on top. These mounds were 3.7 to 12 meters (12 to 40 feet) high and varied in area from 1.5 to 16 hectares (4 to 40 acres). The terpen were built mainly from the third to tenth centuries A.D., and some 1500 of them still survive at least in rudiment. Somewhat later, in the 900s A.D., the Dutch began placing obstructions along the coast to catch and hold accretions of sand and silt and built walls to trap silt being washed down the rivers, gradually enlarging delta islands (Figure 2.6).

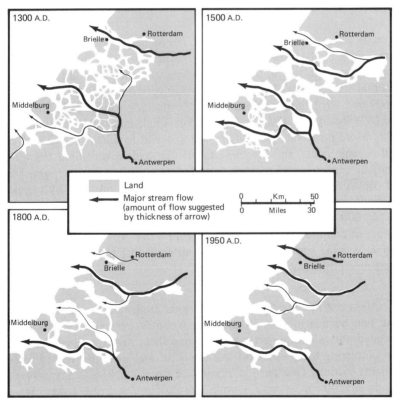

Figure 2.6 Man the modifier at work on the Dutch coastline, 1200–1950. Both the advance of the North Sea and the subsequent work of man to push back the waters are evident in these maps of the Rhine–Maas–Schelde Estuary in the Zeeland province of the Netherlands. The Delta Project is not shown. (After Westermann.)

DIKES AND POLDERS.   Dike-building began about A.D. 1000 in the extensive tidal marsh areas of Flanders and Zeeland, provinces of the southern Netherlands and adjacent Belgium. The dikes protected lands above the low-tide level that were subject to periodic flooding, and sluice gates were opened at low tide to allow discharge of the water which had accumulated through seepage. Such protected areas, drained by gravity flow of water at low tide, became known as *polders,* a term first used in 1138 in Flanders. Dike-building and poldering spread northward into the province of Holland, where Count William the Diker directed poldering in an area of peat bogs, lakes, and marshes south of Amsterdam in the early 1200s. A peak of dike construction occurred in the 1300s to protect cropland from the unpredictable seas, lakes, and rivers. Human reaction remained largely defensive.

The development of polders in areas too low to be drained by gravity at low tide awaited the invention of a mechanical water-lifter. The windmill had been known in the Low Country at least since the late 1100s, and it may well have been independently invented there, though it was known much earlier in a quite different form in the Middle East. For several centuries it served the Dutch only as a grinder of grain, but in the year 1408 the windmill was first employed as a water-lifter. The same westerlies which pushed the waters against the Dutch shores and caused the retreat of the protective sand dunes was harnessed to reclaim the land. Within several centuries nearly all of the marshes and bogs had been converted into polders, with a resultant increase in population and food production.

DRAINAGE OF LAKES.   Drainage of the numerous freshwater lakes dotting the coastal fringe of the Low Country was the next advance in Dutch reclamation technology. Two centuries of experimentation with the windmill had convinced engineers that sizable water bodies could be converted to agricultural use, and between 1609 and 1612 the combined work of forty-nine windmills laid dry a 7,300-hectare (18,000-acre) freshwater lake. Other small lakes were drained in quick succession. More powerful water-lifters were needed to allow reclamation of large lakes and oceanic inlets, and for these the Dutch had to wait until the nineteenth and twentieth centuries, when steam- and, later, electric-engine pumps became available. Between 1840 and 1846, a dike was built around the 60-kilometer (37-mile) circumference of the Haarlemmer Sea, a freshwater lake covering 17,800 hectares (44,000 acres) west of Amsterdam. Then three British-built steam-engine pumps worked continually for five years, from 1847 to 1852, to drain the lake. Haarlemmer was the largest water body yet to surrender to the Dutch at that time, and the greatest projects were still to come.

ZUIDER ZEE PROJECT.   The treacherous Zuider Zee, whose origin has been described, had been a menace to the Low Country ever since its formation. Its waters needed only a strong north wind to send them raging against the vulnerable sea dikes protecting the polderland to the south, and over the years the Zee had claimed many victims. One particularly severe flood in 1916 finally prompted the Netherlands government to take action. The Zuider Zee Project was approved in 1918, and actual work began seven years later. The key to the project was the building of a huge sea dike, the Afsluitdijk, across the narrow mouth of the Zuider Zee to cut it off from the ocean, a task completed in 1932 (Figure 2.4). The streams which flooded into the Zee soon flushed it clean of salt water, creating a freshwater body, IJssel Lake. Sluices to allow for outflow of water and locks to accommodate shipping were built into the dike. The hated name Zuider Zee disappeared from the map, and perhaps the only group of people who mourned its demise were the salt-water fishermen, mainly Frisians, whose livelihood was destroyed. The highway and railroad built on the new dike provided greatly shortened transport links between western and eastern parts of the Netherlands, and also reduced the mileage of exposed ocean dike to a small fraction of the former total.

The second part of the project has involved the diking and draining of five large polders from the floor of the old Zuider Zee. The Wieringer Polder in the far northern part was actually drained before all of the sea dike was finished, falling dry in 1931. Experimentation established the best sequence of crops to remove salinity from the soils, and soon the Wieringer Polder was being colonized by Dutch farmers. Settlement was completed under German occupation in 1941, and today the area is a fully integrated part of the Netherlands, largely undistinguishable from surrounding districts. Humor prompted the Dutch to name one of the new Wieringer towns Middenmeer, or "Middle-of-the-Sea." The other polders are (1) the Noordoost (Northeast), drained by electric pumps in 1936–1942 and completely colonized by the early 1960s; (2) Eastern-Flevoland, named for the ancient Roman lake and laid dry in 1957; (3) Southern-Flevoland, laid dry in 1968; and (4) Markerwaard, scheduled for completion in 1980. The latter two are still in varying stages of development, and it will probably be 1985 before the Zuider Zee project is finally completed. A sizable part of the IJssel Lake will remain undrained, serving as a freshwater supply and recreational area. The total land gained in new polders will be almost 2300 square kilometers (900 square miles).

DELTA PROJECT.   With the Zuider Zee Project, the Dutch have turned back the major marine encroachment on their northern coast. The other principal danger area lies in the southwestern province known as Zeeland, where the Rhine–Maas–Schelde estuary passes through six large gaps in the old sand-dune barrier. This delta country was no stranger to storm floods from the sea, but the attention of the Dutch government was finally attracted by an especially severe disaster in 1953. Between January 31 and February 2 of that year, 100-mile-per-hour winds from the northwest pushed river water back up into the estuary, breaking down dikes and spilling into the farmlands and towns of the islands in the estuary. More than eighty breaches were made in the dikes, and some 150,000 hectares (375,000 acres) were flooded with sea water. About 1,800 persons drowned, 100,000 were evacuated, and damage reached half a billion dollars (1953 value). Bad as the damage was, the storm could easily have been much worse. The strategic dike along the north bank of the Rhine–Maas channel called the New Waterway (Nieuwe Waterweg), protecting the densely settled heartland of Holland to the north, held—barely. Had it collapsed, the homeland of three million people would have been inundated and many persons drowned in a catastrophe of almost unimaginable proportions.

To prevent such an occurrence in the future, the government gave quick approval to the *Delta Project* (Figure 2.4). Four large sea dikes are being built to close off most of the mouths of the Rhine–Maas–Schelde estuary, with a freshwater lake on the landward side. The New Waterway is being left open so as not to disrupt Rhine River shipping, but elaborate water-diversion systems are being built to direct the flow of the Rhine and Maas into the adjacent lake in case a storm tide backs up the river as in 1953. The lake can absorb the river flow for several days without spilling over its dikes, and the excess water can then be released through sluices to the sea when the storm subsides. The western Schelde estuary is being left open, since it serves the major Belgian port of Antwerpen, but the dikes along the estuary shore are being raised and strengthened. Little land reclamation is involved in the Delta Project, only about 16,200 hectares (40,000 acres), for the goal is preservation rather than expansion. The project is rapidly nearing completion, and will definitely be finished before the Zuider Zee effort.

Holland, then, is a man-made land. Without the human effort that has been applied in the Low Country, the seacoast would lie far to the interior (Figure 2.4), and Europe would be deprived of some of its richest farmland and largest cities.

2.3 CLIMATE

Europe is far from being uniform in climate, though mild, humid conditions generally prevail. A number of factors contribute to regional climatic differences, of which the most important are *airmasses*. These are exactly what the name implies —large masses of air which are relatively uniform in temperature and moisture content, several different types of which compete for influence in Europe. *Marine* airmasses, moisture laden and mild in temperature, originate over the adjacent Atlantic Ocean and move onshore from the west, while the vast interior of the Eurasian continent and the frozen ocean of the north spawn cold, dry *continental* airmasses given to extremes of temperature, especially in winter. The Sahara Desert of North Africa is the birthplace of still another distinctive airmass, labeled *tropical continental,* which on occasion invades southern Europe, bringing hot, dry weather. Also influencing climate is *latitude,* or distance from the equator. Increased latitude means a weakening of incoming solar energy and a gradual cooling toward the north. Also important are the prevailing winds in Europe's latitudes, the *westerlies,* in which are embedded numerous low-pressure centers, or storms. Airmasses follow this same west-to-east migration pattern.

Elevation, or distance above sea level, can also affect climate, as increased elevation produces lower temperatures. In addition the *terrain* is important to European climate, in particular the distribution of mountain ranges. Many of the ranges are aligned in an east–west direction, parallel to the westerlies blowing in from the Atlantic, thereby allowing marine airmasses to penetrate far into Europe. In contrast, the mountains of the United States and Canada run roughly at right angles to the western coastline, blocking the entry of marine influence from the Pacific Ocean.

All of these factors, and others as well, help explain the map of climate regions (Figure 2.7). The classification of climatic types used here is that of W. Köppen as modified by G. T. Trewartha, and it should be recognized at the outset that, as in all classification systems, a great deal of generalization is involved. Although sharp lines are drawn on the map, in actuality there is a gradual transition from one region to the next.

Figure 2.7   Climate types. (After Köppen and Trewartha.)

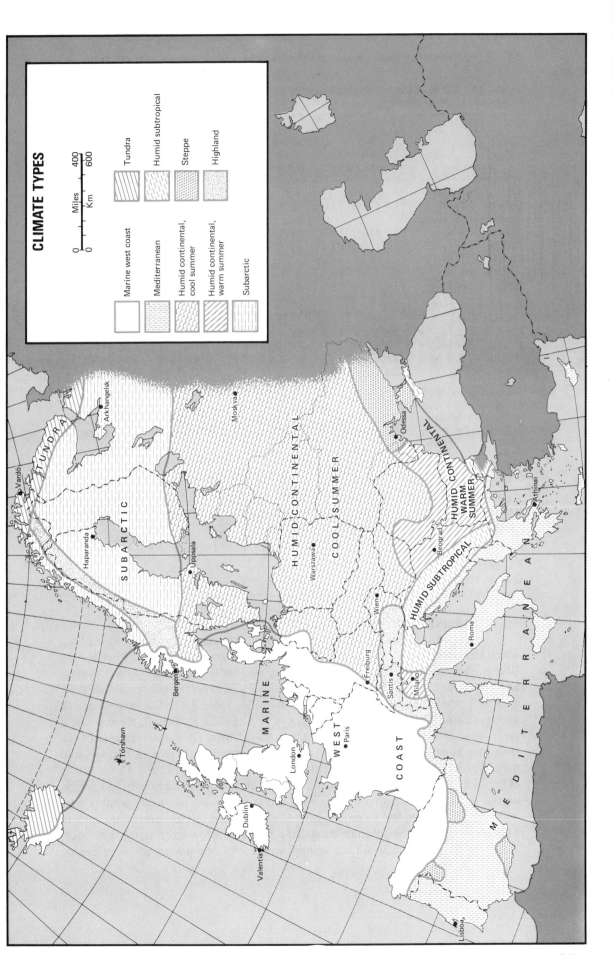

CLIMATE TYPES

Miles 0 400
Km 0 600

Marine west coast

Mediterranean

Humid continental, cool summer

Humid continental, warm summer

Subarctic

Tundra

Humid subtropical

Steppe

Highland

TABLE 2.1   Climatic Data for Selected Marine West Coast, Humid Continental, Subarctic, Tundra, Steppe, and Highland Stations

Station	July average temperature	January average temperature	Average annual temperature range	Average annual precipitation
Marine west coast				
Valentia, Ireland	15° C (59° F)	7° C (44° F)	8° C (15° F)	142 cm (56 in.)
Freiburg-im-Breisgau, West Germany	19° C (67° F)	1° C (33° F)	18° C (34° F)	86 cm (34 in.)
Paris, France	19° C (66° F)	3° C (37° F)	16° C (29° F)	58 cm (23 in.)
Tórshavn, Færoe Islands	11° C (51° F)	3° C (38° F)	8° C (13° F)	145 cm (57 in.)
Bergen, Norway	14° C (58° F)	1° C (34° F)	13° C (24° F)	213 cm (84 in.)
Cool-summer humid continental				
Moskva, USSR	19° C (66° F)	−11° C (12° F)	30° C (54° F)	53 cm (21 in.)
Uppsala, Sweden	17° C (62° F)	−4° C (24° F)	21° C (38° F)	53 cm (21 in.)
Warszawá, Poland	19° C (66° F)	−3° C (26° F)	22° C (40° F)	56 cm (22 in.)
Wien, Austria	20° C (68° F)	−2° C (29° F)	22° C (39° F)	64 cm (25 in.)
Warm-summer humid continental				
Beograd, Yugoslavia	22° C (72° F)	−2° C (29° F)	24° C (43° F)	61 cm (24 in.)
Milano, Italy	24° C (75° F)	−1° C (31° F)	25° C (44° F)	102 cm (40 in.)
Subarctic				
Arkhangelsk, USSR	16° C (60° F)	−13° C (8° F)	29° C (52° F)	43 cm (17 in.)
Haparanda, Sweden	16° C (60° F)	−10° C (14° F)	26° C (46° F)	53 cm (21 in.)
Tundra				
Vardö, Norway	9° C (48° F)	−6° C (22° F)	14° C (26° F)	66 cm (26 in.)
Highland				
Säntis, Switzerland	5° C (41° F)	−11° C (16° F)	14° C (25° F)	244 cm (96 in.)
Steppe				
Odessa, USSR	23° C (73° F)	−4° C (25° F)	27° C (48° F)	41 cm (16 in.)

MARINE WEST COAST CLIMATE

One of the three major climate types of Europe is the marine west coast, which indicates both its location and predominant airmass. Areally it includes the British Isles, northern Iberia, most of France, western Germany, the Low Country, and part of the fjord coast of Norway (Figure 2.7). Temperatures are mild all year, with cool summers and relatively pleasant winters (Table 2.1). The coldest month averages above freezing and generally below 7° C (45° F). Overall, there is not a great range of temperature between winter and summer. Dublin, the capital of the Irish Free State, averages only 10° C (18° F) warmer in July than in January, and the difference at Tórshavn in the Færoe Islands is only 7° C (13° F). The mildness of the winters is illustrated by the fact that the majority of January nights in London do *not* have frost. Occasional bitter cold waves do occur, but many winters pass without one. London has recorded −16° C (4° F), and in one severe cold spell in February 1929, the temperature remained constantly below freezing for 226 hours in the British capital. The surprising appearance of a few palm trees at places on the southwest Irish coast, however, suggests the overall mildness of the winters. The summers are cool, and sweaters or coats feel comfortable on many days. Heat waves, with temperatures above 32° C (90° F), do occur in parts of the marine west coast area, but they are also rare. The record high temperature at Paris is 38° C (100° F).

Because the marine airmasses contain great amounts of moisture, the west coast climate is quite humid, with adequate precipitation all year round. Normally between 50 to 100 centimeters (20 and 40 inches) fall each year, though some stations record more. In plains areas, the amounts are rather modest, as for example Paris, which receives only 58 centimeters (23 inches) annually, and London 62 centimeters (25 inches). However, the cool temperatures retard evaporation, as does prevalent cloudiness, and the precipitation is adequate to produce humid conditions. Stations situated in or at the western edge of hills and mountains receive considerably more precipitation. Freiburg-im-Breisgau, West Germany, at the foot of the Black Forest (Schwarzwald), averages 86 centimeters (34 inches) annually, and the slopes above Bergen, Norway, on the west flank of the Kjölen Range, receive 213 centimeters (84 inches) in an average year. This increased amount is the product of the so-called *orographic* factor. The humid airmasses moving from the west into Europe are forced to rise over hill and mountain barriers which block the path, such as the Black Forest (Schwarzwald) and Kjölen Range. In the process of rising, the airmass cools, thereby lowering its ability to hold moisture in an evaporated state, and the excess is precipitated on the west-facing slopes.

Very little precipitation typically falls on any given day in the marine west coast areas. Gentle showers or drizzles are the rule. Paris, for example, has its annual 58 centimeters (23 inches) spread over 188 days, or about 0.30 centimeter (0.12 inch) per rainy day, involving over half of all days in the year. On one occasion London had 72 consecutive days in which precipitation was recorded. Clouds obscure the sun most of the time, and the marine west coast climate is not regarded by most people as a pleasant one. Travel-folder pictures convey a quite misleading image of western Europe, because they are invariably taken on rare sunny days. Seventy percent or even more of the daylight hours each year are marred by cloudiness, and the British Isles average less than 1500 hours of sunshine annually, about 4 hours per day or less. Fog and mist are also common, and one town in Denmark reports an average of 54 foggy days each year. This cheerless climate drives numerous of its inhabitants to seek vacations in the sunny southern part of Europe.

Local winds can greatly modify weather within limited areas of the marine west coast climate. One of the best known is the *föhn* of southern Germany, a type of wind known in the United States as *chinook* and elsewhere in Europe under a variety of names. The föhn, a warm, dry wind from the south, results when one of the low-pressure centers, or storms, embedded in the westerlies moves across southern Germany. The low pressure serves to attract air over the Alps from the Mediterranean region. The winds are drawn up the southern slope of the Alps, dropping orographic precipitation and growing cooler in ascent, then descending into Germany, warming as they progress downslope. A föhn blowing in midwinter can produce a sudden false springtime, with fair skies and pleasant temperatures, a delightful though short-lived respite from the dreary, damp winter conditions.

Another trait of the marine west coast climate and, indeed, of climate throughout Europe, is the relative absence of violent types of weather. Europeans do not suffer the ravages of tornadoes or hurricanes such as plague the inhabitants of other mid-latitude areas such as the United States. Largely absent too are the potentially lethal blizzards, in which extreme cold is combined with high winds and snow, such as occur in the Great Plains of the central United States. Climatic extremes, including many forms of violent weather, are alien to Europe in almost all respects.

MEDITERRANEAN CLIMATE

Southern Europe, in particular the three southward-reaching peninsulas of Iberia, Italy, and Greece, is dominated by the Mediterranean type of climate. Also included are the various European islands of the Mediterranean, southern coastal France, and the Adriatic coast of Yugoslavia (Figure 2.7).

Certainly the most distinguishing trait of the Mediterranean climate is the concentration of precipitation in the winter season, with exceptionally dry summers. Generally, less than one-tenth of the annual precipitation falls in the quarter-year comprising the summer months of June, July, and August (Table 2.2), and the month of July is almost totally rainless. Lisboa, Portugal, averages only 0.5 centimeter (0.2 inch) in July; Roma, Italy, but 1.8 centimeter (0.7 inch); and Athínai (Athens), Greece, only 0.8 centimeter (0.3 inch). This seasonality of precipitation reflects the transitional position of the Mediterranean basin between the humid marine west coast to the north and the parched Sahara in the south. In winter the Mediterranean lands lie in the belt of westerlies and receive the impact of precipitation-producing airmasses and migrating storm centers, while in summer the region comes more under the influence of a great high-pressure center over the South Atlantic, which causes fair weather in Sahara and Mediterranean alike. Winter precipitation usually is in the form of rain in the thickly populated plains, but snow is common in the numerous mountain ranges. The accumulated snow in the highlands is of crucial importance to the farmers of the region, because the meltwater runoff in spring and summer provides a source of irrigation water for the drought season.

The temperatures in the Mediterranean climate are somewhat warmer than those of the marine west coast area because of a more southerly location and a lower incidence of cloudiness. The summers are hot, except along the Atlantic shore and some other windward coastlines, with July averages in the 21° C to 29° C (70° F to 85° F) range. The record high temperature at Athínai is 40.5° C

TABLE 2.2   Climatic Data for Selected Mediterranean Stations

	Lisboa, Portugal	*Roma, Italy*	*Athínai, Greece*
Average annual precipitation	74 cm (29 in.)	84 cm (33 in.)	41 cm (16 in.)
Average precipitation, June through August	3.0 cm (1.2 in.)	8.4 cm (3.3 in.)	3.8 cm (1.5 in.)
Month receiving most precipitation	November	October	November and December
Month receiving least precipitation	July and August	July	July
July average temperature	21° C (70° F)	24° C (76° F)	27° C (80° F)
January average temperature	11° C (51° F)	7° C (45° F)	9° C (48° F)
Average annual temperature range	10° C (19° F)	17° C (31° F)	18° C (32° F)

(105° F). However, the relative humidity in summer tends to be low, and fairly rapid nighttime cooling is common.

The winters are particularly mild, and extended periods of frost are unknown, except in the mountains. Groves of citrus fruit dot the lowlands of the Mediterranean, a good indicator of the absence of severe cold. The record low of −7° C (20° F) for Athínai is typical of the region.

Cloudiness is at a minimum, particularly in the summer, a striking contrast to the marine west coast. Parts of Italy receive over 2500 hours of sunshine per year, almost twice as much as the British Isles.

The local winds of the Mediterranean reflect its location between the marine west coast and the desert. Winter storm centers moving through the basin draw cold, damp winds down from the north, including the *mistral* and the *bora*. The mistral blows with some fury down the Rhône–Saône corridor into the Mediterranean coastal fringe of France and on beyond to the islands of Corse and Sardegna, while the bora strikes the eastern coast of Italy from across the Adriatic Sea. From the opposite direction, dry, hot *sirocco* winds (pronounced "shiroko") are drawn up from the Saharan region, parching already dry cropland when they occur in response to the low pressure produced by rare summer storms.

It was in the Mediterranean climate that the European culture area was born. These pleasant latitudes were home to the Minoan, Mycenaean, classical Greek, Etruscan, Roman, and Byzantine cultures, upon which much of Western Civilization is based. Moreover, periodic changes in the Mediterranean climate, especially a prolongation of the drought season, may have contributed to the decline of certain of these cultures. In particular, the curious abandonment of the cities of Mycenae and Tiryns in the Greek Pelopónnisos about 1150 B.C., centers of the great Mycenaean civilization, can perhaps be explained as the result of repeated crop failures due to drought. The classical scholar Rhys Carpenter proposed this desiccation theory, and he further suggested that the limited evidence of destruction by fire found in the ruins of Mycenae may have been caused by a starving peasantry seeking to gain access to the city's granaries. Continued drought presumably would have prompted mass emigration from Mycenae to better-watered lands, and in this way the city, whose king, Agamemnon, had only shortly before returned triumphant from the Trojan wars, was abandoned. So completely were its glories forgotten that superstitious Dorian Greek peasants in later times developed the myth of the giant Cyclops to explain how the massive stones of Mycenae's abandoned walls were put into place. According to Carpenter, another Mediterranean drought cycle in the seventh century A.D. helps explain the lack of cultural achievements in that period.

COOL-SUMMER HUMID CONTINENTAL CLIMATE

The third of the three major climate types found in Europe dominates the eastern part of the culture area, from central Germany on through Poland, Czechoslovakia, and Hungary into Russia, including southern Scandinavia as well (Figure 2.7). The cool-summer humid continental climate lies just to the interior, or east, of the marine west coast, and its name suggests the basic difference between the two. Here the battle of airmasses is won more often by those which originate over the great land expanse of Eurasia. The most apparent result of dominance by continental airmasses is a greater contrast between summer and winter temperatures (Table 2.1). In particular, the winters are colder and become progressively more bitter toward the east. The disasters which befell the armies of Hitler and Napoleon in Russia were in no small part the work of numbing cold. January averages in the cool-summer humid continental area range from about −12° C to 0° C (10° F up to freezing), and low readings far below −18° C (0° F) are common. The difference between January and July averages runs double or more the annual range of many marine west coast stations. Winter temperatures are low enough to cause a durable snowcover to develop, with usually at least one month in which the ground remains blanketed. In more eastern areas, the continuous snowcover can last for three or four months. Rivers, lakes, and shallow ocean inlets freeze over, including the Baltic Sea.

Summer temperatures are remarkably similar to those in the marine west coast area. The July average at Moskva and Warszawá is identical to that at Paris, and most stations fall in the 16° C to 21° C (60° F to 70° F) range for the warmest month average.

Precipitation is adequate at all seasons, due in part to the low evaporation rate associated with cool and cold weather. Between 50 and 63 centimeters (20 to 25 inches) of precipitation can be expected each year at typical humid continental stations, only slightly less than is the rule in marine west coast areas.

Closely akin to the cool-summer humid continental climate is the *warm-summer humid continental,* a subtype found in the lands along the lower Danube River, just south of the main body of the cool-summer region, and in the upper Po Valley (Figure 2.7). Temperaturewise, its summers are more akin to those of the adjacent Mediterranean, but there is no drought season. Any humid continental station which has an average of 22° C (72° F) or more for the warmest month belongs in the warm-summer variety of this climate (Table 2.1).

OTHER CLIMATE TYPES

The greater part of Sweden and Finland lie in the zone of the *subarctic climate,* more severe than the humid continental (Figure 2.7). Only one to three months average over 10° C (50° F), and the proximity to the pole in a continental location means bitter winters. Summers are very cool and short, and winter is clearly the dominant season (Table 2.1). Somewhat less precipitation falls than in areas to the south, but the total is still adequate to produce a humid climate, as evaporation is low in the cool summers. Few Europeans choose to live in this cold zone, and most of those who do have come as a result of a severe shortage of good land, as in Finland, or to exploit the fisheries or mineral wealth such as northern Sweden's iron ore.

The polar tree line marks the northern border of the subarctic, beyond which lies a narrow strip of *tundra climate,* a region largely devoid of trees (Figure 2.7). The tundra lacks a summer altogether, and the warmest month averages below 10° C (50° F, Table 2.1). Surprisingly, the adjacent Barents Sea, part of the Arctic Ocean, does not freeze in winter, and the entire Norwegian coast and the Soviet tundra port of Murmansk remain open to shipping, thanks to the influence of the easternmost branch of a warm ocean current known as the North Atlantic Drift.

The Dinaric Range and coastal portion of the Po Valley are characterized by the *humid subtropical climate,* identical to the Mediterranean area in temperature but lacking the pronounced summer drought. Here the summers are hot with high humidity, and the July visitor to Venezia may well be reminded of New Orleans or Brisbane.

Nearly all of the European region receives adequate precipitation, even if it is seasonal as in the Mediterranean. The only exceptions are some small, scattered semiarid areas of *steppe climate* (Figure 2.7, Table 2.1), where evaporation from the surface of the ground and the vegetation is potentially greater than the amount of moisture added through precipitation. The result is a chronic deficiency of water. In the Iberian Peninsula small dots of steppe climate are found in locations where mountain ranges block rain-bearing winds from the ocean to the west. The Almería region, centered in one of the several huertas between the Betico Mountains and the Mediterranean Sea, is semiarid, as are parts of the Ebro Valley, bordered on the west by the Iberian Mountains. Another steppe zone lies just north of the Black Sea in the Ukraine, part of the Soviet Union, the product of increased distance from the moisture-giving Atlantic.

Finally, the climatic influence of increased elevation is recognized in the largest European mountain range, the Alps, in the form of a special highland climate (Figure 2.7). It is impossible to characterize the Alpine climate, for variations are found with each difference in height and sun exposure, but in general, temperatures are lower and precipitation is greater than in the adjacent plains. For example, at Säntis in Switzerland, the effect of elevation is to create tundralike temperatures and almost 250 centimeters (100 inches) of precipitation annually (Table 2.1).

2.4 MAN'S INFLUENCE ON CLIMATE AND WEATHER

It is becoming increasingly apparent that man, particularly modern industrial man, is beginning to alter climate. Perhaps nowhere has this anthropoclimatology been so thoroughly studied as in the London area, the largest single urban complex in Europe. As early as 1661, the Englishman John Evelyn wrote in reference to London that "the weary traveller, at many miles distance, sooner smells, than sees the city to which he repairs." When the coal smoke poured through a myriad of chimneys, "the City of London resembles the face rather of Mount Etna, the Court of Vulcan, Stromboli, or the suburbs of hell, than an assembly of rational creatures. . . ." In recent times geographers studying climate have come to speak of London's "heat island," a reference to the fact that temperatures are consistently higher over the built-up portion of the city than over the surrounding rural Greenbelt (Figures 2.8, 2.9). Minimum nighttime temperatures are at times 7° C (12° F) higher over the central portion of London than in the Greenbelt, and daytime maximums are also higher. This is a result of several causal factors, including the inability of heat radiation from the surface to penetrate the pollution haze which hangs over the city; the retention of heat by paved streets and buildings; and the heat produced locally by fuel combustion in vehicles, factories, and homes. At times, isotherms, lines connecting points with the same temperature, take on the same shape as the London urban area (Figure 2.9).

Human activity also influences the rainfall and humidity characteristics of the London area. There are more thunderstorms over the city, more thunderstorm precipitation, and a distinctly higher absolute humidity than in adjacent rural areas. Observation suggests a tendency for thunderstorms to develop or intensify over north London. The cause apparently lies both in the greater amount of thermal convection resulting from more surface heating and in the superabundance of microscopic particulate matter associated with air pollution. Drops of condensation are built around such nuclei. A decrease in coal-burning has lessened somewhat the degree of air pollution in London since about 1960, but one can still observe the pronounced effect of man on the local climate. This same effect can be detected in other areas of dense human settlement.

Decreasing air pollution in the London area, the result of effective legal restrictions, has reduced the human modification of local temperatures and precipitation in recent years. Still, pollution of the air is increasingly common through much of Europe, even in cities such as Beograd and Athínai, which are outside the major industrial complex.

2.5 VEGETATION

The original vegetation cover of Europe has been so drastically modified by man that only minor vestiges remain today. Even the ablest and most experienced scholars cannot tell with certainty what the full extent of this human impact has

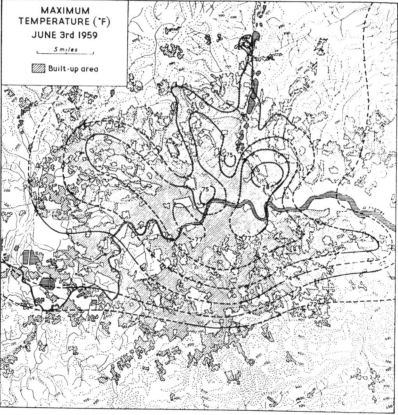

Figure 2.8 Stimulation of daytime heating in the built-up area of London. The temperatures, shown in degrees Fahrenheit, reveal the greater amount of heating in the urban area as opposed to the surrounding countryside. (Reproduced from T. J. Chandler, "The Changing Form of London's Heat Island," *Geography,* Vol. 46 (1961), p. 300, with the permission of The Geographical Association and the author.)

been, for the process began with the first arrival of men in Europe far back in prehistoric times. In the final analysis, the greater proportion of the plants which surround settlements are directly or indirectly the result of human activity, and it is
safe to say that the most impressive vegetation alteration has been accomplished
within the last 2000 years. The map of vegetation regions (Figure 2.10) is a rough
approximation of the pattern which existed before this major period of modifying
activity began.

MEDITERRANEAN OPEN FOREST

The coastal lands of the Mediterranean were once covered by an open
forest of broadleaf evergreen trees, interspersed with woody shrubs and grasses.
The plants were by necessity able to withstand the pronounced summer drought of
the area, and most can be described as *sclerophyllous,* or possessing exceptional
development of a protective supporting tissue, as in the thickening of leaves and
bark. The purpose is to retard evaporation, as is well illustrated by the thick, deeply
fissured bark of the cork oak or the stiff, leathery leaf of the olive tree. In addition,

Figure 2.9 Retardation of night cooling in the built-up area of London. The temperatures,
shown in degrees Fahrenheit, indicate a difference of twelve degrees from the heart of London
to the suburban "Greenbelt." Most of this climatic contrast is apparently the result of human
activity. (Reproduced from T. J. Chandler, "The Changing Form of London's Heat Island,"
Geography, Vol. 46 (1961), p. 303, with the permission of The Geographical Association
and the author.)

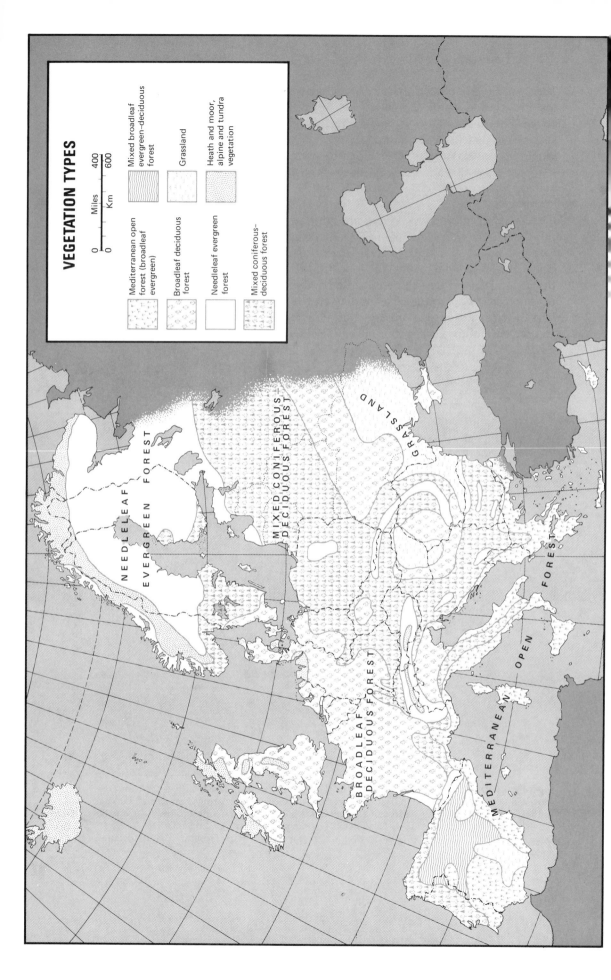

VEGETATION TYPES

Miles
0   400

Km
0   600

Mediterranean open forest (broadleaf evergreen)

Broadleaf deciduous forest

Needleleaf evergreen forest

Mixed coniferous–deciduous forest

Mixed broadleaf evergreen–deciduous forest

Grassland

Heath and moor, alpine and tundra vegetation

NEEDLELEAF EVERGREEN FOREST

MIXED CONIFEROUS–DECIDUOUS FOREST

GRASSLAND

BROADLEAF DECIDUOUS FOREST

MEDITERRANEAN OPEN FOREST

the leaves are small and shiny, further retarding evaporation. Laurel, cypress, chestnut, lavender, and myrtle join the live oaks as major Mediterranean species. Typically the trees are widely spaced, of medium to low height, with massive trunks and gnarled branches. In higher elevations, some poplar, ash, birch, and pine trees are found, as in the famous pines of Rome.

Man's destruction of the Mediterranean woodlands began in prehistoric times, long before the classical period. Homer's *Iliad,* apparently based on an oral tradition dating back to the twelfth century B.C., contains the earliest references to the plant life of the Mediterranean, pointing to a much more complete forest cover than exists at present. Homer wrote of "wooded" Samothráki and of Itháki "with quivering leafage," the former an island in the northern Aegean, the latter Ulysses' home island in the Ionian Sea west of the Grecian mainland, neither of which is well wooded at present (Figure 2.11). Mediterranean forests were destroyed in a variety of ways for many purposes, and the clearing continued over thousands of years. Fire was used to create more pastureland for the numerous herds of sheep and goats, as well as additional farmland for grains, orchards, and vineyards. Often the fires were accidentally set in the drought season, for Homer wrote that ". . . fierce fire rages through the glens on some parched mountainside, and the deep forest burns. The wind driving it whirls the flames in every direction. . . ." Shipbuilding also took a heavy toll, including the "thousand" ships launched for the sake of fair Helen of Troy. Homer, in describing the incredible carnage on the battlefield in front of Troy, was fond of comparing the deaths of warriors to the felling of trees, and a soldier speared in the throat "fell as an oak, or a poplar, or tall pine tree which craftsmen have felled in the hills with freshly whetted axes to be a ship's timber," while another warrior, speared just below the ear, "fell as an ash, on the crest of a distant hill, which is smitten by the bronze axe and falls to the ground." Timber was cut also to provide charcoal for smelting, particularly after the use of iron replaced bronze. Timber was also used in the construction of buildings, including temples and palaces, until finally a shortage of wood forced acceptance of stone as the primary Mediterranean building material. An example from the non-European Mediterranean, where historical records are more complete, is the great temple of Solomon in Jerusalem, built in part of cedar wood from the famous forests of Lebanon. Considerable damage had already occurred by the 400s B.C., prompting Plato to compare deforested, eroded Attica to "the skeleton of a sick man, all the fat and soft earth have been wasted away, leaving only the bare framework of the land."

Man, then, using both fire and axe, assaulted the Mediterranean woodlands in preclassical times and continued the destruction for many centuries. What made this attack all the more significant was the fact that the forest was not able to reestablish itself after being cleared. The removal of trees tended to be permanent for two major reasons. First, the Mediterranean open forest was, more often than not, situated on steep slopes, for this southern part of Europe is dominated by mountainous terrain. When the trees were removed from the slopes, the soil was soon washed away by the winter rains, stripping the mountains to bare rocky skeletons unfit for reforestation. The second retarding factor in woodland regeneration was the lowly goat, a domestic animal of great importance to most

Figure 2.10   Vegetation types.

Figure 2.11   Deforested, rocky landscape on the Aegean island of Patmos. Thousands of years of grazing, accidental fires, and the need for lumber have left this Greek hillside denuded of forest, with much exposed rock. Tall stone fences have been built to separate adjacent herds of goats and sheep. Most of the Greek islands were once much more forested than they are today. (Photo by the author.)

Mediterranean rural people. The goat, quite at home in the rugged terrain, devours with pleasure the tender young shoots of trees newly broken through the soil. This single animal was probably responsible for the permanence of deforestation in many of the lands along the Mediterranean shore.

Still, much timber survived in the classical period, as is indicated by the writings of numerous scholars of the time. The same destruction continued in post-classical times. Venetian and Genoese merchant fleets and Byzantine, Spanish, and Portuguese imperial navies made the same demands on the forests as had their Greek and Roman predecessors. The craftsmen of Firenze, Toledo, and Constantinople needed charcoal as had their classical forerunners, and the ever-present herdsmen and farmers continued to regard the woodland as an enemy to be conquered.

The most extreme result of man's activity are expanses of bare rock devoid of any vegetation. More common, however, are regions covered with thickets of low evergreen shrub growth, known in French as *maquis,* in Italian as *macchia* or *maki,* and in Spanish as *matorral.* These thickets were used as hiding places by the French underground in World War II, with the result that the entire resistance movement became known as the Maquis. There are also areas of *garigue* vegetation, a thin cover of scattered evergreen scrub rooted in very shallow soil or in fissures in bare rock. In either case, maquis or garigue, man has produced a badly damaged environment which is of little further use. If the Mediterranean lands which supported the great civilizations of antiquity could be compared photographically to modern Greece or Italy, the differences revealed would be shocking, and perhaps the present backwardness and poverty of the region could be linked in part to a drastic environmental decline.

DECIDUOUS BROADLEAF FOREST

Large parts of Europe were formerly covered with forests of deciduous broadleaf trees, those which drop their leaves during the dormant season in winter. In part, the distribution resembled that of the marine west coast climate, including the British Isles, most of France, western Germany, and southern Scandinavia (Figure 2.10); and there is, indeed, a certain amount of cause-and-effect relationship between climate and vegetation. However, large zones of broadleaf deciduous forest were once found in eastern Europe, in the region of humid continental climate, serving as a caution against acceptance of a climatic determinism of vegetation. The most common trees of the European broadleaf deciduous forest include various oaks, the dominant species, as well as the elm, beech, linden, and ash. Wherever three-quarters or more of the woodland is composed of such trees, the designation broadleaf deciduous forest is appropriate.

In general, the soils underlying these woodlands were very well suited for farming, due partly to the dominance of plains terrain and the rich deposits of leaf mold which had accumulated over the centuries. Consequently, man has largely destroyed the broadleaf deciduous forest. The major period of clearing began later than in the Mediterranean, not until about A.D. 500. While it is likely that Neolithic man used fire, and perhaps the axe as well, to create open land in northwestern Europe, particularly on the loessial soils of the North German Plain, this early phase of clearing was of minimal importance. The great deciduous broadleaf woodland of France was sufficiently intact at the time of the Roman conquest to afford a refuge to the beleaguered Gauls, for Julius Caesar in his *Commentaries* made frequent reference to the role of the forest in Gaulic defensive strategy.

During Roman times "forest" became virtually synonymous with "border" in many parts of the Empire, especially in the broadleaf deciduous lands of the north. The god Sylvanus was, significantly, the Roman protector of both woodlands and borders. Indeed, forests continued to serve as buffer zones between hostile European peoples long after Roman times, especially in the Middle Ages. Slav and German were thus separated and the German word *"Mark"* (English "march"), as in the Mark Brandenburg, came to mean "border region," though the word originally designated "forest." To Roman and German alike, then, woodlands often acquired the status of political borders, separating the clearings of adjacent hostile peoples.

The Roman occupation of the deciduous broadleaf forest of northwestern Europe led to accelerated clearing, but still the greater part of the conquered provinces remained wooded. Centuries later, when the legions retreated from the banks of the Thames, Rhine, and Seine to defend the core of a crumbling empire, they left behind densely forested lands.

Coincident with the fall of the Roman Empire, for reasons still inadequately understood, there was a major period of population increase and westward migration by Germanic tribes, including the Frankish invasion of modern France and the Anglo-Saxon penetration of Great Britain. Soon thereafter, in the Middle Ages,

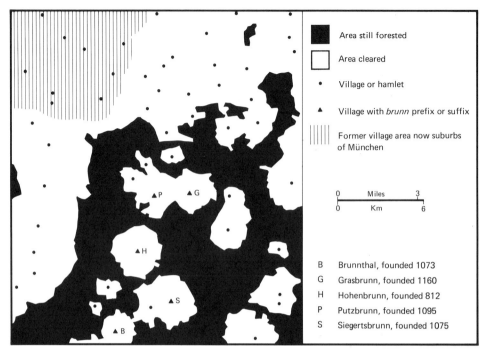

Figure 2.12 Stages of forest clearance on the southeastern outskirts of München, West Germany. This map reveals typical Germanic forest clearance at almost every stage, curiously preserved to the present day. The smaller clearings are suggestive of an early stage; the Hohenbrunn clearing, almost perfectly circular, of a somewhat later stage. The Siegertsbrunn–Brunnthal area reveals the earliest phase of coalescence of adjacent clearings, while the Putzbrunn–Grasbrunn area is an example of more mature coalescence. To the north and west more complete clearing occurred, producing the typical western European pattern of isolated remnant groves. Place names containing the word element *brunn* indicate that the original clearing was accomplished with fire (compare English "burns"). (After Brunhes.)

the Germanic folk began major forest-clearance activities, centered in northern France, western Germany, the United Kingdom, and the Low Country. Many new agricultural colonies were founded by small groups of settlers, over the centuries, acting under the direction of monarchs, landlords, or the church. Often, evidence of the initial clearing is contained in the present-day village and town names. In Germany, the common suffixes *-rod, -rot, -rodt, -roth, -rode, -reuth,* and the like, as in Wernigerode, Heiligenroth, and Bayreuth, are all related to the modern German verb *roden,* which means "to root out," or "to clear." The Flemish and Dutch forms of this suffix, found in portions of Belgium and the Netherlands, are *-rode, -rath, -raedt,* and *-rade,* and in Norway it appears as *-rød* or *-rud.* The German and English suffixes or prefixes *brand, brent, brind, bronn, brunn,* and the like, exemplified by Branderoda, Oberbränd, and Brindley, indicate that the original clearing was accomplished by burning, for all are derived from a Germanic root word meaning "fire" (modern German "der Brand" and English "to brand"). In England the frequently encountered suffixes *-ley, -leigh,* and *-lea,* as in Woodley or Mariansleigh, are derived from an old Germanic word meaning a "clearing" or "open place" in the woods, as is the Flemish equivalent *-loo,* as in Waterloo and Beverloo. In French language areas, the word element *sart,* from the verb meaning "to grub up" or "to clear," appears in many place names, such as Cul-des-Sarts in Belgium and Les Essarts in France.

Germanic forest removal typically began with small, roughly round clearings. As the population grew, the settlers worked communally to push the perimeter of farmland outward at the expense of the forest, until finally the clearings of adjacent villages joined, sometimes leaving small isolated groves of trees at points farthest from the settlements (Figure 2.12). Less common, and confined mainly to valleys in the hill lands of central and eastern Germany, was the pattern of clearing which began with a long, narrow cut along the valley to serve as a road. The colonists each received a ribbon-shaped farm stretching in a narrow strip back away from the road. Farmsteads were built at the front of the holdings, and each colonist was responsible for clearing his own property. Since no communalism was involved, the more ambitious settlers or those richer in sons rapidly cleared the forest toward the hinter portions of their land, while their neighbors lagged behind, producing an uneven line of farmland advancing from the valley toward the adjacent ridgecrest.

The Germanic devastation of the broadleaf deciduous forest continued unabated through the Middle Ages to about 1350, when pestilence and warfare drastically reduced the population in many areas, causing a temporary halt in the expansion of farmland. In fact, the forest was able to reclaim some districts depopulated by the Black Death or military activity (Figure 2.13). The Hundred Years' War in France was so destructive of peasant life as to give rise to a folk-saying of the northern part of the Basin of Aquitaine lamenting that "the forests came back to France with the English."

The great era of clearing which ended in the mid-fourteenth century was primarily the work of agriculturists, though other demands were also made on the forests. As in the Mediterranean, charcoal was needed for smelting. In Belgian Brabant the great *Silva Carbonnaria,* or "forest of the charcoal makers," is today an unwooded plain.

After a brief respite of a century or so, the surviving deciduous forests were subjected to a renewed attack by Germanic axemen. Population decline had proven to be temporary, and a final phase in the clearing of the western European woodland

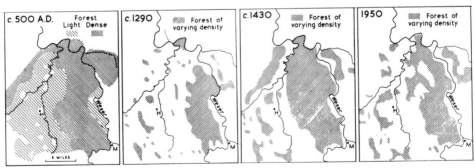

Figure 2.13 Extent of forests in the far northern part of Hessen, West Germany, at various periods. H = Hofgeismar, M = Münden. Note the major forest clearance in the Middle Ages, followed by a spread of woods in the period of population decline caused by the plague after about 1350. (After Jäger.) (Reproduced with permission from H. Clifford Darby, "The Clearing of the Woodland in Europe," in *Man's Role in Changing the Face of the Earth,* ed. William L. Thomas, Jr., The University of Chicago Press, 1956, p. 199.)

occurred in the 1500s and 1600s. To the renewed demands of an expanding farm population were added the needs of English, French, and Dutch shipbuilders, as well as other artisans. By 1550 England suffered from acute timber shortages, and France was in the same position a century later. Both came to rely on their American colonies to supply much-needed lumber. Considerable forests remained in Ireland during the late 1500s, for there are Elizabethan documents containing comments on the difficulty of conducting military campaigns against Irish rebels in their refuge woodlands. It seems likely that some woods in Munster and Ulster, the southwestern and northeastern parts of the island, were felled for military reasons, to destroy the refuges. The process of deforestation was completed in Ireland in the 1600s by profit-hungry landlords, who sold the timber abroad. By the year 1700, woodlands had vanished from the Irish scene, as is suggested by the virtual absence of oak from the pollen record after that time.

The severity of deforestation decreased eastward through the broadleaf deciduous woodland. Today, only 6 percent of the United Kingdom remains forested, compared to 7 percent in the Netherlands, 20 percent in France, and 27 percent in Germany (Figure 2.14).

A conservation movement arose in time to save only small remnants of the deciduous broadleaf woodland. The nobility of Europe provided early leadership in the drive to save forests, prompted by a desire to maintain hunting preserves for recreational purposes. Sherwood Forest in England acquired royal protection for this reason. Another hunting ground spared the axe was the *Tiergarten,* literally "animal garden," unusual because it was situated in the center of the city of Berlin. There it survived until the winter of 1945–1946, when the desperate inhabitants of the destroyed capital cut the trees for firewood. The Tiergarten has since been replanted. Terrain also protected some of the forest, for woodland cover on steep slopes was generally spared by the farmers (Figure 2.15). So close is the identification between forest and hilly or mountainous areas in Germany that the word *Wald,* "forest," is used as the name for areas of rough terrain, as in Schwarzwald (Black Forest) or Thüringerwald. Similarly, hilly areas in England sometimes bear the suffix -*wold,* as in Cotswold.

Figure 2.14   The retreat of woodland in central Europe, A.D. 900–1900 (After Schlüter.) (Reproduced with permission from H. Clifford Darby, "The Clearing of the Woodland in Europe," in *Man's Role in Changing the Face of the Earth,* ed. William L. Thomas, Jr., The University of Chicago Press, 1956, pp. 202–203.)

Figure 2.15 Forest survival on an English escarpment. The steep slopes of Wenlock Edge in western England, near the Welsh border, were unattractive to farmers, and much of the woodland cover survived the era of forest clearance. In contrast, the fertile vales below were almost completely stripped of trees and are well cultivated. The remnant forests resemble dark caps on the steep leading edges of a succession of great earthen "waves." In Europe as a whole, forests have survived mainly on steep slopes, in hilly and mountainous terrain. (Copyright Aerofilms Limited, London.)

Scientific forestry has arisen in the past two or three centuries in response to the need to preserve remaining forests, and the Germans have been pioneers in this field. The scattered woodlands are now carefully tended, with heavy penalties for unauthorized cutting. Villagers gather dead wood from the forest floor, and it is unusual to find fallen trees or limbs. Often these tidy groves resemble parks more than natural woodlands, particularly to the American eye. In more recent times, however, a rising standard of living and adoption of oil and gas heaters has decreased the use of firewood and caused the forest floors to become littered with fallen wood in countries such as West Germany. Europeans value the remnant forests as recreational areas and have laid out a splendid network of hiking trails. It is rare to find a forest area that is not open to the public.

NEEDLELEAF EVERGREEN FOREST

A portion of northern Europe, as well as scattered mountainous and sandy lowland regions further south, are characterized by needleleaf evergreen softwoods, including spruces, firs, and pines (Figure 2.10). These are represented by European species such as the Norway spruce and Scottish pine. Approximately three-quarters or more of all trees in this forest are conifers.

Man has treated the needleleaf evergreen forest much more gently than the woodlands of southern and western Europe, for two principal reasons. First, the major zone of conifers in Scandinavia lies in the inhospitable subarctic climate, a region unfit for intensive agriculture because of low temperatures and infertile soils. The mountain conifers in the Alps and elsewhere were similarly spared from the agriculturist's axe, due not only to adverse soil and weather conditions, but also to steep slopes. As a consequence, Finland remains 64 percent forested, Sweden 53 percent, and Alpine-dominated Austria 37 percent. The needleleaf evergreen forests are major suppliers of lumber for Europe, but the industry carefully manages the cutting operation so as to replace trees as rapidly as they are removed. Sweden and Finland together export over half of the sawn lumber produced in Europe, and Austria provides an additional 20 percent. The Scandinavian countries are also world leaders in wood-pulp and paper processing, one result of the high literacy rate in Europe.

The limited afforestation accomplished by the Europeans has been primarily to the advantage of needleleaf evergreen woodlands. The infertile, sandy Landes District of the Basin of Aquitaine in southwestern France has been planted to pines and thereby changed from a wasteland to an important supplier of lumber and naval stores for an otherwise timber-poor nation.

MIXED FORESTS

Wide areas of Europe were once covered by a woodland transitional between the broadleaf deciduous and needleleaf evergreen forests, containing a mixture of these two basic tree types, in which neither was dominant. The eastern Germanic lands, southern Sweden, and much of the Slavic domain in eastern Europe once possessed such forests, as did certain mountainous areas in the Mediterranean peninsulas. In general, the percentage of broadleaf deciduous trees increases and the conifers decrease southward and westward through the main body of the mixed-forest region.

The Germanic farmers who decimated the broadleaf deciduous woodland spread into the mixed forest in the Middle Ages, moving east along the North German Plain and Danube River valley. In time, a sprinkling of German agricultural colonies dotted most of eastern Europe. The Slavs, who had already made a modest attack on the mixed forest, received an added impetus from the Germans and soon expanded the cleared area into the East European Plain. Slavic clearance is indicated by place names containing the word elements *trebynja, kopanice, lazy,* and *paseky,* all of which specifically indicate clearing, as in the Slovenian town Trebnje. Still, the destruction did not quite equal that in western Europe, and countries such as Czechoslovakia, Bulgaria, Yugoslavia, and Russia remain about one-third forested today. Even Poland, a plains nation which offers few mountain refuges for woodland, remains over 20 percent forested.

Another transitional forest is the mixed zone of broadleaf evergreen and broadleaf deciduous trees in northern Iberia, blending the traits of Mediterranean lands and northwestern Europe. Here little remains of the original woodland.

GRASSLAND, MOOR, HEATH, AND TUNDRA

Regions covered with grass, also called steppes, are uncommon in Europe. In the east, a finger of grassland lying along the shore of the Black Sea points toward the heart of Europe, a remarkable steppe corridor which has served as a natural routeway for many groups of mounted Asiatic invaders, who found the treeless country well suited to their mode of warfare. The western tip of the grassland finger is the Valachian Plain of southern Romania, and just beyond in the Hungarian Basin is the Alföld, an outlier of the steppe. It is significant that the Magyar invaders of Europe, linguistic ancestors of the modern Hungarians, established a permanent foothold in the grassy portions of the Hungarian Basin, an area perhaps vegetationally similar to their previous homeland, while in the closed forestlands of Europe they suffered military defeat and were expelled.

The only other sizable grass-covered districts lie in the drier portions of Spain, including parts of the Ebro Valley and the Basin of New Castilla. Still today, windmills are powered by the winds which blow across the treeless expanse of La Mancha, a portion of New Castilla.

Once an expanse of tall grasses covered these open areas of Europe, but man has long since removed the original vegetation. The prairie soils were too fertile to be spared the plow, and grazing by domestic livestock completed the destruction. Only the absence of even remnant forest groves suggests that woodlands were not common. The story of man's modifying activity probably goes back much further, however, for the open grassy country, in particular the Alföld, may itself have been the result of removal of a forest cover by prehistoric humans.

Small areas of moor and heath are found in the British Isles, Low Country, and North German Plain. A variety of low plants, including grasses, juniper, brambles, heather, and furze (gorse) are typical of the moors and heaths, and the surface is often sandy or overlaid with peat. In general, these are poor areas agriculturally and have attracted very small populations.

North of the treeline in Scandinavia and above the limit of tree growth in mountain areas, tundra or Alpine vegetation is found. Lichens, mosses, sedges, grasses, and a variety of low bushes and dwarf trees are found, sufficient to support grazing herds of livestock. Reindeer nomads spend the summer in the tundra of Scandinavia, and dairy cattle are taken at the same season to graze on the highland *almen* and *seter* pastures of the Alps and Kjölen Range. The short summer brings an outburst of flowery plants of unique coloring and beauty.

2.6 SOILS

While conditions vary greatly within Europe, soils suitable for intensive agriculture are quite widespread. Over much of the area once covered by broadleaf deciduous woodlands, fertile brownish soils with adequate humus developed. These were sufficiently attractive to motivate the difficult work of forest removal, and they support still today a large farm population. Through the centuries, repeated plowing and manuring, establishment of pasture grasslands, and the absence of fallen leaves from forest trees have produced soil more nearly man-made than natural. Surprisingly little erosion has occurred, in part because much of the land is in pasture grasses which hold the soil in place.

The greater part of the needleleaf evergreen and mixed needleleaf–deciduous forests are underlaid with infertile, acidic soils known as *podsols,* from the Russian *pod zola,* or "ash-colored soil." Before the podsols can produce satisfactory harvests, the farmer must add large amounts of manure to correct a humus shortage and lime to counteract the acidity. Nevertheless, podsols are widely used for agriculture in the zone of original mixed forest.

Much of the zone of Mediterranean climate and vegetation is characterized by pink or reddish soils of varying depth and fertility, known by the Italian name *terra rossa,* or "red earth." These are derived from limestone, and rarely extend to any considerable depth. Of all the soils of Europe, the terra rossa have probably been most abused by man. About half of all land in the central and southern provinces of Spain is seriously or severely eroded, and all cultivated land with a slope of 3 percent or more has been damaged. Abandonment of land no longer fit for crop farming is occurring, and some of the orchards, vineyards, and fields have lost more than three feet of soil and subsoil. Irrigation reservoirs are silting up, and the debris of erosion clogs many streams and drainage channels. Fragmentation of the cropland into tiny parcels through the practice of divided inheritance makes difficult such conservation measures as contour plowing, terracing, and strip-cropping. The Spanish government is acting to improve the situation, but it will prove difficult to correct a process of deterioration already thousands of years old.

Among the best European soils are the *chernozems* of the former grasslands in the Hungarian Basin, the Valachian Plain, and the Ukraine. "Chernozem" is Russian for "black earth," and the dark color is the visible mark of a very high humus content, derived from decomposed grasses. Wheat, in particular, thrives on the chernozems and has long been the major bread grain there.

Wind-deposited *loess,* related to the chernozems, is present in an extensive fragmented belt from Russia to France through the heart of the European peninsula. Loess is easy to work and very fertile, a sandy loam rich in lime, but careful treatment of the land is necessary to prevent erosion, because it is very fine textured.

Scattered about in small strips along rivers and lesser streams are *alluvial* soils, composed of material deposited by flowing water. Countless alluvial lowlands dot the Mediterranean area, including the previously mentioned *huertas* of Betico coastal Spain, and such soils support just about all of the intensive agriculture of southern France. A very large alluvial area is found in the Low Country of the Netherlands and Belgium, where several rivers built up a collective delta. Man greatly speeded the process of alluviation in the Mediterranean area by removing the soil-holding forests on the mountain slopes. One consequence has been the rapid silting up of harbors, in some cases adequate to make inland towns out of places which were seaports as recently as the classical period. The Greek geographer Strabo, writing just prior to the beginning of the Christian Era, noted that the Adriatic tides reached to Ravenna in the Po Valley, a city which is today ten kilometers (six miles) inland. Even more impressive is the silting which occurred in the area of Monte Circeo, a mountain on the western coast of Italy. According to the Homeric epic *Odyssey,* Monte Circeo formed an island, but today the mountain is on a peninsula attached to Italy by a wide belt of silt deposited in the three thousand years since Ulysses' visit.

Tundra and high mountain regions have at the surface either bare rock, as is the case in much of the Kjölen Range, where it is called *fjell,* or very poorly developed, highly acidic bog soils. The cold temperatures retard both chemical weathering of bedrock and biological decay of plant life, two main processes by which soils are created. Crop farming is absent from such regions, and at best the land supports small groups of herdsmen.

*   *   *

NATURE WAS BOUNTIFUL in Europe, providing climates surprisingly mild for latitudes so high, extensive zones of fertile soils, an advantageous arrangement of terrain, and a rich and abundant plant life, all of which man has modified to some extent. Yet Europe was not more blessed environmentally than many other parts of the world. Nothing in the physical makeup of Europe is not duplicated in other lands across the seas. The nonagricultural Indians of pre-Columbian times lived in Mediterranean and marine west coast climates on the Pacific shore of North America, while their counterparts in what is now the eastern United States occupied a broadleaf deciduous woodland strikingly like that of Europe. The geographer Carl Sauer suggested that it would have been impossible for western European emigrants to cross any ocean and find a land environmentally more like their old homeland than was the eastern seaboard of the United States. Yet the American Indians living in this physical twin of Europe had developed quite un-European cultures. Similar environments do not necessarily produce similar cultures.

European man has more nearly molded his physical surroundings than he has been shaped culturally by his environment. At best the study of the physical Europe provides a description of the man-modified stage upon which Europeans, the activists, play out their largely self-written drama. The remainder, and appropriately larger part, of the book is devoted to the variety of areal patterns created by the peoples of Europe.

SOURCES AND SUGGESTED READINGS

Edgar Anderson. "Man as a Maker of New Plants and New Plant Communities." In *Man's Role in Changing the Face of the Earth,* ed. William L. Thomas, Jr. Chicago: University of Chicago Press, 1956, pp. 763–777.

Ian Y. Ashwell and Edgar Jackson. "The Sagas as Evidence of Early Deforestation in Iceland." *Canadian Geographer.* Vol. 14 (1970), pp. 158–166.

B. W. Atkinson. "A Further Examination of the Urban Maximum of Thunder Rainfall in London, 1951–60." *Institute of British Geographers, Transactions and Papers.* Vol. 48 (1969), pp. 97–119.

Hugh H. Bennett. "Soil Erosion in Spain." *Geographical Review.* Vol. 50 (1960), pp. 59–72.

J. Blüthgen. "Klimawerte der Länder der Erde." *Geographisches Taschenbuch 1960–1961.* Wiesbaden, Germany: Franz Steiner, 1960.

Ernst Brezina and Wilhelm Schmidt. *Das künstliche Klima in der Umgebung des Menschen.* Stuttgart, Germany: Enke, 1937.

Jean Brunhes. *Human Geography.* Translated by Ernest F. Row. Skokie, Ill.: Rand McNally, 1952.

Rhys Carpenter. *Discontinuity in Greek Civilization.* London: Cambridge University Press, 1966.

T. J. Chandler. "London's Urban Climate." *Geographical Journal.* Vol. 128 (1962), pp. 279–302.

T. J. Chandler. "The Changing Form of London's Heat Island." *Geography.* Vol. 46 (1961), pp. 295–307.

T. J. Chandler. *The Climate of London.* London: Hutchinson, 1965.

Victor Conrad. "The Climate of the Mediterranean Region." *Bulletin of the American Meteorological Society.* Vol. 24 (1943), pp. 127–145.

H. Clifford Darby. "The Clearing of the Woodland in Europe." In *Man's Role in Changing the Face of the Earth,* ed. William L. Thomas, Jr., *op. cit.,* pp. 183–216.

John H. Davis. "Influence of Man upon Coast Lines." In *Man's Role in Changing the Face of the Earth,* ed. William L. Thomas, Jr., *op. cit.,* pp. 504–521.

H. J. Fleure. "The Loess in European Life." *Geography.* Vol. 45 (1960), pp. 200–204.

Alice Garnett. "The Loess Regions of Central Europe in Prehistoric Times." *Geographical Journal.* Vol. 106 (1945), pp. 132–143.

R. Louis Gentilcore. "Reclamation in the Agro Pontino, Italy." *Geographical Review.* Vol. 60 (1970), pp. 301–327.

George W. Hoffman. "The Zuider Zee Reclamation Project." *Papers of the Michigan Academy of Science, Arts and Letters.* Vol. 35 (1949), pp. 197–211.

Homerus. *Chapman's Homer: The Iliad, the Odyssey, and the Lesser Homerica.* Edited by Allardyce Nicoll. Princeton, N.J.: Princeton University Press, 2nd ed., 1967.

M. H. M. van Hulten. "Plan and Reality in the IJsselmeerpolders." *Tijdschrift voor Economische en Sociale Geografie.* Vol. 60 (1969), pp. 67–76.

Wladimir Köppen, Rudolph Geiger *et al. Handbuch der Klimatologie.* Berlin: Borntraeger, Vols. I, III, 1930–1936.

Albert Kratzer. *Das Stadtklima.* Braunschweig, Germany: Vieweg-Verlag, 2nd ed., 1956.

A. W. Küchler. "Vegetation [of Europe]." In *Goode's World Atlas,* ed. Edward B. Espenshade, Jr., Skokie, Ill.: Rand McNally, 13th edition, 1970, p. 125.

H. H. Lamb. "Britain's Changing Climate." *Geographical Journal.* Vol. 133 (1967), pp. 445–466.

Audrey M. Lambert. *The Making of the Dutch Landscape: An Historical Geography of the Netherlands.* London and New York: Seminar Press, 1971.

C. Milleret. "La Forêt d'Orléans." *Annales de Géographie.* Vol. 72 (1963), pp. 426–458.

A. R. Orme. *Ireland.* Chicago: Aldine, 1970.

Erwin Raisz. "Physiography [of Europe]." In *Goode's World Atlas, op. cit.,* pp. 122–123.

Clifford T. Smith. *An Historical Geography of Western Europe Before 1800.* New York: Praeger, 1967.

Joseph E. Spencer and Gerry A. Hale. "The Origin, Nature, and Dispersal of Agricultural Terracing." *Pacific Viewpoint.* Vol. 2 (1961), pp. 1–40.

S. E. Steigenga-Kouwe. "The Delta Plan." *Tijdschrift voor Economische en Sociale Geografie.* Vol. 51 (1960), pp. 167–175.

Ch. A. P. Takes and A. J. Venstra. "Zuyder Zee Reclamation Scheme." *Tijdschrift voor Economische en Sociale Geografie.* Vol. 51 (1960), pp. 162–167.

Arthur G. Tansley. *The British Isles and Their Vegetation.* London: Cambridge University Press, 1939.

Glenn T. Trewartha. *An Introduction to Climate.* New York: McGraw-Hill, 3rd ed., 1954.

Johan van Veen. *Dredge, Drain, Reclaim: The Art of a Nation.* The Hague: Nijhoff, 5th ed., 1962.

Michael Williams. *The Draining of the Somerset Levels.* London: Cambridge University Press, 1970.

Raphael Zon. "Forests and Human Progress." *Geographical Review.* Vol. 10 (1920), pp. 139–166.

CHAPTER THREE

Population geography

3.1 POPULATION NUMBERS AND DISTRIBUTIONS

Of all the human areal patterns, none is more basic than the distribution of population, and therefore the study of the location and numbers of people is an appropriate first topic in the geographical analysis of the European culture area. Europe is one of the most densely settled parts of the world, surpassed only by the Orient. Within the confines of the traditional Uralian border live some 622 million (1971), almost one out of every six human beings. Even if all parts of the Soviet Union and Turkey are excluded, the total is still an impressive 466 million, as of the middle of 1971.

At the beginning of the Christian Era, perhaps thirty or thirty-five million people were found west of the Urals and north of the Mediterranean, only about 6 percent of the present total (Table 3.1, Figure 3.1). The disruption caused by the decline and fall of the Roman Empire, followed by epidemics, famines, and invasions by Arabs and others, caused a drastic decline in population over the first six or seven centuries of the Christian Era. A period of major growth in the Middle Ages, lasting to the mid-fourteenth century and characterized by numerous colonization projects in the forestlands of central Europe, was abruptly ended by the ravages of the Black Death and the Hundred Years' War. In the 1500s, Europeans recovered numerically from these losses, and only the destructive effect of the

TABLE 3.1   The Estimated Population of Europe at Selected Dates, with the Proportion in Each Major Subdivision

Year A.D.	Population in area west of Ural Mts. (millions)	Southern Europe (Iberia, Italy, Greece)	Western Europe (France, Low Countries, Luxembourg)	British Isles	Northern Europe (Scandinavia, Finland, Iceland)	Central Europe (Germany, Switzerland, Austria)	Eastern Europe (Poland, Czechoslovakia, Romania, Hungary, Bulgaria, Albania, Yugoslavia)	European USSR
1	33	50%	20%	1%	<1%	10%	9%	9%
350	27	37	19	1	<1	12	16	13
600	18	40	17	4	<1	11	16	11
800	29	35	17	4	<1	14	13	17
1000	38	37	16	4	<1	10	12	20
1200	49	36	20	6	<1	14	11	12
1340	70	30	27	8	<1	16	7	12
1400	41							
1500	56	27	29	7	1	13	13	11
1650	100	26	30	7	2	11	12	13
1700	113	23	24	7	4	13	14	15
1750	140	22	23	7	4	13	15	16
1820	210	20	17	10	3	13	18	19
1900	392	18	14	10	3	15	18	22
1930	500	16	12	10	3	15	19	25
1950	550	18	13	11	3	14	17	24
1970	620	17	12	10	3	15	17	26

Source: The material in this table was gathered from Russell, Carr-Saunders, and Haliczer.

Figure 3.1   Population density, circa A.D. 1. (After Usher and Russell, in part.)

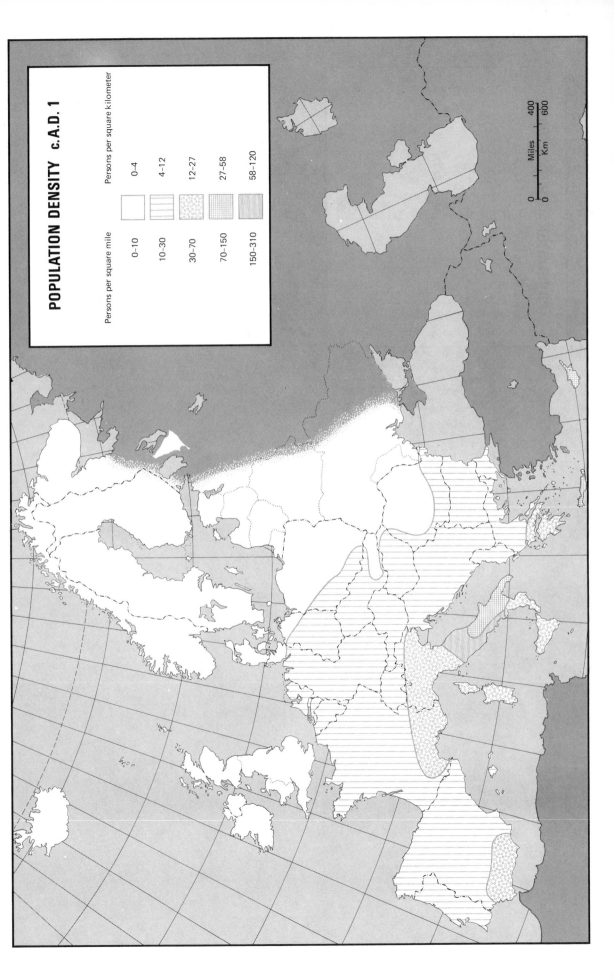

POPULATION DENSITY c.A.D. 1

Persons per square mile		Persons per square kilometer
0–10		0–4
10–30		4–12
30–70		12–27
70–150		27–58
150–310		58–120

Miles

0   400
0   600
Km

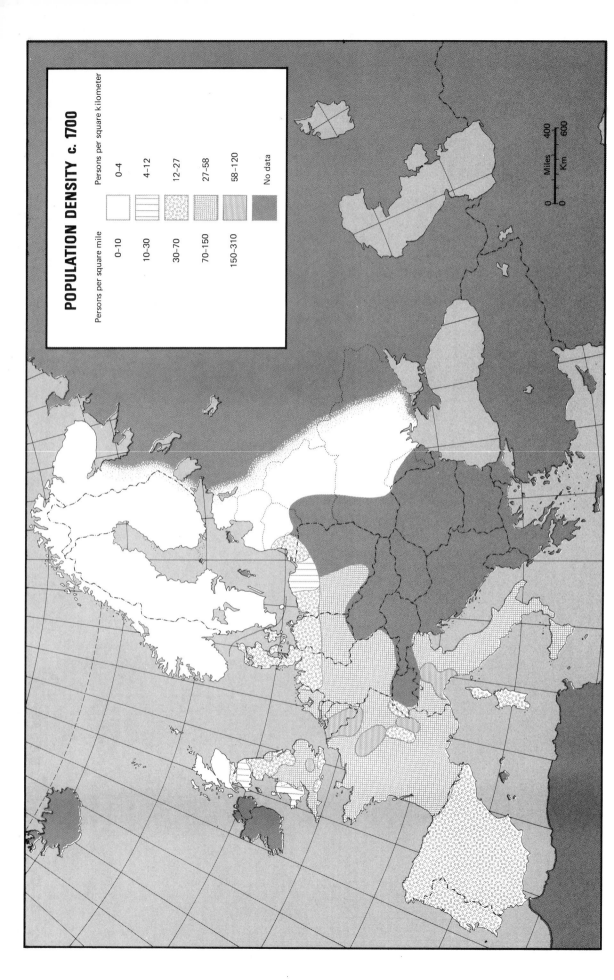

POPULATION DENSITY c. 1700

Persons per square mile		Persons per square kilometer
0–10		0–4
10–30		4–12
30–70		12–27
70–150		27–58
150–310		58–120
		No data

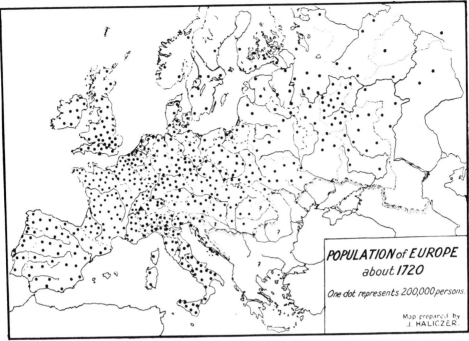

Figure 3.3 Population of Europe about 1720. (Reproduced from Josef Haliczer, "The Population of Europe, 1720, 1820, 1930," *Geography*, Vol. 19 (1934), p. 265, with the permission of The Geographical Association.)

Thirty Years' War (1618–1648) has interrupted the continuous growth since then. About 100 million persons inhabited the European culture area by 1650, over three times the estimated total of the first century A.D. (Figure 3.2). A period of spectacular growth associated with the Industrial Revolution occurred from around 1750 to World War I (Figures 3.3, 3.4), in spite of massive emigration during the same period, and the European population reached 500 million. Gradual increase has been the rule over the past half-century or so, and at present Europe has more nearly approached a stabilized number of people than has any other sizable culture area.

The numerical changes through the past two millennia have been paralleled by areal shifts in the population (Table 3.1). At the birth of Christ, southern Europe, including the Iberian Peninsula, Italy, and Greece, contained fully half of the inhabitants of Europe, while the British Isles were home to only one of every one hundred Europeans. At present the Mediterranean peninsulas account for less than one-fifth of the population, and one of every ten Europeans is British. The greatest concentrations of people have typically been found in those lands which had achieved political and economic dominance, and it is interesting to note that the largest European population is now found in the Soviet Union.

If the people presently living west of the Urals and north of the Mediterranean were evenly distributed over the land area of Europe, each square kilometer

Figure 3.2 Population density, circa 1700. (After Usher and Haliczer, in part.)

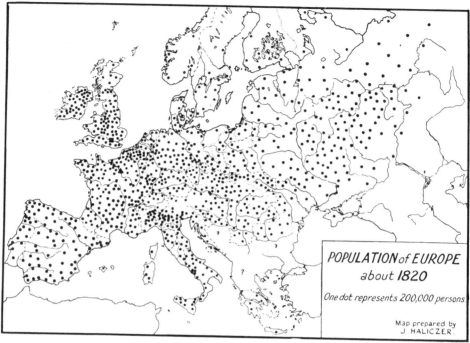

Figure 3.4   Population of Europe about 1820. (Reproduced from Josef Haliczer, "The Population of Europe, 1720, 1820, 1930," *Geography*, Vol. 19 (1934), p. 266, with the permission of The Geographical Association.)

would contain over 60 persons (about 160 per square mile). This is, however, a meaningless figure because the population density varies greatly from one part of Europe to another, ranging from the totally uninhabited glaciers of interior Iceland to over 200 per square kilometer (500 per square mile) on the fertile plains of Flanders and many thousands per square mile in the urban centers. Representing the latter is the city-state of Monaco on the Mediterranean Riviera, which contains 15,400 persons per square kilometer (40,000 per square mile).

The accompanying map of population distribution (Figure 3.5) is a generalization, a simplification of an extremely complex spatial pattern. It does allow, however, recognition of the broader features of the distribution. Readily visible is the great corridor of dense population stretching east from lowland Great Britain across the Low Country, through central Germany, western Czechoslovakia, southern Poland, and on into the Soviet Union, a corridor containing over 100 persons per square kilometer (250 per square mile) and five cities of over one million population. In the same density category are certain coastal portions of Italy and Iberia, the lands along the lower course of the Seine River in France, and the Po Valley. At the opposite extreme, low population density is typical of northern Scandinavia, the Meseta of Spain, and various mountain areas such as the Alps, Appennini, Pyrenees, and Carpathians. It can be said that Europe is typified by a densely populated core, represented in the major east–west corridor, and by a sparsely settled

Figure 3.5   Population density, 1970.

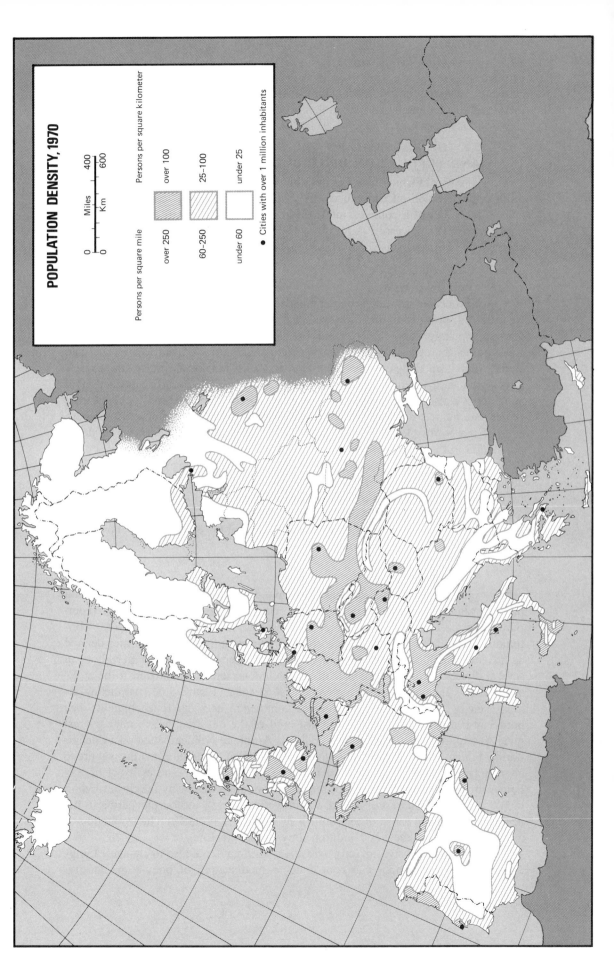

POPULATION DENSITY, 1970

Miles
0 ___ 400
0 ___ 600
Km

Persons per square mile

▨ over 250

▧ 60–250

☐ under 60

Persons per square kilometer

over 100

25–100

under 25

● Cities with over 1 million inhabitants

periphery, including northern Scandinavia, Iceland, the Scottish Highlands, most of Iberia, and the mountainous Balkan Peninsula.

3.2 THE PHYSICAL ENVIRONMENT AND POPULATION DISTRIBUTION

The way in which man has distributed himself across the face of Europe, a result of the decision-making process in choosing where to live, can be understood only as the result of a complex interworking of numerous environmental and cultural factors. The causes of population distribution can be found in such diverse phenomena as terrain, inheritance laws, coal deposits, and forced migrations.

TERRAIN AND SOIL

European man's affinity for plains areas has been mentioned previously, in Chapter 2. It bears repeating, however, that almost without exception, the areas of densest population are characterized by flat terrain, while the mountain ranges stand out as lines of sparse settlement (compare Figures 2.1 and 3.5). The cold climate and steep slopes of the mountains and hills did not appeal to the agriculturists who until recent times dominated Europe's population. The attraction of good soils is also based on the ancient cultural-economic decision to be farmers rather than hunters and gatherers. The fragmented belt of loess along the southern edge of the North German Plain parallels the great east–west corridor of dense population in the core of Europe, and all of the loessial *Börde* are thickly settled. Prior to the acceptance of agriculture in Neolithic times, however, the Mesolithic inhabitants of this part of Europe showed no preference at all for the loessial districts. A human group tends to view the physical environment in the light of its own technology and needs, and soils became a locational factor only after farming ascended to a predominant position, only after man of his own free will chose to be a farmer.

CLIMATE

For the most part, Europeans have avoided settlement in colder climates, in particular the subarctic and tundra areas of central and northern Scandinavia (compare Figures 2.7 and 3.5). A detailed study was made of the border between "continuous" and "discontinuous" rural settlement zones in Sweden, the former defined as areas in which all persons live within 5 kilometers (3 miles) of neighbors in several directions. The northern limit of continuous settlement proved to be a W-shaped line running east–west across central Sweden (Figure 3.6), paralleling almost exactly the border between humid continental and subarctic climates. The border also duplicated the northernmost limit of the oak tree, where mixed forest gives way to evergreen needleleaf woodland. A unique political situation in neighboring Finland, however, produced a quite different evaluation of the subarctic climate as a zone of settlement. The Finns were faced with the necessity of finding homes for hundred of thousands of refugees from areas seized by the Soviet Union in World War II, and part of the answer proved to be agricultural pioneering in the needleleaf evergreen forest of the Finnish subarctic (Figure 3.7). The evaluation of an environment can, then, be conditioned by political factors.

Man is responsive not only to severity of climate, but also to changes. Long-range climatic fluctuations can contribute to modification of population density,

Figure 3.6 (*Below left*) Swedish inhabited areas. In the areas shaded black, all persons live within 5 kilometers (3 miles) of neighbors in several directions. The boundary parallels very closely that between humid continental and subarctic climates. (Redrawn; used by permission from the *Annals* of the Association of American Geographers, Volume 52, 1962, from an article by Kirk H. Stone.)

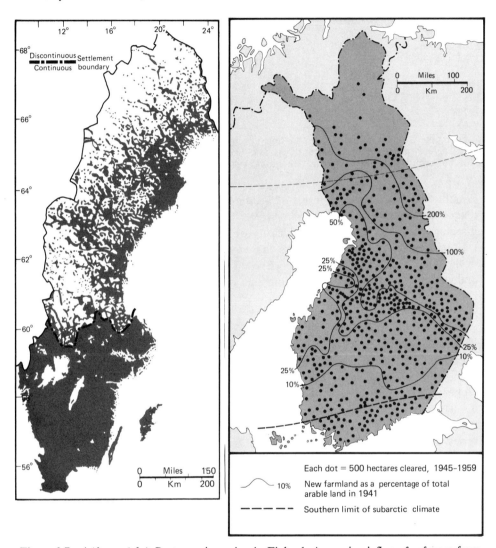

Figure 3.7 (*Above right*) Postwar pioneering in Finland. A massive influx of refugees from areas annexed by the Soviet Union forced the Finns to undertake pioneering in the inhospitable subarctic climate zone. (After Sømme.)

especially in marginal areas. Evidence accumulated by a variety of scholars points to a deterioration of the climate of Iceland from the 1200s into the 1800s, with progressively colder temperatures and a southward expansion of Arctic marine drift ice. The permanent snow line on the south side of the great glacier called Vatnajökull moved ever lower, a good indicator of cooling climate. During this same period, the Icelandic population declined almost 30 percent and the average height of males was reduced by five centimeters, or about two inches (Table 3.2), pre-

TABLE 3.2   The Icelandic Population, 1200–1970

Year	Estimated population	Estimated average height of males
1200	70,000	172 cm (5 ft 8 in.)
1400	65,000	172 cm (5 ft 8 in.)
1600	57,000	172 cm (5 ft 8 in.)
1703	50,000	169 cm (5 ft 7 in.)
1784	38,000	167 cm (5 ft 6 in.)
1800	47,000	167 cm (5 ft 6 in.)
1901	78,000	172 cm (5 ft 8 in.)
1961	177,000	177 cm (5 ft 10 in.)
1972	210,000	178 cm (5 ft 10 in.)

Source: Sigurdur Thorarinsson, "Population Changes in Iceland," *The Geographical Review,* Vol. 51 (1961), pp. 519, 525, 531–533. Used with the permission of the American Geographical Society.

sumably in large part as a result of a diminished food supply caused by climatic deterioration. By the 1700s, humans were on the verge of extinction in Iceland, and it seems reasonable to attribute at least part of the numerical dwindling and physical shrinkage to economic hardships caused by the cooling climate. The population of the country has rebounded in the last hundred years in a period of urbanization and milder climate to reach an all-time high of about 200,000.

NATURAL RESOURCES

To the preagricultural hunters of Europe, the great natural resources were wild game and the raw materials for making weapons of the hunt. The location of wild animal herds or of types of wood well suited for spears and bows attracted them. Modern man, having created a different form of economy, has become a seeker of coal and iron ore, of uranium and bauxite, and these resources influence his settlement distribution just as herds of deer attracted his ancestors. As a consequence, every area with sizable deposits of high-grade coal acquired in recent centuries a large population, and the correlation between the distribution of coal and people is quite striking. The deposits of lowland England, the Sambre–Meuse district, the Ruhr, Upper Silesia, and the Don Basin outline nearly the major corridor of dense population in Europe. Here the distribution of people reflects the choice to be manufacturers, just as the attraction of good soils and level terrain is indicative of an agricultural way of life.

INSOLATION

The amount of *insolation,* or exposure to sunlight, can also influence man's selection of a place to live. In the Alps of Switzerland, northern Italy, and Austria, where the mountain ridges are oriented in an east–west direction, the south-facing slopes receive much more sunlight than do the shadowy north-facing slopes. The local inhabitants have long recognized this contrast, and the Alpine French coined the words *adret* for sun slope and *ubac* for shade slope. Almost invariably, adret sides of the longitudinal valleys in the eastern and western Alps contain more population than the ubac, in some cases twice as many people (Figure 3.8). North-facing slopes are commonly left in forest, for the local farm folk know that crops

Figure 3.8   Concentration of settlement on the adret of the Upper Rhône Valley, Swiss Alps. The shaded area is in shadow at noon at the winter solstice. Villages and scattered dwellings are shown in black. (From an article by Alice Garnett, reprinted by permission from *The Geographical Review,* Volume 25, 1935, copyrighted by the American Geographical Society of New York.)

which ripen early on the sunny slopes may fail to ripen at all on the opposite side of the valley. So strong is the distinction between the adret and ubac in some districts that the residents of the former consider themselves socially superior to the "shady characters" from the ubac and frown upon intermarriage. Many different insolation characteristics influence the choice of settlement site, including the area in noonday shadow at the winter solstice, the number of hours of potential sunlight, and the noon *intensity* of insolation, which varies with degree of slope. Through centuries of trial and error, the inhabitants of these mountains have been able to discern the areas of optimum insolation and have distributed themselves accordingly. Even so, members of different cultures interpreted the Alpine adret and ubac in contrasting ways. Near the point where Italy, Switzerland, and Austria join, the Alps are settled by a mixture of Romance- and German-speaking peoples. The Latins, reluctant to abandon warmth-loving crops such as corn and the gravevine, established their highest permanent adret settlements some 200 meters (650 feet) *lower* than those of German dairy-cattle raisers on the inferior ubac adjacent on the north. The more complete German utilization of the mountain environment is in part a result of their greater reliance on hearty crops such as hay and oats.

NATURAL DISASTERS

Natural disasters such as volcanic eruptions and earthquakes can alter the population of small areas over short periods of time. Mention has already been made of the million victims of Mt. Etna on the island of Sicilia, the Minoan disaster produced by the explosion of Thíra, and the destruction of Pompeii by Vesùvio. To these should be added the 1783 eruption of the volcano Laki in southern Iceland, when ash was deposited on pastures and cropland, causing famine and a population reduction of 20 percent to only 38,000 by 1784. One of the worst earthquakes in European history, another Sicilian disaster, claimed 60,000 lives in the early 1900s.

DISEASE

The spread of major diseases has also greatly altered the numbers and distribution of population in Europe. Among the exotic Oriental exports which moved westward over newly opened caravan routes between China and Europe in the late Middle Ages was the *bubonic plague*. Together with silks and tapestries it reached Istanbul (then still called Constantinople) in 1347, spreading quickly on beyond to Kriti, Genova, and southern France. In 1348 the plague made major inroads into Italy, Spain, and much of France, and in the following year it entered the Germanic lands and Hungary. Scandinavia and eastern Europe felt its effect in 1350, and epidemics recurred through much of the remainder of the fourteenth century. Eventually the plague became endemic. Some believe that the plague, or Black Death, claimed twenty-five million victims in the 1300s, including two-thirds of the people in parts of Italy. The English population is said to have declined from 3.7 million in 1350 to only 2 million by 1377. Less spectacular but still significant was the impact of *malaria,* introduced into the lowlands of the European Mediterranean in the third and fourth centuries B.C., presumably from North Africa. The Campagna, a large plain of about 2000 square kilometers (800 square miles) lying between the city of Roma and the Mediterranean coast, was intensively cultivated in antiquity, reaching a peak of productivity at the height of the Roman Empire. Then, as the centuries passed, the elaborate system of drainage ditches built by the Romans was neglected and cropland abandoned. Malaria soon spread into the Campagna and became endemic, and the disease was particularly widespread in the 1600s and 1700s. In consequence, the once-thriving Roman province had become a thinly populated wasteland by 1800, a curious empty area on the outskirts of one of Europe's great cities. The view to the west from towers perched upon the hills of Roma was bleak indeed, perhaps not duplicated in desolation by the fringes of any other city in the world. Reclamation and resettlement of the Campagna followed eradication of malaria early in the present century. In certain other parts of Italy, there is still today a concentration of towns and villages on hilltops, a reflection of the desire to escape malarial lowlands as well as the need for defense.

COAST VERSUS INTERIOR

The environmental contrast of seacoast and interior has been evaluated variously in different parts of Europe. In the Mediterranean peninsulas and Scandinavia, which are mountainous or cold, man has more often chosen to settle on or near the coasts, while in the remainder of Europe, the bulk of the population is in the interior. The coastal rim of Iberia is more densely peopled than the Meseta, while in Norway almost all of the population is clustered in or near port settlements. In the nations of Greece, Italy, Spain, Portugal, Norway, Sweden, and Finland, almost 80 percent of all cities of 500,000 or more population are on or within 40 kilometers (25 miles) of the seashore, while for the remainder of Europe, excluding the Soviet Union, only 30 percent are so situated. The Greeks, Portuguese, and Norwegians have long turned to the sea for a livelihood as traders and fishermen, and the merchant marine of little Norway has traditionally been one of the largest in the world. In contrast, most of the French, Germans, and Irish, in spite of ample coastlines, traditionally concentrated in the interior as farmers.

3.3 CULTURAL FACTORS IN POPULATION DISTRIBUTION

The physical environment and its evaluation by man can provide only part of the explanation for population distribution. For a more complete answer, the activities of man must be studied, for even minor regional variations in culture and economy can produce contrasting densities of settlement.

INHERITANCE LAWS

One such cultural difference has to do with inheritance laws, for Europe was divided traditionally into two major zones on the basis of *legal systems*. In the south, in areas once part of the Roman Empire, the practice of divided inheritance was long dominant, forming one of the cornerstones of Roman law. This tradition, by which landholdings and other possessions were divided equally among all heirs, has only recently been restricted in many of the Romance-language nations. Farms were allowed to become ever smaller, and in some instances, the miniaturization of landholdings actually reached the point where farms were too small to support the families living on them. Roman law, then, tended to produce very dense rural population.

In contrast, Germanic law and its English common law offspring support the principle of *primogeniture* or some other means of undivided inheritance. Land is passed intact from parent to one child, with the remaining offspring gaining compensation in other ways, if at all. Often the landless children emigrated or, in more recent times, moved to the cities, though many remained as tenant farmers. The overall impact of Germanic law was to hold down rural population growth. In Germany the contrast produced by the two legal systems was particularly evident in the early nineteenth century before the rise of industrialism, and to a degree the differences persist even today. In the provinces along the Rhine, Lahn, Main, Neckar, and Mosel rivers, once under Roman rule, including Baden-Württemberg, Rheinland-Pfalz, and parts of Hessen, farm miniaturization had reached a critical degree by the 1840s, and rural overpopulation was a major problem, while in the North German Plain, a traditional stronghold of Germanic law which the Romans never conquered, rural population densities even in the fertile loess districts were not so great.

VOLUNTARY MIGRATION

Man can greatly alter population distribution through *voluntary mass migration,* a process perhaps best exemplified by the island of Ireland. In 1841 the census of the United Kingdom listed over eight million Irish, a density of over 97 per square kilometer (250 per square mile), and by the middle of the decade the Irish population had reached an all-time high of almost eight and one-half million (Table 3.3). Then came the great famine of the mid-1840s, which brought death to hundreds of thousands, and in its wake a massive and persistent out-migration to Great Britain and overseas. In a five-year span from 1846 to 1851, some 800,000 Irish starved or perished from disease, and another million emigrated to foreign lands. Hardest hit was interior Ireland, where one county lost over 20 percent of its population through emigration (Figure 3.9). Today little over half as many people reside in Ireland as did in 1841, and the present trend suggests continued gradual decline.

The claim to the greatest per capita voluntary out-migration not spurred by famine or natural disaster belongs to Scandinavia. In 1865 the total population of Norway, Sweden, Iceland, and Denmark was about 8.8 million. Within the span of only thirty-five years, a third of a century, these four lands contributed 1.4 million of their sons and daughters to the United States, an impressive 16 percent of the 1865 total, not to mention the numerous other emigrants who went to Canada. The motive behind the Irish and Scandinavian migrations was economic, the desire to escape poverty. In post–World War II Germany, a political stimulus sent hundreds of thousands of migrants from the Russian-occupied German Democratic Republic to the west, a migration which caused the stabilization or slight decline of East Germany's population and contributed to steady, significant growth in the Federal Republic before being forcibly halted in 1961. Many of the migrants were young and of child-bearing age, making the exodus all the more harmful to Communist Germany.

Voluntary migration has also been produced by differential rates of industrialization. The factories of the Po Valley are attracting large numbers of southern and Alpine Italians, just as the industries of lowland Scotland once con-

TABLE 3.3   The Declining Irish[a] Population

Year	Population	Density of population	
		Per square mile	Per square kilometer
1800	5,000,000	153	59
1841	8,175,000	251	97
1845	8,450,000	259	100
1851	6,552,000	201	78
1861	5,765,000	177	68
1968	4,400,000	135	52

[a] The Republic of Ireland plus Northern Ireland.

1978   4,800,000

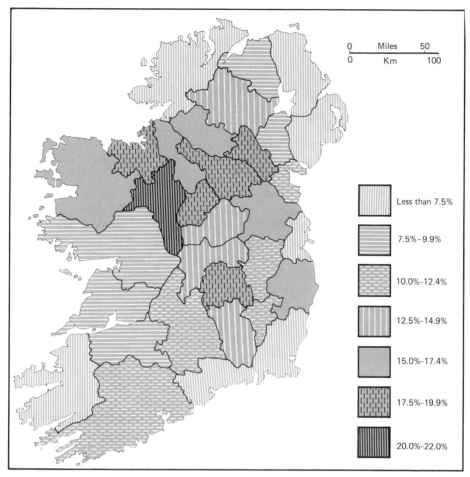

Figure 3.9   Emigration from Ireland, 1846–1851, as a percentage of the population in 1841. (Redrawn; used with permission from the *Transactions* of the Institute of British Geographers, Volume 28, 1960, page 121.)

Legend:

- Less than 7.5%
- 7.5%–9.9%
- 10.0%–12.4%
- 12.5%–14.9%
- 15.0%–17.4%
- 17.5%–19.9%
- 20.0%–22.0%

tributed to the partial depopulation of the adjacent, agricultural Highlands and the steel mills and coal mines of the German Ruhr district drew workers from as far away as the Slavic lands and Belgium. Similarly, millions of southern Europeans, especially Greeks, Iberians, and Yugoslavs, have migrated north since World War II to find employment in industrialized nations such as West Germany.

BIRTH RATES

For cultural reasons not clearly understood, different European national and linguistic groups have had markedly contrasting birth rates, a phenomenon which has an obvious relationship to population density. The French people in particular long multiplied at a much slower rate than did Germans, British, and Italians (Table 3.4). In 1720, and even as recently as 1850, Frenchmen outnumbered each of their neighbors, and yet by the 1960s France ranked fourth behind Germany, the United Kingdom, and Italy. In the early 1700s one in every six Europeans was French, but at present the proportion has fallen to only one of every twelve. A

TABLE 3.4 The Growth of the French, German, British, and Italian Populations, 1720–1968 (in millions)

Nation	1720	1800	1850	1900	1930	1968
France	19	27	36	38	42	50
Germany[a]	14	25	35	56	64	77
Italy	13	18	23	32	41	53
Great Britain and Northern Ireland	7	11	27	37	46	55

[a] East and West Germany together. Germany subject to changing borders.

steady decline in birth rates was noted in France beginning about 1820, falling to thirty births per thousand population in 1830. The German rate did not decline to thirty per thousand until 1910, fully eighty years later.

What makes the case of the French even more puzzling is that millions of Germans, British, and Italians migrated overseas in the 1700s, 1800s, and 1900s, mainly to the Americas, while relatively few French left their homeland. Furthermore, the Germans suffered much more disastrous war casualties and still managed to out-multiply the French. From 1800 to 1970 the population of France has not even doubled, despite repeated efforts by the government to promote a bumper baby crop. During the same period the Germans and Italians have tripled in number, and the British have multiplied fivefold. Curiously, the phenomenon of low French fertility extended across international borders into Belgium, where the Germanic Flemings outstripped the French Walloons to become the linguistic majority, a position traditionally held by the French. At the same time the German-speaking inhabitants of Alsace, the easternmost area of France, multiplied roughly at the German rate, even though Alsace was ruled by France for most of the period in question. In Switzerland the French-speaking population also lagged behind the German and Italian groups in rate of natural increase (Figure 3.10). In short, the birthrate contrast ran along linguistic rather than international borders. After about 1930, the speakers of French, German, Italian, and English increased at about the same rate, as the birthrate of most of the non-French groups finally fell to the low French level. In Belgium, however, the Germanic Flemings continued to multiply more rapidly than the French Walloons.

Several possible explanations have been suggested for the slow growth of the French population, none of which is entirely satisfactory. It is asserted that the French Revolution removed class restrictions on individual economic advancement, thereby encouraging the masses to restrict family size in order to improve their standard of living. Furthermore the revolution created an anticlerical attitude in France which supposedly allowed the French people to turn a deaf ear to Vatican pronouncements against birth control. Another demographer argued that the French tradition of arranged marriages was not conducive to marital love and large families, and still other experts point to the high degree of French urbanization, centered in the city of Paris, noting that urban populations generally have lower birth rates. Yet none of these theories is adequate. The British enjoyed the same political freedom which supposedly depressed the French birth rate, and the majority of British and Germans were free of Catholic influence by virtue of being Protestant. In addition, the anticlerical attitude in France is not evident in French-

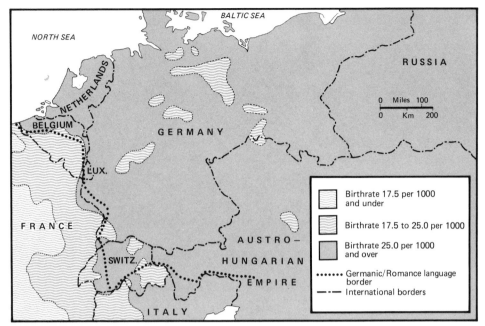

Figure 3.10 The contrast of Germanic and French birth rates, 1910. In nearly all of Germany, the birth rate in 1910 was 25 or more per 1000 population, while in France it was much lower. Note how the birth rate border paralleled the linguistic boundary, with Germanic Flemings, Dutch, Germans, and German–Swiss on the higher side and French-speaking Belgian Walloons, French, and French–Swiss on the low side. This curious pattern has never been adequately explained, but it indicates clearly that the French were multiplying less rapidly than the Germans. By about 1930, the birth rates of the two linguistic groups were about equal, but the Germans had far surpassed the French in numbers by that time.

speaking portions of Belgium, where the birth rate is also very low. Both Germany and the United Kingdom have long been more urbanized than France, and arranged marriages are no more typical of the French than the Italians. Certainly there is nothing genetically wrong with the French, for their emigrant kinfolk in the province of Quebec, Canada, have traditionally had one of the highest birth rates in the world, increasing from 10,000 in the 1600s and 1700s to about 7 million today. The answer is obviously cultural, but it has thus far escaped detection.

WAR CASUALTIES
Warfare, man's obsession with decimating his own kind, can and has greatly modified patterns of population distribution. One of the conflicts most destructive of human life was the Thirty Years' War, fought from 1618 to 1648 in central Europe. The population of some German districts was reduced by two-thirds or more in that terrible war, and major losses of life also occurred in western Czechoslovakia (Figure 3.11). More recently the estimated 20 million casualties suffered in World War II by the Soviet Union, representing about 10 percent of her inhabitants, caused a decline in population that has only recently been overcome. Germany counted almost 6 million soldiers and civilians dead in the same war, a loss of over 8 percent of the total, and little Yugoslavia was deprived of fully 11 percent of her population, some 1.7 million persons.

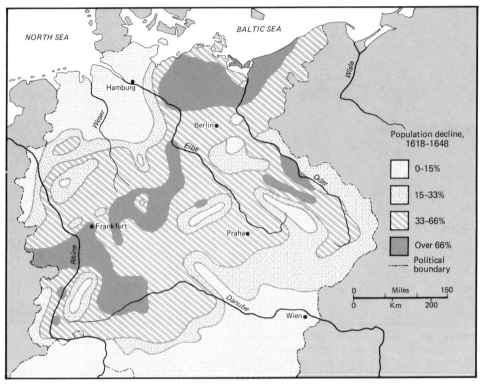

Figure 3.11 Population loss due to warfare and disease in central Europe, 1618–1648. The Thirty Years' War and associated epidemics drastically reduced the number of people in parts of Germany and western Czechoslovakia, producing a long-lasting change in population density and distribution. (After Franz and Keyser in Westermann.)

FORCED POPULATION MOVEMENTS

The sinister twin of voluntary migration is forced population movement, a practice so common in Europe and bearing such far-reaching consequences that it merits special attention in a discussion of European population geography. In the short span of about thirty-five years, 1920 to 1955, an astounding total of well over thirty million persons were forced to leave their homelands in Europe and prevented from returning, a violation of what Albert Schweitzer has called "the most basic of all human rights"—the right to live in one's ancestral homeland (Table 3.5). These movements included forced transfer of linguistic minorities, emigration to avoid religious and political persecution, deportation for forced labor or extermination, and flight to escape zones of military activity. Many additional Europeans were uprooted temporarily but succeeded later in returning to their homelands. Sudden and drastic changes in population density, language, and religion have resulted from these transfers.

Forced population movements have become closely identified with twentieth-century Europe, but precedents for such expulsions are scattered through many centuries and various parts of the world. The Roman dispersal of Jews from Palestine in the early decades of the Christian Era, the British expulsion of French-speaking Acadians from Nova Scotia in the 1750s, and the resettlement of the "Five Civilized Tribes" of Indians from the southeastern United States to Oklahoma

TABLE 3.5 Selected European Ethnic Groups Involved in Forced Permanent[a] Migrations, 1920–1955

Ethnic group	Number of persons forced to migrate	As an approximate percentage of total ethnic group at time of migration
Germans	15,800,000[b]	20
Poles	6,300,000[c]	24
Jews	6,000,000	67
Czechs and Slovaks	2,000,000[c]	16
Greeks	1,250,000[c]	18
Turks	800,000[c]	
Byelorussians and Ukrainians	553,000[c,d]	13
Finns	480,000[c]	14
Serbs and Croats	410,000[c]	4
Bulgars	361,000[c]	<1
Hungarians	355,000[c]	4
Latvians	310,000[c]	30
Lithuanians	244,000[c]	12
Estonians	235,000[c]	25
Italians	140,000[c]	<1
Romanians	100,000[c]	<1
Swedes	6,000[c]	<1

[a] All persons expelled, exchanged, evacuated, or imprisoned who were never able to return to their homeland, including those who perished.
[b] Excludes Jews and all ethnic Germans resident in the Soviet Union within the pre–World War II borders.
[c] Excludes Jews.
[d] Excludes transfers within the USSR.

in the first half of the nineteenth century are several of the numerous earlier examples. But only in modern Europe have such movements become a common method of solving ethnic minority "problems" (Figure 3.12). The widely accepted twentieth-century procedure has been to establish political borders, with varying degrees of attention to ethnic boundaries, and then move groups of people back and forth across the lines until political and ethnic borders corresponded. The major modern precedent for this ugly business was the Greek–Turk exchange of the early 1920s.

THE GREEK–TURK EXCHANGE. Greeks and Turks have long been enemies. For many centuries they have engaged in intermittent warfare, a struggle not just between Greek and Turk, but also a holy war between Christian and Moslem.

The Turks had conquered and annexed all of the Greek lands by the 1500s, but in the early nineteenth century a successful independence movement developed with British support in southern Greece. Through a series of minor wars the Greeks pushed the Turks back, annexing more and more territory, until by 1918 only the Anatolian Greeks, who lived on the eastern shore of the Aegean Sea in Asia Minor, had not been liberated. Greeks had lived there since before the days of Homer, and the coastland of Asia Minor therefore constituted an ancient Hellenic domain. The armies of Greece made an attempt after World War I to seize the eastern Aegean

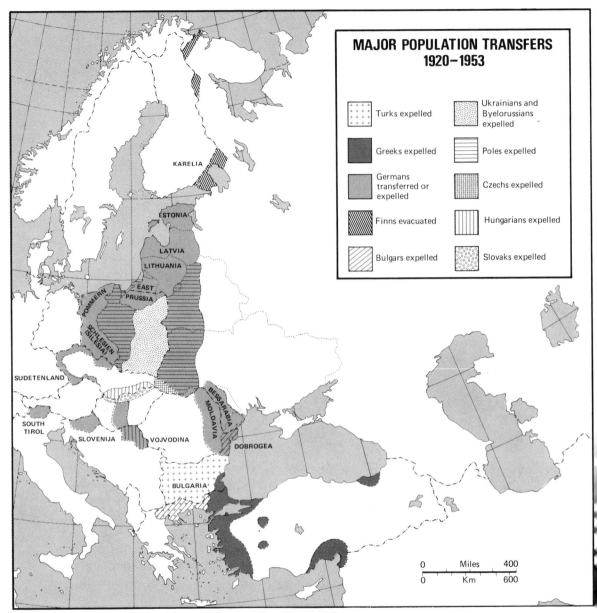

Figure 3.12   Major population transfers, 1920–1953.

shore, but the Turks repelled the invasion and eventually drove the attackers back to the sea.

Having failed to make their eastern political border correspond to the linguistic boundary, the Greeks reluctantly agreed to an exchange of population with Turkey, an agreement which also involved numerous Christian Armenians in Turkey. Many Greeks had fled Asia Minor with the retreating army, and most of the remainder were quickly uprooted and sent to Greece, a total refugee population of over one million persons. At the same time, hundreds of thousands of Turks and even some Greek-speaking Moslems who resided in Greece, a living human heritage of centuries of rule by the Ottoman empire, were shipped across the Aegean to Turkey. The precedent was established. Peoples whose only fault was residence on the wrong side of an artificially created political border were deprived of the right to continue to live in the land of their ancestors. Henceforth, few Europeans were secure in their homelands.

NAZI POPULATION TRANSFERS. The next series of major population transfers were carried out at the instigation of Nazi Germany. Contrary to what might be expected, the people involved were often ethnic Germans, Teutonic minorities from the Alps and plains of eastern Europe who were "called home" by Hitler against their will.

The Alpine province known variously as the *South Tirol* or *Alto Adige* was peopled by German-speaking folk who had traditionally, before 1918, been ruled by the Austro–Hungarian Empire (Figure 3.12). As German Austrians, they were members of the ruling ethnic group in the empire, and their position seemed quite secure. After World War I, however, Italy demanded and was granted a new northern border, a "natural" frontier which followed one of the Alpine ridges. Deliberately ignored was the fact that the revised border placed the German-speaking South Tirolers on the Italian side. A campaign of Italianization was soon directed at their newly created German minority by the Mussolini government, involving suppression of German newspapers and clubs, dismissal of German-speaking local government officials, requirement of Italian given names for all newborn children, and even the chiseling away of German tombstone inscriptions. Years of such persecution created desperation among the South Tirolers, and when Hitler annexed adjacent Austria they looked to the German *Reich* for support. But Hitler betrayed them, for as early as the 1920s he had expressed in *Mein Kampf* his willingness to sacrifice all claims to the South Tirol in exchange for an alliance with Italy. With Hitler's approval the Italian government forced South Tirolers to choose in 1939 between continued compulsory assimilation in their homeland and resettlement in Germany. Thus pressured, 70 percent of them chose to move, and the Roma–Berlin axis was secure. The war interrupted the transfer, but about 72,000 persons were actually moved, some of whom later returned.

In the three *Baltic states* of Latvia, Lithuania, and Estonia lived a small German minority of about 130,000 persons, the heritage of a small current of migration dating back to the Teutonic Knights of the Middle Ages (Figure 3.12). The Baltic Germans were mainly landowners and urban dwellers, preserving their language and culture through a network of German schools, churches, clubs, and newspapers. They had fared well during the long Russian rule of the Baltic states, forming somewhat of an aristocracy. In 1920 *half* of the total land area of Latvia was owned by Germans, who composed only 3 percent of the population, and many of the Baltic Germans were engaged in white-collar and professional employment in cities such as Riga. Independence was granted to the three Baltic republics after World War I, and the Germans quickly lost their privileged position. Nazi Germany, again cementing an alliance, signed the famous Soviet–German nonaggression pact in 1939, one secret clause of which involved Nazi agreement that the USSR should invade and annex the Baltic states. Further, to avoid future friction, it was stipulated that the Baltic Germans should be "repatriated," a transfer which was completed in 1939–1941. By the same treaty Hitler agreed to the expulsion of an additional 136,000 ethnic German peasants from numerous agricultural folk-islands in eastern Poland, an area to be occupied by the Soviet Union, in exchange for about 35,000 Ukrainians and Byelorussians expelled from German-annexed western Poland. Elsewhere Hitler demanded the removal of over 200,000 ethnic Germans from trans-Carpathian areas in Romania, especially the provinces of Dobrogea and Moldavia (Figure 3.12). Another 50,000 ethnic Germans were removed from southern and central Yugoslavia.

Most of the displaced Germans were resettled in the Polish Corridor area which the *Reich* occupied in 1939, especially the province of Posen (Polish Poznań). To make room for them, the Nazis moved out a large segment of the resident Polish and Jewish population. Smaller numbers representing almost every ethnic group in eastern Europe were transferred by Nazi Germany and its allies, in addition to perhaps six million Jews (see Chapter 5). People were being shipped around like so much freight, and the worst was yet to come.

EVACUATION AND EXPULSION OF THE EASTERN GERMANS, 1944–1951. The largest forced movement of peoples ever to occur involved the removal of the population of the eastern German provinces of East Prussia (Ostpreussen), Schlesien, and Pommern, as well as the old free city of Danzig (Polish Gdańsk) and parts of Brandenburg and Sachsen. It involved the large majority of some ten million inhabitants of an area about 130,000 square kilometers (50,000 square miles) in extent (Figure 3.12). Major revisions in political, linguistic, and religious borders thereby resulted, and Germany lost about one-quarter of its prewar territory.

German agricultural pioneers had colonized these eastern provinces between about 1125 and 1400, assimilating the numerically inferior resident Slavic population. By 1945 Schlesien, Pommern, and East Prussia had served as German homelands for 600 years or more, and the inhabitants were long accustomed to rule by German states.

Soon after the German–Soviet partition of Poland in 1939, various Polish organizations in exile began making proposals for a new German–Polish border which involved considerable territorial gain for Poland. In May 1940, for example, an exile group in France suggested the Odra (Oder) River and Sudetes Mountains as the most desirable new line. Certain verbal promises were made to the Poles by representatives of the great powers, including Churchill, who recommended the separation of East Prussia from Germany and the systematic expulsion of the German population, citing the precedent of the Greeks in Turkey. The actual new border, called the Odra-Neisse line, established in 1945, followed very closely the proposal of the 1940 exile group in France.

Forced emigration of the resident German population began as a normal war refugee flight in the fall of 1944 in the province of East Prussia. Red army thrusts caused 500,000 civilians to flee from the eastern part of the province, while others evacuated the northern port city of Memel, the present Lithuanian Klaipeda. A winter offensive produced still more refugees, and by April of 1945 about three-quarters of the East Prussians had fled the province, a total of almost 2 million

TABLE 3.6 Expulsion of Germans from the Eastern
Territories

Year	Number expelled
1945 (June–December)	650,000
1946	2,000,000
1947	500,000
1948	150,000
1949	150,000
1950 + 1951	50,000
	3,500,000

people. Similar evacuations, involving lesser proportions of the population, occurred in Schlesien and Pommern, leaving behind in the Russian-occupied eastern provinces about 4.5 million Germans, just less than one-half of the preinvasion total.

After hostilities ceased, many refugees sought to return to their homes, but only a relative few succeeded, because the Russians and Poles had sealed the new Odra–Neisse–Sudetes border. In the summer of 1945 the systematic expulsion of the remaining German population began, continuing until the early 1950s (Table 3.6). Approximately a million of the original population remained in the east, principally those persons with Slavic surnames or possessing the ability to speak Polish. Added to the numbers expelled were another 2.5 million Germans removed from the area of the old Polish Corridor, including many who only five years earlier had been uprooted by the Nazis from their original homes in the Baltic states and other parts of eastern Europe. The evacuation and expulsion produced temporarily a wasteland of untended farms and unrepaired towns and cities in Schlesien, Pommern, and East Prussia, a condition which persisted well over a decade until the provinces were fully resettled by Slavs. A massive renaming process was necessary, extending down to the smallest village and brook. The German Breslau, capital of Schlesien, became the Polish Wroclaw; East Prussian Königsberg gave way to the Russian Kaliningrad; and Stettin, provincial capital of Pommern, preserved only its pronunciation in Polish as Szczecin. The German town of Grünberg, meaning "green mountain," was directly translated into Polish as Zielona Gora.

EXPULSION OF THE SUDETENLAND GERMANS. The highland rim of western Czechoslovakia, the Sudetenland, had been peopled by Germans in the medieval expansion eastward, leaving only the interior plains of České and the hills of Morava as Czech-language strongholds (Figure 3.13). Traditionally, the Sudetenland Germans had been ruled by their linguistic brothers, the Austrians, and occupied a position in the Austro–Hungarian Empire similar to that of the South Tirolers. However, after World War I, the Sudetenland Germans were placed in Czechoslovakia as a minority group, and by 1930 the German element in this fringe of the Czech state numbered about 3.2 million (Figure 3.13). Nazi agitators stirred up the Sudetenlanders in the mid-1930s, and anti-Czech sentiment ran high among the populace, producing an international crisis which led to Nazi German annexation of the district in 1938.

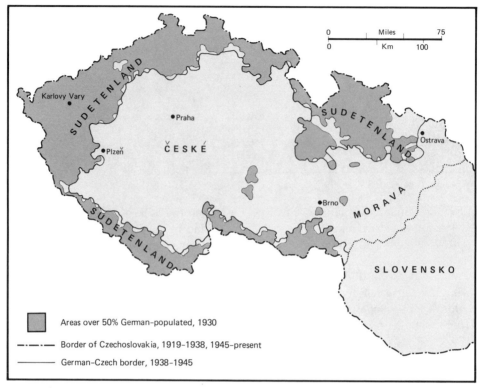

Figure 3.13 The Sudetenland German areas prior to the forced expulsion. The boundary of western Czechoslovakia drawn after World War I left a German-populated rim, the Sudetenland, within the Czech state. By the agreement made at München in 1938, the Sudetenland was given to Germany, and the new boundary was much more just in an ethnographic sense. However, the Czechs reclaimed the Sudetenland in 1945 and expelled the German inhabitants, causing a major decline in population density (see Figure 3.14). (After Winkler.)

After World War II the original Czechoslovak–German border was reinstated, again placing the Sudentenland Germans on the wrong side of the line. There had been little refugee movement from the area, since American rather than the feared and hated Russian troops occupied western Czechoslovakia.

Between 1945 and 1947, the Czech government carried out the systematic expulsion of some three million Sudeten Germans, leaving only about 200,000 in their homeland. As in the Polish territories, there was gradual resettlement by Slavs, causing ethnic and political borders to coincide. The population had still not reached preexpulsion density by the early 1960s (Figure 3.14).

OTHER POPULATION TRANSFERS. In the ethnic housecleaning which followed World War II, numerous groups other than Germans were moved about. There was an exchange of Slovaks and Hungarians in 1946, a Russian–Polish trade involving over two million persons, and an expulsion of 118,000 Czechs from the far-eastern tip of Czechoslovakia which was annexed by the Soviet Union. In the early 1950s, Bulgaria transferred remaining Turks "back" to Turkey, completing an expulsion begun in the 1920s. Finland, which shared Germany's wartime defeat by the Russians, was forced to cede certain eastern territories to the Soviet Union,

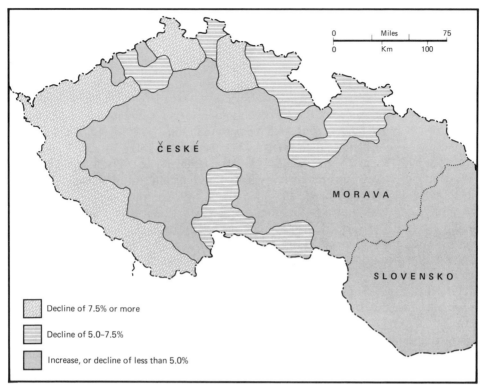

Figure 3.14 Population decline in western Czechoslovakia, 1921–1961. The long-lived effect of forced population movement on population density is clearly revealed in a comparison of Figures 3.13 and 3.14. The Sudentenland rim of Czechoslovakia, from which about three million German inhabitants were expelled in 1945–1947, still showed the effects of depopulation a decade and a half later. Some districts remained more than 15 percent below 1921 population figures in 1961. (After Gottmann.)

causing a flood of 480,000 displaced Finns to enter the remnant Finnish nation. The sudden influx of so many new people, well over 10 percent of Finland's existing population, led to a much fuller utilization of the subarctic zone for agricultural purposes, including the establishment of many new farms, called "cold farms," in the northern forests.

3.4 CHARACTERISTICS OF THE POPULATION

While the numbers and distribution of population are of great significance, it is equally important to know *what kind* of people are involved. Six hundred million half-starved, diseased, illiterate people are by no means the equal in potential for achievement of the same number who are well fed, healthy, and highly educated. The Europeans enjoy a standard of living far higher than that of most human beings, and partially for this reason they have been better able to exert influence in the world as a whole than have peoples of Africa or Asia. To be born in Europe is to have as a birthright the expectancy of long life, high income, good health, nutritious diet, and thorough education. But while Europeans as a group live better than the vast majority of Africans and Asians, the standard of living is not equally high throughout Europe, and significant regional differences exist. Some marginal European lands are in many respects more closely akin in quality of life to adjacent Africa or Asia than to the European core.

PER CAPITA INCOME

One measure of economic well-being is the per capita national income (Figure 3.15). In this respect there is a major contrast between north and south in Europe, with the highest per capita incomes found in Scandinavia and the lowest in the nations of Iberia and the Balkan Peninsula. According to recent statistics from the late 1960s, the income per person in Denmark was $2183, and Iceland, Sweden, and Norway also ranked very high. On the mainland of Europe, Switzerland ranked highest, with over $2454 per capita. In effect, the peoples who occupy some of the least desirable physical environments of Europe—the cold northland and the rugged Alpine district—have achieved the highest incomes.

At the opposite extreme are the nations of southern Europe. In Portugal the per capita national income is only $460, and even lower figures are found in Albania and some other Balkan countries. The southern peoples are not, however, as deprived as these figures suggest, for their economy is much more subsistent and rural in character, less reliant on cash exchange. Most of the farm families of southern Europe produce a large proportion of their own food and clothing, and consequently have less need for money. Furthermore, in the urbanized, industrial nations of northern and central Europe, the governments take a large share of personal income through taxes to help support ambitious social-welfare programs. Still, it is northern and central Europeans, and not the Iberian or Balkan peoples, who can afford various luxuries, including travel and automobile ownership. The affluent West Germans and Swedes can be found as tourists all over Europe and adjacent North Africa, but it is unusual to encounter a Portuguese, Yugoslav, or eastern European vacationer outside his home country. At the same time, southern Europeans are much better off economically than neighboring Africans on the opposite shore of the Mediterranean. Per capita incomes in Spain and Portugal, among the lowest in Europe, are about twice as high as those of adjacent Morocco.

EDUCATION

Europe has been the world center of learning, academic progress, and innovation for at least the past five centuries, and today the European population is much better educated than the other peoples of the Old World. The origin of the modern educational system lies in the era of urban rebirth in the Middle Ages. In almost every civilization, development and appreciation of learning has been centered in the cities and towns rather than the countryside. Both city and educational institution rest, however precariously, on the base of an agricultural surplus which allows part of the population to be freed from the task of food production. The city was the intellectual focal point of classical Greece and the Roman Empire, and when Europe finally emerged from the decline of learning following the fall of imperial Roma, it was the medieval city which witnessed the renewal of scholarship. Bologna, a city of the Po Valley, lying at the northern foot of the Appennini Mountains, was the location of the first European university, founded in the eleventh

Figure 3.15 Per capita income, in dollars.

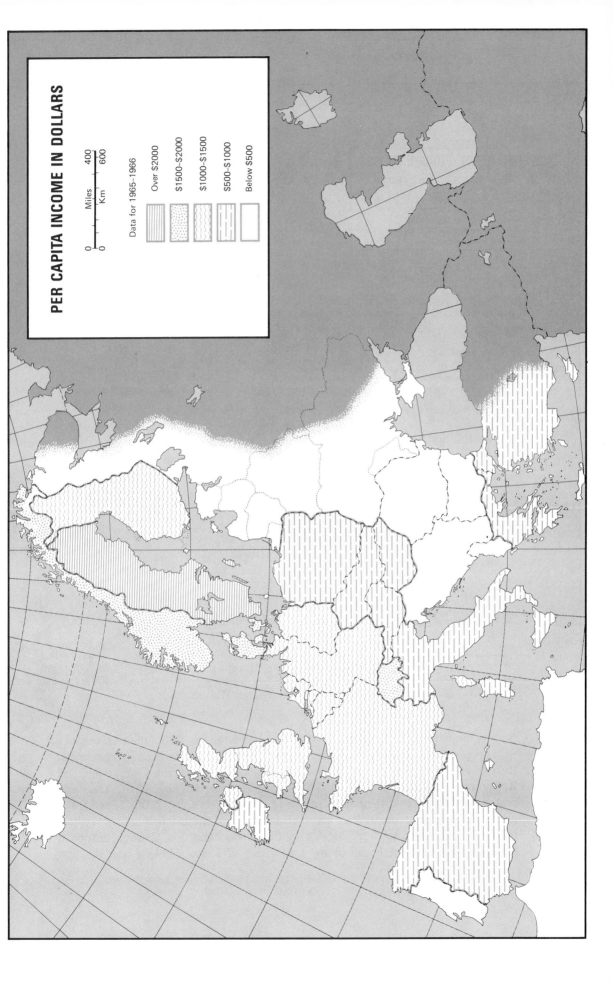

PER CAPITA INCOME IN DOLLARS

Miles
0   400

Km
0   600

Data for 1965–1966

Over $2000

$1500–$2000

$1000–$1500

$500–$1000

Below $500

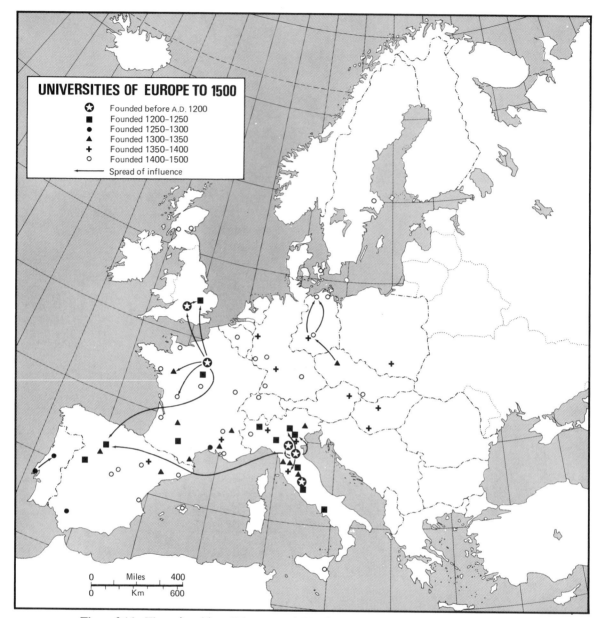

Figure 3.16   The universities of Europe, to 1500 (Source: Westermann.)

century though it had existed as a law school as early as A.D. 890. Other universities were soon established, often evolving slowly from cathedral and monastery schools. By the year 1200, additional universities with complete facilities were found at Reggio, near Bologna, at Paris, and Oxford in England (Figure 3.16). The early center of university development remained in Italy, but by 1500, France had numerically equaled the Italian accomplishment, and almost half of the institutions of higher learning were located in those two countries. Central European university development began in the Czech city of Praha (1348), and the first

Spanish university was located at Palencia in Old Castilla (1208). In the period since 1500, the lands north of the Alps and Pyrenees have replaced Italy as the center of higher education, with famous universities such as the Sorbonne, Cambridge, Lund, and Heidelberg. Traditionally, university education was confined to persons of the upper class, a restriction only recently abolished in some areas. Today, the average European is still much less likely to attend a university than is his American counterpart.

Access to even rudimentary education for the great majority of Europeans has come about in the nineteenth and twentieth centuries, beginning in northwestern Europe and spreading southward and eastward. German peasants were being taught to read and write in the first half of the 1800s while most Russians, Italians, and other Mediterranean and Slavic farm folk remained illiterate. Only after the Communist take-over was education made available to the average Russian. In most of Europe, education has spread to the masses because of ambitious government-supported education plans. Usually, private schools coexist with those financed by the state, but it is typical for even church schools to receive government funds, as in the Netherlands and the United Kingdom. In France the government maintains control over the schools through the Ministry of Education, and most other countries have a similar arrangement. The state requires children to remain in school for a certain number of years. A basic difference between European public schools and those of the United States is that European central governments direct the operation of schools, while in America local governments play a greater role. In part, this is because European countries are smaller, with less importance or need for local government.

Today the peoples of northern and eastern Europe are virtually all literate, and in some nations it is illegal not to be able to read and write (Figure 3.17). Over 99 percent of the adult Germans are literate, a proportion matched throughout northwestern Europe and the Soviet Union. Only slightly behind are Poland, with 4 percent illiterate, and Hungary with 3 percent. Southern Europe is the only remaining zone of widespread illiteracy, and even there the majority of the population have been educated. Most backward is Portugal, where only three of every five persons aged fifteen or more are literate, followed by Albania, which has educated 72 percent of its population. Just over four of every five Yugoslavs and Greeks are literate. Even the lowest European educational levels are high when compared with those of adjacent Asiatic and African lands, as for example Turkey (40 percent literate), Morocco (14 percent), and Tunisia (16 percent).

The literacy rate is, at best, a very crude measure of level of education, and better indicators are to be found in the field of publications. Daily-newspaper circulation is highest in the Scandinavian lands, Finland, Britain, Iceland, Germany, and Switzerland, where over 300 copies per 1000 inhabitants are distributed each day (Figure 3.18). Sweden claims the leadership with 505 copies per 1000, or one newspaper for every two inhabitants, followed by the United Kingdom with 479. The figures decline markedly to the south, falling to only 68 in Portugal and 47 in Albania, but even fewer newspaper copies are published in nearby African and Asian countries. It can be argued that newspaper readership is influenced by factors other than educational level, including degree of press freedom and even the frequency of bad weather, but still, the distribution is interesting and suggestive of differences in desire to learn more about the world.

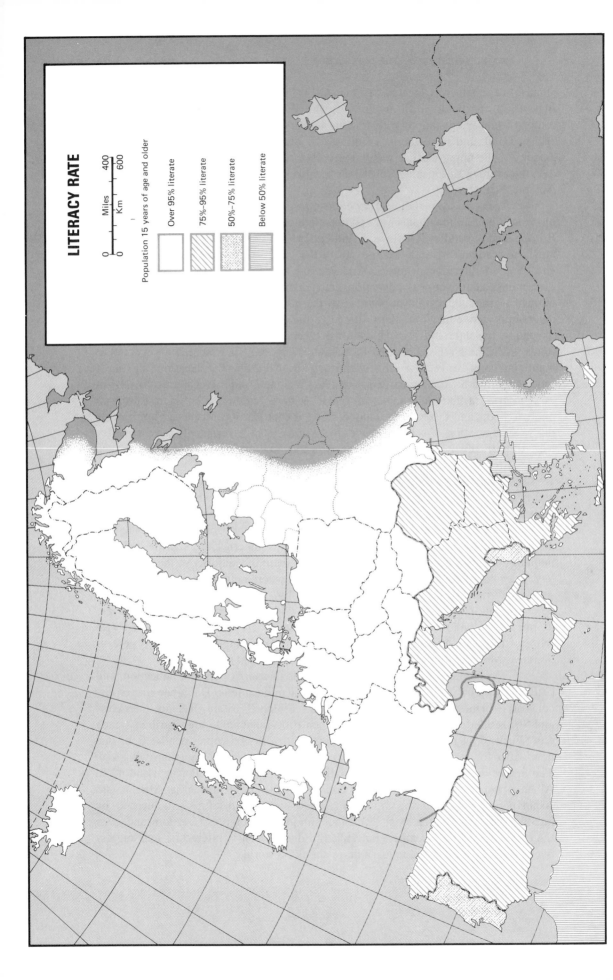

LITERACY RATE

Population 15 years of age and older

Over 95% literate

75%–95% literate

50%–75% literate

Below 50% literate

Miles
0   400

Km
0   600

Northern Europe also leads in the number of book titles published each year. If the Soviet Union is excluded as only partially European, then the United Kingdom ranks first with just over 26,000 different books printed annually, followed by West Germany, France, Spain, and the Netherlands. The high position of Spain is due in part to the demands of a huge overseas Spanish-speaking population. On a per capita basis, Iceland, Finland, and Switzerland are the leaders, and in the former nation one book title is published annually for each 391 people, the highest proportion in the world. The Icelandic and Finnic achievements are made even more remarkable by the fact that there is little or no foreign demand for books in the languages of those nations. Lowest levels of book production per capita are found in Ireland, Cyprus, Greece, Albania, and Poland.

HEALTH

In no European nation is the life expectancy at birth of males less than sixty years, a tribute to the extensive health-care programs which have been established. Northern Europeans live somewhat longer than their neighbors in the southern part of the culture area, but the difference between these two zones has been decreasing (Figure 3.19). In Sweden, Norway, and the Netherlands, the average male life expectancy is seventy-one years, the highest in Europe, while Portugal (sixty years) and Yugoslavia (sixty-two years) rank lowest. Even the worst European averages are far higher than those of nearby African nations, as for example Egypt, where the newborn male lives only fifty-one years, and Algeria, with a thirty-five year expectancy. Great improvements in life expectancy have been made in the twentieth century, particularly in southern Europe. Bulgaria, whose male population in 1928 averaged only forty-five years of life, now has raised the figure to sixty-seven years, and Greece experienced a corresponding rise from forty-nine to sixty-seven years between 1930 and 1965.

Another index of health conditions is the infant mortality rate, the number of children per thousand live births who do not survive to the age of one year. In this respect, the contrast between different parts of Europe is much sharper than was the case with male life expectancy (Figure 3.20). Sweden reports the lowest infant mortality rate, a remarkable thirteen per thousand, followed closely by the Netherlands, Iceland, and Norway, all in northern Europe. Ranking lowest are Albania, with eighty-six per thousand; Yugoslavia, with seventy-one; and Portugal, with sixty-four. Once again the southern portion of Europe exhibits a lower standard of living, transitional between northern Europe and Africa. Similarly, the infant mortality rates of eastern Europe are intermediate between those of Asia and the nothern and western nations of Europe.

Access to a physician is readily available to almost all Europeans, regardless of their nation of residence. Only in Albania are there more than 1500 persons per doctor. The lowest doctor:patient ratio is found in the Soviet Union (1:490), followed by Czechoslovakia, Austria, and Hungary (each 1:560). The higher ratios are typical of Albania (1:2,310), Cyprus (1:1,380), and Portugal (1:1,200), but even these compare favorably with adjacent African Tunisia (1:10,000), Asiatic Turkey (1:3,220), or African Morocco (1:9,700).

Most of the great epidemic and endemic diseases, such as smallpox, cholera,

Figure 3.17 Literacy rate: (Source: United Nations, *Statistical Yearbook,* 1964.)

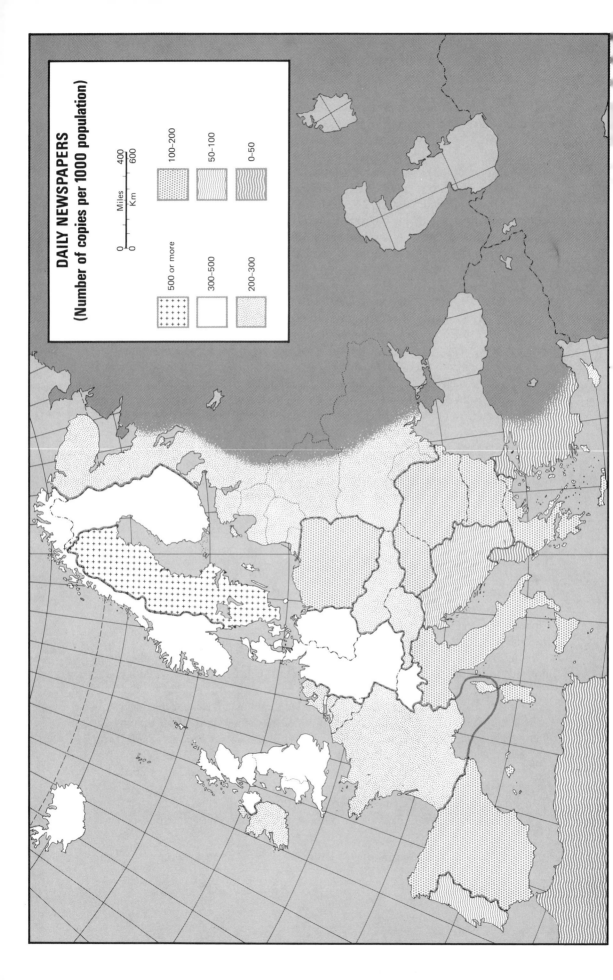

DAILY NEWSPAPERS
(Number of copies per 1000 population)

500 or more

300-500

200-300

100-200

50-100

0-50

Miles
0   400
0   600
Km

malaria, bubonic plague, and diphtheria, which once killed or debilitated millions of Europeans, have been eradicated. The last major epidemic of cholera in Europe occurred in 1923, and malaria was finally conquered in low-lying Italian lands by the early part of the present century. The Communist regime of Albania, the most backward European state, claimed that malaria was under control there by about 1960, though the difficulty of malaria eradication and the primitive character of the nation cast doubt on the governmental pronouncement. Tuberculosis is still rather widespread, and as recently as 1955, this disease affected almost 15 percent of the Albanian population. The Mediterranean practice of consuming raw goat's milk, coupled with a fairly high incidence of diseased milk cows, helps spread not only tuberculosis, but also brucellosis. Furthermore, the farmers of this region sometimes sell animals known to be diseased to unwary purchasers, thereby spreading the diseases even more widely.

In the United Kingdom, respiratory tuberculosis remains a serious problem not only in certain cities with unclean air, but also in the rural northern Welsh shires of Caernarvon, Merioneth, and Flint, where the disease is a heritage of mining, overcrowded dwellings, and perhaps hereditary susceptibility strengthened by inbreeding (Figure 3.21). Most respiratory disorders occur with greatest frequency in polluted cities and industrial districts in Europe, such as the Ruhr area of West Germany and the English Midlands. The cities of Birmingham, Liverpool, and Manchester, together with the adjacent provinces of Staffordshire and Lancashire, report some of the highest bronchitis and respiratory-cancer mortality rates in England and all of Europe (Figure 3.21). In contrast, British deaths caused by stomach cancer are highly concentrated in rural Wales (Figure 3.21), perhaps due to highly mineralized drinking water which has been polluted by runoff from mine tailings or to the dietary preference for fried foods and the customary reuse of cooking fats.

There is, then, a pronounced areal character to the geography of death and disease in Europe, with some regions far more healthful than others. As a whole, however, the European culture area offers a much more salubrious setting in which to live than do any of the African or Asian lands, and even surpasses the United States in this respect. The high health standards of the European culture area can, in large part, be related to the existence of elaborate national plans for providing health care. Regardless of whatever criticisms may be directed against socialized medicine, the obvious fact is that the people of Europe have utilized it to become the healthiest in the world. Medical care is free, which means that even persons in the lowest income brackets have access to whatever treatment is needed. Socialized medicine is found in both Communist and non-Communist countries and has a tradition reaching back almost one hundred years in parts of northwestern Europe. The money needed to provide for national health-care systems is, of course, derived from taxes. Europeans pay far higher taxes than do Americans.

DIET

Health and the consumption of proper foods are closely related, for a well-balanced diet, including adequate calories for energy, a combination of fats, carbohydrates, and proteins for tissue building, and a satisfactory amount of minerals

Figure 3.18 Daily newspapers, number of copies per thousand population. (Source: United Nations, *Statistical Yearbook,* 1966.)

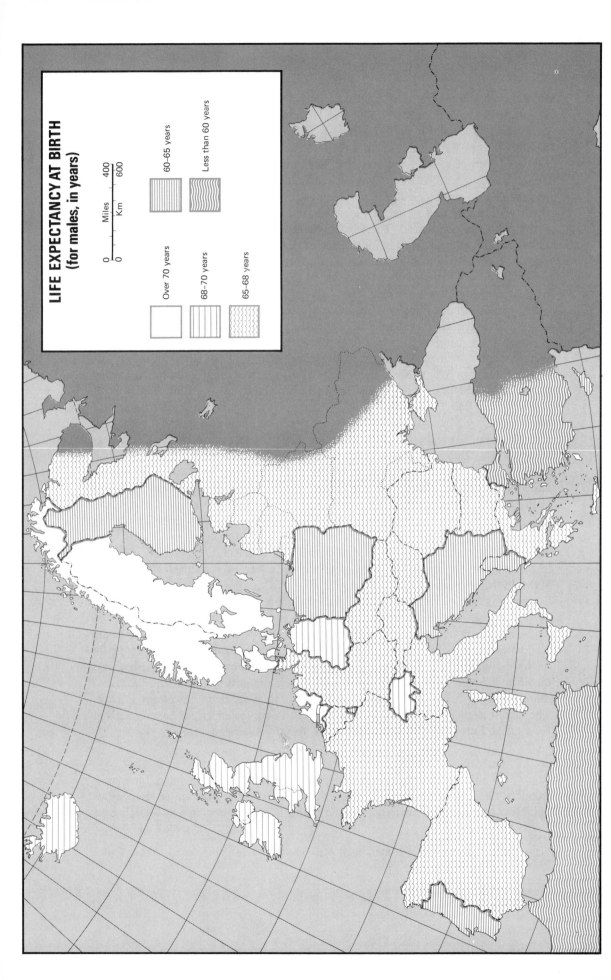

LIFE EXPECTANCY AT BIRTH
(for males, in years)

Over 70 years

68–70 years

65–68 years

60–65 years

Less than 60 years

Miles
0   400
0   600
Km

and vitamins, is necessary for the development and maintenance of a healthy human being. Not all Europeans enjoy such a diet, but most do.

The minimum average daily calorie intake recommended by the United Nations nutrition experts as necessary to produce a healthy person is estimated at around 1800 to 2000. None of the peoples of non-Communist Europe and Yugoslavia consume less than 2600 calories daily, and the Irish gorge themselves with 3430, on the average, to claim the title of best-fed, or most thoroughly overfed Europeans (Figure 3.22). Close behind are the Danes, Swiss, and English, while the Portuguese rank lowest in western Europe with 2610 calories per day. Recent figures are not available for Communist eastern Europe, but in all probability the calorie intake there is far above the suggested minimum. Even prior to World War II, the Albanians, who might be expected to have the lowest intake of all Europeans, averaged 2000 calories per day, a figure which has no doubt risen somewhat in the years since. Many Europeans suffered hunger during and immediately after World War II, but this condition was temporary. At that time the Albanian consumption dropped to only 1276 per day, a level certain to produce malnutrition.

Of course *what* is consumed is just as important as how much. Even a high-calorie diet can be inadequate if sufficient protein, vitamins, and minerals are not present. Protein deficiency was traditionally found in some European lands, including Greece, but recent dietary improvements have all but eliminated protein malnutrition. In western and southern Europe, nearly all peoples now consume over eighty grams of protein per capita daily, a quite adequate amount (Figure 3.23). Yugoslavia reports ninety-nine grams per capita, the highest European average, followed by France and Greece. The Portuguese, who consume seventy-two grams of protein per capita each day and the Italians, with seventy-nine grams, rank lowest in non-Communist Europe. Comparable data for eastern Europe are again lacking, but other sources suggest that only Poland still has a problem of protein malnutrition in some districts. In contrast, shortage of protein is typical for the large majority of Asians and other peoples of underdeveloped lands. The average resident of India, for example, consumes only fifty-one grams of protein daily, definitely an inadequate amount.

Multiple vitamin deficiences have long been typical of southern European areas, extending on beyond into the Balkans and Poland (Figure 3.23). A recent study suggests that in Yugoslavia, for instance, the intake of vitamin A is only slightly over one-fourth the recommended level, while in Poland the consumption of both vitamins A and C is low.

Mineral deficiencies are rather rare, with the possible exception of iodine. Many hilly or mountainous districts, particularly in southern Europe, have inadequate amounts of this mineral in the soil and consequently in the food (Figure 3.23), leading to the condition known as goiter, a swelling of the area of the neck. Goiter can be prevented simply by the use of iodized salt, but the ailment can nevertheless still be found in some parts of Europe. The Ministry of Health in Poland was still combating goiter in the early 1960s in some rural areas.

Economic distress, particularly food shortages resulting from the disruptions caused by war, have been a leading cause of malnutrition in Europe. In addi-

Figure 3.19 Life expectancy at birth for males, in years. (Source: United Nations, *Demographic Yearbook,* 1967.)

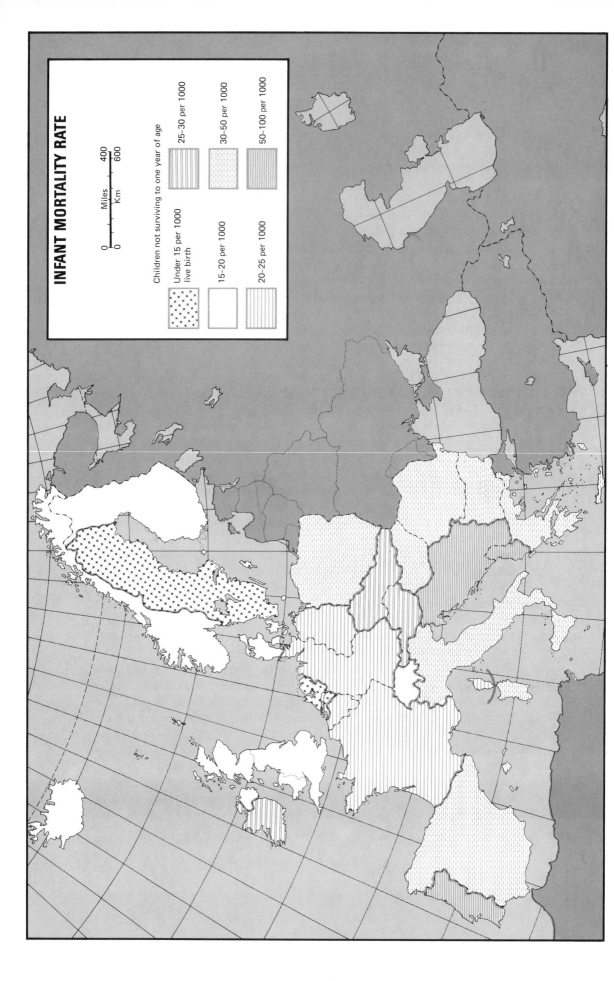

INFANT MORTALITY RATE

Miles
0   400
Km
0   600

Children not surviving to one year of age

Under 15 per 1000 live birth

15–20 per 1000

20–25 per 1000

25–30 per 1000

30–50 per 1000

50–100 per 1000

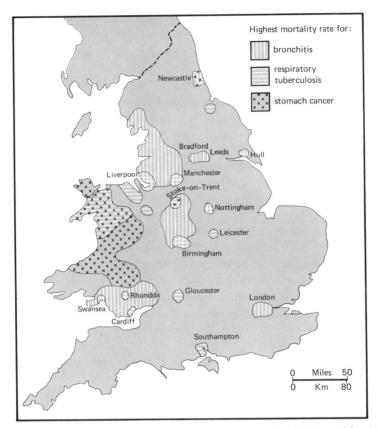

Figure 3.21 The geography of selected fatal diseases in England and Wales. (After Murray.)

tion, the disruption of production associated with the collectivization of agriculture in Communist lands after World War II caused some dietary deficiency. More often than not, however, unsatisfactory diet results from ignorance, tradition, and other cultural causes, for diet is a most characteristic expression of culture, often reflecting many of the beliefs of a people, both positive and negative. In some Balkan countries, until quite recent times, religious fasts occurred so often and for such long periods as to impair the health of the people. A six-week fast in Advent, another six weeks in Lent, one week to a month at the time of the feast of St. Peter, plus regular Wednesday and Friday fasts throughout the year were typical of parts of southeastern Europe, totaling 206 days each year when the consumption of meat was forbidden. Albanians are, and have historically been, vegetarians, consuming mainly corn bread, vegetables, whey, and cheese, with mutton rarely present even in the soup prepared for festive occasions. Indeed, most southern Europeans eat little meat. In the Portuguese, Greek, Spanish, and Italian diets, only 15 to 17 percent of calories are of animal origin. Of course, vegetarianism is not necessarily detrimental to health, but adequate substitutes for meat must be available, which is not always the case in these countries. In contrast, 42 percent of the English calorie intake is animal in origin. Other regional dietary differences include the Hungarian

Figure 3.20 Infant mortality rate. (Source: United Nations, *Statistical Yearbook,* 1966.)

reliance on cereals, which provide fully 90 percent of their carbohydrates and 70 percent of the protein. Dietary imbalance rather than absolute insufficiency affects certain European groups, and the cause is often cultural rather than economic in nature.

The role of tradition as an influence in diet can hardly be overestimated. Almost every European country has a distinctive cuisine, so that the linguistic–political mosaic is duplicated by a crazy-quilt of food preferences. Among the basic contrasts are olive oil versus butter in cooking, the former confined to southern Europe; wheat bread versus rye bread, the latter found mainly in northern and northeastern Europe; and maize (corn)-eating versus maize-avoidance. Most Europeans will not eat corn, raising it instead only as a livestock feed, but some peoples such as the Albanians do use it in their diet. In choice of alcoholic beverages, the preference runs from wine in southern Europe to beer in most Germanic areas and to hard liquors of various kinds in some parts of peripheral northern and eastern Europe. Almost inevitably, Europeans are quite proud of their ethnic or national dishes and speak derisively of the cuisine of other groups and nations. Foods remain to the present day a vital expression of ethnic differences in Europe. For example, until quite recently northern Italians were either ignorant of or disrespectful toward pizza, a southern dish. Only with the massive migration of southern Italians to the factories of the North has pizza spread to that region. Indeed, pizza is now found as far afield as West Germany. Ethnic pride can also be detected in the chauvinistic attitude adopted toward the cheeses, wines, sausages, and other distinctive foods of individual small districts, and it is typical for varieties of these foods and beverages to bear the name of the town or province of origin. In Europe, one does not speak simply of cheese but rather of "Roquefort," "Limburger," "Cheddar," or "Edam." Wine is not merely wine, but instead "Mosel," "Port," or "Champagne." Disdain for the daily fare of foreigners is evident still today and can be traced back as far as the historical record exists. The revulsion expressed by the Roman writer Tacitus for the crude Germans with their "butter-smeared beards" finds echoes yet today in a multitude of culinary prejudices. Foods are part and parcel of the diversity found within the European culture area.

The differences in distribution and characteristics of population discussed in this chapter are indicative of many other regional human contrasts in Europe. In the following three chapters, consideration will be given to the areal diversities in human physical traits, in language, and in religion.

SOURCES AND SUGGESTED READINGS

Roberto Almagia. "The Repopulation of the Roman Campagna." *Geographical Review*. Vol. 19 (1929), pp. 529–555.

Marcel Aurousseau. "The Arrangement of Rural Populations." *Geographical Review*. Vol. 10 (1920), pp. 223–240.

Henri Bastide and Alain Girard. "Les tendances démographiques en France et les attitudes de la population." *Population*. Vol. 21 (1966), pp. 9–50.

E. Behm and H. Wagner. "Die Bevölkerung der Erde." *Petermanns Geographische Mitteilungen, Ergänzungsheft Nr. 35.* Gotha, Germany: Justus Perthes, 1874.

Figure 3.22 Average daily calorie intake per capita. (Source: United Nations, *Statistical Yearbook,* 1964.)

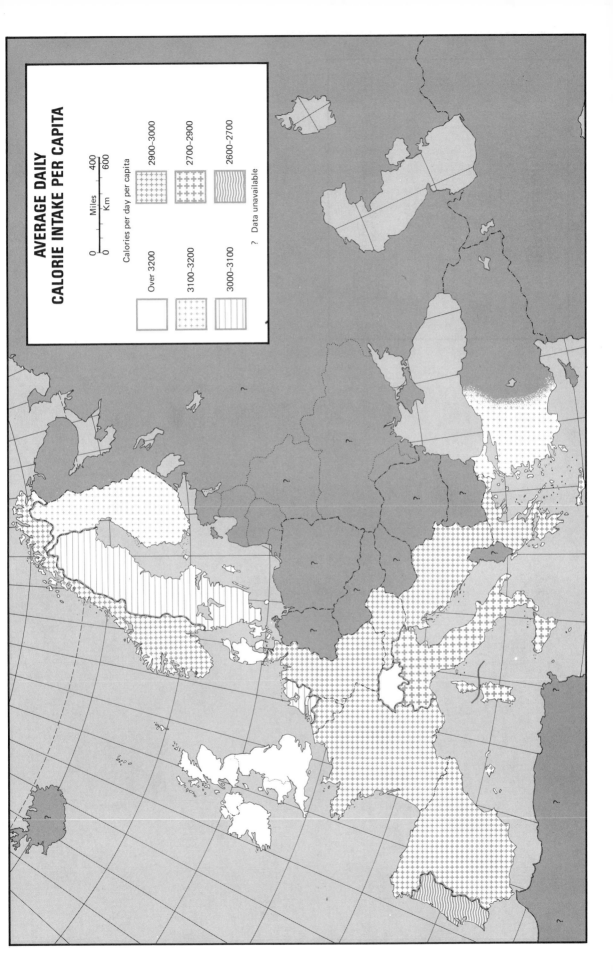

AVERAGE DAILY
CALORIE INTAKE PER CAPITA

Miles
0   400
0   600
Km

Calories per day per capita

Over 3200

3100-3200

3000-3100

2900-3000

2700-2900

2600-2700

? Data unavailable

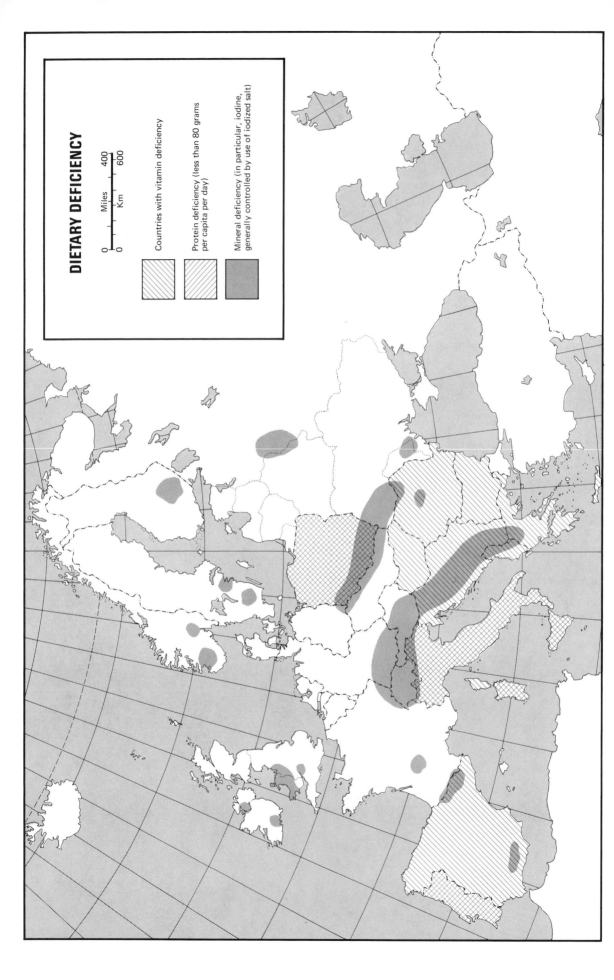

DIETARY DEFICIENCY

Miles
0   400
Km
0   600

Countries with vitamin deficiency

Protein deficiency (less than 80 grams per capita per day)

Mineral deficiency (in particular, iodine, generally controlled by use of iodized salt)

J. Beloch. *Die Bevölkerung der griechisch-romanischen Welt.* Leipzig: Duncker & Humbolt, 1886.

Raoul Blanchard. "The Exchange of Populations Between Greece and Turkey." *Geographical Review.* Vol. 15 (1925), pp. 449–456.

Jan O. M. Broek and John W. Webb. "The Differential Growth of Population." Chapter 18 in *A Geography of Mankind.* New York: McGraw-Hill, 1968.

Alexander M. Carr-Saunders. *World Population: Past Growth and Present Trends.* Oxford: Clarendon Press, 1936.

S. H. Cousens. "The Regional Pattern of Emigration During the Great Irish Famine, 1846–51." *Institute of British Geographers, Transactions and Papers.* Vol. 28 (1960), pp. 119–134.

Robert E. Dickinson. *The Population Problem of Southern Italy: An Essay in Social Geography.* Syracuse, N.Y.: Syracuse University Press, 1955.

Alice Garnett. "Insolation, Topography, and Settlement in the Alps." *Geographical Review.* Vol. 25 (1935), pp. 601–617.

Josef Haliczer. "The Population of Europe, 1720, 1820, 1930." *Geography.* Vol. 19 (1934), pp. 261–273.

James M. Houston. *A Social Geography of Europe.* London: Duckworth, 1953, chapter 10.

G. Melvyn Howe. "The Geographical Distribution of Cancer Mortality in Wales, 1947–53." *Institute of British Geographers, Transactions and Papers.* Vol. 28 (1960), pp. 199–214.

Dudley Kirk. *Europe's Population in the Interwar Years.* Genève: League of Nations, 1946.

Leszek A. Kosinski. *The Population of Europe: A Geographical Perspective.* Harlow, Essex, England: Longman, 1970.

Huey Louis Kostanick. "Turkish Resettlement of Bulgarian Turks 1950–1953." *University of California Publications in Geography.* Vol. 8 (1940–62), pp. 65–163.

Jacques M. May. "Medical Geography: Its Methods and Objectives." *Geographical Review.* Vol. 40 (1950), pp. 9–41.

Jacques M. May. *The Ecology of Malnutrition in Central and Southeastern Europe.* Darien, Conn.: Hafner, 1966.

Jacques M. May. *The Ecology of Malnutrition in Five Countries of East and Central Europe.* Darien, Conn.: Hafner, 1963.

Kurt B. Mayer. *The Population of Switzerland.* New York: Columbia University Press, 1952.

William R. Mead. "The Cold Farm in Finland, Resettlement of Finland's Displaced Farmers." *Geographical Review.* Vol. 41 (1951), pp. 529–543.

Malcolm Murray. "The Geography of Death in England and Wales." *Annals, Association of American Geographers.* Vol. 52 (1962), pp. 130–149.

Alan C. Ogilvie. "Physiography and Settlements in Southern Macedonia." *Geographical Review.* Vol. 11 (1921), pp. 172–197.

Clyde P. Patton. "On the Origins and Diffusion of the European Universities." *Yearbook, Association of Pacific Coast Geographers.* Vol. 31 (1969), pp. 7–26.

Norman J. G. Pounds and Charles C. Roome. "Population Density in Fifteenth Century France and the Low Countries." *Annals, Association of American Geographers.* Vol. 61 (1971), pp. 116–130.

Figure 3.23 Dietary deficiency.

Malcolm Proudfoot. *European Refugees: 1939–52, A Study in Forced Population Movement.* Evanston, Ill.: Northwestern University Press, 1956.

J. C. Russell. "Late Ancient and Medieval Population." *Transactions of the American Philosophical Society.* New Series Vol. 48 (1958), part 3.

Joseph B. Schechtman. *Postwar Population Transfers in Europe 1945–1955.* Philadelphia: University of Pennsylvania Press, 1963.

Gabriele Schwarz. *Allgemeine Siedlungsgeographie.* Berlin: Walter de Gruyer, 2nd ed., 1961.

Max Sorre. "La géographie de l'alimentation." *Annales de Géographie.* Vol. 61 (1952), pp. 184–199.

L. Dudley Stamp. *The Geography of Life and Death.* Ithaca, N.Y.: Cornell University Press, 1964.

Kirk H. Stone. "Finnish Fringe of Settlement Zones." *Tijdschrift voor Economische en Sociale Geografie.* Vol. 57 (1966), pp. 222–232.

Kirk H. Stone. "Swedish Fringes of Settlement." *Annals, Association of American Geographers.* Vol. 52 (1962), pp. 373–393.

Sigurdur Thorarinsson. "Population Changes in Iceland." *Geographical Review.* Vol. 51 (1961), pp. 519–533.

A. R. Toniolo. "Studies of Depopulation in the Mountains of Italy." *Geographical Review.* Vol. 27 (1937), pp. 473–477.

Glenn T. Trewartha. *A Geography of Population.* New York: Wiley, 1969.

United Nations. *Demographic Yearbook. Annuaire Démographique.* New York: UN, various issues.

United Nations. *Statistical Yearbook. Annuaire Statistique.* New York: UN, various issues.

Abbott Payson Usher. "The History of Population and Settlement in Eurasia." *Geographical Review.* Vol. 20 (1930), pp. 110–132.

J. Velikonja. "Postwar Population Movements in Europe." *Annals, Association of American Geographers.* Vol. 48 (1958), pp. 458–481.

Hedwig Wachenheim. "Hitler's Transfers of Population in Eastern Europe." *Foreign Affairs.* Vol. 20 (1942), pp. 705–718.

Guido Weigend. "Effects of Boundary Changes in the South Tyrol." *Geographical Review.* Vol. 40 (1950), pp. 364–375.

Westermanns Grosser Atlas zur Weltgeschichte. Braunschweig, West Germany: Georg Westermann, 1956.

Kurt Witthauer. "Die Bevölkerung der Erde: Verteilung und Dynamik." *Petermanns Geographische Mitteilungen, Ergänzungsheft Nr. 265.* Gotha, East Germany: Justus Perthes, 1958.

Kurt Witthauer. "Verteilung und Dynamik der Erdbevölkerung." *Petermanns Geographische Mitteilungen, Ergänzungsheft Nr. 272.* Gotha, East Germany: Justus Perthes, 1969.

Wilbur Zelinsky. *A Prologue to Population Geography.* Englewood Cliffs, N.J.: Prentice-Hall, 1966.

CHAPTER FOUR

Physical traits of the Europeans

One of the three basic human traits which, in the narrower sense, helps define "Europe" is the dominance of lighter-complected peoples, normally referred to as *caucasoids*. The geographer is concerned with such physical characteristics of the population for several reasons. First, the peoples of Europe, despite the basic caucasoid unity, exhibit some rather pronounced regional physical differences, many of which are readily apparent even to an untrained observer. Some Europeans are tall, others short; some are blond, others brunet; some have long heads, others round heads; and so on. These areal variations have at times been the basis of conflict and discrimination between groups, as in the Nazi episode. More recently, an immigration of exotic physical types of darker complexion has led to segregation and discrimination in countries such as the United Kingdom. The important fact is that European people are aware that they differ physically and that this awareness has on occasion influenced their interactions.

In addition, the distribution of physical traits can often provide some suggestion of past migrations of peoples and related diffusion of culture, evidence sometimes not otherwise available. Such traits may be an aid in understanding the diffusion of domestic plants and animals through Europe in prehistoric times, or they may help explain why a high civilization arose in remote parts of Britain as far back as 2000 B.C.

The geographer is also attracted to the study of human physical features because such traits are in part the result of local or regional differences in culture and environment. For example, diet can affect the size of people, as can climate, and the shape of the head can be influenced by the use of cradleboards for infants. The geographer, by training and inclination, is attracted to the study of such inter-related areal variations.

4.1 AREAL VARIATIONS OF PHYSICAL TRAITS

Human physical traits differ in Europe on several scales. Within the same area or region, there are differences between individual persons, even those who share some degree of common ancestry. On another level, averages or means of physical features compiled for groups living in one area often reveal contrasts to those for other groups elsewhere. This second type of variation is of more interest to the geographer than the first, though averages do conceal marked individual differences.

There are numerous group traits which have been shown to vary areally in Europe. Of these, only a few are presented here as representative.

PIGMENTATION

One of the most visible characteristics of people is the pigmentation of the skin, hair, and eyes. In the lands around the shores of the North and Baltic seas, including most of Scandinavia, northern Germany, Poland, Finland, Estonia, Latvia, the Netherlands, and eastern coastal Great Britain, most of the population is light-complected (Figure 4.1). The same is true of Iceland, eastern Ireland, and parts of northwestern Russia. Hair is blond, red, or light brown; eyes are most often blue, gray, or hazel; and the skin is unusually fair. This northern zone of depigmentation is divided into at least two subregions. In the west, including Scandinavia, the Netherlands, northwestern Germany, and the British Isles, golden-blond hair and blue eyes are the commonest forms of light coloring, while to the east, in Finland and the lands of the northern Slavs, grayish eyes and ash-blond hair are more typical. Red hair is commonest in the Scottish Highlands, but even there only about 10 percent of the population exhibits that trait. The fairest-skinned Europeans are those living to the east of the Baltic Sea and in certain Norwegian valleys. Nowhere else in the world is depigmentation of hair, eyes, and skin so common as in northern Europe.

Dark-complected people are dominant in the Iberian Peninsula, the Balkan Peninsula, Italy, southern France, and Wales (Figure 4.1). Dark brown or brown hair and eyes, together with swarthy skin, are most common in these southern European areas. The darkest-skinned Europeans are the Portuguese, southern Spaniards, Romanians, and southern Italians. Beyond the limits of Europe, in North Africa, the Middle East, and central Asia, even darker-complected peoples are found, though most of these peripheral populations are still caucasoid (Figure 4.1).

Between the northern region of depigmentation and the southern brunet zone is an east–west belt of medium complexion. Overall, pigmentation tends to decrease steadily to the north through Europe, with some local irregularities. There are no sharp pigmentation borders, and complexion lightens gradually with in-

Figure 4.1   Distribution of hair color. (After Struck, Günther, and Biasutti.)

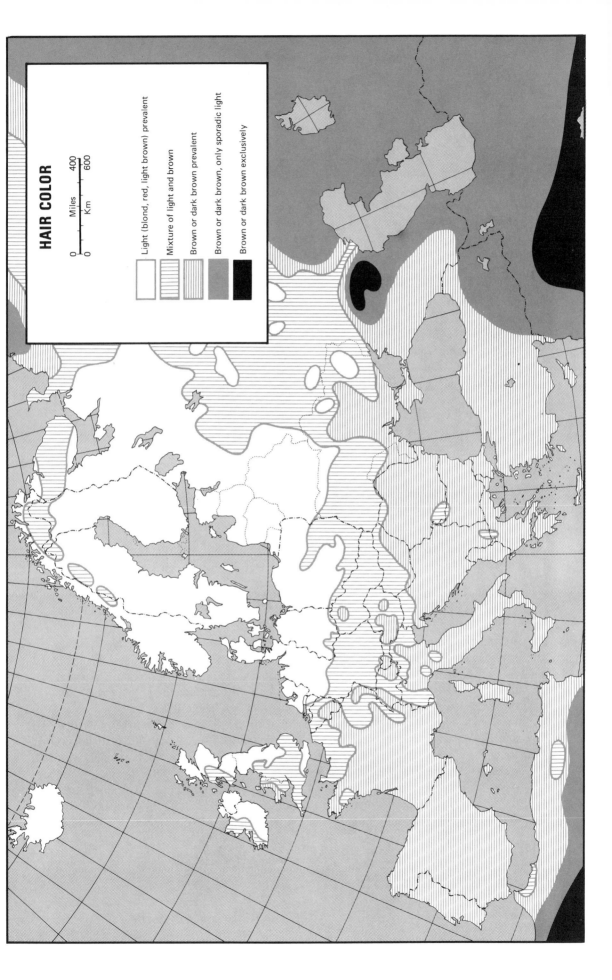

HAIR COLOR

Miles
0   400
Km
0   600

☐ Light (blond, red, light brown) prevalent

▨ Mixture of light and brown

▥ Brown or dark brown prevalent

▦ Brown or dark brown, only sporadic light

■ Brown or dark brown exclusively

creasing latitude. A geographical transition of this type, from lower to higher incidence of a human physical trait, is called a *cline*. All physical differences between
Europeans are clinal in character.

While the pigmentation averages compiled for the various peoples of
Europe do reveal a clinal distribution, a continuum, it is important to recognize
that blond *individuals* can be found in southern areas such as Spain, Italy, and
Greece, while some brunet persons live in Sweden, Iceland, or Norway. Indeed, the
northern Europeans are only secondarily and partially blond, for brunet pigment
survives in nearly all areas of depigmentation. Even at the blond extreme, in certain
eastern valleys of Norway, only about half of the population is wholly blond. Moreover, the incidence of brunet traits has been increasing in recent times in countries
such as Sweden.

In all probability, depigmentation is a response to reduced sunlight. The
pigment map of Europe closely resembles the climatic distribution of cloudiness.
Sunny climates such as the Mediterranean appear to be more conducive to brunet
populations, while cloudy climates, including the marine west coast, seem to encourage depigmentation. The key to this cause-and-effect relationship is a dark-
colored chemical substance called *melanin,* which is deposited in the lower strata
of the epidermis. Melanin production is stimulated by exposure to ultraviolet light,
as the body seeks to deposit a barrier to protect itself from overpenetration by
ultraviolet rays which can damage living cells. Pigmentation of the hair and eyes is
affected in the same way as that of the skin. Depigmentation may also be a result
of the greater use of clothing for thousands of years in the colder lands of the north.

The central zone of medium pigmentation in Europe is perhaps the product
of mixing between southern brunets and northern blonds. More likely, however, it
represents a response to a climate which is intermediate in degree of cloudiness.

STATURE

A second standard for physical comparison of Europeans is stature, or
height. Taller caucasoids populate the lands bordering the Baltic and North seas,
the Dinaric Range of Yugoslavia and Albania, and the Ukraine (Figure 4.2). The
Po Valley and middle Rhine districts also have relatively tall populations. Even
untrained observers can hardly fail to notice the large number of unusually tall
people in parts of Yugoslavia. Tallest of all, however, are highlanders and island
folk from parts of western Scotland, where the average stature for males and females
together is 178 centimeters (5 feet 10 inches) or greater.

Short stature is typical of peoples in parts of Spain, southern Italy, France,
the plains of interior Poland, and inland northern Scandinavia (Figure 4.2). In
these regions, average stature for the population as a whole is less than 163 centimeters (5 feet 4 inches). The shortest Europeans are the Lapps of northern Sweden
and Norway, who average less than 158 centimeters (5 feet 2 inches) in some districts. As was true of pigmentation, stature appears to vary in a clinal manner, with
transition areas of medium stature between regions of tall and short peoples.

Stature appears to be partially the result of genetic reaction to temperature,
for the tallest Europeans tend to live along the $-4°$ C ($25°$ F) January isotherm.
It has long been recognized that the larger and heavier representatives of individual

Figure 4.2   Distribution of average stature (males and females together). (After Biasutti.)

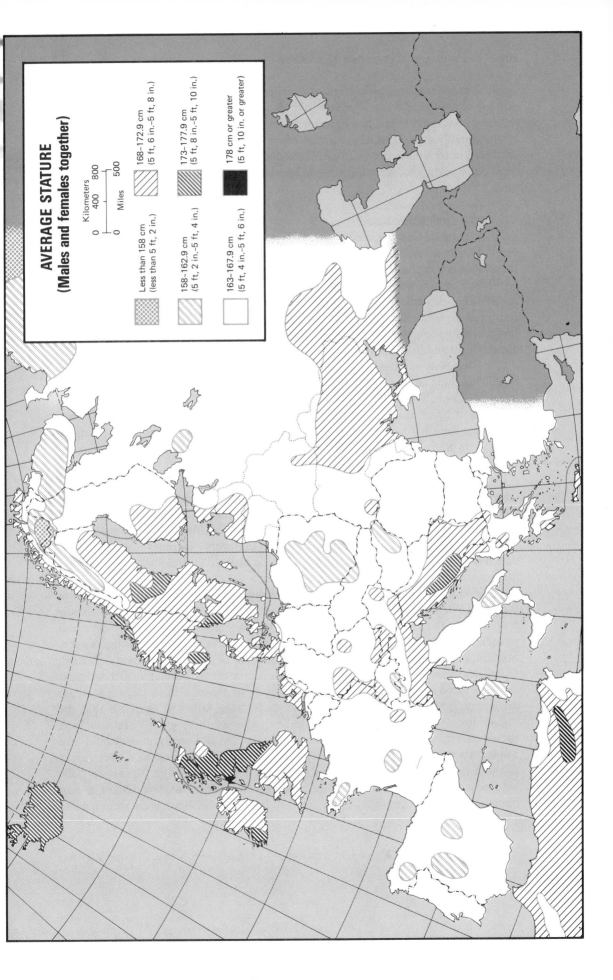

AVERAGE STATURE
(Males and females together)

Kilometers

0   400   800

0   500

Miles

Less than 158 cm
(less than 5 ft, 2 in.)

158–162.9 cm
(5 ft, 2 in.–5 ft, 4 in.)

163–167.9 cm
(5 ft, 4 in.–5 ft, 6 in.)

168–172.9 cm
(5 ft, 6 in.–5 ft, 8 in.)

173–177.9 cm
(5 ft, 8 in.–5 ft, 10 in.)

178 cm or greater
(5 ft, 10 in. or greater)

animal species lived in colder regions. European man appears to vary in this way, at least in a general sense. Perhaps still more important, stature is influenced by nutrition. Average stature has been increasing in many countries since World War II, presumably as a result of a more satisfactory diet. Similarly, the decline in stature noted in Iceland between A.D. 1200 and A.D. 1700 (Table 3.2) during a period of colder climate was likely due to food shortages caused by the decreased temperatures.

CEPHALIC INDEX

Another common measure of physical differences in people is the *cephalic index,* the breadth of the head as a percentage of the head length. An oblong skull, then, has a low cephalic index, in which case the individual is referred to as *dolicho-cephalic*. Zones of dolichocephalic averages are found in both northern and southern Europe, particularly in Scandinavia, the British Isles, Iceland, Iberia, southern Italy, and the southeastern Balkan Peninsula (Figure 4.3). In these areas the population averages less than 79 in cephalic index, reaching the lowest averages in northern Portugal and in central Sardegna.

Broad-headed, or *brachycephalic,* people are found in central Europe, in a belt stretching from Atlantic coastal France eastward into the Soviet Union (Figure 4.3). Cephalic index averages of 83 or more are typical of this zone, reaching extremes of 87 or more in parts of southern France and Albania. Another brachycephalic cluster is found in northern Scandinavia. *Mesocephalic* averages, ranging from 79 to 83, are found in the transition zones between the broad- and narrow-headed peoples.

While brachycephalic people have lived in Europe since pre-Neolithic times, including one specimen 30,000 years old found in Yugoslavia, there has been a pronounced increase in cephalic index throughout most of Europe in recent times. Since about A.D. 600, and particularly since the year 1000, the average cephalic index has risen significantly, especially in central Europe. During the same period, dolichocephalism has been almost everywhere in retreat. The majority of Europeans are now either brachycephalic or mesocephalic.

Areal differences in cephalic index and the changes which have occurred in the past 1500 years or so have been explained in various ways. The brachycephalic trait may be the result of racial mixture with mongoloid peoples, most of whom have high indexes. Those who support the mixture thesis point out that the brachycephalic zone of Europe is astride the historic axis of invasion by Avars, Tartars, Huns, and other possibly mongoloid groups. Moreover, since many of these invasions occurred after A.D. 600, the invasion thesis would explain the recent increase of brachycephalism. Detailed studies, however, have failed to establish that the Asiatic invaders were broad-headed. Rather, many of these groups seem to have been rather diverse in head shape. Moreover, the invasion explanation would lead one to expect an increase in brachycephalism to the east, toward the source region of the invaders, but the map reveals no such cline. Some of the highest cephalic indexes are found in France, near the *western* end of the zone. In addition, a pronounced mongoloid contribution to cephalic index should have been accompanied

Figure 4.3   Distribution of average cephalic index. (After Biasutti.)

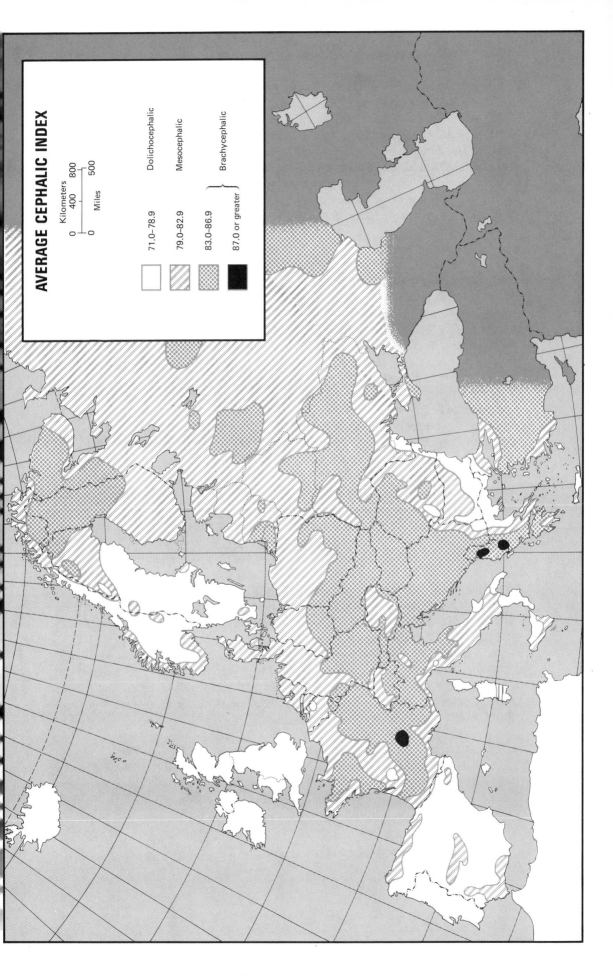

AVERAGE CEPHALIC INDEX

Kilometers
0   400   800
0   500
Miles

71.0–78.9   Dolichocephalic

79.0–82.9   Mesocephalic

83.0–86.9
} Brachycephalic
87.0 or greater

by the implantment of numerous other mongoloid traits, but such was not the case.

Perhaps more plausible is the suggestion that brachycephalism is a mutation within the caucasoid population, the result of an evolutionary process. A broad head may provide a more efficient container for the brain in man's erect posture, and the spread of brachycephalism might be viewed as the result of this inherent superiority. Ironically, some misled racists earlier in the twentieth century had concluded that dolichocephalic people were mentally superior to those with broad heads. No evidence exists, however, to support the notion that intelligence is in any way related to shape or size of the skull.

BLOOD GROUPS

Human blood groups are based on the presence or absence of substances called *agglutinogens* in the red blood cells. The most important agglutinogens, or factors, are designated by the symbols A, B, and Rh. Presence or absence of factors A and B has led to the designation of four *blood types:* (1) type A, containing only factor A, (2) type B, containing only factor B, (3) type O, in which neither factor A nor B is present, and (4) type AB, containing both factors. This classification is further refined by the presence of factor Rh (Rhesus) in most people, divided into Rh+ and Rh− categories.

Blood types are not evenly distributed in Europe (Figure 4.4). Type A is more common in western Europe than elsewhere, accounting for 30 percent or more of the population in parts of western Iberia, eastern France, Scandinavia, northern Italy, and the Carpathians. The concentration of type A in marginal and highland areas suggests that it is a very old blood trait in Europe. In contrast, type B, which is not as common as type A, appears usually in eastern Europe. Type B is common among the mongoloid peoples of Asia, and it is possible that the greater occurrence in eastern Europe is the result of fairly recent mongoloid mixture with caucasoids there. Nowhere in Europe does type B account for more than 18 percent of the population. By far the most common blood type in Europe is O, which reaches greatest frequencies in the coastal periphery of western and southern Europe. In Iceland, Scotland, Ireland, Corse, Sardegna, and the Basque area of the Spanish–French borderland, over 70 percent of the population has type O. Nearly all parts of Europe have at least half of the population with type O blood. The dominance of type O in the far-western peripheries of Europe has led some geneticists to regard it as the oldest European blood type.

The Rh positive and negative traits are also unevenly distributed. Northwestern Europeans are more likely to have Rh− blood than are residents of the Mediterranean region or eastern Europe. The Basque people of Spain and France have a high frequency of Rh−, as do the inhabitants of certain Alpine valleys in Switzerland.

OTHER TRAITS

There are many other traits which can be used to classify people into physical groups. One is the *nasal index,* a measure of the width of the nose as a percentage of length. Northern Europeans and Iberians have very low indexes, less than 67, while central and most of southern Europe fall in the 67-to-72 category.

Figure 4.4   Distribution of A–B–O blood groups. (After Mourant, Vallois, and Marquer.)

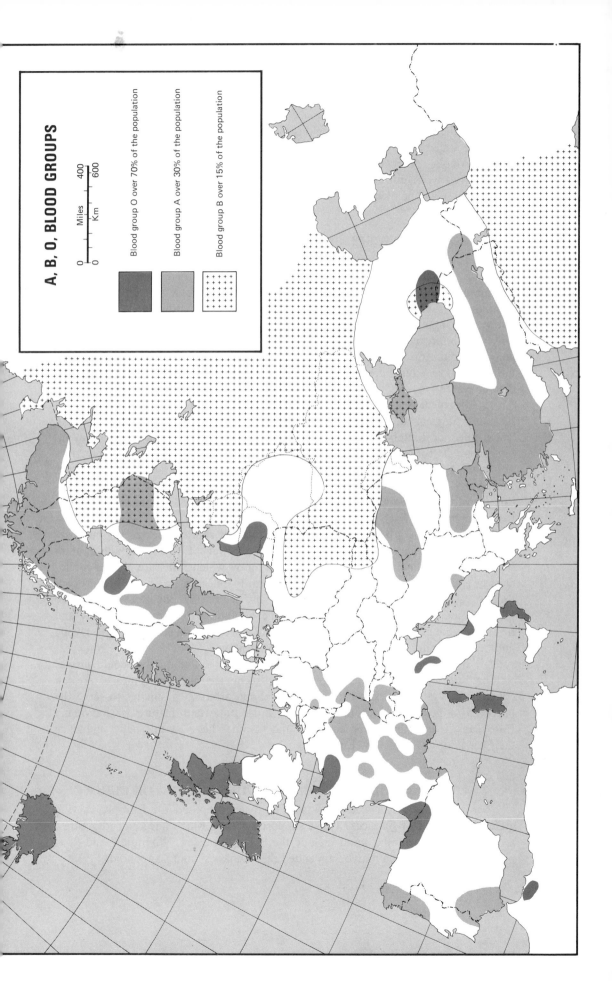

A, B, O, BLOOD GROUPS

Miles
0   400

Km
0   600

Blood group O over 70% of the population

Blood group A over 30% of the population

Blood group B over 15% of the population

Another commonly measured physical trait is *head size*. The Europeans having the largest head size live mainly in northwestern areas and in the Dinaric Ranges of the Balkan Peninsula, regions also characterized by tall people. To these should be added the residents of the Dordogne area in southwestern France.

Among other traits which differ regionally in Europe are hair form (straight, wavy, or curly), face profile, face width, nose profile, and eyelid form. Some of these will be mentioned later in this chapter.

4.2 THE CONCEPT OF RACE

It was long the practice of scholars who study the physical traits of man to designate separate *races* and *subraces*. Many definitions of race were proposed, but perhaps most commonly it was understood to be a group possessing *an aggregate* of common physical traits which served to distinguish them, individually and collectively, from other races or subraces. Properly used, the term race was employed only with reference to physical traits, not to cultural characteristics such as language, religion, or nationality. A few writers used the term *geographical race* to mean a people having features in common and extending over a geographically definable area.

In recent years the concept of race or geographical race has been discarded by many physical anthropologists and geneticists. Races, they say, do not exist. Their objection centers on the fact that the various physical variations in mankind are not areally concordant, that the distribution of cephalic index, for example, does not match the distribution of blood types, head size, pigmentation, or any other trait. There are no aggregates of physical traits which have the same areal distribution, and the entire concept of race was built on the assumed existence of such inherited aggregates. Each trait varies areally in a unique way.

At best the grouping of peoples into races or subraces serves the purposes of generalization, and any racial classification is arbitrary. Literally an infinite number of such classifications is possible, depending on which traits are chosen for inclusion and what numerical limits are arbitrarily selected on the cline, or continuum, as dividing points. One classifier of races may choose to emphasize pigmentation, blood type, and stature, while another prefers cephalic index and head size. One may set 82 as the breaking point between cephalic index types, while another may prefer 81 or 83 or some other percentage.

Five Caucasian subraces are mentioned below. The number could just as well be fifty or five hundred. It is essential to recognize that these subraces are not concrete, separate entities, but rather artificial and arbitrary groupings to serve the purposes of generalization. Perhaps their most important feature is that many Europeans *believe* these subraces exist and at times have let this belief influence their behavior toward fellow Europeans.

4.3 THE TRADITIONAL CAUCASOID SUBRACES OF EUROPE

Numerous racial classifications have been proposed for Europe, varying greatly in number of subraces. Those supposed groups which have gained greatest acceptance in the popular mind include the "Mediterranean," "Nordic," and "Alpine" subraces, to which may be appended the "Dinarics" and Lapponoids."

THE MEDITERRANEAN SUBRACE

In the southern extremities of Europe is the *Mediterranean* subrace, a group characterized by relatively short stature, low to very low cephalic index, and fairly dark complexion. Most often, Mediterranean people have a slender body build, narrow face, straight and prominent nose, small jaw, and small to medium head size. The form of the hair varies but is often curly, and the face profile is *orthognathous,* meaning that the lower parts of the face are not projecting. In most cases the upper face is relatively long in proportion to the total face height.

Iberia is the principal Mediterranean subrace area, but such people are also found in southern Italy, parts of Greece and the eastern Balkans, southern France, and Wales (Figure 4.5). In non-European areas, Mediterranean people are typical of North Africa, the Middle East, and northern India.

Mediterranean types have lived in Europe for at least 10,000 years, but a more recent infusion of such people apparently occurred in Neolithic times with the coming of agriculture to southern Europe. Iberia received an additional influx of Mediterraneans with the Moorish invasion in historic times. Sculpture from the period of classical Greece and the Roman Empire most often portrays individuals with Mediterranean traits.

The influx of the Mediterranean subrace has been linked by some writers to the rise of higher civilization in Europe. They have been portrayed as the bearers of the technology of Mesopotamia and Egypt who established the first high civilization in the European culture area.

THE NORDIC SUBRACE

The *Nordic* subrace, as the name implies, is centered in northern Europe, especially southern and central Scandinavia, the British Isles, and Iceland (Figure 4.5). Nordic people tend to be light-complected, tall, and dolichocephalic to mesocephalic (82 or less cephalic index). The nasal index is usually low, 65 or less, the face profile is orthognathous, and the head is large. Overall, the Nordics are a big-boned people, physically larger than most of their southern neighbors.

Many believe that the Nordics are derived from the Mediterranean subrace, representing a depigmented phase of that group. They are said to have reached central and northwestern Europe from the east in the third millennium B.C., following the plains pathway north of the Alps while their Mediterranean kinsmen went south of the mountain complex. Depigmentation was presumably the result either of mutation, in response to cloudy climate, or of mixing with light-complected earlier residents of northern Europe. Similarly, the increased stature may have been due to colder climates. Supporting the thesis that Nordics are simply "bleached" Mediterraneans is the survival of brunet pigment in all supposedly Nordic areas.

THE ALPINE SUBRACE

Much of the central section, wedged between the Nordic and Mediterranean zones, is dominated by the *Alpine* subrace (Figure 4.5). Actually the term "Alpine," though long used by students of race, is somewhat misleading, for members of this subrace are found all the way from Bretagne on the Atlantic coast of France to the interior provinces of China. It is true, however, that the Alpine peoples are more common in mountainous or hilly areas than on the adjacent plains.

The principal and sole distinguishing trait of the Alpines is a high cephalic

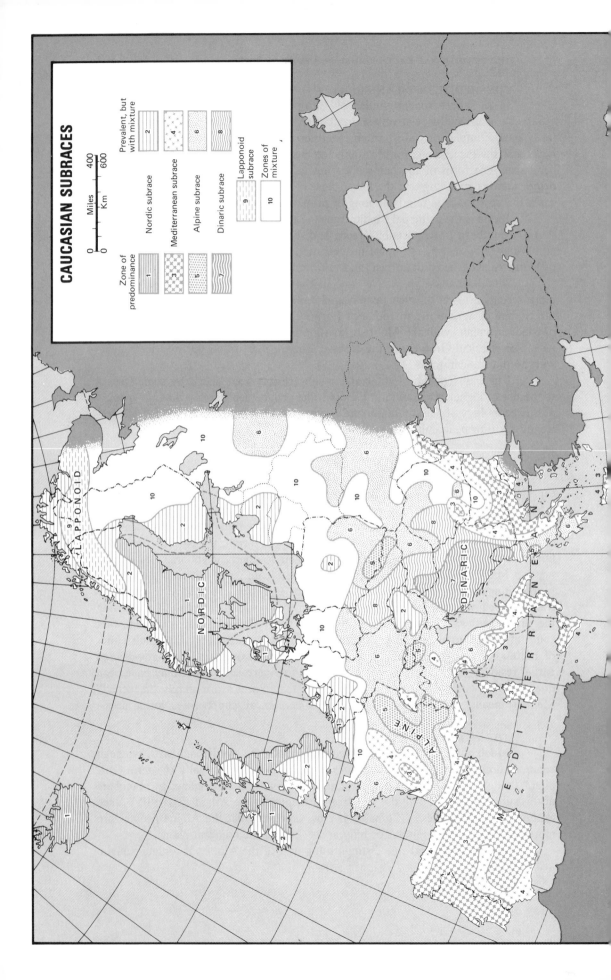

CAUCASIAN SUBRACES

Miles
0   400
Km
0   600

Zone of predominance

1 Nordic subrace
3 Mediterranean subrace
5 Alpine subrace
7 Dinaric subrace
9 Lapponoid subrace
10 Zones of mixture

Prevalent, but with mixture

2
4
6
8

LAPPONOID

NORDIC

ALPINE

DINARIC

MEDITERRANEAN

index, in excess of 83 generally. They are of medium stature and stocky build, with short arms and legs, large hands and feet, and abundant body hair. The face is quite broad or round, and the nose usually has a low bridge.

THE DINARIC SUBRACE

The *Dinaric* subrace, like the Alpine, consists mainly of mountain-dwelling people. Their home is principally the Dinaric Mountain Range of Yugoslavia and Albania, along the eastern shore of the Adriatic Sea (Figure 4.5). Similarity to the Alpines is also seen in the brachycephalism of the Dinarics, but in most other ways they are distinct from the Alpines. The face is usually long and narrow, somewhat triangular in shape, with a broad forehead and narrow jaw. A long, narrow, convex nose is typical. Still more distinctive is the tall stature of the Dinarics, a trait which distinguishes them from neighboring Mediterraneans and Alpines. They are closely akin to the Mediterraneans in pigmentation.

The Dinarics may be the result of a mixture between round-headed, broad-faced people and others who were long-headed and narrow-faced. It is equally possible that their distinguishing traits are the result of mutation. Their brachycephalism may be partly the result of cultural practices, in particular the traditional use of cradleboards for infants, which tends to flatten the occipital area of the skull. Dinaric types have lived in the mountains of Albania for at least 2500 years, though probably at first as a minority group. Similar people are found to the east in Armenia and the Caucasus.

THE LAPPONOID SUBRACE

One of the most distinctive groups in Europe is the *Lapponoid* subrace, confined areally to the northern parts of Sweden, Norway, Finland, and the Karelian Autonomous Republic of the Soviet Union (Figure 4.5). These people are of short or very short stature, with small hands and feet. They are normally brachycephalic and have broad faces. The eyes are widely separated, the chin is pointed, the teeth are small, and the hair form is straight. Lapponoids have snub noses with a nasal index of 70 or more. Their complexion is somewhat darker than that of the Nordics to the south, and they are more likely to be mesognathous (some projection of lower face). The Lapponoids are very small people, with short arms and legs. Blood types are also distinctive, for the Lapponoids have charactistically different frequencies of nearly all blood-group genes.

Lapponoid origins are hotly disputed. The traditional view was that these people were partially or even largely mongoloid rather than Caucasian, based on their short stature, brachycephalism, darker complexion, and moderately high frequency of blood type B. More recently it has been suggested that the Lapponoids have no mongoloid ancestry, that they may be related to the Alpine subrace or perhaps represent a survival of a very early caucasoid group.

SUBRACE AND THE MYTH OF SUPERIORITY

No sooner had the first classification of Europe's subraces appeared than various writers began attaching *behavioral* images to each group, so repeatedly that the images became stereotyped. The Nordics supposedly possessed genius for leadership and were work-loving, efficient, and militaristic, while the Mediterrane-

Figure 4.5   Caucasian subraces. (Based principally on Biasutti.)

ans were labeled as artistic, lazy, inefficient, and hot-blooded. The poor Alpines were said to be unimaginative, plodding, and reserved. A satirical poem by Hilaire Belloc sums up these popular images quite well:

> Behold, my child, the Nordic man,
> And be as like him as you can.
> His legs are long—his mind is slow;
> His hair is lank and made of tow.
>
> And here we have the Alpine race,
> Oh! what a broad and brutal face.
> His skin is of a dirty yellow.
> He is a most unpleasant fellow.
>
> The most degraded of them all
> Mediterranean we call.
> His hair is crisp and even curls
> And he is saucy with the girls.[1]

These stereotypes have no basis in scholarship, and Belloc rightly pokes fun at them, but they appear again and again, and their imagined truth and importance reached truly absurd and tragic proportions in Nazi Germany. Strangely, the most influential advocates of Nordic supremacy were Adolf Hitler and his propaganda minister Josef Göbbels, both of whom were exceptionally short and rather dark-complected. There is no "master" race or subrace, though it is perhaps human nature to regard groups of people who are physically different as undesirable inferiors.

4.4 RECENT EXOTIC IMMIGRATION

A modern influx of exotic physical types has accompanied the establishment and decline of European colonial empires in the tropics, mainly since World War II. Hundreds of thousands of negroid West Indians have exercised the privileges of their British citizenship and migrated permanently to the United Kingdom, and they have been joined by large numbers of dark-complected Mediterranean caucasoids from India and Pakistan, who are also regarded as "coloured" by the English. These immigrant groups, numbering about one million in all, are readily distinguished racially from the dominantly Nordic Britons. France has received numbers of Negroes from African and West Indian areas, and the black-populated islands of Martinique and Guadaloupe in the West Indies have been incorporated as provinces of the French state, politically as much a part of France as Paris. Some blacks from nations within the French economic community in Africa have come seeking temporary employment in France, including such un-African tasks as snow removal in winter. The Netherlands received some 50,000 Indonesian immigrants. At least one European nation, Iceland, has consistently forbidden residence by noncaucasoids, even to the point of excluding black military personnel at the United States base at Keflavik. West Germany has acquired a small population of mulattoes as a result of the American military presence.

---

[1] Reprinted by permission of A. D. Peters & Company.

Still another exotic racial immigration may have occurred in the northern portion of formerly German East Prussia (Ostpreussen) annexed by the Soviet Union in 1945. It seems likely that some mongoloid settlers were among the Soviet citizens brought in to replace the expelled German population.

All in all, however, the caucasoid character of Europe is largely undisturbed and remains one of the traits which provides a visible human definition for the western peninsula of Eurasia.

4.5 PHYSICAL TRAITS AND CULTURE

While human physical features do not determine ability or behavior, it is still true that certain cultural traits and events have, or once had, genetic connotations. There are sometimes correlations between the distribution of physical and cultural traits.

LANGUAGE

The mosaic of languages in Europe will be dealt with in the following chapter, but it is important to recognize here that a certain amount of areal correlation exists between physical and linguistic features. This is not wholly unexpected, since individuals normally inherit both physical features and form of speech from their parents. The manner of inheritance is fundamentally different, of course, since physical traits are genetically inherited while language is the result of social transmission, but the end result is usually the same.

The best correlation is that between Lapponoid peoples and the language known as Lappish (compare Figures 4.5 and 5.1). Somewhat less precise is the areal correspondence between light-complected people and the various Germanic tongues (compare Figures 4.1 and 5.1). People speaking the Basque language in France and Spain display unusual frequencies of blood factors B and Rh−. Indeed, the speakers of Basque and Lappish are at opposite blood type extremes, with other European groups occupying intermediate positions. Interestingly, residents of Wales who have Welsh surnames have a higher frequency of blood type O than those in the same area who have English family names.

MIGRATIONS AND CULTURAL DIFFUSION

In some cases physical traits can be linked to migrations and the resultant diffusion of culture. The remarkably high culture which evolved some 4000 or more years ago in western Great Britain and left behind such awesome ruins as Stonehenge has long puzzled experts because of its peripheral location, far from other great civilizations. The survival to the present day of dark complexion in western Britain, especially Wales (Figure 4.4), provides some evidence that the Stonehenge builders may have migrated from the Mediterranean Basin, bringing with them an advanced culture along with dark complexion to implant on British shores.

Another remarkable migration was that of the Vikings in the ninth and tenth centuries A.D. From their homes at the heads of northern fjords, Norse, Swedish, and Danish Vikings steered their dragon ships as far as Iberia, Iceland, Italy, and Turkey. The seas and rivers of western Europe were the Viking warpaths, and they were feared far and wide. In many areas they remained as conquerors, as in French Normandie (Norman = "Northman" = Viking). They were few in number but usually successful in battle. Part of their success was probably due to their large physical size, which gave them an advantage over smaller foes in the era of hand-to-hand combat.

RACE AND POLITICS

Political interaction between groups has at times been based on physical traits. In Nazi Germany, blond, blue-eyed persons were favored, while persons displaying the "wrong" physical traits, such as dark-complected Gypsies, were often marked for imprisonment or extermination. To a degree, German nationalism became identified with a specific racial type, and persons who did not fit the "ideal" Nordic stereotype often found it difficult to be accepted as rightful members of the German nation.

More recently, the immigration of Asian Indians, Pakistanis, and Negroes from the West Indies has stirred racial prejudice in the United Kingdom. A degree of residential segregation of races is evident in cities such as London or Birmingham. Certain politicians in Britain have appealed to racial prejudice to win election to public office. In this way, voting patterns are being influenced by racial distributions.

*   *   *

THE PEOPLES of Europe, then, are physically diverse, within the basic caucasoid framework. They differ in a great variety of ways, only a few of which were selected for consideration here. More important, these areal contrasts can be related to certain cultural patterns, past and present, and can serve as an aid in tracing and understanding ancient cultural diffusion and, at times, the basis of nationalism.

SOURCES AND SUGGESTED READINGS

Renato Biasutti *et al. Le Razze e i Popoli della Terra,* Vol. 2, "Europa-Asia." Torino, Italy: Unione Tipografico-Editrice Torinese, 4th ed., 1967.

William C. Boyd. "Genetics and the Human Race." *Science.* Vol. 140, No. 3571 (1963), pp. 1057–1064.

William C. Boyd. *Genetics and the Races of Man.* Boston: Little, Brown, 1950.

Jan O. M. Broek and John W. Webb. "Race: Biological Facts and Social Attitudes." Chapter 4 in *A Geography of Mankind.* New York: McGraw-Hill, 1968, pp. 73–96.

Karl W. Butzer. *Environment and Archaeology: An Ecological Approach to Prehistory.* Chicago: Aldine, 1971.

P. B. Candella. "The Introduction of Blood Group B into Europe." *Human Biology.* Vol. 14 (1942), pp. 413–444.

Carleton S. Coon. "The Mountains of Giants: A Racial and Cultural Study of the North Albanian Mountain Ghegs." *Papers of the Peabody Museum of American Archaeology and Ethnology.* Vol. 23, no. 3 (1950).

Carleton S. Coon. *The Origin of Races.* New York: Knopf, 1962.

Carleton S. Coon. *The Races of Europe.* New York: Macmillan, 1939.

Carleton S. Coon, Stanley M. Garn, and Joseph B. Birdsell. *Races: A Study of the Problems of Race Formation in Man.* Springfield, Ill.: C. C Thomas, 1950.

Carleton S. Coon and Edward E. Hunt, Jr. *The Living Races of Man*. New York: Knopf, 1965.

David J. de Laubenfels. "Australoids, Negroids, and Negroes: A Suggested Explanation for Their Disjunct Distributions." *Annals, Association of American Geographers*. Vol. 58 (1968), pp. 42–50.

Josef Deniker. *The Races of Man*. New York: Scribner, 1900.

Leslie C. Dunn and Theodosius G. Dobzhansky. *Heredity, Race, and Society*. New York: New American Library, 1952.

Herbert J. Fleure. *The Races of England and Wales: A Survey of Recent Research*. London: Benn, 1923.

John Geipel. *The Europeans: An Ethnohistorical Survey*. Harlow, Essex, England: Longmans, 1969.

Hans F. K. Günther. *The Racial Elements of European History*. Translated by G. C. Wheeler. Port Washington, N.Y.: Kennikat Press, 1970.

Ellsworth Huntington. *The Character of Races as Influenced by Physical Environment, Natural Selection and Historical Development*. New York: Scribner, 1927, chapters XIV–XX.

K. L. Little. "Race Relations in English Society." *Man*. Vol. 42 (1942), pp. 90–91.

Frank B. Livingstone. "On the Non-Existence of Human Races." *Current Anthropology*. Vol. 3 (1962), pp. 279–281.

Ashley Montagu (ed.). *The Concept of Race*. New York: Free Press, 1964.

Ashley Montagu. *Man's Most Dangerous Myth: The Fallacy of Race*. New York: Columbia University Press, 2nd ed., 1945.

A. E. Mourant. *The Distribution of Human Blood Groups*. Springfield, Ill.: C. C Thomas, 1954.

A. E. Mourant, A. C. Kopec, and K. Domaniewska-Sobczak. *The ABO Blood Groups*. Oxford: Blackwell, 1958.

Marshall T. Newman. "Geographic and Microgeographic Races." *Current Anthropology*. Vol. 4 (1963), pp. 189–192.

Martin P. Nilsson. "The Race Problem of the Roman Empire." *Hereditas*. Vol. 2 (1921), pp. 370–390.

G. C. K. Peach. "Factors Affecting the Distribution of West Indians in Great Britain." *Institute of British Geographers, Transactions and Papers*. Vol. 38 (1966), pp. 151–164.

William Z. Ripley. *The Races of Europe, A Sociological Study*. New York: Appleton, 1899.

Giuseppe Sergi. *The Mediterranean Race: A Study of the Origins of European Peoples*. London: Walter Scott, 1901.

Griffith Taylor. *Environment, Race, and Migration*. Chicago: University of Chicago Press, 1937, chapters XI–XIV.

Griffith Taylor. "The Evolution and Distribution of Race, Culture, and Language." *Geographical Review*. Vol. 11 (1921), pp. 54–119.

H. V. Vallois and P. Marquer. "Le Répartition en France des Groupes Sanguins A B O." *Bulletins et Memoires de la Société d'Anthropologie de Paris*. 11th series, Vol. 6, No. 1 (1964), pp. 1–200.

Franz Weidenreich. "The Brachycephalization of Recent Mankind." *Southwestern Journal of Anthropology*. Vol. 1 (1945), pp. 1–54.

Andrzej Wierciński. "The Racial Analysis of Human Populations in Relation to Their Ethnogenesis." *Current Anthropology*. Vol. 3 (1962), pp. 2, 9–20.

CHAPTER FIVE

The geography of languages

Language is the bearer of culture, the principal means by which communication within cultural groups is achieved, and as such it is of major interest to the geographer. While the study of internal structure of languages is principally the concern of linguists, the areal distribution of languages and of the groups which speak them are of geographical concern. Because language determines to a great degree who talks to whom, it can exercise a decisive influence on political, social, and economic phenomena. Areal distributions of types of economy and forms of worship often are closely related to linguistic patterns, as is the territorial extent of political states and provinces. Typically, language borders are sharp, dividing an area such as Europe into an assemblage of relatively uniform blocs, areas which tend to differ in many ways other than speech. In addition, the areal patterns of the physical environment are often related to the linguistic map. The distribution of languages and the interplay between speech and other areal variations, both environmental and cultural, are the topics of concern in this chapter.

5.1 THE KINSHIP AND ORIGIN OF EUROPEAN LANGUAGES

Linguistically, Europe presents a crazy-quilt pattern surpassed in complexity by few other parts of the world. Since 10,000 years ago, a veritable Babel of tongues has passed across Europe. Some languages have spread and prospered,

TABLE 5.1   Comparative Vocabularies of Selected Indo-European and Non–Indo-European Languages

Language family	Group	Language	Word meaning "three"	Word meaning "mother"
Indo-European	Romance	Latin	tres	mater
" "	"	Italian	tre	madre
" "	"	Spanish	tres	madre
" "	"	French	trois	mère
" "	"	Romanian	trei	mama
" "	Germanic	English	three	mother
" "	"	German	drei	mutter
" "	"	Swedish	tre	moder
" "	"	Icelandic	thrír	módir
" "	Slavic	Russian	tri[a]	mat'[a]
" "	"	Czech	tri	matka
" "	"	Polish	trzy	matka
" "	"	Serbo-Croatian	tri	mati
" "	Celtic	Erse (Irish)	tri	mathair
" "	Thraco-Illyrian	Albanian	tre	motrë
" "	Hellenic	Greek	treis[a]	meter[a]
" "	Baltic	Lithuanian	trys	motyna
Uralic	Finnic	Finnish	kolme	äiti
" "	Ugrian	Hungarian	három	anya
Basque	Basque	Basque	iru	ama

[a] Word transliterated from non-Latin alphabet.

some have clung tenuously to inhospitable refuges, others have vanished, leaving behind a few words in surviving tongues or perhaps a sprinkling of place names. In the face of the linguistic diversity, however, it is possible to detect some measure of unity, for most of the tongues spoken in Europe today are related, belonging to the great language family called *Indo-European* or Indo-Aryan. Indeed, the relationship is close enough to warrant the status of Indo-European as one of the three major defining human traits of "Europe." The linguistic kinship of the various Indo-European languages can be very well illustrated by comparing their vocabularies, especially those words which describe commonplace things encountered in everyday life, as for example numbers or blood relations (Table 5.1). The Indo-European relationship is immediately apparent from such comparisons and is underscored by the different form of the same words in non–Indo-European languages (Table 5.1).

Linguistic kinship implies that all related languages are derived from a single, ancient parent tongue. The earliest written specimen of an Indo-European tongue dates from about 1900 B.C., but even at that early date the parent language had apparently spread widely and given birth to mutually unintelligible offspring. A written form of the Indo-European language Greek, the Linear B script of the great Minoan civilization in the Aegean area, dates from as early as 1500 B.C.

The approximate area of origin of Proto–Indo-European, as well as many of its sounds and words, can be derived from a comparative analysis of vocabularies, both modern and archaic. If a word describing an element of the physical or cultural environment is similar in numerous Indo-European languages, then in all probability the element described was known to speakers of the parent tongue. Conversely, diverse words suggest that the object or trait in question was not familiar to the original Indo-Europeans. Using this method, philologists have ascertained that the Proto–Indo-Europeans lived in an environment which had "snow," "cold," and "heat," indicating a mid-latitude land of pronounced seasons. "River" was known to them, as were "wolf," "bear," "oak," "pine," "willow," "beech," and "birch." "Sea," "lion," and "tiger" were absent, however, as were "donkey," "camel," and "elephant," thereby ruling out coastal lands, India, Africa, and the Middle East as possible places of origin. The original Indo-Europeans were farmers apparently acquainted with "plow," "ox," "pig," "sheep," "goat," "apple," and the small grains, but they did not know of such typical Mediterranean plants as the "fig" or "grapevine." To find common words for the varied phenomena associated with the environment of the first Indo-Europeans, experts often had to refer to obsolete or archaic vocabularies. For example, Spanish *oso* and modern German *Bär* would seem to indicate quite different words for "bear" in these two languages, but the archaic German *Ursel,* also meaning "bear," is derived from the same root word as *oso.*

In sum, the vocabulary evidence points to a temperate, well-wooded continental interior, an area north of the Alps and Black Sea, as the birthplace of Proto–Indo-European. This original home was possibly northern Germany, southern Scandinavia, the Baltic lands, the Danubian region, or the southern part of the East European Plain. Perhaps noteworthy is the fact that the modern language believed to be most like the parent Indo-European, Lithuanian, is spoken on the eastern shore of the Baltic.

As the speakers of the original language spread through Europe in prehistoric times, beginning about 3000 B.C., linguistic fragmentation occurred. It is believed that initially two major Indo-European tongues were derived from the parent —*Centum* and *Satem,* names taken from the two variant pronunciations of the word meaning "hundred." From these, in turn, came still more. The Centum group eventually gave birth to Celtic, Germanic, Greek, Romance, and others, which further divided to form many modern languages, as well as some now extinct. Through a similar procedure, the Satem group was the parent of Slavic and Baltic, among others. Fragmentation of the original Indo-European was largely responsible for the present-day diversity of languages in Europe (Figure 5.1, Table 5.2).

5.2 DISTRIBUTION OF THE INDO-EUROPEAN LANGUAGES

The geographical distribution of the various languages reveals a complex mosaic, with no large areas of uniform speech (Figure 5.1). Each subfamily of Indo-European occupies its own corner of the culture area, the result of many centuries of territorial conflict with adjacent linguistic groups.

THE ROMANCE LANGUAGES

One of the most important offshoots of the Centum branch of Indo-European is the Romance, or Romanic group, also called Italic. There are between 160 and 170 million persons in Europe speaking one or another of these closely

Figure 5.1   Languages of Europe.

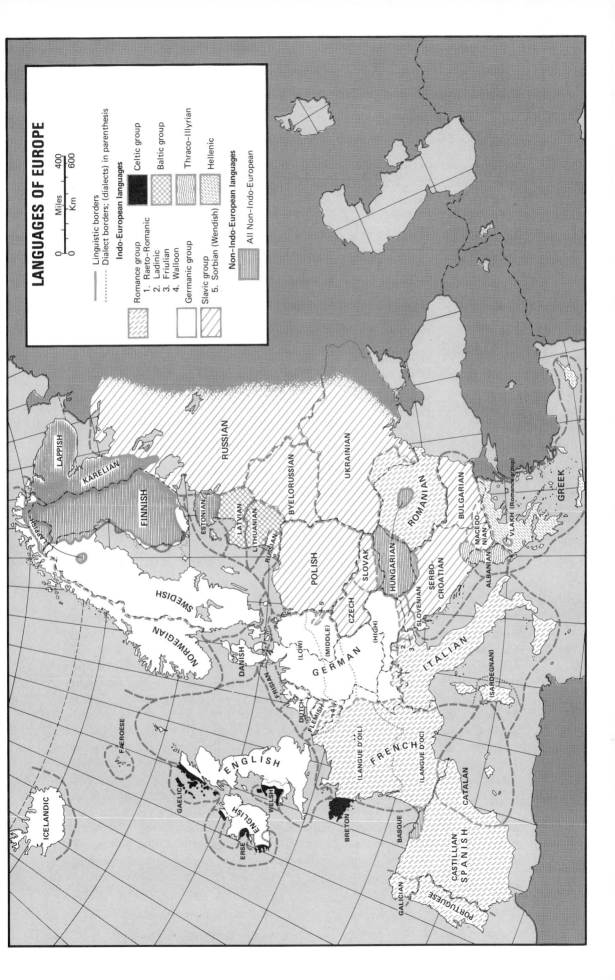

LANGUAGES OF EUROPE

Miles 0 400 600
Km 0

Linguistic borders
.... **Dialect borders; (dialects) in parenthesis**

Indo-European languages

Romance group
1. Raeto-Romanic
2. Ladinic
3. Friulian
4. Walloon

Germanic group

Slavic group
5. Sorbian (Wendish)

Celtic group

Baltic group

Thraco-Illyrian

Hellenic

Non-Indo-European languages

All Non-Indo-European

LAPPISH
KARELIAN
FINNISH
LAPPISH
RUSSIAN
ESTONIAN
LATVIAN
LITHUANIAN
RUSSIAN
BYELORUSSIAN
UKRAINIAN
ROMANIAN
BULGARIAN
MACEDO-NIAN
ALBANIAN
VLAKH (Romance group)
GREEK
POLISH
CZECH
SLOVAK
HUNGARIAN
SLOVENIAN
SERBO-CROATIAN
SWEDISH
NORWEGIAN
DANISH
GERMAN (HIGH)
(MIDDLE)
(LOW)
FRISIAN
DUTCH
FLEMISH
ITALIAN
(SARDEGNAN)
ICELANDIC
FAEROESE
ENGLISH
GAELIC
ENGLISH
WELSH
ERSE
BRETON
FRENCH
(LANGUE D'OIL)
(LANGUE D'OC)
BASQUE
CASTILLIAN SPANISH
CATALAN
GALICIAN
PORTUGUESE

TABLE 5.2   Major European Languages Ranked According to Number of Speakers in Europe

Rank	Language	Main areas where spoken	Approximate number of (in millions) speakers in Europe, 1970
1	Russian	USSR	130[a]
2	German	East and West Germany, Austria, Switzerland, Luxembourg, eastern France, northern Italy, central Hungary, central Romania	85
3	Italian	Italy, Corse, parts of French Riviera, Swiss Ticino	56
4	English	United Kingdom, Republic of Ireland	55
5	French	France, southern Belgium, western Switzerland	51
6	Ukrainian	southwestern USSR	45
7	Polish	Poland, western USSR	31
8	Castillian Spanish	Spain	30
9	Romanian	Romania, Moldavian SSR	18
10	Dutch-Flemish	Netherlands, Belgium, northern France	17
11	Hungarian	Hungary, central Romania	14
12	Serbo-Croatian	Yugoslavia	12
13	Portuguese-Galician	Portugal, northwestern Spain	10
14	Czech	western Czechoslovakia	9
	Byelorussian	western USSR	9
	Greek	Greece, Cyprus, southern Albania	9
17	Swedish	Sweden, coastal Finland	8
18	Bulgarian	Bulgaria	6

[a] Total includes many speakers outside of nuclear Europe.

related languages today (Figure 5.1). Iberia is home to no fewer than four of the Romance tongues. Dominating the nation of Spain from the Meseta interior is *Castillian Spanish,* spoken by some thirty million people. Speakers of the *Catalan* language, numbering six million and found in the eastern coastal fringe of Spain, the Baleares Islands, a tiny corner of southern France, and a foothold on Italian Sardegna, are struggling to preserve their speech against the inroads of Castillian Spanish, French, and Italian. Spain in particular is the scene of this linguistic-political competition, with Castillian Madrid attempting to subjugate Catalonian Barcelona. The Atlantic front of Iberia is home to the *Portuguese* and *Galician* (Gallegan) languages, really two dialects of the same tongue, with some ten million speakers. The survival of Portuguese is guaranteed by political independence, but Galician faces the same Castillian pressure as Catalan within the Spanish nation.

Northward from Iberia, beyond the Pyrenees, is found *French,* the speech of the large majority of France's population as well as the southern Belgians, or Walloons, and the western Swiss, a grand total of over fifty million persons. The southern of two principal French tongues, *langue d'oc,* has succumbed to assimilation, giving way to the *langue d'oïl* originally spoken only in the Parisian north. *Italian,* with just slightly more speakers than French, some fifty-six million, is found not only in Italy but also on the island of Corse, which belongs to France, Canton Ticino in southern Switzerland, and the Nice (Nizza) district on the French Riviera. The Italian character of Corse is revealed in the family name of the island's greatest son, Bonaparte. Sardegnan is a major dialect which has survived in the Italian language zone with one million speakers. Elsewhere the Tuscan dialect has become standard Italian speech, a heritage of the cultural greatness of Firenze.

Along the northern fringe of the Italian area, sheltered in Alpine valleys, are found the Romansh tongues—*Raeto-Romanic* in eastern Switzerland and *Ladinic* and *Friulian* in Italy. These mountain folk long had the reputation of being outlaws who raided the adjacent plains from their highland fastness. Indeed, the very name "Ladin" is related to the Romance root-word for thief (Latin "latrones," modern Spanish "ladron").

Romanian is an eastern outlier of the Romance languages, separated from the larger western area by the interposed South Slavs. This language, spoken by more than eighteen million persons in Romania and the adjacent Moldavian Republic of the Soviet Union, has somehow survived in spite of invasions by Slavs, Magyars, and other groups, though the vocabulary is infiltrated with Slavic words. Closely related to Romanian is *Vlakh,* presumably derived from Valachia in southern Romania but today spoken by a few nomadic herding tribes in interior northern Greece and adjacent countries. The Vlakhs are apparently descended from Romanians who migrated southward after the collapse of the Roman Empire to find refuge in the Dinaric–Pindhos mountain region. Still today the crude shelters of the Vlakhs may be seen at the foot of Mt. Ólimbos in Greece and elsewhere.

Another minor eastern Romance tongue is *Ladino,* spoken by some of the Balkan Jewish population. It is a mixture of corrupted Spanish and Hebrew implanted by Jewish migrants fleeing persecution in Iberia.

THE GERMANIC LANGUAGES

A second major group within the Indo-European family is composed of the various Germanic languages, encompassing a speaking population of over 170 million in Europe, somewhat greater than the total for the Romance languages (Figure 5.1). The single most important tongue is *German,* spoken by 85 million people in eight principal nations—East and West Germany, Austria, Switzerland, Luxembourg, the Alsace region of France, Liechtenstein, and the South Tirol area of northern Italy. In addition, German folk islands are still found in Romania, remnants of numerous colonies which dotted eastern Europe before the population transfers during and after World War II. In spite of the multinational character of German, it has been standardized in written and spoken forms, and dialects are rapidly fading. The major dialect zones of Low, Middle, and High German formerly lent further complexity to a land of severe political fragmentation, but the Luther Bible led the way in creating a uniform language. Low German was once dominant in the northern German lands, High German in the south, and Middle German in a central zone (Figure 5.1). Next to Russian, German is by far the single most important language in Europe, both in terms of number of speakers and in the degree of internationality (Table 5.2). In six separate nations it is the speech of the large majority of the people, a claim no other European tongue can rival.

While in Germany proper Low German is declining and disappearing, several variant forms have survived elsewhere as distinct languages mainly because of the political independence of their speakers. *Dutch* and *Flemish,* almost identical and certainly mutually intelligible, are both basically Low German and have a collective speaking population of about 17 million in the Netherlands, northern Belgium, and the Dunkerque area in northern France.

To the north are the Scandinavian Germanic languages, including *Danish* with 5 million speakers, *Norwegian* with almost 4 million, *Swedish* with over 8 million in Sweden and coastal Finland together, *Icelandic* with only 200,000, and *Færoese* spoken by the 40,000 inhabitants of a small island cluster in the ocean north of Great Britain.

Frisian is a Germanic language of little consequence today, spoken only by a relative handful of North Sea fisher folk, about 300,000 in all, living in the Netherlands, West Germany, and Denmark. The importance of Frisian is historic, for it is the closest Germanic kin of *English,* the native tongue of about fifty-five million Europeans and now established as the greatest world language. The Anglo-Saxon–Jute invaders of England came principally from the Frisian coastal districts of the mainland, leaving behind only a relic ethnic minority. Both English and Frisian are basically Low German, but English absorbed a large number of Romance words as a consequence of the Norman French conquest in the eleventh century. Gradually, the speech of victor and vanquished blended, producing an unusually large vocabulary with numerous synonyms.

Mention should also be made of *Yiddish,* the language of many East European Jews. It was derived from German in the Middle Ages, before a large-scale Jewish migration from the Rhine into the borderlands of Poland and Russia (Yiddish = Jüdisch = Jewish). Once the streets of Bialystok, Vilnius, and other eastern cities rang with this colorful speech, which pleasingly blended corrupted German with some Hebrew and Slavic. Wherever a remnant of East European Jewish population is found today, Yiddish is still spoken.

THE SLAVIC LANGUAGES

The third of the three major Indo-European groups, the Slavs, differ from their Romance and Germanic cultural kinsmen in that their speech was derived through the Satem rather than the Centum offshoot of Proto–Indo-European. Areally they are split into a large northern and eastern zone and a much smaller southern region, with alien Germans, Hungarians, and Romanians wedged in between (Figure 5.1). In the north, *Polish* can claim about thrity-one million speakers, and is confined mainly to the nation of Poland; *Czech* is the language of about nine million residents of Česke and Morava, the two western provinces of Czechoslovakia; and *Slovak* is spoken in the mountainous province of Slovensko in eastern Czechoslovakia. In the marshy East German forest district southeast of Berlin known as the Spreewald live the 10,000 Wends or *Sorbs,* a small Slavic relic which survived a medieval eastward expansion of the Germans.

Eastward, in the Soviet Union, are found the two most important Slavic languages, *Russian* with about 130 million speakers both in and out of Europe proper, and *Ukrainian* with about 45 million. The former, of course, is the dominant speech of the Soviet Union. The Ukrainians occupy a republic on the north shore of the Black Sea within the Soviet Union, a status which constitutionally guarantees the perpetuation of their speech and customs. However, they have long desired complete political independence, even to the point of welcoming German invaders as "liberators," and the intent of the constitution of the USSR is regularly ignored by the ruling Russians. In much the same position as the Ukrainians are the *Byelorussians,* or White Russians, a Slavic group of 8 or 9 million living in a Soviet republic adjacent to the Ukraine on the north.

Beyond the non-Slavic corridor in the Balkans are found the South Slavs, only slightly more than one-tenth as numerous as the northern branch. The most important language is *Serbo-Croatian,* spoken by nearly 12 million in Yugoslavia ("South Slavia"). The Serbs use the Cyrillic alphabet, but the Croatians, who occupy lands north and west of the Serbs, employ the Latin characters, resulting in two written forms for what is basically one language. The remaining South Slavs speak three other languages. In far northern Yugoslavia and across the border in the Klagenfurt Basin of Austria live about 1.5 million *Slovenes,* while in the southern extremity of Yugoslavia and a corner of Bulgaria live over 1 million Slavic *Macedonians.* The remainder of the south Slav domain is occupied by the *Bulgars,* about 8 million in number.

THE CELTIC LANGUAGES

A once-great Indo-European group, the Celts, are now withdrawn into small hilly refuges in Great Britain and France and apparently have hopes for long-term survival only in Ireland (Figure 5.1). The surviving Celtic tongues are *Welsh,* spoken by about 650,000 in the hills of Wales; *Gaelic,* the ancestral Scottish language which survives only among some 75,000 persons in the northwest Highlands of Scotland and the isolated Hebrides Islands offshore; *Breton,* the speech of perhaps 900,000 Celts in the western part of French Bretagne; and *Erse,* or Irish Gaelic, one of the two official languages of the Republic of Ireland (Eire) but concentrated as a mother tongue mainly in scattered localities along the hilly coastal fringe of the island among some 30,000 rural Irishmen. The Erse-speaking regions are collectively known as the *Gaeltacht.*

THE HELLENIC LANGUAGE

Only one language represents the Hellenic Indo-European group—modern *Greek.* Its survival is principally the result of the unifying influence of the Greek Orthodox church and the earlier cultural greatness of classical Greece and Byzantium. Some nine million people speak modern Greek, which differs from the classical form about as much as modern Italian does from Latin.

Greek has a remarkable record of locational stability. In spite of invasions and conquests by Romans, Germanic tribes, Slavs, and Turks, the language is spoken today in essentially the same locations as in the time of Homer, eight centuries before Christ (Figures 5.1, 5.2). The Aegean lands are today and have for at least 3500 years been the Greek home.

THE THRACO-ILLYRIAN AND BALTIC LANGUAGES

The only Thraco-Illyrian language is *Albanian,* which has several dialects and perhaps three million total speakers. While centered in the nation of Albania and adjacent southern Yugoslavia (Figure 5.1), the language is also found in

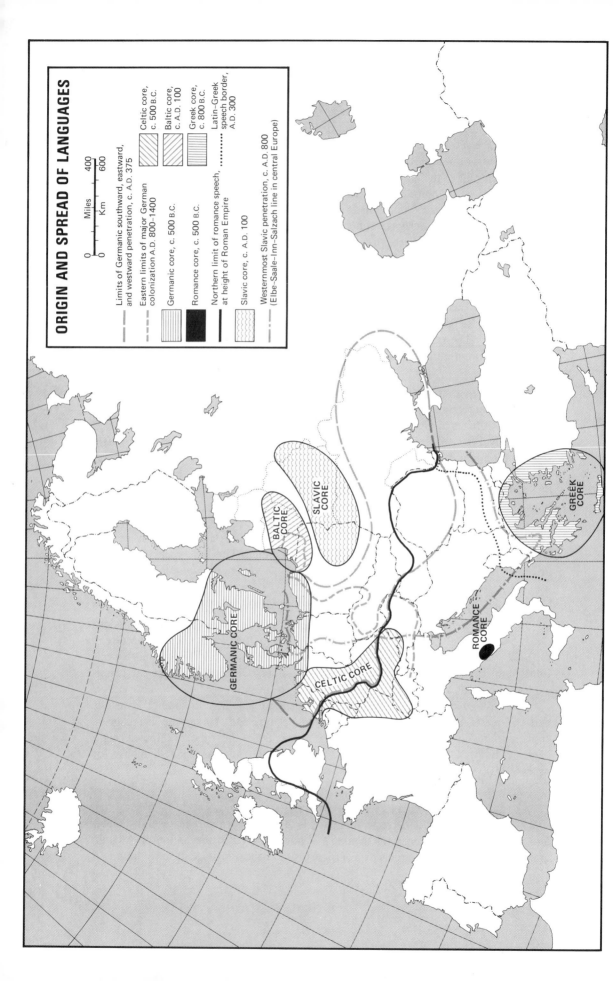

ORIGIN AND SPREAD OF LANGUAGES

Miles
0   400
0   600
Km

Limits of Germanic southward, eastward, and westward penetration, c. A.D. 375

Eastern limits of major German colonization A.D. 800–1400

Germanic core, c. 500 B.C.

Romance core, c. 500 B.C.

Northern limit of romance speech, at height of Roman Empire

Slavic core, c. A.D. 100

Westernmost Slavic penetration, c. A.D. 800 (Elbe–Saale–Inn–Salzach line in central Europe)

Celtic core, c. 500 B.C.

Baltic core, c. A.D. 100

Greek core, c. 800 B.C.

Latin–Greek speech border, A.D. 300

GERMANIC CORE

BALTIC CORE

SLAVIC CORE

CELTIC CORE

ROMANCE CORE

GREEK CORE

mountain folk-islands scattered in the southern Appennini of Italy, Sicilia, the Greek Pelopónnisos, and the Aegean isle of Evvoia.

Another branch of Satemic Indo-European found in Europe is composed of the Baltic languages, *Lettish* (Latvian) and *Lithuanian,* spoken in two Soviet republics on the eastern Baltic shore (Figure 5.1). The former has about 1.5 million speakers, and Lithuanian about 2.5 million. Baltic speech, as is the case with Hellenic, has not undergone any important territorial change (Figure 5.2). Some of the eastern part of Baltic territory was lost to Slavic expansion, but the shore line was held. Later German colonists annexed some southern areas, extinguishing the Baltic tongue *Prussian* in what became East Prussia. The Balts have historically struggled to escape political domination by the Slavs and Germans, a struggle which has largely failed.

ROMANY

One of the most interesting Indo-European languages is Romany, not to be confused with Romanian or the Romance tongues. Romany is the ancestral speech of Europe's wandering Gypsies, whose horse-drawn caravans can be seen throughout Europe, especially in the Balkans. While Gypsies are able to converse in the language of the countries where they live, many still use various dialects of Romany when talking with others of their kind. This language is of the Satemic branch and was brought to Europe from the Indian subcontinent. Gypsies are descended from members of a lower caste of itinerant Hindus in northwestern India, and their ancestors migrated westward into Europe, first appearing in the Balkans during the fourteenth century. The Gypsies' ties to the East are further indicated by their blood types, which reveal similarity to those of the Indian source region. Moreover, the Gypsies generally have darker skin, hair, and eyes than do most other Europeans.

5.3 DISTRIBUTION OF NON–INDO-EUROPEAN TONGUES

There are a few isolated exceptions to the dominance by Indo-European languages in the culture area of Europe. Certain groups speak tongues unrelated to those already mentioned, belonging to completely different language families.

BASQUE

Basque is the great mystery language of Europe, spoken by perhaps 600,000 or more people along a segment of the Bay of Biscay shore and in the adjacent Pyrenees, straddling the western sector of the French-Spanish border (Figure 5.1). Basque is puzzling because it is apparently unrelated to any other language in the world. The best theory seems to be that Basque is a lone survivor of pre–Indo-European languages in Europe. People who speak it are a remarkably cohesive group, inbred because of their reluctance to marry outsiders. The language perimeter is shrinking slowly, under pressure particularly from the Spanish government, which desires to destroy Basque separatism.

Figure 5.2 Origin and spread of languages.

URALIC LANGUAGE FAMILY

The other non–Indo-European languages within Europe all belong to the *Uralic* family, or more exactly to its Finnic, Lapp, and Ugrian subdivisions. *Hungarian* is the Ugrian Uralian speech of about fourteen million people in Hungary, Romania, and fringes of all other nations of the Hungarian Basin (Figure 5.1). The major group living outside of Hungary proper are the Szekely, who occupy the Magyar Autonomous Region in the very heart of Romania, surrounded by Romance-language speakers.

Distant kinfolk of the Hungarians are the *Finnic* Uralic peoples. Of these, the speakers of the *Finnish* language are the most important, numbering over 4.5 million in the nation of Finland (Figure 5.1). Closely related are *Estonian,* the speech of about 1.5 million people in a Soviet republic just south of Finland, and *Karelian,* spoken in the far northwestern corner of the USSR, adjacent to Finland on the east (Figure 5.1). The Finnic peoples presumably originated in the eastern and northern parts of the great plain of Russia, where many of their linguistic kinsmen still live today, and then spread west and north to occupy their present location early in the Christian Era. Pressure from Slavs and Balts gave the move added impetus, pushing the Finnic tribes for the most part into the undesirable subarctic zone. Closely related to the Finns are the *Lapps,* a small Uralian group who survive today in the least desirable areas of northern Scandinavia, Finland, and the Kol'skiy Peninsula (Figure 5.1).

With the exception of Hungarian, the non–Indo-European languages are found on the peripheries of the culture area, in regions which are only marginally "European." Tundra waste, subarctic expanses of coniferous forest, and broad areas of grassland, the domain of Lapp, Finn, and Hungarian, are hardly typical European environments, and the presence of these exotic linguistic groups adds still more non-European flavor.

5.4 LANGUAGE AND THE PHYSICAL ENVIRONMENT

The linguistic mosaic of Europe is in many ways related to patterns of the physical environment. In particular the distribution of terrain types is reflected in the language map.

TERRAIN

Mountains and hilly areas often mark linguistic borders, as in the Pyrenees, where French and Spanish meet. Only at the narrow beach strips on the Mediterranean and Bay of Biscay shores do Catalan and Basque occupy both Pyrenean flanks. In places Alpine ridges divide German and French from Italian, and southern Slavic from German. To pass south through the famous St. Gotthard Pass in Switzerland is to move from German to Italian-speaking lands. Various areas of rough terrain in Iberia have helped isolate Castillian Spanish from neighboring Catalan, Portuguese, Galician, and Basque. The forested, hilly Vosges district in eastern France has been the German–French language border for well over one thousand years. Such linguistic borders defined by sparsely populated broken terrain have generally been stable over the centuries.

Conversely, language boundaries which cut across plains have usually been subject to change. The Romance-Germanic border, so stable in the hilly

Vosges and on the Alpine crests, has migrated in areas of level terrain. In the upper Rhône Valley of Switzerland, German is steadily advancing westward, village by village, while French retreats, and a similar spread in eastern Swiss valleys is allowing German to bring Raeto-Romanic to the verge of extinction. On the flat plains of French Flanders, however, Germanic Flemish is retreating before French and survives only within an ever-smaller perimeter around historic Dunkerque.

Terrain, in the form of hills and mountains, has often provided refuge or isolation for people unable to cope with alien groups on adjacent plains, and has consequently allowed their language to survive. Such is the fate of the Celts, who have been in retreat for about the last 2000 years. The Celtic language core area before about 500 B.C. was perhaps in the southern German lands (Figure 5.2), where Celtic place names such as "Rhine" (Celtic *renos*, "flow") and "Alps" (modern Erse *ailp*, "high mountain") were left behind. From there, the Celts spread over much of Europe from the Atlantic to the Black Sea, only to be displaced or assimilated by Germanic and Romance linguistic groups. Eventually only the British Isles were left for refuge. The Celts survived the Roman occupation in Britain but were sent scurrying to the western hills or across the English Channel to hilly Bretagne by the numerically superior Anglo-Saxons. Celtic tongues survive today only in hilly refuge areas. The Vlakhs, Ladins, Appennini Albanians, and Transylvanian Germans of interior Romania have also been able to preserve their speech partly because of mountain refuges. In some instances, mountain groups ventured out of their highland refuge after danger had passed to reclaim the adjacent plains. This was the case with the Romanians in the Middle Ages who left their Carpathian stronghold to reacquire Valachia, Moldavia, and much of the Hungarian Basin.

THE ROLE OF INSULARITY

Islands can influence the linguistic pattern in two ways. If the island is isolated, the remoteness often helps preserve archaic tongues. Icelandic, of all the Scandinavian German languages, is the closest to Old Norse speech, mainly because it is spoken on an isolated European outpost island in the North Atlantic. Catalan is spoken in its purest form on the Baleares Islands, and the isolation and protection afforded by islands has also helped preserve the Sardegnan dialect, Færoese, and Italian on Corse.

Other islands, because of their situation on major trade routes, have attracted many seafaring peoples and acquired a polyglot character. Cyprus is shared by Greek and Turkish, while Sicilia is home to Italian, Albanian, and Greek.

THE ROLE OF VEGETATION

Natural vegetation can also influence the linguistic map. Hungarian was implanted in Europe by Magyar invaders from the steppe grasslands of interior Eurasia. These newcomers apparently moved westward through the low Carpathian passes into the Hungarian Basin in the year 895. Accustomed to a grassland environment, the Magyars were at home in the grassy Alföld, and their skills at mounted warfare allowed them to hold the area and preserve their speech. Thrusts into wooded country to the west invariably met with military failure, and Hungarian has remained principally a language of the open grasslands.

Conversely, the forest was a refuge for some other linguistic groups. The

Russians found some respite from the invasions of Asiatic hordes in the Steppe Corridor by withdrawing northward into their thickly wooded heartland in the Middle Ages.

THE ROLE OF MARSHES
Protection has also been afforded by marshes and other poorly drained districts. The Slavic Wends or Sorbs were able to survive an eastward spread of German people by retreating to the watery refuge of the marshy Spree Forest near Berlin, where they remain today. Frisians have clung tenaciously to the North Sea coastal marshes of the Netherlands, West Germany, and Denmark. Marshes and poorly drained glacial till plains also helped protect the Baltic languages from Slavic and Germanic expansion.

Linguistic borders are, in some instances, marked by poorly drained country. The sparsely populated Pripyat Marshes have long helped separate Byelorussians from Ukrainians and both of these from Poles.

THE ROLE OF CLIMATE
Severe climates can offer the same protection as marshes, mountains, forests, and islands. In particular the subarctic and tundra climates of northern Europe have proven unattractive to most invaders, serving as a refuge for the numerically small Lappish and Finnic peoples.

Climatic changes have perhaps also altered the language map. A pronounced southward spread by many Germanic tribes in the thousand years between about 500 B.C and A.D. 500 may have been in part the result of climatic deterioration in the northern cradleland of these people (Figure 5.2).

5.5 LANGUAGE AND MIGRATION

Language is the principal bearer of culture and perhaps the best key to the identification of culture areas. When peoples migrate, their language goes with them. The linguistic map has been shaped in large part by numerous migrations back and forth across Europe, movements which have involved almost every language group. Such migrations have been more common at certain times in European history than at others. One mass migration, called the *Völkerwanderungen*, literally the "Folkwanderings" or "Migration of Peoples," occurred in the first five centuries of the Christian Era. Another briefer period of movement of peoples in Europe took place between about 1920 and 1950. In both instances the Germanic and Slavic peoples were the groups most deeply involved.

GERMANIC MIGRATIONS
The original Germanic core was probably centered in southern Scandinavia and far-northern Germany (Figure 5.2). From there Teutonic tribes spread initially to the east and south in the pre-Christian Era, reaching the shores of the Black Sea. Later, in the Folkwanderings, the Germanic tribes evacuated eastern Europe to invade lands to the west and south. All lands east of the line formed by the Elbe and Saale rivers in East Germany, the present West German–Czech border, and the Inn and Salzach rivers of Austria (Figure 5.2) were abandoned as Germanic tribes invaded Italy, Spain, France, and North Africa. The Angles, Saxons,

and Jutes made England their new home at this time, and somewhat later the
Norse colonized Iceland. The resettled Teutons generally failed to preserve their
language, and only relatively small areas were wrested away from the Romance
speakers. Most of the invaders suffered the fate of the Franks, who were assimilated
into the French language even in the process of giving their Germanic name to
France. As a rule, invaders who were culturally inferior to the people they conquered accepted the language of their new homeland.

No sooner had the rush to the west ended than the Germans started back
east. From about A.D. 800 to 1300, agricultural pioneers moved eastward to colonize
the lands beyond the Elbe and Saale on the North German Plain and east of the
Inn and Salzach in the Danube Valley and eastern Alps of Austria. Another major
retreat from the east came in 1945–1951, when millions of Germans were forcibly
expelled from provinces in present-day Poland, Czechoslovakia, and the Soviet
Union, as was described in Chapter 3.

SLAVIC MIGRATIONS
The most impressive change in the language map over the past 2000 years
has been the areal expansion of Slavic speech, a spread which is still under way.
At the time of the birth of Christ, the Slavic core area was probably a small
district between the upper Dnepr River in the far western USSR and the middle
Wisla River of Poland, a heavily wooded, marshy land of poor quality (Figure 5.2).
Apparently there was a great numerical increase of Slavs between about A.D. 100
and 400, for they began pushing out of their dreary homeland in all directions,
driving back Finnic peoples to the north, following the westward evacuation of the
Germans, thrusting southward into the former Balkan realm of imperial Roma,
and venturing out onto the alien steppes of the Ukraine (Figure 5.2). Medieval
losses to the readvancing Germans, coupled with the intrusion of the Magyars and
the movement of Romanians from their Carpathian refuge down onto the adjacent
plains, thrust a barrier between north and south Slav and cost considerable territory
on the North European Plain. These losses were more than compensated for by
the huge gains of eastward expansion beyond the Urals, a drive which continues
today as the Slavs carry the culture of Europe into Asia.

5.6 LANGUAGE AND THE POLITICAL PATTERN
A very close relationship exists between linguistic and political borders in
modern Europe, and nationality has become almost synonymous with language.
The political map is nearly a duplicate of the language map (compare Figures 5.1
and 7.1). More attention will be devoted to this relationship in Chapter 7, but
suffice it to say at this point that the interaction of state and language has been of
great importance in determining both the fate of languages and the destiny of states
in Europe. Language has become the principal basis of nationalistic sentiment, and
minority linguistic groups have generally not fared well in European nations.

ASSIMILATION OF LINGUISTIC MINORITIES
Assimilation of linguistic minorities in European states has been under way
for well over a thousand years. French advances at the expense of the Germanic
tongues in France, but retreats before German in Switzerland; Basque and Galician

gradually are replaced by Castillian in Spain; and Swedish surrenders to Finnish in Finland. In East Germany the Slavic Wends or Sorbs declined in number from 142,000 in 1849 to 10,000 today, and their language perimeter steadily shortened. Such assimilation generally occurs even if the minority speech has firm legal standing, as in Switzerland or Finland, and it applies to dialects as well as completely different languages. Dialects of French, Italian, and Greek have all declined as a result of political unification.

DECLINE OF THE CELTIC LANGUAGES

The unhappy fate of minority tongues is perhaps best illustrated by the Celtic languages. In the British Isles the English state, created by the Germanic invaders, militarily subjugated the Celtic hill refuges one by one. Once under English rule, the Celts drifted toward assimilation. Cornish, a Celtic tongue of southwestern Great Britain, died out about 1750, approximately one thousand years after the English conquest of Cornwall. The same fate befell Manx, the ancestral speech on the Isle of Man between Ireland and Great Britain. Gaelic is on the verge of death in northern Scotland, for all but 1000 of its speakers can also speak English. Welsh has proven more durable, but its shrinking perimeter, slowly declining number of speakers, and the bilingual character of nearly all of its population do not bode well for the future (Figure 5.3). Similarly, the Celtic refuge in Bretagne was annexed politically by France, and the Breton language has retreated steadily before French (Figure 5.4).

The basic problem facing most of the Celts is that they lack independent political status, the only exception being the Irish. In the Republic of Ireland (Eire)

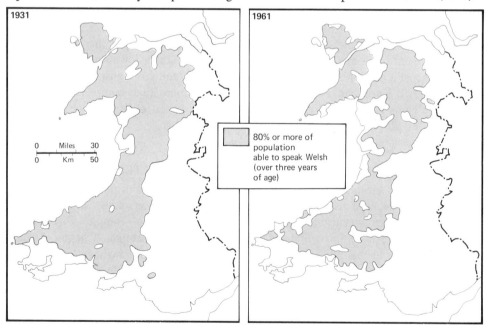

Figure 5.3 The gradual retreat of the Welsh language, 1931–1961. In thirty years, the Welsh area has been split into three main remnant "islands" by English encroachment in the valleys of the upper Severn River in central Wales and the Conway River in the north. Additional Welsh retreat occurred along the coastline. During this time span, the number of persons able to speak Welsh declined from 909,261 to 659,022. (After Williams, Jones, and Griffiths.)

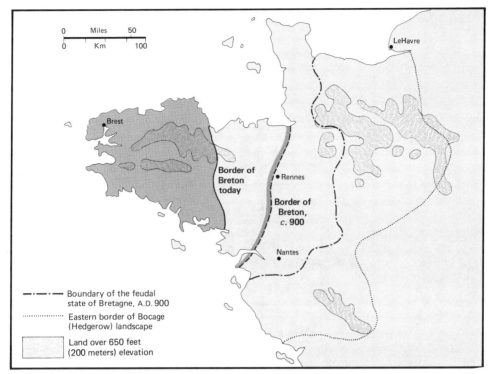

Figure 5.4 One thousand years of Celtic retreat in Bretagne. The Celtic Breton language has retreated slowly west toward the port town of Brest, surviving mainly in the hilly interior of the peninsula. To a degree, the Celtic domain in France can be identified with the *bocage,* or hedgerow, cultural landscape.

Celtic Erse has acquired legal standing and is taught as a required course in the schools, although the large majority of the population speaks English, a heritage of the long period of rule by the United Kingdom. The goal of the Irish govern- ment is apparently a fully bilingual population, making its way in the world using English and preserving its rich Celtic cultural heritage through Erse (Figure 5.5). Some 500,000 Irish now have at least some knowledge of their ancestral tongue.

Modern communications within the United Kingdom and France, especially radio and television, are serving to hasten the Celtic decline. The era of electronic communications has ended the isolation in which linguistic distinctiveness was bred and nourished. Today not even the most remote Celtic vale can escape the English voice of the BBC.

LANGUAGE AND EMPIRE
The areal spread of certain languages has occurred as a result of empire- building. This was the principal device by which Romance speech was diffused through Europe, a contrast to the mass migrations which produced the spread of the Germanic and Slavic languages. Originally, in about 500 B.C., Latin, the parent of the Romance group, was spoken only in a small district on the west flank of the Appennini, the Plain of Latium (modern Lazio), from which the language derived its name (Figure 5.2). Latin spread with Roman victories, slowly at first, for the conquest of Italy alone required two centuries. About A.D. 100 the Roman Empire,

Figure 5.5 Bilingual road sign in the Republic of Ireland. The Celtic Erse version of the place names appears in smaller print above the English form. Such signs are visible evidence of Irish efforts to preserve their ancestral language while at the same time retaining English, the mother tongue of most of the population. (Photo courtesy Irish Tourist Board.)

and with it Latin, reached its greatest territorial extent, and the Romance tongue was heard on the banks of the Thames, Rhine, and Danube, as well as in North Africa. Few of the cultural groups ruled by the empire were able to resist linguistic assimilation, though the Greeks did succeed because of their high culture. The Romance languages retreated but did not disappear with the Empire. Barbarian German invaders brought their own language to Great Britain, the west bank of the Rhine, and the Alps, while Slavs and Magyars surged into the Balkans, leaving the lonely linguistic outpost in Romania as a reminder of the former eastern greatness of the Romans. In these forfeited areas, only place names survive today as remnants of the Latin tongue. In England for example, *-caster* and *-chester* suffixes, as in Lancaster or Manchester, are derived from *castria,* Latin for "military camp."

The fragmentation of Latin into separate dialects and languages was accelerated by the destruction of the empire. Disappearance of central political control caused regional isolation in the Romance areas, and isolation, coupled with illiteracy, fostered linguistic drift.

5.7 LANGUAGE AND THE CULTURAL LANDSCAPE

The cultural landscape, that assemblage of man-made features which has been imprinted on the physical face of Europe, is related to the map of languages in a variety of ways. One such relationship is that between language and rural settlement form.

RURAL SETTLEMENT FORM

In rural Europe, most people live in clustered villages, but in some areas a pattern of dispersed farmsteads is found (see Chapter 9). As a rule, the isolation resulting from dispersed settlement tends to favor the survival of minority languages, while clustering in villages promotes assimilation. Some European languages owe their survival in part to the pattern of scattered farmsteads in the areas where they are spoken (compare Figures 5.1 and 9.1). In France the Flemish language has long been identified with a zone of dispersed settlement in the north, and the same is true of Welsh in the United Kingdom. The remarkable survival of Basque may be due in part to the pattern of scattered farmsteads in the Spanish–French borderlands. Similarly, Castillian inroads in the area of Galician speech in northwestern Iberia were perhaps blunted by the dispersal of the population there. Village settlement, on the other hand, may have facilitated German assimilation of the Slavic farm population of the North German Plain east of the Elbe–Saale line during the Middle Ages. Large numbers of German settlers moved into the Slavic villages in that period of Teutonic colonization, and the Slavs were quickly absorbed into German culture.

VISIBLE LANGUAGE

Because the large majority of Europeans are literate, their languages are much in evidence visibly in the form of written signs. Linguistic borders are often easily detected by the traveler for this reason, particularly if the language changes at an international boundary. At the Austrian–Hungarian border, for example, the linguistic change is strikingly visible, in part because German and Hungarian are completely unrelated tongues. Visibility of the language frontiers is heightened when an alphabet change accompanies the linguistic transition, as occurs along the Danube River where it divides Romania from Bulgaria. Zones of mixed language can often be detected by the presence of bilingual signs (Figure 5.5).

There are some areas, however, where the visible language is not a true indicator of the local speech. In the small state of Luxembourg, located between France and West Germany, nearly all signs are in French, yet the people speak a form of German. Even the name of the country is a French form of the German Luxemburg (derived from archaic German *Lucilinburhuc,* "little fortress"). The people of Luxembourg use the visible language to distinguish themselves from Germans, while their speech differentiates them from the French. They thereby establish an identity as neither German nor French, an identity which facilitates their continued political independence. Elsewhere, language may be invisible if a linguistic minority is being suppressed by a hostile central government.

5.8 LANGUAGE AND ECONOMY

Ties frequently can be found between language and economic phenomena. For example, linguistic diffusion may be aided by commerce and transportation facilities, while shopping patterns and market areas are in some instances restricted by language contrasts.

LANGUAGE AND COMMERCE

Trading peoples have often carried their languages to distant lands as a side effect of commerce. The Greek language was diffused in this manner by the merchants of antiquity. Isolated Greek folk-islands are scattered from the toe of the boot of Italy to the Russian Caucasus, from coastal Syria to the steppes of the Ukraine, remnants of the commercial interests of classical and Byzantine Greece. Similarly, Russian fur-traders were the first to carry the Slavic language east of the Urals, beginning in 1580.

In zones of linguistic mixing, one language often attains the status of *Umgangssprache,* or "language of association." People in such areas often speak one language at home and another in the marketplace. In the Klagenfurt Basin of Austria, where speakers of both Slovenian and German live, the latter tongue is the language of association. Not infrequently linguistic assimilation results from such an arrangement.

If two language groups living in an area are hostile to one another, the result will likely be economic segregation, with no *Umgangssprache* employed. In Brussels, for example, the decision of individuals as to where they should do their shopping is often influenced by the mother tongue of the shop owner. Flemings are more inclined to purchase at Flemish-operated stores than at those run by French personnel, even if the proprietor is bilingual. When a linguistic group is small and socially cohesive, the speakers may form what amounts to a closed society economically. In still other instances, a blend of mercantile language may result. Residents of the strategically situated island of Malta in the Mediterranean speak Maltese, a mixture of Arabic and Italian. If such mixtures exist principally as languages of commerce, they are referred to as *pidgins.* Examples of European pidgins, now extinct, are *Sabir,* a blend of Spanish, Greek, Italian, French, and Arabic used by Mediterranean merchants and seaman in the Middle Ages, and *Russenorsk,* a mixture of Russian and Norwegian spoken by fish-traders in port towns of northern Norway as recently as the early twentieth century.

LANGUAGE AND TRANSPORT

If language is the bearer of culture, transport routes are often the paths of linguistic diffusion. Highway and railroad building have at times influenced the areal distribution of languages. In France the development of a system of post roads radiating from Paris in the 1700s hastened the spread of Parisian French (langue d'oïl) and the decline of the southern dialect, langue d'oc (see Figure 13.3). Further to the east, the Russian language has spread rapidly through southern Siberia in the twentieth century along the line of the Trans-Siberian Railroad, completed in Czarist times.

LANGUAGE AND FORM OF EMPLOYMENT

In a general way certain language groups can be "identified" with particular livelihoods. The Romance-speaking Vlakh people of southeastern Europe are almost exclusively nomadic herders, and a surprisingly large proportion of the Basques were sheepherders and fishermen before industrialization came to their homeland. Romany-speaking Gypsies also form a distinctive economic group, engaging in a wandering life as peddlers and the like.

Form of employment may also influence the vocabulary of a linguistic group. The Vlakh language contains an unusually large number of words having to do with sheep and forage, a reflection of the herder economy of these people. Similarly, the wandering life of the gypsies brings them into contact with a variety of language groups, and the various dialects of Romany have incorporated words from a great many other languages.

*   *   *

OF ALL CULTURAL PATTERNS in Europe, that of languages is one of the most complex and important. While the modern trend is toward progressively fewer languages as minor ones retreat and die out, considerable linguistic diversity will characterize Europe for the foreseeable future, retarding contacts between peoples and perhaps undermining attempts to create a European political unity. Speech is one of the principal traits which make the cultural tapestry of Europe so varied and interesting.

SOURCES AND SUGGESTED READINGS

Gino Bottiglioni. "Linguistic Geography: Its Achievements, Methods and Orientations." *Word*. Vol. 10 (1954), pp. 375–387.

Jan O. M. Broek and John W. Webb. "The Mosaic of Languages." Chapter 5 in *A Geography of Mankind*. New York: McGraw-Hill, 1968, pp. 97–123.

Carl D. Buck. *A Dictionary of Selected Synonyms in the Principal Indo-European Languages*. Chicago: University of Chicago Press, 1949.

Jovan Cvijić. "The Geographical Distribution of the Balkan Peoples." *Geographical Review*. Vol. 5 (1918), pp. 345–361 (color map).

Albert Dauzat. *La géographie linguistique*. Paris: Flammarion, 1922.

C. M. Delgado de Carvalho. "Geografia das linguas." *Boletim Geográfico*. Vol. 1 (1943), pp. 45–62 (translated as "The Geography of Languages," in *Readings in Cultural Geography*, ed. Philip L. Wagner and Marvin W. Mikesell. Chicago: University of Chicago Press, 1962, pp. 75–93.

Leon Dominian. *The Frontiers of Language and Nationality in Europe*. New York: American Geographical Society, Special Publication No. 3, 1917.

Alb. Drexel (ed.). *Atlas Linguisticus*. Innsbruck: Kartographisches Institut, 1934.

J. S. Dugdale. *The Linguistic Map of Europe*. London: Hutchinson University Library, 1969.

Paul Friedrich. *Proto–Indo-European Trees: The Arboreal System of a Prehistoric People*. Chicago: University of Chicago Press, 1970.

John Geipel. *The Europeans: An Ethnohistorical Survey*. London: Longmans, 1969.

Walter Geisler. "Die Sprachen- und Nationalitätenverhältnisse an den deutschen Ostgrenzen und ihre Darstellung." *Petermanns Mitteilungen Ergänzungsheft* No. 217. Gotha: Justus Perthes, 1933.

Hugh Hencken. "Indo-European Languages and Archaeology." *Memoirs, American Anthropological Association*. No. 84 (1955).

Marvin I. Herzog. *The Yiddish Language in Northern Poland: Its Geography and History*. The Hague, Netherlands: Mouton, 1965.

Adelheid Heuberger-Hardorp. *Volkstumsprobleme im Sprachgrenzgebiet des Bozner Unterlandes*. München: Wagner, 1969.

Karl Jaberg. *Aspects géographiques du langage*. Paris: Droz, 1936.

Emrys Jones and Ieuan L. Griffiths. "A Linguistic Map of Wales, 1961." *Geographical Journal*. Vol. 129 (1963), pp. 192–196.

Olinto Marinelli. "The Regions of Mixed Populations in Northern Italy." *Geographical Review*. Vol. 7 (1919), pp. 129–148 (color map).

Antoine Meillet. *The Indo-European Dialects*. Translated by Samuel N. Rosenberg. University, Ala.: University of Alabama Press, 1967.

Antoine Meillet. *Les langues dans l'Europe nouvelle*. Paris: Payot, 2nd ed., 1928.

Sandor Rado (ed.). *National Atlas of Hungary*. Plates on "Mother Tongue." Budapest: Cartographia, 1967. p. 41.

Irwin T. Sanders. "The Nomadic Peoples of Northern Greece: Ethnic Puzzle and Cultural Survival." *Social Forces*. Vol. 33 (1954), pp. 122–129.

W. Schmidt. *Die Sprachenfamilien und Sprachenkreise der Erde*. Heidelberg: C. Winter, 1926.

Wolf-Dieter Sick. "Die Siebenbürger Sachsen in Rumänien." *Geographische Rundschau*. Vol. 20 (1968), pp. 12–22.

United Nations. *Demographic Yearbook, Annuaire Démographique*. New York: UN, various years.

Philip L. Wagner. "Remarks on the Geography of Language." *Geographical Review*. Vol. 48 (1958), pp. 86–97.

Henry R. Wilkinson. *Maps and Politics: A Review of the Ethnographic Cartography of Macedonia*. Liverpool: University Press, 1951.

D. Trevor Williams. "A Linguistic Map of Wales According to the 1931 Census, With Some Observations on Its Historical and Geographical Setting." *Geographical Journal*. Vol. 89 (1937), pp. 146–151.

Bogdan Zaborski. "Europe Languages" (map). In *Goode's World Atlas*, ed. Edward B. Espenshade, Jr. Skokie, Ill.: Rand McNally, 13th Edition, 1970, pp. 126–127.

CHAPTER SIX

The geography of religions

The third of the three basic European traits is Christianity, traditionally the strongest of the triad. As recently as A.D. 1500, Christianity was confined almost exclusively to Europe, and the culture and the religion were nearly synonymous. Had it not been for the vitality of the Christian Church, Europeans might well have remained mired in the cultural sink which existed after the fall of the Roman Empire. It was, to a quite remarkable degree, the Church which lifted Europe to the great artistic and commercial exploits of the Middle Ages and, finally, the Renaissance. Only in the Christian monasteries was any notable preservation of learning and appreciation of knowledge achieved in the Dark Ages; it was often the settlement dependent on an abbey or monastery that kept alive any sort of urbanism as cities disappeared one by one after the fall of the empire; and it was the Church which directed much of the woodland colonization that converted Europe north of the Alps from a wilderness into a prosperous, cultivated land. From the latter days of the Roman Empire, for a thousand years and more, Christianity was the bearer and preserver of Western Civilization. Conversion to Christianity was synonymous with acceptance of civilization. It is no accident that the alphabet advanced with the Church.

The Christian Church and the vital message it bore provided the inspiration for the large majority of works of art, literature, philosophy, and architecture produced by European culture until quite recent times. It is true that the Church at times was an obstacle to creativity and the advancement of learning, but on the whole it had a positive influence. One cannot imagine a European cultural heritage devoid of the magnificent cathedrals, altarpieces, crucifixes, and religious statuary. Christianity gave us the *Commentaries* of St. Thomas Aquinas, da Vinci's *Last Supper,* Michelangelo's *David* and Sistine Chapel, the Kremlin and the cathedral at Chartres, Dante's *Inferno,* and Milton's *Paradise Lost.* For many centuries, the Church was Europe and Europe was the Church. All Europeans and their overseas offspring, regardless of their present religious beliefs, bear the permanent stamp of Christianity.

The geographer is interested in the spatial or areal characteristics of religions, in the ways in which religious phenomena differ from place to place. Above all, his interest focuses on the cause-and-effect relationships which exist between religious distributions and other areal patterns, both cultural and environmental. It is possible to distinguish at least four major themes in the geography of religions, including (1) the areal distribution and areal interaction of religious groups, (2) the imprint of the physical environment on the evolution, character, and distribution of religions, (3) the impact of religions on the environment, especially the religious contribution to the *cultural landscape,* the visible imprint man has made on the countryside, and (4) the areal interrelationship between religion and other cultural phenomena, such as languages, agriculture, politics, transportation, and industry.

6.1 DISTRIBUTION AND INTERACTION OF RELIGIOUS GROUPS

As was true of physical traits and languages, the basic unity provided by Christianity conceals a great deal of internal diversity in Europe. Christianity, the last of the three major human traits to fall into place, came to Europe as a unified faith, but it has since separated into three major divisions—Roman Catholicism, Eastern Orthodoxy, and Protestantism (Figure 6.1). The latter two of these have further fragmented into numerous constituent groups. To help understand the present pattern, it is useful to consider the early spread of unified Christianity into Europe.

THE DIFFUSION OF CHRISTIANITY TO EUROPE

Christianity was preceded in Europe by a hodgepodge of lesser religions, most of which were on a rather primitive level. The ancient religious tradition of the Indo-European peoples was decidedly polytheistic, a marked contrast to the monotheism of the Christian faith. Everywhere the Indo-European tribes spread, a heavy baggage of multiple divinities was carried along. The ancient Greeks placed a rather eccentric assemblage of gods and goddesses on Mt. Ólimbos and wove a fascinating mythology around the personalities and deeds of these deities. The Romans inherited this rather lovable group of gods from the Greeks, changing only the names. The Germanic, Celtic, and Slavic tribes also worshiped multiple divinities, many of whom were associated with the woodlands and marshes of their northern homelands.

In the Greco–Roman world the traditional deities later shared importance with various other cults, including the "mystery religions" derived from the orig-

Figure 6.1   Religions of Europe.

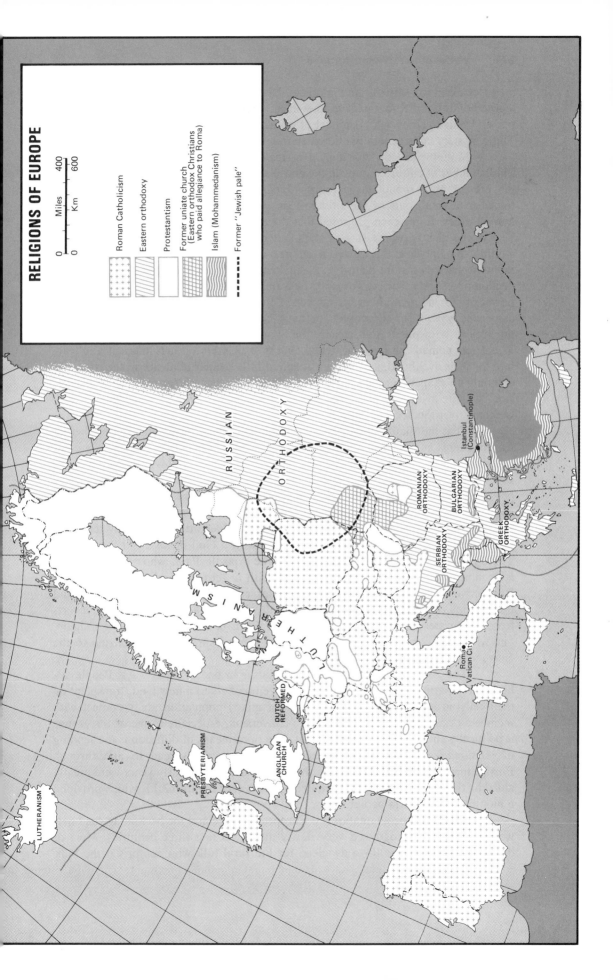

RELIGIONS OF EUROPE

Miles 0   400
Km 0   600

Roman Catholicism

Eastern orthodoxy

Protestantism

Former uniate church (Eastern orthodox Christians who paid allegiance to Roma)

Islam (Mohammedanism)

Former "Jewish pale"

LUTHERANISM

PRESBYTERIANISM

ANGLICAN CHURCH

DUTCH REFORMED

L U T H E R A N I S M

RUSSIAN

O R T H O D O X Y

SERBIAN ORTHODOXY

ROMANIAN ORTHODOXY

BULGARIAN ORTHODOXY

GREEK ORTHODOXY

Roma
Vatican City

Istanbul (Constantinople)

inally localized worship of, among others, Isis, the Egyptian goddess of fertility and motherhood; Cybele, the great mother-earth goddess of the Anatolians; and Mithras, an Iranian god of light, defender of truth, and enemy of the powers of darkness. These mystery cults generally offered eternal life to the faithful.

Monotheism, the worship of a single god, originally typified only a very small number of culture groups in the entire world. In fact, the origin of all three of the present great monotheistic faiths—Judaism, Islam, and Christianity—can be traced to a small part of the Middle East, where it perhaps arose among desert nomad.tribes. It has been proposed that the clear desert skies, by providing a vivid view of the nightly progression of stars and planets, suggested a single divine hand guiding the universe. However, a cultural rather than environmental basis for monotheism seems more plausible. A single male deity was a logical theological reflection of a secular society governed by a single male tribal chieftain possessing the power of life and death over his subjects. Female deities such as Isis were normally associated with farming peoples, perhaps because women had been the original domesticators of plants and because the female was the human symbol of fertility. The desert nomads, in contrast, relied almost exclusively on herd animals and warfare for their livelihood, and women acquired little secular influence in the tribe and certainly no chance to attain godly status. Nomadic concern for the welfare of livestock is quite evident in numerous biblical references to God as a keeper of sheep, watching over the flock of faithful.

That the shepherd God of desert nomads should have come to polytheistic Europe seems at first glance unlikely, for it would be difficult to imagine a greater contrast than that between the complex polytheism of most Indo-Europeans and the simple, stern monotheism of the Hebrew herders. The difficult transition was made possible first of all by the sedentarization of the Hebrews, their abandonment of the nomadic life followed in Sinai for agricultural pursuits in Palestine, an event which led to certain modifications in their religion. Jesus added attractiveness by replacing the forbidding, vengeful Old Testament deity with a God of love and forgiveness. The other key figure in the transition was the Apostle Paul, who used his Greek education to interpret the infant Christian faith in terms appealing to the Greco–Roman world, including the removal of observation of traditional Jewish law and the addition of emphasis on miraculous events, the latter a necessity to win converts from the mystery cults. In effect Paul made Christianity a *universalizing* religion, one which actively sought converts with the aim of spreading its doctrine to the entire world.

The areal spread of a religion can occur in one of three ways. People adhering to a particular faith may move in large numbers to a new land, transplanting their religion in the process; or, in areas of mixed population, daily contact with members of another religion can lead to conversion, especially if one of the groups is politically and economically dominant. The third means of diffusion is the sending of *missionaries* by universalizing religions. Christianity spread to and through Europe mainly by this third method. Its missionaries in the early years were greatly aided by the splendid system of Roman highways (see Figure 12.1), which provided a mobility unknown in earlier times.

In spite of the adaptations to European culture and the beckoning road network, Christianity progressed very slowly during its first three centuries. Most of the early converts were town dwellers, for the rural folk who comprised the bulk of the population did not flock to the new faith. Indeed, so urban was the character of the early Christian church in Europe that the Latin word *pagus,* meaning "rural district," became the root of both modern *pagan* and *peasant,* implying a connection between the two. Little progress was made until after A.D. 313, when the Christian Roman Emperor Constantine issued an edict of toleration for Christianity which led eventually to its status as state religion. From that date into the 1300s, missionaries crisscrossed Europe, gradually winning over the population to Christianity (Figure 6.2).

ROMAN CATHOLICISM

The Roman Catholic church is the most important of the three main Christian groups in Europe, both areally and in number of adherents. It is found in Iberia, France, Italy, Ireland, Belgium, the southern German lands, and in several Slavic countries (Figure 6.1). The large Catholic domain stretches from the Irish hills of Donegal to central Romania and from Lithuania to Portugal.

The Roman Catholic church emerged in the fourth century as the area presided over by the bishop of Roma, who shared leadership of Christianity with bishops in four other cities, including Constantinople (present Istanbul). The Roman bishop claimed leadership of the entire Christian movement, based on Jesus' statement to Peter, but the other bishops did not wholeheartedly accept the Roman claim, and the church drifted steadily toward a schism between Roma and Constantinople. Division was further encouraged by the political split of the Roman Empire into eastern and western sections and by the use of different languages in the two churches. A final official split into two separate churches occurred in 1054.

The Roman church spread rapidly in the western Mediterranean during the fourth and fifth centuries. Before the fall of the empire, Italy, France, and Iberia were converted, and the Germanic tribes who subsequently overran these areas were quickly won over to the church, losing their ancestral speech in the process. Christianization of the German invaders was accomplished in part by the device of contact conversion rather than by missionary activity.

From the western Mediterranean core, Roman Catholic missionaries quickly spread far to the north (Figure 6.2). Patrick arrived in Ireland in 432, and a major cultural flowering occurred among the Celtic converts there. For a time, the Celtic Christians remained outside of Roman control, but by 800, all recognized the authority of the pope, as the bishop of Roma was by then called. Peoples of Great Britain were converted from the 400s through the early 600s (Figure 6.2).

The pagan tribes of Germany received missionaries from Ireland and Great Britain, aided by others from France, in the period from the early 600s to the early 800s, and the Germans in turn carried the church to Scandinavians and Slavic Poles, missions completed by about 1100. The pivotal event in Poland occurred in 966, when the principal local ruler allowed himself to be baptized, an event duplicated in Hungary in 973. The European work of Roman missionaries ended in 1386 with the conversion of the Balts in distant Lithuania. In carrying Christianity to the heathen north of the Mediterranean core of Catholicism, the missionaries of Roma also took the Latin alphabet, and still today the zone of Roman mission work is fairly well indicated by the use of Latin characters.

The impressive Catholic gains in the north were partially offset by losses to Islam in the Mediterranean area. North Africa, where the Roman church was

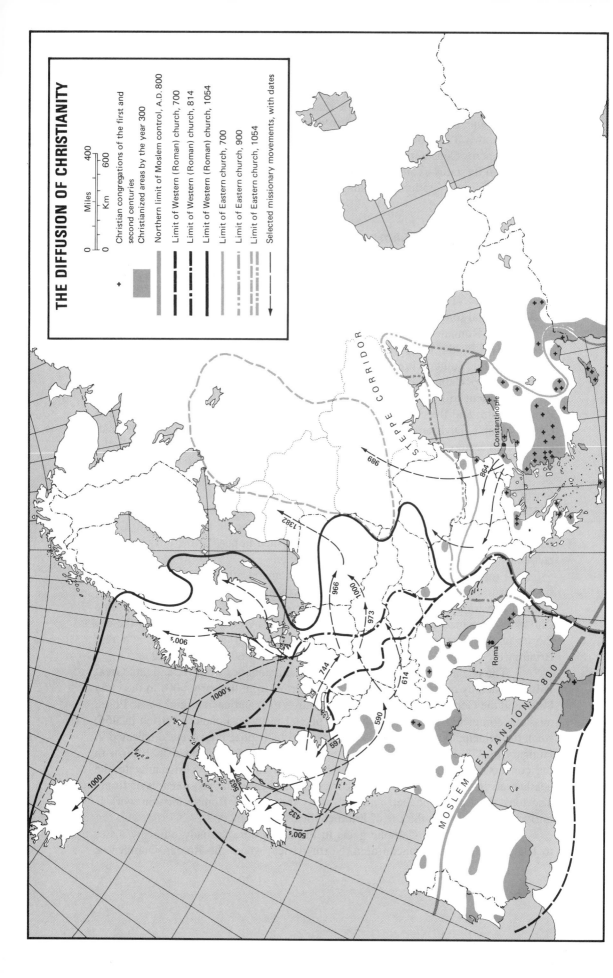

THE DIFFUSION OF CHRISTIANITY

+	Christian congregations of the first and second centuries
	Christianized areas by the year 300
	Northern limit of Moslem control, A.D. 800
	Limit of Western (Roman) church, 700
	Limit of Western (Roman) church, 814
	Limit of Western (Roman) church, 1054
	Limit of Eastern church, 700
	Limit of Eastern church, 900
	Limit of Eastern church, 1054
	Selected missionary movements, with dates

Miles
0 — 400
Km
0 — 600

STEPPE CORRIDOR

Constantinople

MOSLEM EXPANSION, 800

Roma

686

864

1382

966

1000

973

744

614

590

597

563

432

1000's

500's

1000

1000's

1006

well established, became permanently Moslem in the 700s, and much of Iberia remained under the control of the Moslems for many centuries. In general, however, the Islamic invaders respected those religions which possessed a written book of beliefs, and both Christianity and Judaism survived in Moorish Iberia.

EASTERN ORTHODOXY

Eastern Europe, including Greece, the Soviet Union, Bulgaria, Cyprus, and parts of Romania and Yugoslavia, is the zone of Eastern Orthodox Christianity (Figure 6.1). This branch of the faith has historical ties to the bishop of Constantinople, paralleling the Catholic relationship to Roma. The Eastern Orthodox church, in Europe at least, was the established religion of the Byzantine, or Eastern Roman, Empire.

The Eastern church was not as active in missionary work as the Roman branch of Christianity, confining its attention for many centuries to winning over the Slavic tribes who had spread south of the Danube River into imperial territory. Initially, then, the prospective converts came to Byzantium rather than vice versa. These South Slavs were soon won for Orthodoxy, except for the Croats and Slovenes, who were converted by Roman missionaries. Mission work north of the Danube was hindered by repeated invasions by Asiatic hordes entering Europe through the Valachian steppe corridor between 567 and 1048 (Figure 6.2). But the church did make a major gain in the north in 989 when the Slavic ruler of Kiev was baptized, an event which led Russia to Eastern Christianity. The Orthodox missionaries working among the Slavs developed the Cyrillic alphabet, derived from the Greek characters, and the distribution of this script today closely parallels the extent of the Eastern church in Europe. The Eastern Orthodox Serbs and Roman Catholic Croats of Yugoslavia, though speaking dialects of the same language, use different alphabets because of their religious background.

The energies of church and empire declined together. Soon after 1200 the Byzantine Empire collapsed under pressure from the Turks and other groups, though the imperial and churchly capital at Constantinople held out longer. The collapse cost the Eastern Orthodox faith the permanent loss to Islam of most of Asia Minor and the northern shore of the Bosporus–Dardanelles. Additional retreat occurred in the 1920s, when the large Greek population remaining in Asia Minor was expelled.

The Eastern Orthodox Church lacks the monolithic, highly centralized organization of Roman Catholicism. Orthodoxy split very early into regional divisions which in time took on a nationalistic character, as in the Greek Orthodox church and the Russian Orthodox church. Nine different, autonomous Orthodox groups are in existence today. The patriarch of Constantinople has functioned more as a titular leader of the faith with no real authority over the far-flung membership. His position was no doubt undermined when the churchly capital city, Constantinople, fell permanently to the Moslem Turks in 1453, a fate spared the Catholic center at Roma.

An intermediate position between Eastern Orthodoxy and Roman Catholicism was long occupied by the Uniate church, found in the borderlands between Romania and the Ukrainian Soviet republic (Figure 6.1). The Uniate group recog-

Figure 6.2   The diffusion of Christianity.

nized the authority of the pope but preserved the Orthodox liturgy. Since World War II the Uniate church has been forced back into Orthodoxy.

PROTESTANTISM

In the northern part of Europe, including Scandinavia, the United Kingdom, Finland, the Netherlands, and parts of Germany, is found an assemblage of various Protestant churches (Figure 6.1). There is no central Protestant authority; even the individual sects are often very loosely organized and split along national lines.

The Protestant movement arose in different places over several centuries as various attempts to bring about reforms or changes within the Roman church. The pivotal event was the challenge to the church issued by Martin Luther at Wittenberg, Germany, in 1517, a challenge which evolved into secession. The Lutheran church quickly spread through northern Germany and the Scandinavian lands, supported by the rulers of the individual states (Figure 6.3). The Protestant cause was also furthered by John Calvin in the mid-1500s. From his headquarters at Genève, in the French-speaking portion of Switzerland, Calvin was instrumental in dispersing Puritanism to England, Presbyterianism to Scotland, the Reformed church to the Netherlands and Germany, and the Huguenot faith to France, as well as lesser Calvinist groups to eastern Europe. In German Switzerland, Ulrich Zwingli led a movement at Zürich and, together with Calvin, produced a Protestant majority in the Swiss Confederation. In the 1520s and 1530s, a number of Anabaptist Protestant sects were founded, including the Hutterites of Morava, the Swiss Brethren, and the Mennonites in the Netherlands. These people rejected infant baptism and offered the rite only to adult believers. An additional breakaway from Catholicism came in 1534, when King Henry VIII created the Church of England, referred to usually as Anglican.

The present Catholic–Protestant border in Europe existed in rough form as early as the 1560s or 1570s (compare Figures 6.1 and 6.3). Later minor areal changes were made, in particular the crushing of Huguenot Calvinism in France by the Catholic-inspired monarchy. The long, dreadful Thirty Years' War, fought in central Europe from 1618 to 1648, a religious war between Catholics and Protestants, resulted in very little change of religious borders. The only significant alteration of the map occurred in 1945–1951, when the German Protestant population in the eastern provinces of Schlesien, Pommern, and East Prussia (Ostpreussen) was expelled and replaced by Polish Catholics, an expulsion undertaken for linguistic rather than religious reasons. The Polish-speaking—but Lutheran—Masurian people were allowed to remain in their southern East Prussian homeland.

The success of the Protestant breakaway may have been due in part to environmental conditions. Natural protection afforded by the English Channel, North and Baltic seas, Dutch marshes, and Swiss mountains perhaps helped preserve infant Protestantism from Catholic reconquest.

NON-CHRISTIAN RELIGIONS

As is the case with languages, the cultural unity of Europe is somewhat disrupted by the presence of small non-Christian religious groups. The long Arabic

Figure 6.3   The Protestant Movement, circa 1570. (After Palmer and Westermann.)

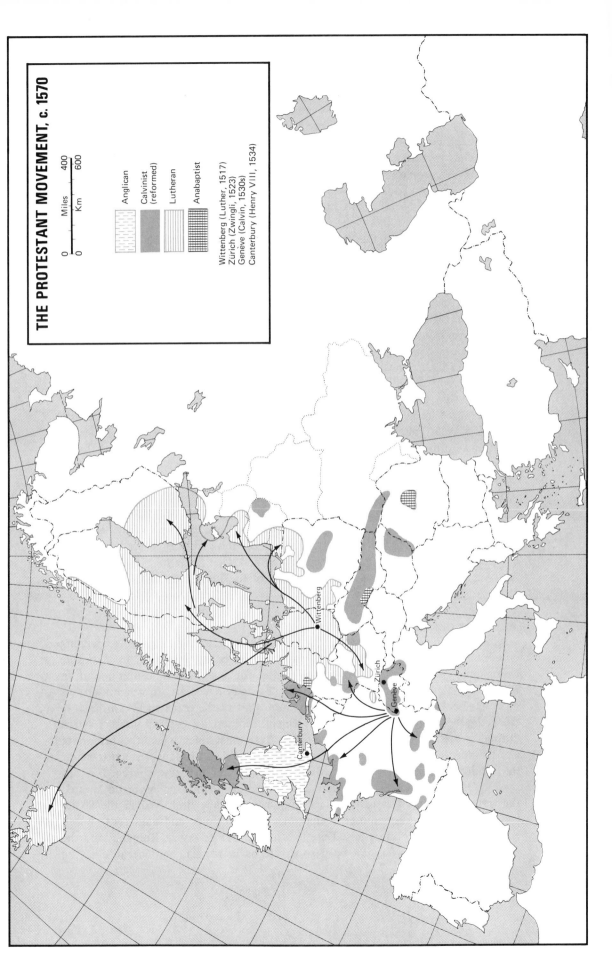

THE PROTESTANT MOVEMENT, c. 1570

Miles 0 400 600
Km 0

Anglican

Calvinist (reformed)

Lutheran

Anabaptist

Wittenberg (Luther, 1517)
Zurich (Zwingli, 1523)
Genève (Calvin, 1530s)
Canterbury (Henry VIII, 1534)

Wittenberg

Zürich

Genève

Canterbury

Muhammad

rule of Iberia failed to leave behind an Islamic residue, but the later and briefer Turkish extension into the Balkans created a permanent Moslem enclave among Albanians and some South Slavic peoples, primarily in Albania and the adjacent Yugoslav provinces of Crna Gora, Kosovo-Metohija, Makedonija, Bosna, and Hercegovina (Figure 6.1). Within the nation of Albania, a majority of about 70 percent of the people are Moslem, amounting to some 1.3 million persons, while the same is true of about 12 percent of the Yugoslavs, a total of about 2.4 million. To the east in Bulgaria, approximately one of every ten inhabitants is Moslem, amounting to about 800,000 souls. All of these outposts of Islam are not far removed in distance from the present shrunken Turkish bridgehead on the north side of the Dardanelles–Bosporus.

Much more important than the small Moslem enclaves has been the traditional Jewish presence in Europe. As recently as 1939, almost ten million Jews lived in Europe and the Soviet Union, well over half of the world total. Poland was home to over three million, followed in order of importance by the Soviet Union, Romania, and Germany.

The mechanism by which Judaism was spread in Europe was quite different from that of Christianity. It involved both forced and voluntary migration of the people adhering to this nonuniversalizing faith. The Jewish presence in Europe originated with the forced dispersal from Palestine in Roman times, which saw Jews scattered to all parts of the Mediterranean Basin. Over the centuries nearly every European country acquired some Jewish residents, though some, such as Spain and Portugal, issued expulsion edicts. In time, the bulk of European Jewry came to be concentrated in the region of the present Russian–Polish border, an area which became known as the "Jewish Pale" (Figure 6.1). A Russian statute proclaimed in 1804 confined Jews to that region.

The Nazi period witnessed the drastic reduction of European Jewry, especially during World War II when the Germans occupied the Jewish Pale. Apparently as many as two-thirds of the European Jews were murdered, including 88 percent of those in Poland. Europe, which had been home to 57 percent of all Jews in 1939, could claim only one-quarter of the much-reduced world total in 1945.

DE-CHRISTIANIZED AREAS

In many parts of Europe, the influence of organized religion is declining or even largely vanished. Eastern Orthodoxy has been suppressed by a hostile Communist government in the Soviet Union for over half a century, and in Romania, Bulgaria, and Yugoslavia for about twenty-five years. In general, Orthodoxy has buckled under Communist pressure. Part of the problem lay in the very close ties between state and church which traditionally typified most Eastern Orthodox areas, ties which date back to Byzantine times when the bishop of Constantinople was deeply involved in imperial politics. In many Orthodox lands, the secular monarch also functioned as titular head of the state church. For this reason, Orthodoxy was especially disrupted when Communist governments severed the traditional church–state ties. The church is virtually destroyed in the Soviet Union. Attendance is composed mainly of elderly persons, and numerous church edifices are now only museums. Deterioration of Orthodoxy in Romania and the southern Slavic lands has not been so severe as in Russia, both because of the shorter period of Communist rule and the less intense governmental anticlerical campaign. Yugoslav Christians are no longer greatly restricted in their worship. Overall, however, it can be said that Orthodoxy as a vital force survives mainly in a southern refuge, a peripheral remnant stronghold in Greece and Cyprus where church–state ties remain strong. Significantly, this refuge area is the original core of Eastern Christianity, the region of greatest Orthodox antiquity, from which it spread north over 1000 years ago.

Roman Catholicism has also suffered severe losses in recent times, but the church has withstood Communist pressure much better than the Eastern Orthodox faith and retains great influence in Russian-dominated Poland. Of all the Communist lands in Europe, only in Poland has any Christian body felt secure enough to criticize openly the government. Harassment by party officials, including planned disruptions of the millennial celebration of Polish Christianity in 1966, has only strengthened popular support for the church. In other Communist countries, however, decline is evident. Catholicism has not fared well in postwar Czechoslovakia and Hungary, nor in Russian-ruled Lithuania.

Furthermore, major Catholic slippage can be detected in many non-Communist countries, as for example in France, where many of the people have been anticlerical since the time of the Revolution almost two centuries ago. The Paris Basin is the region of greatest defection from Catholicism in France, but the church does retain a strong position in peripheral provinces such as Bretagne, Alsace-Lorraine, French Flanders, Cévennes in the Massif Central, and Navarre adjacent to the Pyrenees in the south (Figure 6.4). Perhaps significant is the presence of linguistic minority groups in all of these districts except Cévennes, groups of Bretons, Flemings, Germans, and Basques who may cling to Catholicism in part *because* the French-speaking majority is abandoning it.

Catholicism in Austria and southern Germany, including Bayern, remains strong only in certain rural districts. Overall, the greatest strength of Roman Catholicism, as of Orthodoxy, is confined to the south, to the Mediterranean peninsulas of Iberia and Italy, where the Church has been established longest and where its headquarters are situated.

The position of the Protestant faiths is even more seriously eroded than that of Catholicism or Orthodoxy. In the Netherlands, where the Calvinist Dutch Reformed church is the largest, fully 17 percent of the population disavowed any religious affiliation by the mid-twentieth century. Dutch de-Christianization is much more pronounced in the Protestant north than in the dominantly Catholic south (see Figure 6.10). As early as 1850, major defections from Anglican and other Protestant faiths were noted in parts of the United Kingdom, including traditionally Methodist Celtic Wales. It is necessary to seek out such remote areas as the Færoe Islands to find a vital Protestantism today. Elsewhere, the faith has been severely downgraded in importance.

A survey conducted in Europe by the American Institute of Public Opinion (Gallup Poll) in 1968, the results of which are reproduced here with permission of the Institute, bears witness to the decline (Table 6.1). Persons interviewed were asked whether they believed in God, life after death, Hell, and the Devil. In Greece, representative of the southern refuge of religion in Europe, the highest percentages of affirmative responses to all four questions were noted, while the greatest amount of defection from the traditional beliefs of Christianity was re-

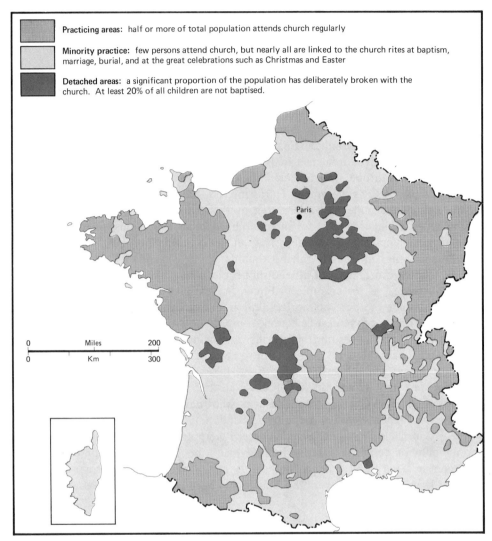

Practicing areas: half or more of total population attends church regularly

Minority practice: few persons attend church, but nearly all are linked to the church rites at baptism, marriage, burial, and at the great celebrations such as Christmas and Easter

Detached areas: a significant proportion of the population has deliberately broken with the church. At least 20% of all children are not baptised.

Figure 6.4 The vitality of the Church in rural France, about 1950. (After Boulard.)

corded in France and Sweden. Only about one-third of all Frenchmen expressed belief in an afterlife, and only 60 percent of the Swedes believed in God. Comparison of the 1968 survey to one taken by Gallup twenty years earlier revealed a marked de-Christianization since World War II (Table 6.1). In general, defection from the church is more pronounced in urban, industrial, Protestant, and Communistic areas.

QUASI RELIGIONS

De-Christianization is in part the result of a rise of various quasi religions, systems of belief which are similar to religions but lack worship services. Communism is a quasi religion and has functioned as a replacement for Christianity in Russia. Indeed, communism exhibits some doctrines apparently derived from

TABLE 6.1   A Gallup Survey of Christian Belief in Europe,[a] 1968 (1948 Responses in Parentheses)

Country	Percent expressing belief in God	Percent expressing belief in life after death	Percent expressing belief in Hell	Percent expressing belief in the Devil	Suicides per 100,000 population
	1968	1968 (1948)	1968	1968	ca. 1965
Austria	85	38	26	23	23
Finland	83	55 (69%)	29	26	19
France	73	35 (58%)	22	17	15
Greece	96	57	62	67	3
Netherlands	79	50 (68%)	28	29	7
Norway	73	54 (71%)	36	38	8
Sweden	60	38 (49%)	17	21	20
Switzerland	84	50	25	25	18
United Kingdom	77	38 (49%)	23	21	10
West Germany	81	41	25	25	20

[a] Based on interviews with more than 12,000 adults in all walks of life, including some in the United States and Uruguay, which were included in the survey.
Sources: The Gallup Report, for release Thursday, December 26, 1968. Used with the permission of the American Institute of Public Opinion (The Gallup Poll). Also United Nations, *Demographic Yearbook*, 1967.

Christianity, such as the image of a victorious proletariat (the meek shall inherit the earth), glorification of honest hard work, and sexual morality.

Nationalistic movements at times acquire the status of quasi religions, as was true of nazism in Germany. To the faithful, nazism offered the frequently encountered religious concepts of a chosen people, an invincible, all-knowing leader, and a mission of world conquest.

DISTRIBUTIONAL RESULTS OF INTERACTION BETWEEN RELIGIONS

When different churches share a district or border on one another, areal interaction occurs. This contact can be of three types: (1) peaceful coexistence, (2) competition and instability, or (3) intolerance and exclusion. In Europe, most interaction has been of the two extreme types, with quite different results for the religious map.

In the highlands of Yugoslavia, Moslems and Christians share many villages and towns, living together in peaceful coexistence. Intermarriage between the two groups is not unknown there, though in such cases the wife is normally expected to accept the religion of her husband. Mutual tolerance has allowed considerable areal intermingling of Christians and Moslems to take place, and there is no sharp border between the two groups.

In marked contrast, areas where intolerance and exclusion are found today, or have been present in the recent past, tend to segregate religious groups. Religious borders are very sharp in such cases, with homogeneous populations on either side. The striking pattern of residential segregation of Catholics and Protestants in Belfast and Londonderry, cities in religiously troubled Northern Ireland, is the product of intolerance and exclusion. In earlier times, the Jewish ghettos of many European cities fit this same pattern. Even when intolerance is replaced by peaceful coexistence, segregation can persist long afterwards. The Catholic–Protestant border in rural Germany remains rather sharp today, over three centuries after open hostility between the two groups ceased. Intolerance can serve to reduce the religious diversity of a country. The map of faiths in Spain under Moorish rule was a crazy-quilt of Christians, Jews, and Moslems, but after the Christian reconquest, Jews (1492) and Moslems (1609–1616) were expelled or forcibly converted to Catholicism, greatly simplifying the religious map.

In some instances there are curious local contrasts in forms of interaction between the same two religious groups. On the island of Ródos, a part of Greece, Moslems and Greek Christians coexist peacefully, even to the point of intermarriage, while in nearby Cyprus the two are bitterly opposed to one another and have fought in recent years. Both Ródos and Cyprus have large Greek majorities and small Turkish minorities, both are islands in the eastern Mediterranean, yet they differ greatly in the degree of tolerance present.

CHRISTIANITY AND EUROPEAN EXPANSION

The impressive areal expansion of European peoples and ideas over the past 500 years, described in Chapter 1, was in no small part the result of a cultural self-image derived from Christianity. Partly because Christianity was a universalizing faith, Europe became a universalizing culture. The Crusades, the first large-scale effort by Europeans to expand their culture area onto foreign shores, came about because of the church, and several centuries later God, Gold, and Glory shared direction of Spanish exploration and colonization. Christianity, in effect, helped turn Europeans outward and in so doing forever altered the human geography of the entire world.

6.2 ENVIRONMENTAL INFLUENCE ON RELIGION

The tie between religion and the physical surroundings is generally stronger among primitive peoples who rely on their priests and medicine men to provide a protective buffer between them and the unknown, mysterious forces of nature. Almost invariably, however, some environmental influence persists even in advanced religions such as Christianity.

VENERATION OF HIGH PLACES

From ancient times high places such as mountain peaks have been regarded as holy sites, originally as the home of gods. The early Greeks venerated or feared high places, such as Ólimbos, Parnassós, and Athos. Ólimbos, generally covered by clouds, was the dwelling place of great Zeus and lesser divinities. Parnassós, a mountain in central Greece, was the holiest site in classical times, home of the famous Oracle of Delfi, who issued important prophecies from her place of honor in the temple of Apollo. The name "Parnassós" was derived from an ancient, pre-Greek language and probably means "place of the temple," indicating that its religious significance in Classical times was simply an inheritance from earlier peoples. Athos, a mountainous peninsula reaching into the Aegean Sea, was feared and shunned by the superstitious pre-Christian Greeks.

This ancestral Greek veneration of high places has survived to the present day in Orthodox Christianity. Athos has preserved its religious significance as the site of numerous monasteries, and to the present day no woman is allowed on the peninsula. In fact, hilltops throughout mainland Greece and the Aegean isles are occupied by monasteries today. It is a common sight to see monks winding their way on zigzag trails, coming to and from their labors in fields and vineyards in the adjacent valleys. Similarly, hilltops are often the site of chapels in the Yugoslav republic of Slovenija and in parts of Austria. Visitors to Paris are almost always attracted by the impressive hilltop church of Sacré Coeur which overlooks the city.

VENERATION OF CAVES

Caves, like high places, were often venerated in pre-Christian religions. The Minoan people on the island of Kriti apparently regarded caves as holy places. Perhaps a survival in modern times is seen in the grotto at Lourdes, where the Virgin Mary is said to have appeared in a vision, or in the grotto of St. John on the Greek island of Patmos, where the book of Revelations was composed. Indeed, Patmos combines survival of cave and high place veneration, for a large monastery crowns the hilltop above the grotto of St. John.

VENERATION OF FORESTS AND TREES

In the tribal religions of the ancient Germans, Slavs, Celts, and Greeks, sacred forests were common, including many temple groves. Often these were regarded as the haunts of the woodland gods. Moreover, specific types of trees were sometimes venerated, as for example the evergreen fir tree which was a religious comfort to the ancient Germans because it remained green through the winter. Modern survivals in Christianity include the custom of the Christmas tree and the presence of remnant forests around monasteries in part of the Mediterranean.

VENERATION OF THE HEAVENLY BODIES

Worship of the sun, moon, and stars was especially widespread in pre-Christian Europe. The awesome ruin at Stonehenge in southwestern England is believed to have been a very sophisticated astronomical observatory built for the star-gazing priests of a remarkable early civilization. Recent detailed studies of Canterbury Cathedral, the center of English Christianity, suggest that the mark of those ancient astronomers may linger yet today in England. The cathedral is in several respects asymmetrical in its construction. There is a misalignment of 2° between nave and choir, and another 2° between choir and the Trinity Chapel section of the cathedral, giving the structure a slightly curved configuration. In all probability the present misalignment is based on the ancient floor plans of three separate religious structures built by people of the Stonehenge culture about 2300, 1900, and 1500 B.C. Each of the ancient buildings had its longitudinal axis fixed on the horizon point of rising of the major star Betelgeuse, a point which changed by 2° every 400 years. This theory is further supported by the fact that the outlines of both the Trinity Chapel section of Canterbury Cathedral and Woodhenge, a ruin near Stonehenge, are based on Pythagorean triangles.

Sun worship by pagan Europeans was perhaps most highly developed in the Mediterranean peninsulas. One such cult worshiped a sun god called Invictus, whose birthday was celebrated at the winter solstice in late December, that time of year when the sun, having reached its lowest annual noontime zenith, begins once more to ascend in the sky. The Christian date for Christmas seems to have been inherited from the devotees of Invictus. Moreover, Sunday ("day of the sun") became the Christian holy day.

6.3 THE RELIGIOUS CULTURAL LANDSCAPE

One of the areal expressions of cultures and subcultures is the visible imprint they place on the landscape. A portion of this imprint is invariably the product of religious beliefs and practices, though the magnitude of religious contribution varies greatly from one group of people to another. Those religions which focus on appeal to the human senses, especially sight and sound, have a maximum impact on the landscape, while those concentrating more on commandment and faith often leave relatively little imprint.

SACRED STRUCTURES

Among the most obvious religious contributions to the landscape are sacred structures, especially the church building. Europe exhibits many regional contrasts in church size, building material, and architectural style (Figure 6.5). In Catholic areas, the church structures tend to be larger and more ornate than those of Protestant and Orthodox districts, in part because the Roman church places great value on providing visible beauty for the faithful. Both Catholic and Orthodox landscapes gain additional distinctiveness from the numerous roadside shrines and chapels which dot the countryside.

Even within Catholic areas, there are regional differences in church size. In parts of France where the rural population is dispersed, as in parts of the Basin of Aquitaine, there are a multitude of small churches. Many of these have long been abandoned and stand in ruins, but originally both the size and dispersal of the churches reflected the distribution of population. Moreover, such rural churches were more often used for defense in times of troubles during earlier centuries, and their architecture often reflects that function.

Architectural styles of European churches are extremely varied (Figures 6.5, 6.6, 6.7). Distinctive types of Anglican church architecture connote England to even the casual observer, just as onion-towered Catholic churches characterize many villages of Austria and German Bayern. Some forms of church architecture are clear indicators of specific cultural groups in zones of ethnic mixture, as in Yugoslavian Istra, where both Italians and Slavs are present. Italian influence there is revealed by churches which have a freestanding bell tower. The minarets of Moslem mosques pierce the skyline of many southern Balkan villages and towns, lending a special exotic character to the landscape.

Building materials used in the construction of churches also vary from place to place, even within small districts (Figure 6.5). Impressive wooden churches are found in parts of Russia and the Moldavian section of eastern Romania, while stone structures dominate southern Europe. Often the church is a strikingly visible part of the landscape because it is built of a different material from the other structures in the village or town. In French Normandie, for example, most houses are half-timbered while the churches are stone, and the same is true of parts of northern Germany (Figure 6.5).

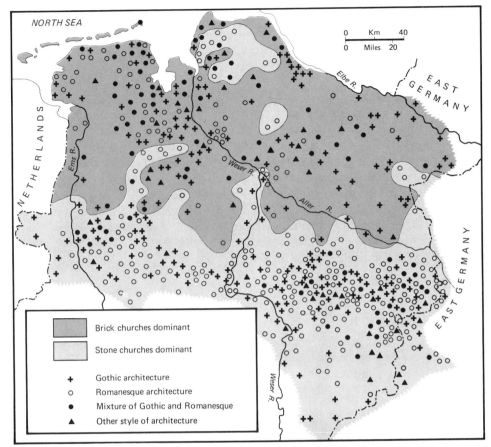

Figure 6.5 Traditional church architecture and building materials in northwestern Germany. The regional contrast between stone and brick churches adds character and diversity to the cultural landscape, and the diversity is heightened by architectural styles. Gothic and partially Gothic churches are dominant in the north, while Romanesque structures are more common in the south. Throughout most of the area where stone churches are dominant, the traditional building method for houses is half-timbering, illustrating a rather common European tendency for houses and churches to be built of different materials. (After Siebert.)

LANDSCAPES OF THE DEAD

The dead also contribute to the religious landscape. Cemeteries vary in site, areal dimensions, and the character of markers for the dead. In places, some persons were buried in the walls and floors of church buildings, as in parts of southern Germany, while in cities such as Roma and Paris, remains of the dead were collected in catacombs. Cemeteries in farm villages of Protestant northern Germany are usually small, with unimpressive markers, for it is the practice there to reuse plots again and again, usually at about fifty-year intervals. Markers in Catholic cemeteries are usually larger and more visibly striking than those of Protestant graveyards. Greater acceptance of cremation for the dead among Protestants still further lessens the visible necrogeography of their areas. Among the most striking landscapes in Europe are those devoted to the war dead, as for example the sea of identical small white crosses which mark American military cemeteries in parts of western Europe, the huge Soviet memorial at Treptow Park in East Berlin, or the almost inevitable stone shafts in the commons of rural German villages commemorating under the sign of the iron cross the list of those who fell in world wars.

PLACE NAMES

The names man has placed on the land of Europe reveal much about the history and culture of the population, and religion is well represented. Catholic areas, especially in Romance-language countries, usually have a large number of places named for saints, often in the form of suffixes added to older, pre-Christian names, as in Alcazar de San Juan in Spain. Eastern Orthodox areas, particularly Greece, also have many religious place names. The frequency of sacred toponyms decreases to the north in Europe, reaching lowest levels in Protestant lands. In West Germany, almost 75 percent of the relatively few towns and villages which bear a prefix of *Sankt* ("Saint") are in the Catholic-dominated southern part of the country, including 21 percent in Bayern alone.

6.4 AREAL RELATIONSHIPS BETWEEN RELIGION AND ECONOMY

Among the most important geographical aspects of religion is the influence belief can exert on economy. The impact of religion can be detected in agriculture, industry, tourism, and trade.

Figure 6.6 A rural Lutheran church in southwestern Iceland. This modest, Gothic-influenced structure is typical of the cultural landscape in Iceland, a barren European outpost island in the North Atlantic. (Photo by the author.)

Figure 6.7   An Orthodox chapel among the olive groves of the Greek island of Kriti. This small church, located at the opposite territorial extreme of Europe from the one pictured in Figure 6.6, is typical of many found throughout Greece. Note the fundamentally different architecture of the Greek and Icelandic churches. (Photo by the author.)

AGRICULTURE
Dispersal of domesticated plants can in some instances be attributed to the spread of a religion, particularly when a certain food crop plays a role in religious ceremony. The Christian sacrament of Holy Communion as practiced in Europe requires the use of wine as the symbolic blood of Christ, and historically this need aided the northward diffusion of viticulture from the sunny lands of the Mediterranean into newly Christianized districts beyond the Alps. The vine-covered valleys of the German Rhine and Mosel rivers owe their dominant crop to immigrant monks of the sixth to ninth centuries. In certain Jewish celebrations, particularly the Feast of Booths in late spring, use was made of the citron, a little-known citrus fruit. When the Romans dispersed Jews from Palestine, the citron and perhaps other citrus fruits were carried by the migrants to the European Mediterranean, the first recorded instance of citrus-raising in Europe. Later, when the religious fervor of the Moslem Arabs led them to conquer Iberia, the orange and lemon, and perhaps also rice, spread into the area as part of the cultural baggage of the Arabic invaders.

Food and labor taboos associated with religious belief can also influence agriculture. In the nation of Albania, for example, swine are found in Christian districts but are largely absent in Moslem areas, a consequence of the Islamic taboo on pork consumption. Christian religious holidays were once so numerous in parts of Europe that the quality of farming suffered, as in fourteenth-century France, where farmers were idled by churchly celebrations about one of every four days.

Numerous fundamental ties exist between the agricultural and religious calendars. The celebration of Easter is derived from Jewish Passover, originally a spring harvest festival. The Hebrew for Passover, *Pesach,* is the root of the Mediterranean European words meaning "Easter," as in Greek *Pascha* or Italian *Pasqua.* As Christianity spread north beyond the Alps, into lands where spring was the season of planting rather than of reaping, the Easter celebration became the substitute for a pagan welcoming-of-spring festival rather than a harvest celebration. Accordingly, the Germanic word for Easter was derived from the name of the goddess of spring, *Eostre* or *Ostara,* and the Christian celebration incorporated pagan fertility symbols of the spring, such as the rabbit and egg. The great ceremonial void resulting from the importation of the Jewish–early Christian Mediterranean cultivation calendar into the Germanic areas north of the Alps was the lack of Christian autumnal harvest festival. As a consequence, the church assimilated and partially sanctified pagan Germanic harvest celebrations such as Michaelmas in England (September 29) and Halloween (October 31).

THE ROLE OF THE CHURCH IN MEDIEVAL LAND COLONIZATION

Another agricultural influence of the church was the active colonization role played by brotherhoods of monks, such as the Benedictine and Cistercian orders, during the Middle Ages. One of the main activities of these orders was the establishment of monastic agricultural colonies in wilderness areas covered by forest or marsh. The Cistercian Order, for example, originated in eastern France and spread to found monastic settlements from Sicilia to Sweden, from Portugal to Poland, mainly in the twelfth century. Much of the task of clearing forests and draining marshes, especially in northern and central Europe, was accomplished by these monks and the peasant colonists under their direction. The Cistercians were engaged in vast land-reclamation schemes in northern Spain and east-central Europe. Land for colonization was obtained either through purchase by the brotherhoods or as donations from landlords who were interested in having agriculture brought to unproductive wilderness regions or areas laid waste by warfare. The peasants involved became tenants on land owned by the brotherhoods, an arrangement which differed little from secular feudalism. Some parts of the estates owned by the orders were worked by the monks themselves as communal farms or *granges* adjacent to the monasteries. A typical grange contained perhaps about one hundred hectares (several hundred acres) of arable land and contained near its center a cluster of buildings equivalent to a secular village, in which the men and animals were housed. In some areas such as northern England, the monks did not promote peasant colonization, but were largely content simply to found granges.

In time, most of the land colonized by the monks was secularized. Granges were converted into villages and became indistinguishable from those of the peasants. The farm folk acquired secular lords to replace the ecclesiastical authority. The labor of the monkish orders thereby became part of the rural economic legacy of most European countries. Even today, sizable amounts of farmland in countries such as Greece are worked by monks and owned by the church.

THE CHURCH AND FISHING

The western Christian tradition of meat avoidance on Friday, and on numerous church holidays, greatly stimulated the development of the fishing industry in Europe. In particular, the Roman Catholic church encouraged the use of fish during periods of fasting and penitence, as well as on Fridays, the latter practice having been abandoned only recently by papal decree. It is not surprising that seashore Catholics, such as Basques, Bretons, and Portuguese, are among the greatest fishing peoples of Europe. St. Peter, the original Christian fisherman, usually holds a place of special veneration in the fishing villages of Catholic Europe, as well as in Orthodox Greece.

The importance of the Catholic church to fishing is suggested by the economic crisis which occurred in English fishing when Catholic dietary restrictions were removed as a result of the Anglican breakaway in the 1500s. Many fishermen were obliged to become sailors, perhaps leading to the great era of English naval exploration, piracy, and overseas colonization.

PILGRIMAGES

In Catholic areas, the church has long been the cause of numerous pilgrimages, temporary movements of people which can have a profound economic impact on the areas involved. Pilgrimage sites are of varying importance, ranging from small shrines which attract only the faithful from the immediate surroundings to internationally known places which are sought out by Catholics from all over Europe and America. Among the major pilgrimage sites are *Lourdes* (Figure 6.8), a French town at the foot of the Pyrenees in the Basin of Aquitaine where the Virgin Mary supposedly appeared in a vision, *Fátima,* north of Lisboa in Portugal, and *Czestochowa,* the hearth of Polish Catholicism. Lourdes alone attracts about two million visitors annually, with the result that this small town of 16,000 population ranks second in France only to Paris in number of hotels.

Of particular geographical significance is the fact that pilgrimage sites are not evenly distributed in Europe, even within Catholic areas. In France, for example, pilgrimage sites devoted to the Virgin Mary are concentrated in the south and west, with a few isolated clusters elsewhere in the country (Figure 6.8). Contrary to what might be expected, the sites are not concentrated in areas of densest population. The flow of pilgrims to the major Virgin Mary shrines is of much greater economic benefit to southern France than to other parts of the country. Similarly, a passion play held every ten years at Oberammergau, a small town in the German Alps of southern Bayern, has developed into a major financial boon to the entire district.

The Vatican City draws millions of Catholic visitors to Roma each year, adding to the already important tourist trade based on antiquities. As recently as the 1700s, almost all of the long-distance travel of people within Europe was that directed toward Roma and a few other religious centers. Many roads were developed mainly for pilgrim traffic, complete with hospices at difficult places such as mountain passes. Monks were active bridge-builders along these routes. Even the directional trend of many European roads was influenced by their function as pilgrimage routes. For example, the ancient route in southwestern France, leading toward Spain, left the banks of the Loire at the town of Amboise, but in later centuries the attraction of the tomb of St. Martin caused the road to be detoured along a less advantageous route through the city of Tours, a change which is reflected in the road map of France still today.

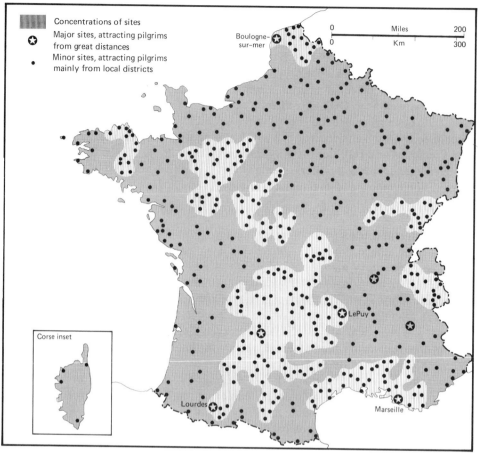

Figure 6.8 Distribution of pilgrimage sites of the Virgin Mary in France. Note the concentration of sites in the west and particularly the south. The distribution is quite different from that of population and tends to correlate to some extent with the map of de-Christianization (see Figure 6.4). Areas where the church is still a vital institution generally have more pilgrimage sites. (After Deffontaines.)

RELIGION AND INDUSTRY

The Protestant Reformation may well have been one root cause of the rise of manufacturing in northwestern Europe, culminating in the far-reaching Industrial Revolution. In the Middle Ages, Christian Europeans were forbidden by the church to lend money for interest, but this usury taboo was removed in Protestant Europe after the Reformation. The increased amount of investment capital may have been a major stimulus to increased mercantilism and manufacturing in Germanic lands. Earlier, many Jews had found an uncontested economic niche in Europe by becoming moneylenders, for usury was not restricted by their religion. Some scholars have suggested that the dynamic character of Protestantism, the willingness of its adherents to accept change and strive for improvement, coupled with the Protestant ethic of hard work, were necessary social precedents to the great Industrial Revolution. Indeed, modern industrialism arose in Protestant lands and only belatedly spread into Catholic and Orthodox areas, though nonreligious factors such as the location of coal deposits help explain industrial origin and dispersal. Earlier, Catholic persecution of Huguenots and Protestant Flemings, many of whom were skilled artisans, caused an emigration of these craftsmen to England, northern Germany, and Holland. The dominantly Protestant countries thereby gained a valuable industrial impetus, while the Catholic lands, particularly France, suffered a setback.

In other ways, however, Roman Catholicism caused advances in manufacturing. Monasteries often housed monks who were highly skilled artisans, manufacturing everything from tapestries to liqueurs. These skills were often spread to the local secular population, greatly improving the economic conditions.

THE CHURCH AND TRADE

Restrictions or needs resulting from religious practice have often stimulated interregional trade. Christianization of Ireland led to an import of wine from the Bordeaux region of France as early as the sixth century, and the movement of wine from south to north greatly increased after the Germanic people in Scandinavia were converted. Catholic dietary requirements made lands such as Italy and Spain, whose adjacent seas are relatively poor fishing grounds, dependent on dried fish imports from the Atlantic front of Europe.

More recently, a "lively" trade in corpses has developed between Luxembourg and adjacent northeastern France. It is unlawful to cremate the dead in Luxembourg, a result of church influence in the legislative process, and French mortuaries across the border are performing this service for Luxembourgers who wish it for their deceased kin.

6.5 RELIGION AND LANGUAGE

Linguistic and religious patterns are often closely related in Europe. There are very strong ties between Catholicism and the Romance languages, and the Catholic area in Europe corresponds fairly well to that of the Latin-derived languages. Most European Catholics speak Romance tongues, and the church long required use of the ancestral Latin in its various ceremonies. Latin survives today *only* as the sacred tongue of Roman Catholicism. It is true that non-Romance groups such as the Irish, Flemings, Poles, and southern Germans are Catholic, but overall the areal correlation between the two is reasonably close (compare Figures 5.1 and 6.1).

Just as Catholicism can be linked linguistically to the Romance speakers, so Eastern Orthodoxy is tied to the Hellenic and Slavic languages. The language of both the Byzantine Empire and the Orthodox faith was Greek, and the only important mission activity was among the Slavs. Protestantism, in turn, is concentrated in the Germanic language area, in part because the Reformation originated in Germany. Judaism, in Eastern Europe at least, was identified with speakers of Yiddish and Ladino.

It is not surprising that religious and linguistic patterns display some correspondence, for language is the principal vessel in which culture, including religion, is transmitted. In turn, the holy writings of the church often serve as a model for the written and spoken form of the language. For example, Luther's translation of the Bible provided the standard for modern German and led to the decline of regional dialects. The very survival of a language can depend on whether or not its literature contains the principal religious books. Translations of the Bible, prayer books, and hymnals into Welsh helped that language to resist the inroads of English better than did Cornish, Gaelic, and Erse.

6.6 RELIGIONS AND POLITICAL GEOGRAPHY

The areal interaction between religion and politics takes many forms in Europe. Perhaps most important is the role religion has played as a basis for nationalism in certain countries.

NATIONALISM

In some nations religion has served as the rallying point for an independence movement. Roman Catholicism is the principal base of nationalism in the Republic of Ireland, for it survived the long English occupation much better than the ancestral Celtic language of the Irish and alone distinguished the bulk of Irishmen from their English enemies.

In Poland, Catholicism is also identified with nationalism, though the Poles have had the added factor of language to indicate their distinctiveness from the adjacent Lutheran Germans and Orthodox Russians. Some of the intense evangelical fervor derived from the Catholic reconquest still lives in Spain, helping bind together an ethnically and physically diverse nation, while in Greece the Orthodox faith has been a potent nationalistic force since the days of Byzantium. It was a Protestant–Catholic religious difference which caused the Dutch and Flemings, who are very closely akin linguistically, to seek different political homes in the nineteenth century. And of course the entire reason for existence of the politically independent Vatican City is its function as residence of the papacy. Indeed, a large part of Europe was directly under church rule in the Middle Ages, including most of central Italy.

The major political dispute in western Europe in recent years has been in Northern Ireland, and the situation there is largely the result of religious contrasts. A Protestant majority was introduced into Northern Ireland through immigration in the 1600s, with the result that the area remained part of the United Kingdom when the Republic of Ireland gained independence in the 1920s. Unfortunately, the political boundary was poorly drawn, leaving large rural Catholic districts in Northern Ireland (Figure 6.9). This unfortunate inclusion of Catholics is part of the cause of the present unrest.

POLITICAL PARTIES AND VOTING PATTERNS

Another political significance of religion is found in voting patterns and political party membership within some European nations. In Germany some political parties have long been based on religious affiliation, and the same is true in the Netherlands and Italy. The Catholic Peoples party in the Netherlands has its strength in Roman Catholic southern portions of that country, and there are several Protestant political parties based mainly in the north (Figure 6.10). Often such parties adopt names like "Christian Democrat" to underline their tie to the church.

As a result, voting patterns within such countries often show a very close correspondence to religious patterns. In Germany, the Center party of pre-World

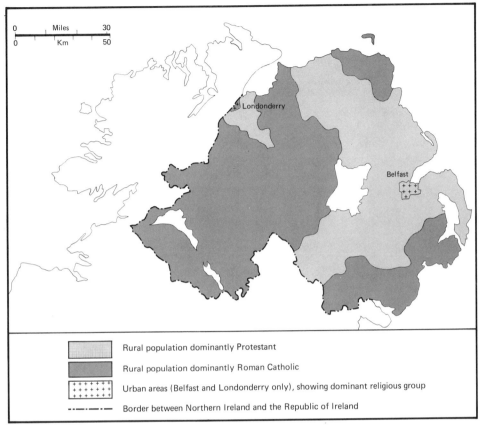

Figure 6.9 Catholics and Protestants in Northern Ireland. The cause of Irish nationalism is based on Catholicism rather than the Celtic Erse language. Therefore, the inclusion of sizable Catholic areas in Northern Ireland has created political instability, including rioting. The boundary drawn in the 1920s was quite unjust to the Catholic Irish, who desired to be included in the Republic of Ireland. Further instability is based on the segregation of Protestants and Catholics in the cities of Northern Ireland. (After Johnson, data for 1951.)

War II times was identified with Catholicism and always drew its heaviest support from Catholic provinces such as Bayern, Westfalen, the Rhineland, and Polish-populated areas in the east. Two political parties in the Netherlands are associated with the Dutch Reformed and Catholic churches, and there are also Catholic parties in Italy and Austria (Figure 6.10).

STATE CHURCHES

The decision by rulers of sundry kingdoms, empires, and principalities to accept, for whatever reason, one particular religious faith has had an immense impact on the distributional pattern of faiths. Indeed, Europe might not have become Christian at all but for the conversion of the Roman Emperor Constantine. Luther would quite likely have perished and his movement with him had not a variety of rulers in Germany and Scandinavia adopted his faith and given him protection.

It mattered a great deal whether a church obtained the status of state religion. Wherever Protestantism was thus protected, as in England, Scotland, various German states, and the Scandinavian nations, it survived and flourished. On the

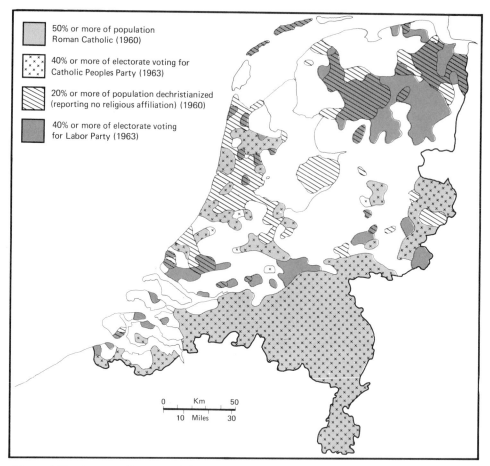

Figure 6.10 Aspects of Dutch religious geography. Some Dutch political parties are closely identified with individual churches. The electorate in all predominantly Roman Catholic areas strongly supported the candidates of the Catholic Peoples party in the election for the Second Chamber of the States General, May 15, 1963. Voting practices in this election are typical. In this way the religious map is related to voting patterns. While the Labor party has no religious affiliation, it draws its strongest support in de-Christianized areas. De-Christianization has occurred mainly in the northern Netherlands, the Protestant section, while Christianity retains its vitality in the Catholic south. (After *Atlas van Nederland*.)

other hand, in areas where Catholicism remained the legally established religion, Protestantism did not fare well. Calvinism in France and Poland was eventually destroyed, while the Anabaptists, persecuted by both Catholics and other Protestants, largely disappeared. Anglican pressure on Calvinist Puritans eventually caused many of them to migrate to New England. In 1817 the independent German state of Prussia, or Preussen, joined Lutherans and Calvinists (Reformed) to form the unified state church. Indeed, as recently as several centuries ago, *most* political borders corresponded to religious borders.

States have differed widely in the degree to which adherence to the state church was required. Spain, where Catholicism has long been strictly enforced as the state religion, retains an afterglow of the fervor of Catholic reconquest, the faded memory of a holy war. Part of this Iberian religious enthusiasm was trans-

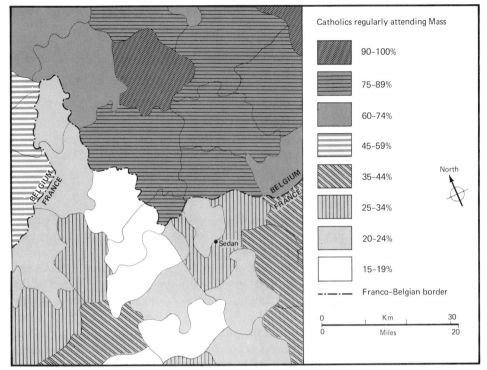

Figure 6.11 Attendance at Mass in the Franco–Belgian border area in the Ardennes. (After Boulard.)

planted to Belgium during the long period of Spanish rule there (1506–1713), with the result that the Belgians are more intensely devoted to the church than are many neighboring peoples. The Spanish influence is seen even in the elaborate religious processions in Belgium. Across the border in France, Catholicism is much weaker, partly as a result of anticlerical sentiment during the French Revolution which led to complete separation of church and state. The difference between Belgium and France can be seen clearly in church attendance, which is very high on the Belgian side but quite low immediately across the boundary in France (Figure 6.11).

POLITICAL ORGANIZATION OF CHURCHES

The three major Christian groups in Europe differ greatly in the degree of centralization and in territorial organization. Protestantism and Eastern Orthodoxy broke down into a large number of independent churches, with little or no unity surviving. Many became autonomous state churches, completely free of international ties. In such cases religious regionalism was fostered.

On the other hand, the Roman Catholic church has retained a remarkable degree of unity and central control. Its political framework, composed of provinces, dioceses, and parishes, grew out of the political organization of the Roman Empire, another link between this church and its Latin heritage. The three orders of political subdivision are administered respectively by archbishops, bishops, and priests. Parishes are relatively uniform in size and small enough to permit each resident to reach Sunday mass without undue inconvenience. Major regional contrasts are found, however, in the size of dioceses, ranging from an average of about 1000 square kilometers (400 square miles) in Italy to 7800 square kilometers (3000 square miles) in Spain. The larger number of dioceses in Italy has been partially responsible for the greater voice Italian bishops have traditionally had in church affairs.

6.7 RELIGION AND DEMOGRAPHY

In various ways the pattern of religions is related to areal variations in other characteristics of the population. Such diverse phenomena as birth rates, suicide, and population distribution can have a religious aspect.

POPULATION DISTRIBUTION

During the centuries when Europe was undergoing Christianization, paganism tended to survive longer in areas where the rural population was dispersed rather than clustered in villages or towns. The cities, where densest population clustering is found, were converted earliest. To the present day, some European rural folk still believe in witchcraft, and very recently some farmers in a part of the West German province of Bayern attempted to burn a woman they believed to be a witch.

For the most part, however, the situation observed during the spread of Christianity is now precisely reversed. The church, whether Catholic, Protestant, or Orthodox, retains its greatest vitality today in rural areas, while the cities tend to be centers of mass defection from the faith. The more highly urbanized countries are generally those in which organized religion is at lowest ebb at present. In this respect it is unfortunate for the church that European population is becoming increasingly clustered with each passing year.

MIGRATION

Movement of European peoples from place to place has often been induced by religious factors. Indeed, Christians have enjoyed a greater potential mobility in part because they are not tied to one place by religious belief, as are some Oriental peoples who engage in ancestor worship and never depart from the area where their forefathers are buried. Such mobility helped allow Europeans to migrate to distant lands such as America and Australia. Conversely, it was the religious memory of a holy ancestral land which led many European Jews "back" to Israel.

In other instances, group migrations have been caused by religious conflict. The expulsion of Jews and Moslems from Spain, the migrations of Anabaptists to eastern Europe, the flight of the Salzburg Protestants to northern Germany, and the exodus of Hussites, a pre-Luther heretical group, from České were all caused by religion.

FERTILITY

In recent times, religion has apparently helped produce some regional contrasts in birth rate. French geographers have noted that fertility is greater in those

Figure 6.12 Suicides per 100,000 persons, annually, circa 1965. (Source: United Nations, *Demographic Yearbook,* 1967.)

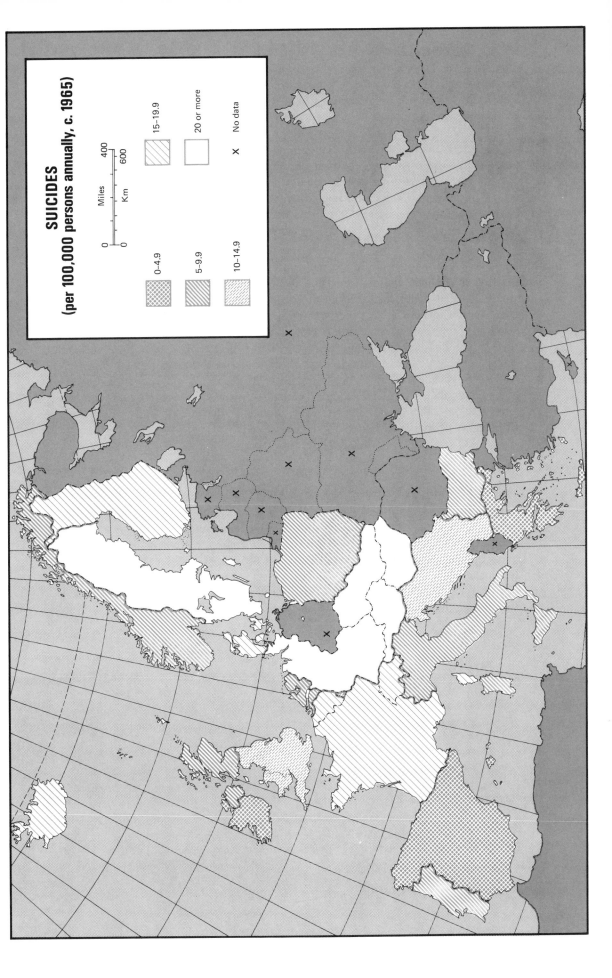

SUICIDES
(per 100,000 persons annually, c. 1965)

0–4.9

5–9.9

10–14.9

15–19.9

20 or more

X   No data

Miles   400
        600
Km

0
0

parts of France where the church is still strong, as in Alsace and Bretagne, while birth rates are lowest in provinces where de-Christianization has occurred, as in Normandie and Aquitaine.

On the other hand, the Catholic and Orthodox requirement for celibacy among priests, monks, and nuns removes part of the population from reproduction and thereby lowers fertility. An extreme example is the autonomous theocratic republic of Athos in northern Greece, an area of about 400 square kilometers (150 square miles) where the entire population of 2700 is male, including nearly 2000 celibate monks. Women are not allowed even to visit Athos.

SUICIDE

In Christian theology, the taking of one's own life is regarded as a sin, and the Roman Catholic church, in particular, has taken a strong stand against suicide. Accordingly, it is not surprising to find that suicide rates in Europe are markedly lower in areas where the church remains strong (Figure 6.12).

In the southern peninsular refuges of Catholicism and Eastern Orthodoxy, suicide is quite uncommon, and the same is true of strongly Catholic Ireland and Poland. Where de-Christianization has occurred, however, as in Sweden and Germany, the suicide rate is higher. Moreover, Protestant countries generally have higher rates than Catholic countries (compare Figures 6.1 and 6.12). There are many factors other than religion which influence the suicide rate, but a vital Christianity obviously does help to keep the rate low.

*   *   *

OF THE THREE LEGS of the tripod supporting European culture, religion seems the most essential. One can easily imagine Europe continuing to thrive should the Indo-European tongues be replaced by alien languages, and there is nothing that binds Europe by necessity to the Caucasian race. What is difficult to envision is the European culture area shorn of Christianity, for the church is intertwined with almost every facet of the culture, economy, and society. So long as there is a Europe, the mark of Christianity will remain.

SOURCES AND SUGGESTED READINGS

American Institute of Public Opinion. *The Gallup Report*. December 26, 1968.

Atlas van Nederland. Plate XI-9, "Religious Denomination." Delft: Topographic Service, 1963–1967.

Lyle B. Borst. "Megalithic Plan Underlying Canterbury Cathedral." *Science*. Vol. 163 (1969), pp. 567–570.

Fernand Boulard. *An Introduction to Religious Sociology: Pioneer Work in France*. Translated by M. J. Jackson. London: Darton Longman and Todd, 1960.

Jan O. M. Broek and John W. Webb. "Religions: Origins and Dispersals." Chapter 6 in *A Geography of Mankind*. New York: McGraw-Hill, 1968.

Pierre Deffontaines. *Géographie et Religions*. Paris: Gallimard, 1948.

Et. Delaruelle. "Contribution à l'étude de la géographie religieuse du Sud-Ouest." *Revue Géographique des Pyrénées et du Sud-Ouest*. Vol. 14 (1943), pp. 48–78.

R. A. Donkin. "The Cistercian Order and the Settlement of Northern England." *Geographical Review.* Vol. 59 (1969), pp. 403–416.

Paul Fickeler. "Grundfragen der Religionsgeographie." *Erdkunde.* Vol. 1 (1947), pp. 121–144. (Translation appears in Philip L. Wagner and Marvin W. Mikesell (eds). *Readings in Cultural Geography.* Chicago: University of Chicago Press, 1962, pp. 94–117.)

Eric Fischer. "Religions: Their Distribution and Role in Political Geography." Chapter 12 in *Principles of Political Geography,* ed. Hans W. Weigert. New York: Appleton, 1957, pp. 405–439.

H. J. Fleure. "The Geographical Distribution of the Major Religions." *Bulletin de la Société Royale de Géographie d'Egypte.* Vol. 24 (1951), pp. 1–18.

Paul Girardin. "Les passages alpestres en liaison avec les abbayes, les pèlerinages et les saints de la montagne." *Geographica Helvetica.* Vol. 2 (1947), pp. 65–74.

Marcus W. Heslinga. *The Irish Border as a Cultural Divide: A Contribution to the Study of Regionalism in the British Isles.* Assen, Netherlands: van Gorcum, 1962.

Gastone Imbrighi. *Lineamenti di Geografia Religiosa.* Roma: Editrice Studium, 1961.

Erich Isaac. "The Act and the Covenant: the Impact of Religion on the Landscape." *Landscape.* Vol. 11, no. 2 (1961–62), pp. 12–17.

Erich Isaac. "Influence of Religion on the Spread of Citrus." *Science.* Vol. 129 (1959), pp. 179–186.

Erich Isaac. "Religion, Landscape, and Space." *Landscape.* Vol. 9, no. 2 (1959–60), pp. 14–18.

Erich Isaac. "Religious Geography and the Geography of Religion." In *Man and the Earth,* University of Colorado Studies, Series in Earth Sciences, No. 3. Boulder: University of Colorado Press, 1965, pp. 1–14.

James H. Johnson. "The Political Distinctiveness of Northern Ireland." *Geographical Review.* Vol. 52 (1962), pp. 78–91.

Emrys Jones. "Problems of Partition and Segregation in Northern Ireland." *Journal of Conflict Resolution.* Vol. 4 (1960), pp. 96–105.

Bernard Jouret. "L'influence du protestantisme dans l'economie douroise." *Revue Belge de Géographie.* Vol. 92 (1968), pp. 61–74.

Hans-Joachim Kress. *Die islamische Kulturepoche auf der iberischen Halbinsel: Eine historisch-kulturgeographische Studie.* Marburger Geographische Schriften, No. 43. Marburg, West Germany: Im Selbstverlag des Geographischen Institutes der Universität Marburg, 1968.

E. Lambert. "Le livre de Saint Jacques et les routes du pèlerinage de Compostelle." *Revue Géographique des Pyrénées et du Sud-Ouest.* Vol. 14 (1943), pp. 5–33.

Pierre Lasserre. "Lourdes: Étude géographique." *Revue Géographique des Pyrénées et du Sud-Ouest.* Vol. 1 (1930), pp. 5–41.

Hermann Lautensach. *Maurische Züge im geographischen Bild der Iberischen Halbinsel.* Bonner Geographische Abhandlungen, No. 28. Bonn, West Germany: F. Dümmler, 1960.

Gabriel Le Bras. "La géographie religieuse." *Annales d'Histoire Sociale.* Vol. 8 (1945), pp. 87–112.

Egon Lendl. "Zur religionsgeographischen Problematik des europäischen Südostens." *Verhandlungen des Deutschen Geographentages 1963.* Vol. 34 (1965), pp. 129–139.

Frederik van der Meer. *Atlas of the Early Christian World.* London: Nelson, 1958.

Alexander Melamid. "The Geographical Distribution of Communities in Cyprus," *Geographical Review.* Vol. 46 (1956), pp. 355–374.

R. R. Palmer. *A History of the Modern World*. New York: Knopf, 2nd ed., 1959.

Xavier de Planhol. "L'islam dans la physiognomie géographique de la Péninsule Iberique." *Revue Géographique des Pyrénées et du Sud-Ouest*. Vol. 33 (1962), pp. 274–281.

Josef Schmithüsen. "Der geistige Gehalt in der Kulturlandschaft." *Berichte zur Deutschen Landeskunde*. Vol. 12 (1954), pp. 185–188.

Anneliese Siebert. "Die Kirchenbauten in Niedersachsen." In *Der Baustoff als Gestaltender Faktor niedersächsischer Kulturlandschaften,* Forschungen zur Deutschen Landeskunde, No. 167. Bad Godesberg, West Germany: Bundesforschungsanstalt für Landeskunde und Raumordnung, 1969, pp. 101–122.

David E. Sopher. *The Geography of Religions*. Englewood Cliffs, N.J.: Prentice-Hall, 1967.

Joachim- F. Sprockhoff. "Religiöse Lebensformen und Gestalt der Lebensräume: über das Verhältnis von Religionsgeographie und Religionswissenschaft." *NUMEN (International Review for the History of Religions)*. Vol. 11 (1964), pp. 85–146.

Joachim- F. Sprockhoff. "Zur Problematik einer Religionsgeographie." *Mitteilungen der Geographischen Gesellschaft in München*. Vol. 48 (1963), pp. 107–121.

Kenneth G. Thompson. "Homicide and Suicide in Latin America and Europe: A Spatial Interpretation." *The Geographical Bulletin*. Vol. 3 (1971), pp. 49–57.

United Nations. *Demographic Yearbook. Annuaire Démographique*. New York: UN, 1966–1969.

Westermanns Grosser Atlas zur Weltgeschichte. Braunschweig, Germany: Georg Westermann, 1956.

CHAPTER SEVEN

Political geography

Political geography is concerned in part with the study of geographical factors, both environmental and cultural, which are at work in the formation, evolution, and disintegration of states and empires. A nation is the product of a complex interworking of numerous internal and external forces, and one task of the political geographer is to identify and evaluate these forces, to learn why states succeed or fail, why they expand or contract. In the study of Europe, political geography is important not only because the culture area is highly fragmented into numerous independent nations, but also because no other part of the earth has given birth to so many significant states, countries which have had major roles to play in the world as a whole. It is perhaps correct to designate the political pattern as the single most important one in the geographical study of Europe. It is, above all, areal diversity which attracts the attention of the geographer, and in this sense the complicated and often fluid political mosaic of Europe offers much potential reward for scholarly investigation. How and why have men created the pattern of political entities which occupy the European culture area, and what prospects for permanence does the present pattern hold?

7.1 THE TERRITORIAL IMPERATIVE

Zoologists have recognized that the behavior of many species of animals is in part motivated by a *territorial instinct,* a compulsion to possess and defend a home area, either as individuals or as members of a group. Such an instinct is found in animals as diverse as the mockingbird, lemur, crab, or prairie dog, and defense of territory generally results only from intrusion by another member or group of the same species. Animal territory often includes a core or heartland, which offers them protection and security, and an outer fringe or periphery where they meet the territorial challenges of rival groups. The territory provides in addition a sense of identity to the animal, satisfying a basic need for belonging. For these animals, the attachment to territory is a genetically determined form of behavior, a need perhaps even stronger than the sex drive.

An increasing number of social scientists, including some geographers, have come to believe that man is himself a territorial animal, influenced by the same instinctive drive that affects the tiger or robin. These scholars feel that human behavior is more a product of our animal background than our recently created civilization, and some, in particular Robert Ardrey, go so far as to describe our primeval African ancestors as territorially motivated predator apes, creatures who used their big brains and manual dexterity to fashion weapons long before tools. Ardrey has beautifully expressed this viewpoint in his two books, *African Genesis* (1961) and *The Territorial Imperative* (1966), both of which should be required reading for anyone concerned with political geography. The thesis of Ardrey's second publication is well expressed on the fifth page, where he suggests that "the dog barking at you from behind his master's fence acts for a motive indistinguishable from that of his master when the fence was built." The concept of instinctive human territoriality is surrounded by much controversy at present, for attachment to territory may be learned rather than instinctive, derived from intellect rather than genetics. The occurrence of territoriality in virtually every human group, however, suggests a genetically inherited trait.

Human territorialism can be seen in private fences or in the Berlin Wall, in cadastral patterns or international borders, in "No Trespassing" signs or the intense patriotism which flares when the homeland is invaded by an alien army, in the cheers for a local soccer team or the thundering "Sieg Heils" on the Nürnberg parade grounds. Quite simply, one of the most basic and primitive needs of man, whether learned or inherited, is to belong to a group and for that group to have its own piece of the earth, its own territory. On the smallest scale, the territorial need finds expression in the homestead and family, ranging upward through extended family, clan, and tribe, through neighborhood, community, district, and province, to reach man's ultimate territorial development—the state or nation. Membership in a group, the sense of belonging, can be based on blood relationship, or on the grander scale on common language, religion, historic experience, allegiance to ruler, and the like. It is this feeling of belonging, of community, which is at the root of nationalism, the raw material of patriotism.

Rarely, if ever, does a human group fail to control some sort of territory, be it a family's suburban yard, the domain of a street gang in New York's ghettos, the hilly refuge of a Celtic clan, or the expanses of a state or empire. A group denied territory on one scale seizes it on another, lower, order or else perishes. The Jews, dispersed from their Palestinian homeland by the Romans, were awarded a needed substitute in the ghetto, and those who escaped the ghetto typically were lost to the Jewish nation through assimilation into the locally dominant ethnic groups.

Learn this

7.2 CENTRIPETAL AND CENTRIFUGAL FORCES

States differ in the degree to which they are supported by the territorial imperative, and accordingly in their degree of unity. In short, it seems desirable that the state's population consists of only one "group" and that the national territory correspond to that group's territory. Inclusion of multiple rival groups can bring grief and possible destruction of the state.

Centripetal forces, in the jargon of the political geographer, are those which tend to draw a population together, to give them a sense of identity as a group. There is one unifying force which stands out above all others in any given state, and this is referred to as its *raison d'être,* its "reason for being." For one state the *raison d'être* may be language, for another religion, for still another allegiance to a popular royal family, and so on. *Centrifugal* forces, in contrast, are those which result from those diversities and contrasts within a state which work to prevent unity. To survive, every nation must obtain a favorable balance of forces, so that the centripetal outweigh the centrifugal.

LANGUAGE

One of the most crucial internal forces in Europe is that of language. National unity tends to be fostered and territorialism best served by linguistic homogeneity of the population, and instability and disruption generally result if more than one language is spoken in the state. In the last several centuries, mainly since the Napoleonic wars, language and nationality have become very closely identified in Europe. It was not always so. The traditional states of Europe extended their borders with no regard to the speech or other cultural traits of the population of annexed territories. A Babel on the Danube was created in the great Austro–Hungarian Empire, where speakers of German, Hungarian, Polish, Czech, Italian, Slovenian, Romanian, Slovakian, and other tongues shared citizenship. The leaders of France long looked to the German-populated Rhine as a "natural" eastern border, disregarding the speech of the people involved, and the German Empire willingly incorporated large Polish areas. England ignored the Celtic claim to political independence, and Russia annexed hundreds of minority groups. With the rise of linguistic nationalism in the nineteenth and twentieth centuries, the map of Europe was gradually modified so that a reasonably close correspondence between nations and languages was achieved, with some notable exceptions. Often it was the people rather than the border which was moved, as was described in the earlier discussion of forced population transfers.

Political geographers and political scientists use the term *nation-state* to describe a country bound together by a cultural trait such as language. A "nation" is a cohesive group of people who share certain traits or beliefs, while a "state" is the organized areal entity which exists as a political expression of the nation. The nation-state is of European origin, but has spread to much of the world in the twentieth century. This idea, which holds that each "nation" has a right to political independence, has brought Europe and the world far more grief than benefit. The numerous forced population transfers of the twentieth century can nearly all be attributed to the nation-state concept, as can several wars. It is one gift of Europe to the world which would have better remained ungiven.

At the present time, language serves as the principal centripetal force in many, if not most, European nations. Major disruptions, or centrifugal forces, have typified polyglot states such as Belgium, where Germanic Flemings vie with French Walloons for dominance; Spain, where Castillians seek to continue their long domination of Catalonians, Galicians, and Basques; and prewar Czechoslovakia, where Czechs and Sudeten Germans were at odds. The large majority of border disputes between nations in recent European history have centered on the matter of linguistic minorities, including the arguments and conflicts over the Alsace-Lorraine, South Tirol, Polish Corridor, and Klagenfurt Basin.

RELIGION

In spite of the recent decline in the significance of religion among most Europeans, the church remains an important political force in many nations. It is desirable, in the interest of national unity, that all or most of the population belong to a single church, for religious diversity can also act as a major centrifugal force. As was pointed out earlier, the recent unrest in Northern Ireland is largely a result of the fact that Catholicism is the only real basis of Irish nationalism, the only survivor of the Celtic culture trinity of language, clans, and religion. As a consequence, Catholics living in Northern Ireland, a part of the United Kingdom, feel deprived of their desired nationhood (Figure 6.9). Even in West Germany, where Christianity is in marked decline, care has been taken since 1949 to balance the governmental offices of chancellor and president between Catholics and Protestants. When the Rhinelander Catholic Konrad Adenauer was chancellor, the Protestant Theodor Heuss occupied the presidency, a tradition which has been continued.

For some European nations, the church serves as the cornerstone of nationalism. This is true not only of the Republic of Ireland, but also of Catholic Belgium, and to a lesser extent of Poland, Greece, Spain, and Italy. Historically, religious minority groups were rooted out as viciously as linguistic minorities have been in the twentieth century. Catholic France expelled or massacred the Calvinist Huguenots, and the same fate befell the Salzburg Protestants in a Catholic German land. Relatively few European states were able to combine successfully peoples of different religious faith, and in some instances where this centrifugal force was overcome, toleration came only after a long, bitter struggle, as in the Thirty Years' War in seventeenth-century Germany. The failure of the Protestant-dominated United Kingdom and the Netherlands to achieve harmony with Catholic minorities led to the eventual secession of Irish and Flemings, respectively. Further, the unification of Germany in 1871 came only when the main champion of German Catholicism, Austria, was defeated and excluded from the union.

RACE

Rarely have racially diverse states escaped the internal unrest or subjugation which typically results from such mixture. Europe has been freer of such strife than most parts of the world, for the simple reason of its almost purely Caucasian population. The "racial" issue raised by Nazis was in reality religious and cultural in character, for the Jews were just as much caucasoid as their German persecutors, and some were even of the Nordic subrace. In contrast to racially troubled states such as Kenya, the Republic of South Africa, the Sudan, and the United States, European nations have little or no problem. Only where sizable populations of alien races have been allowed to immigrate in recent times, as in the United Kingdom, does the potential for racially based political disturbance exist.

COMMON HISTORICAL EXPERIENCES

Patriotism derives much of its vital force from past experiences shared by the members of a group and their ancestors. The common memory of a war of independence, as in Greece and Switzerland; the repulsion of alien invaders, as in France in World War I or the Soviet Union in World War II; and the deeds of great national heroes such as Wilhelm Tell, Jeanne d'Arc, and El Cid, all serve the cause of group cohesiveness and, consequently, national unity. In fact, the memory need not be a happy one to bind a people together. Defeats and long periods of subjugation, the fate of the Poles, Balts, and Czechs, may well strengthen nationalism and the sense of group identity. Nor need the heroes be real, for mythical deeds and fictional personages can stimulate national feeling just as well as flesh-and-blood heroes. It matters little whether Jeanne d'Arc was a peasant girl burned at the stake or, as some have suggested, a noblewoman participating in a plot to dupe the French peasantry into supporting the crown in a long struggle against the English. What is of consequence is that the French believed in her humble origins, heroism, and martyrdom.

Ideally, a people should feel that the state exists because they or their ancestors willfully brought about its establishment and defended it against alien forces. Where such sentiment is lacking, in states created by outside forces rather than by the member population, nationalism is generally weak and a *raison d'être* absent. East Germany, created by the Soviet Union as part of a scheme to keep Germany fragmented and weak, lacks much of the raw material from which nationalism is made.

POLITICAL-ECONOMIC PHILOSOPHY

No great divergences in political and economic philosophy should exist within the population of a state, at least not with numerous advocates of rival ideologies. A people should preferably be fairly united in their desire for democracy, monarchy, theocracy, or dictatorship, for free enterprise, socialism, or communism. Their preference need not be the actual system presently in power in the state, for national unity can also be promoted by a universal desire for change.

When major rival political-economic factions exist within a state, the resulting instability leads in extreme cases to secession, civil war, and destruction of the state. Spain was threatened with permanent fragmentation in the Spanish civil war of the 1930s, in which the Loyalists fought against the forces of Franco. Had one of these groups not gained the upper hand, there might well be two Spanish states today.

Germany was less fortunate than Spain, for it has been imprinted with a political-economic dualism maintained by outside forces. If, through some unexpected letup in the East–West power struggle, it should become possible for the two Germanies to reunite, major problems might result. A quarter of a century of education under communism and nondemocratic rule in East Germany may well have produced a population basically unsympathetic to the form of government and economy in West Germany. In such an event, reunification might founder on disagreements among the Germans themselves.

STANDARD OF LIVING

If one sizable part of a population has a much lower standard of living than another part, and particularly if these two economic factions reside in separate parts of a state, the national unity may be adversely affected. Italy has traditionally been characterized by a prosperous, industrial north and a rural, poverty-stricken south, a contrast which can be traced back to the Middle Ages. Fortunately, unrestricted migration of poor southerners to the north has been possible in modern times, minimizing tension which might otherwise have gotten out of hand. Southerners were thereby allowed access to a higher living standard. In addition, the Italian government has taken great pains to attempt industrialization of the backward Mezzogiorno—the south—for the purpose of reducing poverty there. Similarly, Czechoslovakia combines backward, underdeveloped Slovensko in the east with urban, industrial České (Bohemia) and Morava in the west, a split further widened by linguistic differences.

CORE AREAS AND CAPITAL CITIES

Many states, including the large majority of surviving European nations, originated in small nuclear or core areas and grew outward over the centuries into surrounding territory (Figure 7.1). Such core areas generally possessed some measure of natural defense against the encroachments of rival political entities, a fairly dense population, at least in comparison to surrounding regions, and a prosperous agricultural economy which produced a surplus capable of supporting a sizable military establishment. Perhaps most important of all, the core area required a government headed by ambitious leaders skilled in the military and diplomatic arts, men bent on territorial aggrandizement. During the process of accretion, the core often retained its status as the single most important area in the state, housing the capital city and the cultural and economic heart of the nation.

The core area may be roughly centered in the national territory, or, if growth occurred mainly in one direction, it may be peripheral. Paris and the Île de France, the capital and core area of the French state, are nearly in the middle of France, but Wessex, the nucleus of the United Kingdom, is eccentric. Spain also has a peripheral core, as does Italy, if Piemonte rather than Roma is considered to be the nucleus of Italian unification. In rare instances, all or part of the core of a state was later lost to a neighboring nation through territorial forfeiture, as happened to Portugal and West Germany. Southern Galicia, part of the nucleus of Portuguese expansion southward against the retreating Moors, was later lost to León and eventually Castillian Spain, though the inhabitants of the old core have retained their Portuguese speech to the present day. The Federal Republic of Germany was deprived of contact with the old Brandenburg core through the ill fortunes of war.

The typical core area contains the capital of the state, which is sometimes a "primate city" containing the largest population and greatest single concentration of economic and cultural functions. Paris, Moskva, and Athínai are such core capitals enjoying national urban primacy. Not infrequently, however, the capital was removed from the original core, a relocation prompted by any one of several factors. In some instances, the political headquarters were relocated to the frontier of

Figure 7.1 Core areas of modern European states. (In part after Pounds, Ball, and McManis.)

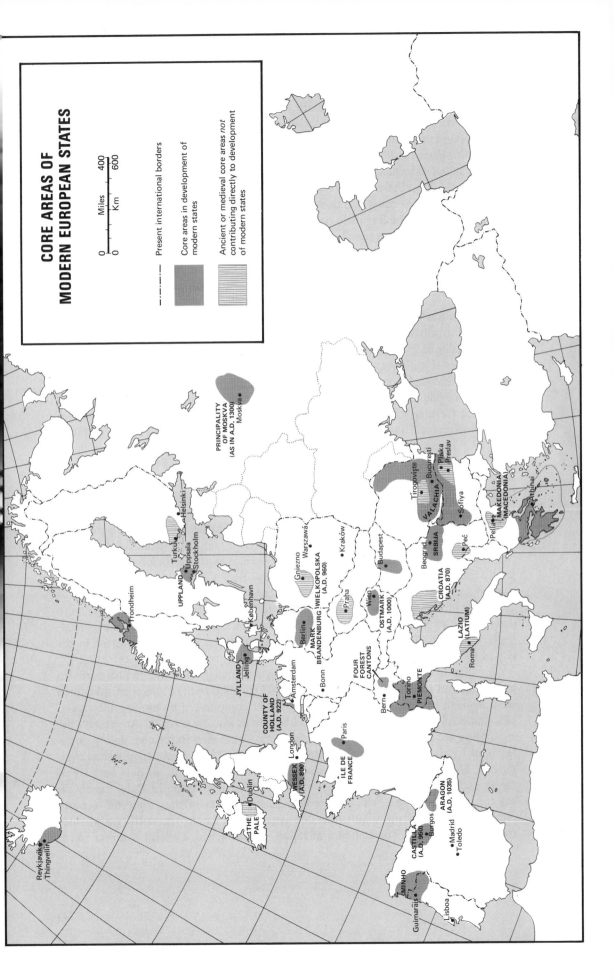

CORE AREAS OF MODERN EUROPEAN STATES

Miles
0   400
0   600
Km

----- Present international borders

Core areas in development of modern states

Ancient or medieval core areas *not* contributing directly to development of modern states

PRINCIPALITY OF MOSKVA (AS IN A.D. 1300)
Moskva●

Helsinki●
Turku●
Uppsala●
Stockholm●
UPPLAND

Trondheim●

Warszawá●
Gniezno●
WIELKOPOLSKA (A.D. 960)
Kraków●

Praha●
Wien●
Budapest●

København●

Jelling●
JYLLAND

Berlin●
MARK BRANDENBURG

Bonn●
Amsterdam●
COUNTY OF HOLLAND (A.D. 922)

FOUR FOREST CANTONS
Bern●

OSTMARK (A.D. 1000)

Tîrgoviște●
Bucureşti●
Pliska●
Preslav●
VALACHIA
Sofiya●

Beograd●
SRBIJA
Peć●

Pella●
MAKEDONIA (MACEDONIA)
Athinai●

CROATIA (A.D. 870)

LAZIO (LATIUM)
Roma●

Torino●
PIEMONTE

London●
WESSEX (A.D. 800)

Dublin●
THE PALE

Paris●
ÎLE DE FRANCE

ARAGON (A.D. 1035)
Burgos●
CASTILLA (A.D. 950)
Madrid●
Toledo●

MINHO
Guimarãis●
Lisboa●

Reykjavík●
Thingvellir●

most active territorial expansion, in which case it is referred to as a *forward-thrust* capital. Sofiya succeeded earlier, more eastern capitals with Bulgarian expansion south and west at the expense of the Turks, while Lisboa and Toledo displaced northern capitals as the Portuguese and Spanish pushed the Moors southward in Iberia. Peripheral St. Petersburg, now Leningrad, temporarily replaced Moskva as the Russian capital when the czars desired closer cultural contacts with Europe, and Oslo replaced Trondheim in Norway as a result of its greater proximity to Sweden and Denmark, which ruled and dominated Norway for many centuries. Switzerland selected Bern, near the linguistic border between German and French, as its capital rather than allowing it to remain in the area of Lake Luzern (Vierwaldstättersee), where the state had its origin. Those core areas which have lost their function as political focus of the state rarely retain any present significance. In other cases, the capital was moved as a response to territorial loss, as occurred in Poland and West Germany.

States which grew up around core areas tend to be more stable than those created arbitrarily at one time to fill a preexistent territorial void, particularly if the core has retained its vitality and dominance. Instability can result if states have no core area, or if multiple, competing cores are present. In the former category are Belgium, Albania, Luxembourg, and West Germany, all born full-grown as children of the power politics of outside forces. The Federal Republic of Germany, deprived of the old German core in Brandenburg, sought out the small university town of Bonn as its capital, thereby overcoming the rivalry of München, Frankfurt, Hamburg, and other major cities which had sought the honor. As a consequence, however, West Germany lacks the cohesive force provided by a core area, though to some extent the great Ruhr industrial district just north of Bonn serves this function.

Competing core areas can prove even more disruptive than the complete absence of one. Historically, such a conflict arose in the German lands between Berlin, in the Prussian nucleus, and Wien, the core-area capital of Austria. These two German powers battled repeatedly over several centuries before the issue was finally decided in 1866 in favor of Prussia and Berlin, but significantly, the Prussians chose to exclude Austria and its rival core area from the unified Germany of 1871. When Hitler annexed Austria to the Reich in 1938, he took great pains to downgrade the political importance of Wien, both because of its potential as a challenger of Berlin and because the Führer had suffered rejection as an artist in the city in his Austrian youth.

Spain is plagued by the regionalism associated with two major northern medieval cores in Aragon (Cataluña) and Old Castilla, both of which are identified with linguistic groups. The situation was further complicated by moving the capital city southward to Toledo and finally Madrid, both in New Castilla. At present, the most bitter competition is perhaps that between Catalonian Barcelona, with a population of 1,650,000, and Castillian Madrid, with 2,450,000 inhabitants. As the capital city, Madrid never quite succeeded in dominating the state, in part because of the sparse population and low productivity of its surroundings. In Italy, the classical core area of Roma, which played no role whatever in the nineteenth-century creation of the modern Italian state, coexists with Piemonte, the northern province from which the drive for Italian unification was launched. Perhaps the attainment of industrial leadership by Piemonte and adjacent Lombardia in the present century is of long-term future significance.

POPULATION DISTRIBUTION

The manner in which the inhabitants of a state are distributed through the national territory can influence political stability. Ideally, people should be clustered in the interior, including the core area, and the boundary zones should have sparse population or be totally devoid of inhabitants. Such a pattern is present in Italy, where the thinly settled Alps parallel the northern border, and also in western Czechoslovakia, where there is a hilly rimland. Instability is encouraged when boundary areas contain more people than the interior, a distribution which can cause the border population to develop closer ties with areas outside the state. Spain is plagued by such peripheral clustering, complicated by linguistic diversity, and France faces a similar, though less serious, problem (Figure 3.5).

THE ROLE OF ENVIRONMENTAL PATTERNS

During the period in which most European states developed, prior to the advent of modern methods of warfare, various physical environmental factors traditionally influenced political viability. Those states which enjoyed some sort of natural protection, such as surrounding mountain ranges, border forests or marshes, insularity, and outward-facing cuestas or escarpments, were more likely to survive. Political geographers call these natural strongholds *folk-fortresses*. France, with a cuesta-ringed core area in the Paris Basin and outer walls of defense in mountains such as the Pyrenees, Alps, Jura, Vosges, and Ardennes, was splendidly equipped by nature for self-protection, as was the original nucleus of Switzerland, which lies astride the Alpine range. The British, who pride themselves on the successful repulsion of all invasion attempts for the last 900 years, owe their achievement in no small part to the natural moat formed by the English Channel. Insularity also was partially responsible for the independence of Ireland and Iceland. The Dutch have on occasion used their precarious sunken location to defensive advantage, allowing the waters of river and sea to flood polders and block the path of invaders. In 1574, the people of the city of Leiden opened the dikes to permit a Dutch naval fleet to sail over the flooded polders and attack Spaniards who were besieging the city. Peninsular location aided the formation of Italy, Spain, and Greece by providing a natural framework for territorial expansion, though such sites rarely offered any defensive advantage.

In antiquity, the role of physical features in the defense of states was even greater. A numerically inferior Greek force of Spartans was able to hold back temporarily the huge Persian army in 480 B.C. at Thermopílai, a narrow mountain pass on the easiest land route between north and south in Greece. Almost exactly two centuries later, Greeks blocked invading Gauls at the same pass for several months.

Just as frequently, the environment hindered the success of states. The fate of Poland might have been much happier had that state not been situated on the expanses of the North European Plain, largely unprotected by terrain from the hostile Germans and Russians on either side. Marshes did at one time offer natural defense to the Poles, but these were eventually colonized and drained by Germanic settlers. In the east, the great Pripyat Marsh provided some protection, but invasion routes lay both to its north and south.

While physical barriers in border areas are desirable for defensive reasons, the same barriers in the interior of a state can prove disruptive. Where mountain ranges, deserts, or the like cut through the heart of a nation, the effect can be definitely centrifugal. Romania, based in the Valachian Plain, is cut in half by the thinly settled Carpathian Range, and perhaps as a consequence, found it difficult to acquire and retain sovereignty over Romanian-populated districts beyond the mountains in the Hungarian Basin. The same refuge range which housed the Romanian folk in the difficult times after the fall of the Roman Empire now serves to divide the nation. Similarly, Spain's problems of internal disunity can be laid partly to the physical barriers between the mountain-rimmed interior Meseta basins of Castilla and the peripheral lowlands. Only a tradition of seamanship allowed the Norwegians to unify the many tiny fjord-head clusters of population separated by the intervening Kjölen Range.

DISTRIBUTION OF NATIONAL TERRITORY

National cohesiveness is promoted by compactness of the state territory. Theoretically, the most desirable shape for a nation is a circle or hexagon focused on a central core area. France and Romania came closer to achieving this ideal model pattern than most other states in the world, for the various apexes of French territory almost perfectly define a circle (Figure 7.2), and Romania's boundaries actually exhibit curvature of a circular character. Poland, Spain, and Hungary also have suitable distribution of national territory.

Instability can be produced by one of several unfavorable territorial patterns, in particular the presence of *enclaves* or *exclaves*. An enclave is a district completely surrounded by a given state but not ruled by it. Within Italy, the Vatican City and San Marino, the latter an independent mountaintop state, are enclaves, as is West Berlin from the viewpoint of the German Democratic Republic (East Germany). An enclave may be either self-governing or the possession of a neighboring state. Even less desirable are those states composed of many separate pieces of territory, including one main area housing the capital and one or more exclaves, a circumstance well illustrated by the independent German states of Braunschweig and Württemberg in the late eighteenth century (Figure 7.3). More recently, West Berlin has developed as an exclave of West Germany, presenting a particularly unstable situation, since the intervening territory which lies between Berlin and the Federal Republic is controlled by a hostile state, Russian-dominated East Germany. West Berlin, then, is an exclave to West Germany and an enclave to East Germany. Similar instability existed between the two world wars, when German-ruled East Prussia was separated from the main body of the nation by the intervening Polish Corridor.

Even if the national territory is in a unit block, difficulties can arise if the

Figure 7.2   The development of France. Growth of the royal domain from the Île de France core area bore only a superficial relationship to the pattern of escarpments. Further, the growth was not continuous, for many areas were gained, only to be lost again. As is shown, gains in the east and south between 1276 and 1328 were partially offset by losses in the north and west. Even parts of the Île de France were later lost. Note the roughly circular shape of modern France. (After Westermann.)

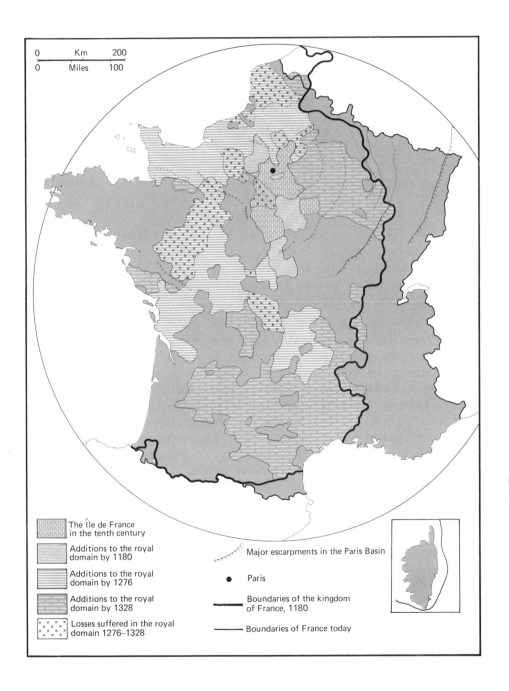

0 Km 200	
0 Miles 100	

The Île de France
in the tenth century

Additions to the royal
domain by 1180

Additions to the royal
domain by 1276

Additions to the royal
domain by 1328

Losses suffered in the royal
domain 1276–1328

Major escarpments in the Paris Basin

●   Paris

Boundaries of the kingdom
of France, 1180

Boundaries of France today

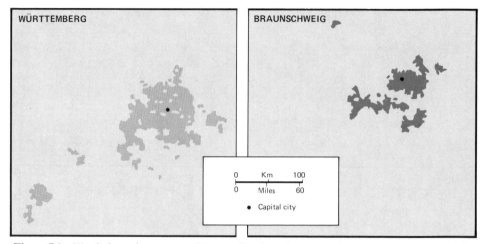

Figure 7.3 The independent states of Braunschweig and Württemberg, 1789. These two fully independent states, largely within what is today West Germany, illustrate unsatisfactory distribution of national territory. Württemberg was riddled with fourteen sizable enclaves, including several on the outskirts of its capital, Stuttgart, and included seventeen exclaves beyond the main body of territory. Braunschweig was composed of three main blocks of territory and a number of small exclaves, one of which was over 100 kilometers (60 miles) removed from the rest of the state. Neither of these states survives today.

shape is awkward. Long, narrow shoestring states such as Norway and Czechoslovakia can experience problems in holding such far-flung territory together. Indeed, the Czechoslovakians, in fifty years of existence as a state, have suffered temporary loss of Slovensko and permanent forfeiture of Ruthenia in the east, losses which may in some measure have been facilitated by the distribution of national territory.

STRENGTH AND POPULARITY OF THE CENTRAL GOVERNMENT

Often, disruptive internal forces can be overcome by strong central governments, sometimes involving dictatorship of one kind or another. East Germany, lacking any real national cement, has been perpetuated through little else than a Soviet-backed totalitarian regime, and Spain's varied ethnic groups have been effectively controlled in the Franco dictatorship. Popularity can be an effective substitute for centralized power, though it is not desirable to place too much of the burden of preserving national unity on a single personality. The British royal family has been able to preserve at least a figurehead status because of its stabilizing ceremonial effect on the government of the United Kingdom.

These, then, are the more important centripetal and centrifugal forces at work within states, lending stability or promoting ruin. Obviously, no state is blessed with all unifying forces. It is enough to obtain a favorable balance, with the factors promoting unity outweighing those causing disruption. The very existence of a state on the political map of Europe indicates that, for the time being at least, such a favorable balance, however precarious, has been found. In some instances, a single viable *raison d'être* is sufficient to overcome many divisive forces, and the same is true of a very powerful central government.

However, even the soundest internal structure does not guarantee the survival of a state. If a people are in some important respect unable to cope with external affairs, their state can perish, regardless of the strength of nationalistic sentiment.

7.3 EXTERNAL FACTORS

STRATEGIC TERRITORIAL RELATIONSHIPS

The cause of peace and political stability is promoted, of course, by mutual recognition or respect of international borders and the absence of desire for territorial expansion on the part of all states. Regrettably, even a brief glance through any text on European history will reveal repeated militaristic violations of sovereignty and persistent attempts to enlarge the areal extent of states. Few peoples of Europe have not at least attempted to grab territory from neighboring states at one time or another.

Consequently, a state must gain one of two objectives to ensure its survival. It should be able to support a military force capable of protecting it by combining its human and natural resources against any potential rival. The effort to obtain such defensive power was traditionally greatly aided by the presence of a folk-fortress and was also directly related to the size of the population and productivity of the economy. Perhaps the most desirable situation is for a state to be surrounded by militarily impotent peoples, as in the Middle Ages, when some empires were flanked by *marches* or marchlands (German *Mark*), zones in which they met the challenge of outside forces without having to fight on home soil. The Frankish Empire was bordered by the Spanish March south of the Pyrenees, the Breton March in the west, and a whole series of marches in the Slavic fringes of the east. The modern equivalent of the march is the buffer state, and many small European nations owe their very existence to such a function. It is unlikely that Luxembourg, a buffer between Germany and France, could have survived under any other circumstances, and the same is true of Belgium and the Netherlands.

If for some reason the state is unable to provide its own defense, then it becomes essential to form favorable alliances with other states facing a common outside threat. Failure to be either militarily self-reliant or to form viable alliances places the state at the mercy of ambitious neighbors, and the history books are littered with the almost-forgotten names of numerous states which have disappeared from the map. The three Baltic states of Estonia, Latvia, and Lithuania, freed from Russian rule after World War I, were too small to defend themselves and unable or unwilling to form protective alliances, and as a result, their independence lasted only two decades. Germany, through military aggression, created more enemies than she could cope with, leading to the destruction of national unity in 1945.

ECONOMIC RELATIONSHIPS

No state is entirely self-sufficient in an economic sense, free from the necessity to exchange goods and commodities with other parts of the world. A viable trade pattern must be set up and maintained if the nation itself is to survive. In the era of medieval city-states, the interruption of trade ties with the hinterland through siege was often sufficient to destroy the independence of the city. Similarly, a naval blockade brought severe hardship to Germany in World War I.

Since the oceans of the world are the single greatest avenues of trade, a free and open access to the sea becomes crucial for all nations. Landlocked states are at a distinct disadvantage in this respect, which perhaps helps explain why very few of the surviving nations of Europe lack a seacoast.

In an economic as well as a military sense, extremely small size is a hindrance to national survival. Miniature states generally must either form economic unions with adjacent, larger states, as Luxembourg did, first with Belgium and the Netherlands and later as a member of the Common Market, or they must develop some economic curiosity to help preserve solvency. In the latter category would be the gambling casino of Monaco, the smuggling and tax-free markets of Andorra, and the postage stamp sales of San Marino and Liechtenstein.

7.4 DEVELOPMENT AND SURVIVAL OF SELECTED EUROPEAN STATES

With these considerations of centrifugal and centripetal forces, of strategic and economic external relationships as a background, the political geography of selected individual European states can be studied, with emphasis on the establishment and maintenance of their viability.

FRANCE

France, one of the oldest and most viable of the European states, possesses a great preponderance of centripetal forces. In spite of its linguistic and religious links to the Mediterranean, France owes both its origin and name to a Germanic tribe, the Franks, who spread westward with the fall of the Roman Empire. Major statebuilding occurred following the invasion, culminating in the great Frankish Empire, which encompassed not only most of modern France, but also northern Italy, Western Germany, and the Low Country. The empire was split into three parts in A.D. 843, of which the westernmost became the basis of the present French state. It included the Basin of Aquitaine, most of the Paris Basin, and the Massif Central, but not the Rhône–Saône Corridor or any of the Rhine drainage. Technically, the unity of France has remained undisturbed for over a thousand years to the present, but in actuality the kingdom of the West Franks fell immediately after 843 into feudal disunity. Local lords paid only lip service to the king and governed their small domains as fully independent rulers. The kingship was largely honorary and the unity of France fictional.

In 987 the empty title of king was passed to the Capets, whose feudal domain was concentrated in a small strip of territory in the heart of the Paris Basin, a domain destined to become the Île de France, the core area of a strongly unified French state (Figure 7.3). The kingship brought with it no additional territory, and the area actually ruled by the Capets remained initially the Île de France. However, partly because the Capet domain possessed greater wealth and a denser population than surrounding districts, and also because this family proved remarkably ambitious, adept, and lucky, they were able to expand the *domaine royale,* spreading their control over much of northern France. To be sure, the physical framework of the Paris Basin, typified by the concentric circles of outward-facing cuestas, offered a splendid natural setting for expansion from the Île de France core, but the dynamic force was human ambition. Furthermore, the Île de France fell short of occupying all of the smallest saucer in the Paris Basin, and subsequent growth of the state only very crudely conformed to the cuesta rims. Expansion was not steady, for there were both pauses and setbacks, but by the late 1200s much of the Paris Basin had become part of the royal domain. The rich district of Champagne was acquired by a most fortunate marriage, and other regions were added through force.

This nuclear French state within the loosely knit kingdom became involved in two great conflicts to expand beyond the Paris Basin. The first of these was the dreadful Hundred Years' War, fought in the 1300s and 1400s against the English, who ruled Normandie and Aquitaine, blocking French expansion to the Atlantic shore. The conflict not only served to expel the English, who were able to retain only the small coastal islands of Jersey and Guernsey, but also provided the first national hero, Jeanne d'Arc. A second great struggle pitted the French kings against the powerful state of Bourgogne, which had arisen to the east of modern France in the 1300s and controlled the important Rhône–Saône Corridor between the Paris Basin and Mediterranean lands to the south. The French rulers defeated Bourgogne in the 1500s and annexed the last remnants of it in the following century. By the year 1700, France had acquired essentially its present borders.

The numerous forces of unity operating within the French state include language, religion, the presence of a dominant core area, compactness of the national territory, a proud historical and cultural tradition, and a favorable terrain pattern which provides both natural borders and a folk-fortress. The close areal correspondence between France and the French language must be regarded as a remarkable historic accident, for the kings of France paid little or no attention to the speech of areas they sought to annex. Some minority linguistic groups were brought into the state, but almost without exception they were small and had no powerful linguistic relatives beyond France's borders who might have challenged the French rule. The Celtic Bretons of hilly Bretagne, annexed in 1491, received no help from their beleaguered brethren in the British Isles, nor did the Basques of French Navarre or the Catalonians of Roussillon obtain aid from Iberian kinsmen. The Italian-speaking residents of Corse and the Riviera too long lacked a unified Italy to champion their cause, and there was no powerful state in Flanders to which the French-ruled Flemings around Dunkerque could look for aid. In fact, the only annexation of a linguistic minority which the French ever had cause to regret involved the German-speaking population of Alsace-Lorraine (Elsass-Lothringen). A powerful, unified German nation has twice seized these provinces since 1870, and over the past century there have been four transfers of sovereignty. Germany has ruled the Alsace-Lorraine for about half of the last hundred years, though France is presently again in control.

Divisive forces are few and weak. A dialect difference, one symptom of regional contrast between a partially Germanized north and a more purely Roman-Mediterranean south, has largely been overcome. Religious conflict flared for a time, but it was resolved through the slaughter and emigration of Calvinist Huguenots.

Much of French stability is based on pride in the rich culture associated with the language, a culture rivaled by few others in quality and consistent productivity. Added to this is the body of common historical memories, reaching from the exploits of Jeanne d'Arc through the Revolution, the era of Napoleonic greatness, and the creation of a far-flung empire.

In sum, France is as stable a state as exists in the world, and there are no significant factors of disunity present. This nation has proven numerous times over the past century that it can survive even the weakest, most mediocre, and ephemeral central governments. A strong ruler such as Charles de Gaulle or Napoleon is simply not needed.

The traditional external threats to France came from the United Kingdom and Germany, which the French statesmen countered by forming alliances with Russia and the United States. Through a major blunder in German foreign policy in the early part of the present century, the traditional enmity between Britain and France was replaced by an alliance, leaving an isolated Germany as the only significant French foe. The German threat was apparently permanently removed after World War II, and today France is not endangered by outside forces.

THE UNITED KINGDOM

There are many similarities between France and the United Kingdom. Both are very old, stable political entities, and both were founded by the descendants of Germanic folk who invaded during the period of Roman collapse. The two states both bear Germanic names, for England, or "Angle-Land," commemorates one of the invading tribes. Jutes and Saxons as well as Angles settled Great Britain, and they were followed later by Norsemen and Danes.

A number of independent feudal states arose among the Germanic settlers, one of which, Wessex (Figure 7.1), or the land of the "western Saxons," proved to be a unifier, capitalizing on the greater freedom from Viking raids provided by its western location. London did not at first serve as the capital of the Kingdom of Wessex, for it lay to the east in Middlesex and was ruled by the Danes for a period in the 800s. Indeed, the Danes once controlled all of England north and east of the ancient Roman road called Watling Street, which runs northwest from London.

The Saxon kings of Wessex, in addition to extending their rule over other Germanic-settled areas, began what was to be the great territorial task of England —the subjugation of the Celts in their highland refuges. Cornwall, the first of the refuges to fall, was conquered by Wessex in the 800s. The Norman ruler William seized the Saxon kingdom in 1066, and he and succeeding monarchs of various royal families continued the drive against the Celts. The end of major resistance in Wales occurred in the 1530s, and the Highland Scots were finally and decisively crushed on the moor at Culloden in 1746. The Irish, though subjugated after many centuries of war, regained their independence in 1922.

The only significant centrifugal force in the United Kingdom has been the discontentment of the Celtic minorities, peoples who unwillingly became English citizens. Gradual assimilation has weakened Celtic nationalism over the centuries, particularly in Cornwall and Scotland. The three culture traits which distinguished the Scots—Gaelic, Catholicism, and the clans—have just about disappeared. The Welsh, somewhat belatedly, are suffering the same fate. Only the Irish, who clung to their Catholicism, proved impossible to assimiliate, and this resistance necessitated, as one scholar put it, the English "regurgitation of the indigestible Irish stew."

The forces of unity are many and varied: a proud history, including nine centuries without an invasion and the building of the greatest empire ever known to man; major achievements in science and literature within the unifying framework of the English langauge; and the figurehead monarchy, a reminder of past glory and greatness. All contribute to the stability of the United Kingdom. The success of the nation has also been furthered by the insular folk-fortress and the presence of a core area and primate city. Assimilation and secession have solved the Celtic minority problem, except in Northern Ireland, where Catholics and Protestants repeatedly verge on civil war.

GERMANY

Unlike the United Kingdom and France, Germany is one of the newer unified states of Europe, or at least it was until its fragmentation in 1945. Still, its origin could have been much the same as that of France, for both arose from the division of the Frankish Empire in A.D. 843. The western Frankish lands, as described, evolved into the French state, while the eastern part of the old empire, an area encompassing approximately the area of the present Federal Republic of Germany, became the Holy Roman or German Empire. In France, however, one royal family expanded its holdings to create a firmly unified state, while in the Holy Roman Empire, a brief early period of unity under the Saxon kings soon gave way to feudal disunity, which grew more intense over the centuries and produced some 300 separate independent states by the 1600s. The title of German emperor became as empty and devoid of authority as the original kingship of France. Unity may have been retarded by the complex pattern of terrain in Germany, with many separate basins, valleys, and intervening hill districts. Certainly no equivalent of the Paris Basin was present, and the German lands are fragmented by landform divisions. It seems more plausible, however, to attribute the persistent disunity to the absence of emperors who desired more than ceremonial rule or were competent enough to achieve a higher goal. Instead, the attention of the best of the German emperors was attracted southward to Italy, where they sought control of Roma, or to the Crusades, away from concerns at home.

The original territorial base of the Holy Roman Empire lay in "original Germany" or *Urdeutschland,* the area which had retained its German population during the great westward movements associated with the Migration of Peoples between A.D. 400 and 800. During the Middle Ages, from about 800 to 1400, German agricultural pioneers pushed back to the east, beyond the Elbe–Saale–Inn–Salzach line into Slavic lands, creating a large new zone of German-speaking peoples (Figure 7.4). This "colonial Germany" was centered in two major lobes of eastward expansion, the North German Plain and the Danube Valley–Eastern Alpine area.

While *Urdeutschland* grew ever more fragmented, powerful states arose in each of the eastern lobes in colonial Germany. Sandy-soiled Brandenburg, covered with pine forests and centered on the insignificant Slavic fishing village of Berlin, originated as an imperial eastern march or *Mark* on the North German Plain, and is probably as unlikely a core area as could be found in all of Europe. Yet once Brandenburg was granted to the ambitious Hohenzollern family, it became equal and eventually superior to the other states of the empire. Brandenburg evolved into the Kingdom of Prussia, lord of colonial Germany in the plains of the north. In no small part, the Prussian success was a consequence of its toleration of religious minorities, which attracted numerous Huguenots, Flemings, Salzburgers, and Anabaptists, who brought needed agricultural and industrial skills to the initially backward state. By 1800, fully one-third of the Prussian population was descended from immigrants who had come to seek freedom, to escape persecution in France, Austria, and other lands.

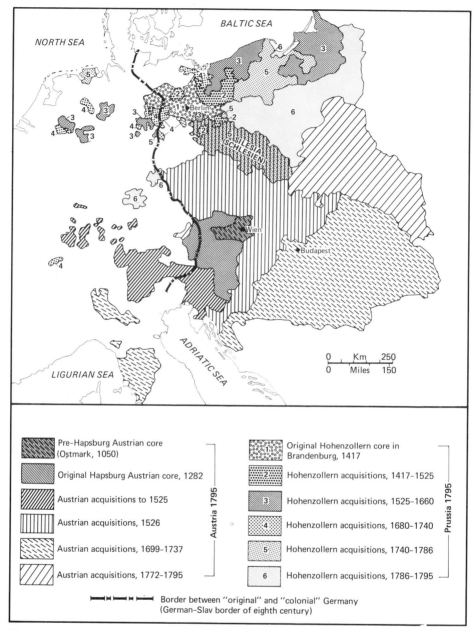

Figure 7.4 The growth of Prussia and Austria, to 1795. Both of the great German states arose in "colonial" eastern Germany, east of the old German–Slav border, and most of their territorial expansion occurred there. However, Prussia and Austria established footholds in "original" Germany and competed for influence there, a competition finally won by Prussia in the 1800s. In the east, only Schlesien was the scene of Prussian–Austrian conflict.

A similar political development occurred in the southern sector of colonial German lands, where the *Ostmark,* or "eastern march" of Bayern, was developed into *Österreich* (Austria) or the "eastern empire," under the skillful guidance of the Hapsburg family. These two powerful states of the colonial east, Prussia and Austria, then turned their attention toward fragmented original Germany, and they competed for influence over the centuries (Figure 7.4). Eventually the Prussians gained the upper hand, finally eliminating Austria as a competitor through warfare in 1866, opening the way for the Prussian unification of Germany in 1871. The German Empire which resulted was nothing more than an extended Prussia, for the Prussian king became the German kaiser and the Prussian capital of Berlin the German capital. Austria was excluded and turned its full attention away from Germany to the Balkans.

The German Empire of 1871 had many ready-made forces of unity, the most important of which was the German language and related brilliant cultural achievement. Few people can rival the German contributions to music, science, and literature. Napoleon's invasion had stirred latent Pan-Germanism early in the nineteenth century, and Prussia successfully assumed the mantle of champion of the German people. Furthermore, the historical deeds and experiences of the Germans as a disunited people were passed intact to the new empire, replete with national heroes such as Hermann (Arminius), a tribal chieftain who routed Roman troops at the Teutoburger Forest in A.D. 9, supposedly preserving the German lands from Romanization; Friedrich Barbarossa, an emperor of the Middle Ages who died on a Crusade; and Gebhard von Blücher, a general instrumental in the defeat of Napoleon. *Deutschland* had long been a distinct human entity; Prussia simply gave it political expression.

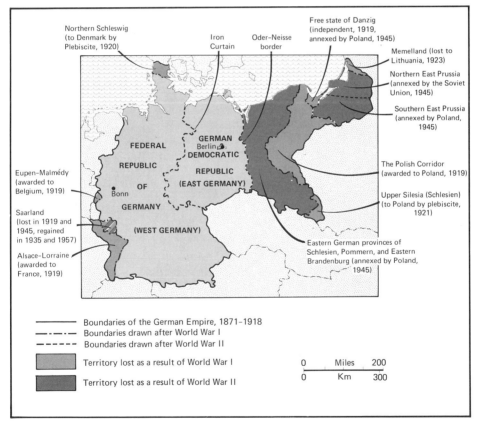

Figure 7.5   The destruction of unified Germany. The German Empire formed in 1871 suffered serious territorial losses after World War I, including German-speaking peoples in Alsace-Lorraine, Eupen-Malmédy, and Danzig. Even more catastrophic losses followed World War II, and the remnant German territory was divided into two separate independent countries.

The unified German state did not survive. Its disintegration began with World War I, when not only alien ethnic areas such as the Polish Corridor, Upper Schlesien, and northern Schleswig were lost, but also German-populated Alsace-Lorraine, Eupen-Malmédy, and the Saar (Figure 7.5). The Saar was later regained through plebiscite and is today part of West Germany. Defeat in World War II produced additional huge territorial losses and, even more critically, the division into two separate independent German states. Disunity returned to the German lands because the state was unable to cope with external hostile forces, and it would appear that the fragmentation may well be permanent. Indeed, disunity appears to be more in keeping with German tradition, for the period of unity was very brief. The German tragedy in the sphere of external strategic relationships may be simply stated: The Germans sought to use their central location as an axis from which to dominate Europe, but they proved unequal to the task and were allotted the fate of fragmented buffer between East and West. Their happiest future would appear to lie in the direction of neutralism.

ITALY

Italy, like Germany, was recently unified, with only the remote unity of Roman times to provide an ancient heritage. For hundreds of years prior to the middle of the nineteenth century, Italy was used as a land bridge by numerous invaders, who poured through the low passes of the Alps in the north or used the

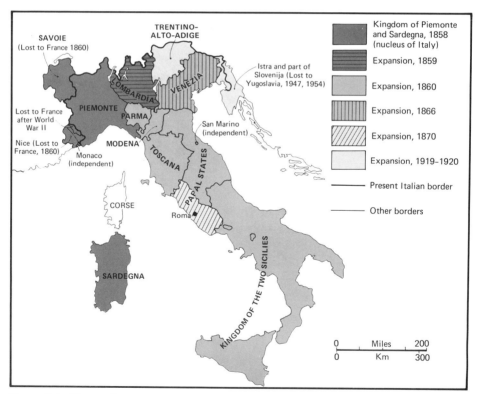

Figure 7.6 The territorial development of Italy. Italy was created largely within a single decade in the nineteenth century through a rapid expansion from a peripheral core area in Piemonte.

island of Sicilia as a stepping-stone from North Africa. Spaniard, German, Byzantine Greek, Frenchman, and Arab came to rule one or another part of Italy during the long period of disunity.

The rising tide of linguistic nationalism engulfed Italy in the 1800s, culminating in a unification drive led by the Kingdom of Piemonte and Sardegna, whose major territorial base was in the province of Piemonte, in the uppermost part of the Po Valley. In spite of opposition from Austria, the pope, and certain local rulers, the various other parts of Italy were joined by force and persuasion to Sardegna–Piemonte from 1859 to 1870 to form the modern state (Figure 7.6). The Piemonte core area lost the capital city to Roma, which had an obvious advantage for historical, locational, and religious reasons. As in Germany, the impetus for union had come from a peripheral area, though the process of amalgamation was accomplished much more rapidly than in the German lands and achieved greater durability. The country survived World War II without serious impairment.

The Italian language and its associated culture form the *raison d'être* of the state, and added unifying forces are suppiled by Catholicism, the classical heritage of the Roman Empire, and the natural framework of the peninsula. Serious internal conflict has been at a minimum, though the economic contrast of north and south, regionalized strength of the Communist party in north-central Italy, and the presence of a discontented German minority in the South Tirol have been troublesome.

SWITZERLAND AND BELGIUM: SUCCESS AND FAILURE ASTRIDE A LINGUISTIC BORDER

The most important language frontier in western Europe is that between Romance speech in the south and the Germanic tongues of the north. Switzerland and Belgium straddle this cultural border and are in certain other respects similar, but only one of the two can claim success.

Switzerland is one of the most viable, stable states of Europe, with perhaps the strongest nationalistic sentiment to be found in the entire culture area. It is not an important state in terms of size, population, or military power, but it is of interest to the political geographer because of its achievement of uniting diverse peoples. Switzerland is split not only linguistically, but also religiously and physically (Figure 7.7). Over 70 percent of its inhabitants speak German, about 19 percent French, 10 percent Italian, and less than 1 percent Romansh. Nearly three-fifths of the Swiss are Protestant, mainly urban people, and most of the remainder are Roman Catholic, confined principally to the rural areas. The human diversity is reflected in the absence of a "Swiss" culture, for German-speaking writers, musicians, scientists and the like are included in German culture, while the French and Italian Swiss belong to France and Italy in cultural allegiance. Additional disunity is provided by the Alps, which cause much of the population to live in isolated valley clusters. Yet in spite of these major centrifugal forces, Switzerland thrives.

The key to the Swiss success lies far back in its history. The residents of the eastern shores of Lake Luzern (Vierwaldstättersee) occupied the northern approach to the great St. Gotthard Pass, which became the main gateway between Italy and the German lands in the 1200s. They were granted exemption by the Holy Roman emperor from the duties of feudalism in exchange for their promise to prevent neighboring lords from dominating the pass. This newly won freedom

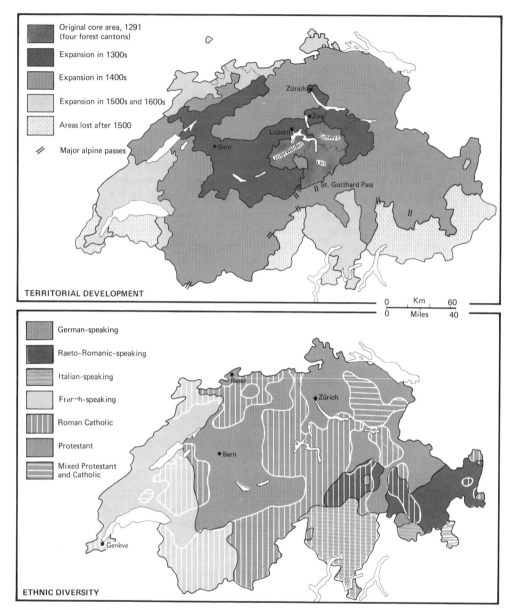

Figure 7.7 Switzerland: Territorial development and ethnic diversity. The Swiss state is a classic example of gradual expansion from a core area. It includes a mixture of Catholics and Protestants and four linguistic groups.

began to erode under the harsh rule of the ambitious Hapsburg family, and in 1291 the free men of Uri, Schwyz, Obwalden, and Nidwalden (the latter two usually grouped as Unterwalden), the "four forest cantons," rose in rebellion to reestablish their rights (Figure 7.7). The uprising of the mountain folk was successful, and the Swiss Confederation was born. The memory of the war of independence and its great hero, Wilhelm Tell, have provided fuel for nationalism ever since. In its formative stage, the state was wholly German in speech and centered on the lake, which afforded easy communication between the various cantons. Schwyz assumed an early leadership and gave its name, distorted as *Schweiz* (Switzerland), to the entire nation. The mountains around the lake shores provided ample protection for the weak infant state. A victory over Holy Roman Imperial forces at Morgarten in Schwyz in 1315 solidified the Swiss claim to independence, as did a victory over the Austrians at Sempach near Luzern in 1386. The success of the rebellion and the subsequent victory at Morgarten impressed the citizenry of nearby city-states such as Luzern, Zürich, Zug, and Bern, causing them to join the Swiss Confederation in the 1300s. With this second phase of territorial growth, the rural core in the four forest cantons gave way to dominance by the towns. On several occasions, the Swiss won territory through military conquest, and in 1476 they purchased the town of Winterthur from the Hapsburgs.

A third phase of expansion occurred in the 1400s and 1500s, bringing control over the Alpine passes and Rhine River crossings. Italian-speaking Ticino was conquered and annexed, as was French-speaking Vaud, creating a polyglot state. The Swiss reputation for military prowess led the papacy and others to hire mercenary troops from the Confederation.

In time, the original Swiss *raison d'être,* mutual aid to maintain freedom, was strengthened by yet another—the *refuge from war.* Once its period of military expansion was over, Switzerland proved remarkably adept at avoiding the great wars which ravaged ·Europe in the past three or four centuries. In spite of the major inroads of Protestantism, including the work of Calvin and Zwingli, Switzerland was spared in the Thirty Years' War, and most recently the Swiss avoided involvement in both of the world wars. Their successful neutralism is based partly on the mountain folk-fortress, defended by a first-rate reserve army composed of nearly all males between twenty and fifty years of age. The rugged terrain which fragments Switzerland also helps protect it. An aggressor even as powerful as Nazi Germany would have found conquest of Switzerland more expensive than it was worth.

The potential conflict between different ethnic groups has been avoided largely through the granting of much local autonomy to the various cantons. The central government remains very weak, and there has been no attempt on the part of the German majority to impose its culture on the Latin minorities. At one time, the Swiss believed that their example of successful unification of diverse peoples might have value for Europe and the world as a whole. In that spirit, they gave full support to the League of Nations and offered their city of Genève as its headquarters. In the wake of the tragic failure of that international organization, the Swiss have declined to join the United Nations.

Belgium also lies astride the Germanic–Romance linguistic border, joining the Flemings of the north with Walloon French in the south (Figure 7.8). It has an advantage in that its population is religiously uniform, adhering to Roman Catholicism. The Belgian state, with about the same territorial size and military strength of Switzerland, has sought to duplicate the Swiss success in establishing neutralism and joining diverse ethnic groups. The Belgians have failed in this attempt, and their state is consequently threatened with possible disintegration.

There are several differences between Belgium and Switzerland which hold the key to the contrast in viability. First, Belgium is a much newer state, dating only from 1830, when its Catholic population broke away from the Protestant-dominated Netherlands. The French-speaking southern Belgians, however, would

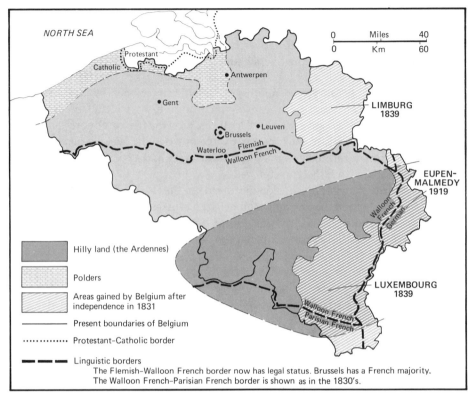

Figure 7.8 Belgium: Political geographical factors. In addition to the problems caused by the Fleming-Walloon conflict, Belgium occupies the natural invasion route between Germany and France, which passes between the hilly Ardennes and the low-lying polderland. The Battle of Waterloo was fought on this route.

have preferred union with France rather than with the Germanic Flemings, a preference rendered futile by British and German opposition to French territorial expansion. Belgium, then, was not created through the desire of the majority of its population, but rather through the decision of several of the great powers. It lacked a *raison d'être,* for Catholicism proved too weak a cement to join Fleming and French, to produce a sense of group membership. Absent was the common memory of a heroic struggle for independence, a pantheon of national heroes, and a core area. The artificiality of Belgium was underscored by the election of a German prince as king, a move favored by the same great powers which directed creation of the state.

Another critical difference has been Belgium's failure to preserve its neutrality. It was established as a buffer state controlling the strategic Flanders narrows of the North European Plain (Figure 7.8), the natural military route between France and Germany, and Belgium has been invaded twice in the present century. No folk-fortress was provided by nature to help the Belgians defend themselves. Consequently, the state failed to offer its citizens a refuge from war, refuge which might well have given rise to nationalistic sentiment and provided a *raison d'être.*

With unifying forces absent or weak, the centrifugal force of linguistic diversity has come to the fore. Early in Belgium's development, the French Walloons dominated the state and formed a majority of about 58 percent of its population. The only official national language was French, and a person aspiring to any position of importance had to be able to speak that language. Flemings were an underprivileged minority. Over the decades, however, the Flemings multiplied more rapidly than the Walloons, in keeping with the higher birth rates in Germanic-language areas as compared to French areas. Eventually, the Flemings replaced the Walloons as the national majority group, and their linguistic standing rose accordingly. In the latter half of the nineteenth century, a Flemish university was established at Gent, and in 1891 the Flemish language first appeared alongside French on the national postage stamps and currency. The greatest Flemish victory was the drawing of an official boundary within Belgium in 1963, north of which the Flemish language is given preference (Figure 7.8).

The Fleming–Walloon rivalry flared into violence in the 1960s, with street-fighting in the capital city, Brussels, which has a French majority but lies north of the linguistic border. Students at the traditionally French University of Louvain (Leuven), in Flemish territory, rioted in successful support of demands that instruction be in the Flemish tongue and that French faculty be dismissed.

In effect, two nations exist within a single state in Belgium. To survive, the government will have to give almost complete autonomy to each group.

POLAND

Eastern Europe, excluding the Soviet Union, has proven to be the least stable political zone in the entire culture area. As the meeting place of Slavic, Germanic, and Romanic speech, of Protestantism, Catholicism, Eastern Orthodoxy, and Islam, it has evolved a complex ethnic pattern which in turn has produced an assemblage of small, weak states. Traditionally, this region was referred to as the "Shatter Belt," in recognition of the political fragmentation. Poland is, unhappily, a typical representative of this region.

About A.D. 960 in the area around Goplo Lake and the town of Gniezno, southwest of the great bend in the lower Wisla River, several local Slavic tribes joined to form the nucleus of the Polish state (Figure 7.1). The dominant tribe, the *Polians* or *Poljane,* gave their name to the infant state, and the original core area came in time to be called *Wielkopolska,* or "great Poland." In less than 200 years, Poland was able to expand south to the Carpathians, west as far as the Odra (Oder) River, north to the Baltic shore, and east to the Bug River—almost precisely the extent of the present Polish state. An absence of politically organized rivals facilitated the early rapid expansion. During a period of weak government and growing feudal disunity from about 1140 to 1333, Poland lost territory in the north and west to Germans, particularly to the military-religious order known as the Teutonic Knights, which seized the entire coastline. In response to these losses, the Polish capital was withdrawn south and east from Gniezno to Kraków, at the foot of the Carpathians.

The golden age of the Polish state, typified by vigorous leadership and great territorial enlargement, extended from the late 1300s through the fifteenth and sixteenth centuries. It began with the kingship of Casimir the Great and included a union of Poland with Lithuania in 1386. The Poles annexed lands from the Baltic to the Black Sea, from Latvia and Estonia to the Dnepr River. The Teutonic Knights were permanently crushed, and all of East Prussia and the later Polish

Corridor were annexed. Poland became the largest state of Europe, and its kings ruled over not only Poles, but also many Germans, Ukrainians, Byelorussians, Lithuanians, and members of other groups.

The rise of strong German states in the west, Prussia and Austria, and a powerful Slavic competitor to the east, Russia, put an end to the greatness of Poland. The state was totally dismembered in three partitions during the latter part of the eighteenth century and disappeared from the map, devoured completely by its three powerful neighbors. Poland, defenseless on the expanses of the North European Plain, had succumbed to more populous rivals on its periphery, and a cruel formula came to govern its fate:

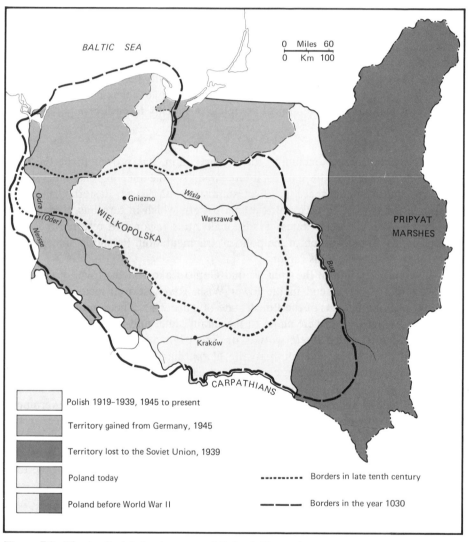

Figure 7.9 The territorial development of Poland. From the core area around Gniezno in Wielkopolska in the mid-tenth century, Poland spread to almost precisely its present limits by the year 1030. Subsequent annexations were later lost. The present Polish state was pushed westward by the Russians in 1945 to reassume its ancient location.

> Strong Germany + weak Russia = German-dominated Poland
> Weak Germany + strong Russia = Russian-dominated Poland
> Strong Germany + strong Russia = no Poland

The eighteenth century produced both strong German states and a strong Russia, and Poland disappeared. The state reappeared ever so briefly when Napoleon brought temporary grief to the Prussians, Austrians, and Russians, but quickly fell again under their control after 1815.

A free and independent Poland is a possibility only when both Germany and Russia are weak, a situation miraculously produced by World War I. In this fertile soil, Poland was reborn, only to disappear again in 1939 in a fourth partition between Germany and the Soviet Union, both of which had recovered from war and revolution to once again become powerful states. In the course of World War II, the German invasion temporarily produced the "strong Germany + weak Russia" pattern, and a puppet Polish state, the Generalgouvernement, appeared on the map under German occupation. The final outcome of the war, however, was "weak Germany + strong Russia," and the Polish state was reborn under Russian domination in 1945. It has never escaped Soviet overlordship in the period since. Indeed, Stalin established Polish dependence on Russia by awarding Poland about one-fourth of all prewar German territory, the previously mentioned provinces of Schlesien, Pommern, and East Prussia (Ostpreussen), from which the German population was expelled (Figure 7.9). The Poles had to rely on Russian protection to retain these new lands. By pure accident, the new borders of Poland closely paralleled those of the years 1000 or 1100.

The fate of Poland, then, is largely governed by outside forces. Alliances with France and the United Kingdom proved to be of no avail in time of need. The modern Polish state has considerable internal unity, based on language, religion, and a long history, but it is not completely independent.

CZECHOSLOVAKIA

If the fate of Poland was to be caught between Germans and Russians, the traditional problem of the Czechs was location between Germans and more Germans. Only since World War II has the Soviet Union come to dominate the Czechoslovak state.

In the folk-fortress of České (Bohemia), wedged in between the two principal lobes of eastern German colonization in Austria and on the North German Plain, the Czech people preserved their cultural identity and developed the state of České about A.D. 900. The group known as the Premyslids, based in the area around Praha, defeated various rivals to unify first České and then Morava, within boundaries similar to those of present-day western Czechoslovakia. České became a kingdom within the Holy Roman Empire and preserved independent status until 1526, when it was annexed by the Hapsburgs of German Austria (Figure 7.10).

České reappeared as Czechoslovakia in 1918, carved from the remains of the defunct Austro–Hungarian Empire, but some mistakes were made in this reincarnation. The worst of these was that the Czechs were linked politically with Slovakians and Ruthenians to form a long, narrow national territory which housed quite different Slavic groups. The areal compactness and ethnic unity of original České were thereby sacrificed. In addition, the German-populated Sudetenland was

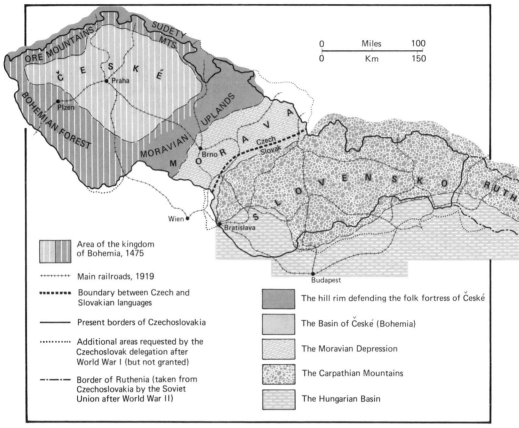

Figure 7.10 Problems of unity in Czechoslovakia. The natural protection and unity offered by the Basin of Česke and its highland rim, which had served so well the old Kingdom of Bohemia (circa 900–1526), was largely negated by the addition of Slovensko and Ruthenia to the new Czechoslovak state in 1919. In addition, Česke had a fine railroad network centered on Praha, but east–west movement in the remainder of the awkwardly shaped country was hindered by a rail pattern centered on Wien, Budapest, and other foreign cities, a pattern inherited from the Austro–Hungarian Empire.

included (Figure 3.13). A poorly developed internal transportation network was one immediate consequence of these mistakes (Figure 7.10).

Hitler's annexation of Austria in 1938 meant that German territory flanked Česke and Morava on three sides, and soon the Czechoslovak state was dismembered, the western part annexed outright or set up as a protectorate by Germany. Slovensko in the east became a separate German puppet state. The Czechoslovak state reappeared after World War II, but quickly fell under Soviet domination. An abortive attempt to reestablish a greater measure of independence and freedom under the Dubcek government was crushed by the Russian invasion of 1968.

YUGOSLAVIA

Yugoslavia is in many respects strikingly like Czechoslovakia. Both arose in the Middle Ages among a Slavic group, thrived for a time and disappeared, only to be re-formed in the present century as polyglot Slavic states. The Serbs won independence in 1180 in the period of Byzantine decline, their state based in the fertile Dinaric *polja* around the ecclesiastical center at Peć (Figure 7.1). Four decades later the rulers of Srbija (Serbia) assumed the title of king, and the state attained a zenith of power in the mid-fourteenth century, expanding to the Adriatic and Aegean from its inland core. A crushing defeat at the hands of the Turks in 1387 led to the extinction of Srbija.

In 1817 the Serb state reappeared as a Turkish satellite, and then won full independence later in the nineteenth century. Before World War I, the Serbs began to champion the cause of Pan-Slavism, protesting in particular the plight of neighboring South Slavs under Austro–Hungarian rule. As a consequence, the new map drawn after the war contained an enlarged Srbija, a South Slavic state including not only Serbs, but also Croats, Slovenes, Bosnians, Macedonians, and others. "Yugoslavia" or Jugoslavija means "land of the South Slavs." It further joined Catholics, Eastern Orthodox Christians, and Moslems.

This union has not been a success. Yugoslavia is held together today mainly by the popularity of Marshall Tito, the resistance leader in World War II who has served as head of state since the expulsion of the Germans. Tito has attempted to overcome the regional ethnic differences by granting each cultural group considerable autonomy. Provincial or republic borders within Yugoslavia are drawn along linguistic and religious lines. The Yugoslav flag is rarely displayed, and the individual republics enjoy a considerable degree of self-government. The principal unresolved rivalry is between Serbs and Croats, both of whom have very old traditions of political independence, dating to the Middle Ages. The Croats, whose republic in the north is called Hrvatska (Croatia), feel that too much of the wealth generated in their relatively prosperous province is being taken by the central government to help develop backward southern republics such as Makedonija (Macedonia). Moreover, the Croats resent the political dominance of Serbian Beograd and the image of Yugoslavia as an extended Srbija. The Croats willingly accepted their status as a separate puppet state under German occupation in World War II. They may well attempt to secede from the Yugoslav state at Tito's death, and it is conceivable that they would look to Russia for support. The principal difference between Croats and Serbs is religious, since both speak essentially the same language. Croats are mostly Roman Catholic while Serbs are Eastern Orthodox.

The future of Yugoslavia is further darkened by boundary disputes with Bulgaria and Albania. Bulgaria feels that the Macedonian Slavs are linguistically best regarded as Bulgarians, while Albania desires to annex the Kosovo-Metohija area of southern Yugoslavia, which is populated by speakers of Albanian.

SWEDEN AND DENMARK

The northern zone of Europe has witnessed political greatness twice, in Denmark and Sweden, both of which acquired considerable power and influence in spite of small populations. The Danish union was accomplished in the mid-tenth century by a tribe headquartered at the old settlement of Jelling on the peninsula of Jylland. The united Danes turned attention first across the North Sea. From 1014 to 1042, all of England was ruled by the Danish King Knut (Canute). After this brief episode as a kingdom of the North Sea, the Danes looked east to the islands of the adjacent Baltic archipelago and on beyond to the southern part of modern Sweden. In the process the focal point of the state shifted from Jylland to the lands bordering the narrow mouth of the Baltic Sea, in particular the island of Sjælland. The town of Roskilde, and later København, succeeded Jelling as the capital. Attempts to become the prime Baltic power, which brought such diverse lands as Estonia, Pommern, and Mecklenburg under Danish rule in the 1200s, eventually were repelled by Germans and Swedes, and Denmark gradually settled into its present position as

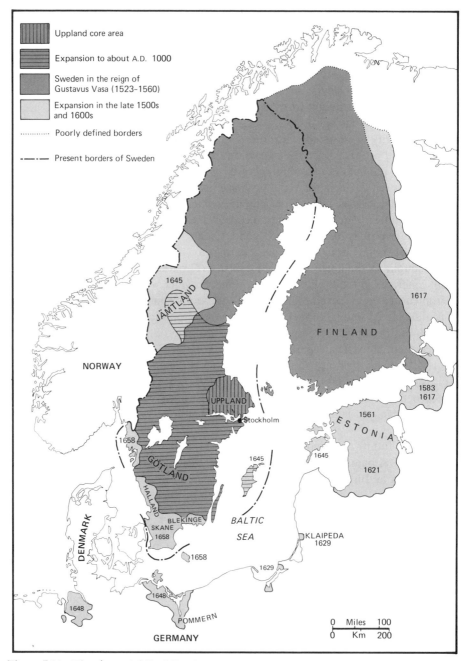

Figure 7.11 The rise and fall of Sweden as a Baltic power. By the mid-1600s, the Baltic Sea had become a Swedish lake, but the present borders of Sweden illustrate the magnitude of retreat since that time.

a small, militarily weak Scandinavian state. Denmark has received some protection from its insular and peninsular situation, and its present unity is based on language and, to a much lesser degree, the Lutheran faith. The monarchy, represented by a king or queen with largely ceremonial powers, was tarnished by a degree of collaboration with the German occupiers in World War II and is no longer very important as a symbol of national unity.

The Swedes initially dwelt in the district of Uppland, centered on the settlement of old Uppsala. The conquest of surrounding tribes, including the Goths of hilly lands to the south, lies early in the recorded history of Sweden, perhaps the 600s A.D. or even earlier (Figure 7.11). The young Swedish state faced eastward to the Baltic, blocked off by Danish and Norwegian territory from access to the Kattegat and Skagerrak channels linking the Baltic and North seas. The richest farming provinces of present Sweden—Skåne, Blekinge, and Halland in the south—remained under Danish rule until 1658. Swedish annexations in the Baltic zone were quite extensive and included Finland (by 1250), southern Karelia (by 1300), Estonia (1561), Latvia (1621), and coastal holdings in Germany (1648). Furthermore, Swedish influence penetrated deep into Russia along the riverine trade routes which led to the eastern Mediterranean. In time the greatness of Sweden was eclipsed by more powerful neighbors and much of its territory annexed by Russia and Germany. The state retreated into a successful neutralism from which it has not emerged since the Napoleonic period, a neutralism facilitated by the peripheral location of Sweden. It lies aside from the major zone of conflict in central and eastern Europe, protected by the Baltic.

The present unity of Sweden is in part the result of linguistic uniformity, with only tiny Uralic minorities, Lapps and Finns, who are unlikely to cause disruption. Sweden's shortcoming as the political expression of the Swedish language was her inability to reclaim the Swedish-speaking populations of coastal Finland and the Åland (Ahvenamaa) Islands. A long tradition of Lutheranism, the state church, adds to unity, and the Swedes recall their important role in preserving Protestantism at the time of the Thirty Years' War. Swedes today enjoy the highest standard of living of all Europeans, providing still more support for the state, and there are no marked class differences which might cause disruption. An economically uniform population was achieved through an ambitious state welfare program, financed by very high taxes.

CYPRUS

The newly independent state is a rarity in Europe; indeed, one must look to the southernmost insular periphery of the European culture area, to Malta and Cyprus, to find such a political phenomenon. The island of Cyprus has housed a high civilization since classical or even preclassical antiquity, but rarely has this crossroads of the eastern Mediterranean achieved self-government. It was ruled at one time or another by every significant power in the Mediterranean area, including Assyria, Greece, Phoenicia, Egypt, Persia, and the empires of the Romans, Byzantines, Arabs, Turks, and British. Surprisingly, only the Greeks and Turks left behind significant ethnic reminders of their rule, and the present Cypriot population is roughly four-fifths Greek Christian and one-fifth Turkish Moslem.

Cyprus was held aside from much of the century-long intermittent Greek–Turk war by virtue of British administration, which was established in 1878. The British desired the island as a guardpost at the northern approach to the Suez Canal.

Egyptian seizure of control over the canal in the 1950s, coupled with anticolonial unrest, made Cyprus less valuable to the British, and soon, in 1960, they granted it independence.

Greek–Turk violence, which broke out in the last years of British rule, has plagued the young nation throughout its existence. The large Greek majority would prefer union (*enosis*) with Greece, while the Turks demand either continued independence with a greater voice in the government or partition of the island into Greek and Turk zones and unification with the respective mother countries. Partition is an impossibility unless large numbers of people are uprooted and moved, for the two groups are presently rather thoroughly mixed in the various settlements around the island. A crisis atmosphere persists today, and the country remains independent under a Greek-dominated government. It does not seem likely that two peoples so bitterly opposed can be successfully united, and continued political instability appears to be unavoidable. The real possibility of civil war persists, and the dangerous possibility of war between Greece and Turkey is ever-present.

7.5 THE HEARTLAND–RIMLAND CONTEST: THE BALANCE OF POWER IN EUROPE

Certainly the study of individual states and the internal and external forces which allow their success or decree their downfall is the heart of European political geography. At the same time, the interest of politically minded geographers can be and has been turned to broader patterns, in particular to the possibility that certain major powers might be able to assume dominance over all or large parts of Europe.

Except for very brief intervals in history, Europe has not fallen under the military control of one great power. Napoleonic France achieved such a position, as did Nazi Germany, but both empires were fleeting. In the opinion of some political geographers, however, there exists a very real possibility, if not likelihood, of domination of Europe by a single power. One of the earliest and best-known theories supporting such a viewpoint was proposed in 1904, with modifications in 1919, by the British geographer Halford J. Mackinder and has come to be known as the *Heartland* theory.

Eurasia, the greatest of the continents, of which Europe forms a western peninsula, was judged by Mackinder to be the only possible base from which a successful drive for world conquest might be launched, not only because of its great size and huge resource base, but also because it housed the great majority of the human race, almost 80 percent of all human beings. In viewing this key continent more closely, he discerned two major subregions—an interior heartland and a coastland fringe, or marginal crescent, around the periphery (Figure 7.12). Of these two, the heartland was believed by Mackinder to possess greater potential for supporting a campaign of world conquest because it was immune to sea power. In contrast, the marginal crescent of Eurasia, including most of Europe, was not immune to invasion by land-based military power. Accordingly, by repeated landpower thrusts outward from the heartland, the marginal crescent could be subjugated and its naval force annexed. This sea power would then be turned against the outlying continents and islands until the entire world was conquered. Initial domination of the heartland was most likely to occur from a power based in the East European

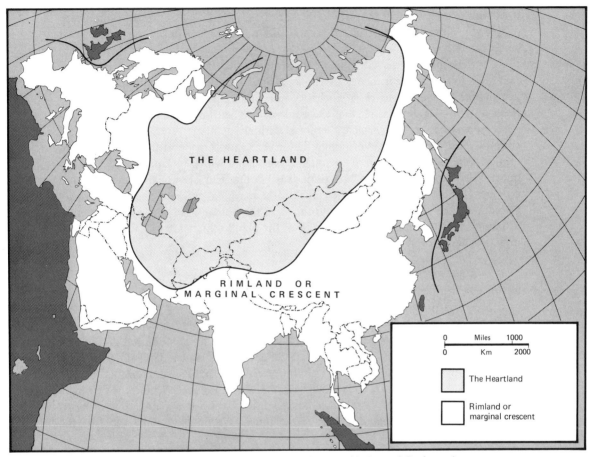

Figure 7.12   Heartland and rimland in Eurasia. (After Mackinder and Spykman.)

Plain, the most densely populated and agriculturally most productive part of the heartland. In sum, Mackinder hypothesized that:

> Who rules East Europe rules the heartland.
> Who rules the heartland rules Eurasia.
> Who rules Eurasia rules the world.

The Russian state had already accomplished the first step at the time Mackinder wrote, and the rise in Russia of the Communist political system bent on world conquest brought considerable attention to the heartland theory. The heartland theory implies that Russian Communist rule of the world is inevitable.

There are several fallacies associated with the heartland theory, the most important of which is the neglect of the role of air power, guided missiles, and nuclear weapons. One might excuse Mackinder these oversights in the first decade of the twentieth century, though one of his fellow members of the Royal Geographical Society, a remarkably perceptive Mr. Amery, commented after hearing his speech in 1904 that "both the sea and the railway are going in the future . . . to be supplemented by the air as a means of locomotion, and when we come to that . . . , the successful powers will be those who have the greatest industrial basis.

It will not matter whether they are in the centre of a continent or on an island; those people who have the industrial power and the power of invention and science will be able to defeat all others."

Perhaps the greatest value of Mackinder's heartland concept lies in the fact that it led to still another theory. Nicholas J. Spykman, an American political scientist, published his famous *rimland* theory in a book entitled *The Geography of the Peace* in 1944. Spykman felt that the value of the heartland area had been greatly overemphasized, and he viewed it more accurately as a sparsely settled wasteland, composed for the most part of nonagricultural expanses of desert, tundra, and subarctic coniferous forests, hardly a suitable base from which to launch a world conquest. While Spykman shared Mackinder's belief that Eurasia was the key or pivotal continent, he placed much greater value on the marginal crescent or rimland, as he called it. In the rimland is found two-thirds of the human race and a huge quantity of natural resources, including nearly all of the peoples and states of Europe. Spykman, in effect, reversed the Mackinder thesis:

Who rules the rimland rules Eurasia.
Who rules Eurasia rules the world.

The rimland, however, is one of the most thoroughly fragmented political zones in the world, and the great potential power of the area is diffused among numerous separate states. Spykman felt that the energies of nonrimland states, including the United States and the Soviet Union, should be focused on attempts to keep it fragmented. The alliance of Nazi Germany and the Japanese Empire, two major rimland powers, and their collective military drive toward a planned meeting in India, was precisely what Spykman feared most—a possible unification of the rimland.

The power balance in the world today, in which Europe is of great importance, differs somewhat from the expectations of either Mackinder or Spykman, though the ideas and influence of both are much in evidence. The great struggle between the Soviet Union and the West is, as Mackinder predicted, the contest of heartland and rimland, though the former has not established the predicted dominance, and air and nuclear power are the key elements rather than land or naval forces. American foreign policy is firmly based on Spykman's theory and directed toward the prevention of rimland unification by the Communists, leaving uncontested the Communist control of the less valuable heartland. Spykman's prediction of a Soviet–American alliance to prevent a unified rimland has not been realized.

Postwar Europe has been caught in the middle of the rimland–heartland conflict. Prior to World War II, European states held a preeminent position in world affairs, and the colonial empires of the British, French, Dutch, and others stretched around the earth. The great decisions guiding the course of mankind were made in London, Paris, Berlin, or Roma, and there was much validity to the European self-image as the political focal point. The war diminished all of the European powers. None, not even the victorious, emerged from the struggle as strong as before. In their weakened condition, the Europeans lost their status in the world power structure, and their colonial empires rapidly dissolved. The Europeans not only ceased to guide the destiny of Africa and other colonial spheres of influence, but also, and much more significant, *lost control over their own political fate*. The decisions governing the destiny of Europe were made in Washington and Moskva rather than the European capitals. All Europe shared the fate of Germany —demotion from powerful axis to buffer—and the culture area became nothing more than a zone of confrontation between two non-European powers, the United States and the Soviet Union. Exhausted and destroyed by two horrible wars and a crippling economic depression in between, deprived of its young men by the staggering number of casualties, Europe in 1945 was an assemblage of second- and third-rate powers, a vacuum quickly occupied by the Soviets and Americans.

The confrontation between the United States and the Soviet Union took shape along a sharp line, the Iron Curtain, in the late 1940s. From Lübeck on the Baltic to Trieste on the Adriatic, the division line snaked across central Europe, paralleling a series of traditional borders which had long divided east and west in Europe (Figure 7.13). The confrontation of Roman and barbarian in the early centuries of the Christian Era, of Slav and German after the Migration of Peoples, of "colonial" and "original" Germany, of free peasantry and remnant feudalism in the nineteenth century, had all preceded the Soviet–American, Communist–non-Communist division along roughly the same line. The essential difference was that the earlier contestants had all been Europeans.

Europe has made a rapid economic recovery from the war, but its political status remains largely unchanged. It is in the interest of Europeans that they disengage from the East–West conflict and evolve toward a third power bloc of neutral, allied states. In effect, the European states can regain power only by putting together the huge human resources of the European rimland to stand free of both Soviet and American domination.

Only rather limited success has thus far been attained in the attempt to disengage (Figure 7.13). Yugoslavia broke away from Soviet domination in 1948, followed later by the defection of Communist Albania. Similar attempts in Hungary and Czechoslovakia were crushed by Soviet troops, though Romania has been able to free itself at least partially from Russian control, including the withdrawal of occupation troops. On the western side of the Iron Curtain, Switzerland and Sweden were able to preserve their traditional neutrality, and they have since been joined in certain respects by France, which withdrew military support from the American-dominated NATO alliance. Weak Austria and Finland were allowed to establish a precarious neutralism in the border zone between East and West. Austria had been divided into four military occupation zones after World War II, suffering the same fate as Germany, but in 1955 the Big Four powers pulled out their troops and permitted the neutralization of the state. Finland finally escaped the imminent danger of Russian takeover in 1952, when the last "war reparation" payments were made to the Soviets, payments which had been designed to destroy the Finnish economy. A default by the Finns would have given the Russians an excuse to invade.

While certain states on both sides of the Iron Curtain have achieved neutralism, the movement still lacks the membership of the most populous and economically powerful nations, such as West Germany and the United Kingdom. Continued alliance, either forced or voluntary, to one side or the other in the Soviet–American conflict can only prevent the reestablishment of the Europeans' control over their own destiny. The dominance by outside powers has ended the intramural warfare which traditionally plagued Europe, but the price paid for such stability is perhaps too high.

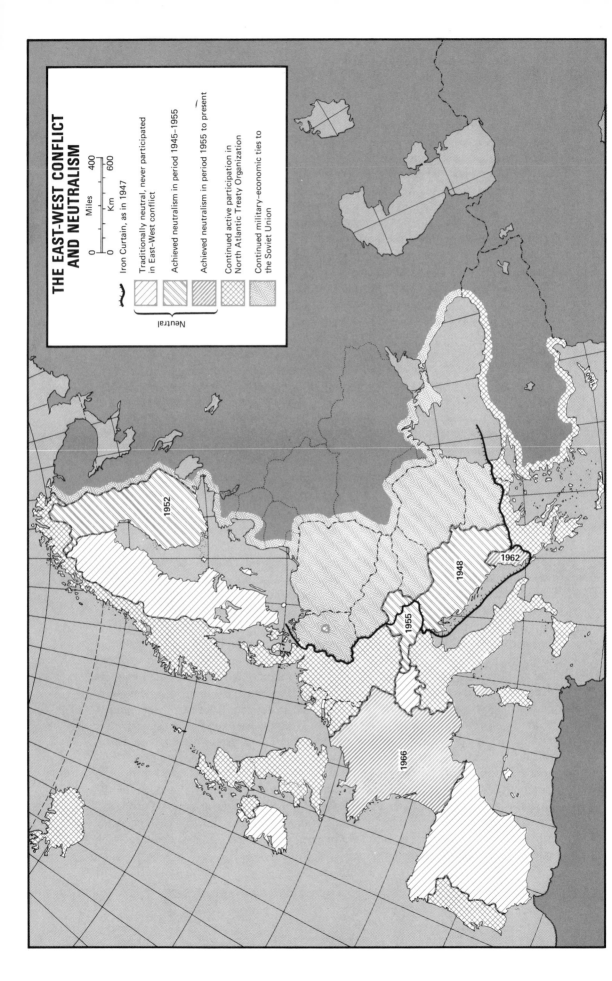

THE EAST-WEST CONFLICT AND NEUTRALISM

Miles
0   400
0   Km   600

Iron Curtain, as in 1947

Traditionally neutral, never participated
in East-West conflict

Achieved neutralism in period 1945–1955

Achieved neutralism in period 1955 to present

Continued active participation in
North Atlantic Treaty Organization

Continued military-economic ties to
the Soviet Union

Neutral

1952

1948

1962

1955

1966

7.6 A UNIFIED EUROPE?

There are many who believe that the political unification of Europe is a possibility and that the brightest future for the culture area lies in that direction. Others have had the same dream in the past and attempted to bring it to realization through military conquest. The new unifiers are using an economic approach, seeking the removal of trade barriers and establishment of complete freedom of movement across borders by workers in search of employment. They note that economic motives lay behind many of the wars of Europe and hope that economic union will promote eventual peaceful political union. One encouraging precedent can be derived from Germany, where economic organizations linking many of the individual separate states were established shortly before the political unification of the nation.

In this spirit, the European Economic Community, or Common Market, was founded in the early 1950s, with initial internal tariff reductions for coal and steel. The Common Market includes six members—West Germany, Italy, France, the Netherlands, Belgium, and Luxembourg. In the near future, the membership will probably be enlarged to include the United Kingdom, Denmark, and the Republic of Ireland. In a surprise move in the fall of 1972, the Norwegians voted against joining. In the economic sphere, the Common Market has already moved far in the direction of federalism.

In the words of the political scientist Howard Bliss, "a surprising consensus exists on the desirability of forming a political union among the Six," though there has been as yet no agreement on the design of the union. Few question that lengthy negotiations, extending over many years, will be required. Walter Hallestein, a West German who has been quite active in Common Market affairs, speaks of "the European nation which we expect the next generations to form."

Success of a unification movement hinges on whether or not the nation-state, that particular expression of human territorialism which developed in Europe, is really obsolete and declining in appeal to Europeans. There is good evidence that two world wars in the twentieth century have permanently damaged the vitality of nation-states in Europe. It is true that the degree of economic intermeshing already achieved has made war between any member nations of the Common Market a practical impossibility.

The unifiers of Europe must proceed with caution. They would be well advised to study thoroughly all facets of the animal instinct of territoriality and its possible application to the affairs of human beings. They must bear in mind that the present political fragmentation of Europe may be in the natural order of things, a manifestation of an instinct which will resist the arguments of intellect. History tells us that successful unification of diverse peoples and large areas is rare and normally accomplished through brute force and dictatorial government rather than by friendly persuasion. In this respect, a comparison of Europe and the United States or Australia can bear little fruit, for while the latter did achieve political unity of large areas, they involved in their formative stages rather homogeneous populations dominantly of British ancestry and voluntary, stateless immigrants who were seek-

Figure 7.13 The East–West conflict and neutralism. Dates indicate time of achievement of effective neutralism.

ing new, economically more promising territorial ties. In both cases, assimilation of non-British immigrant ethnic groups was reasonably rapid and fairly effective, preserving a critical degree of homogeneity in the population. In Europe, on the other hand, a myriad of separate groups reside in ancient ancestral homelands, resisting forfeiture of their group identity.

It seems probable that unification can succeed only if the member states retain a large measure of local autonomy as a bastion for territorialism. The energy of territoriality must be carefully shifted from nation to subnation. Borders must not be completely obliterated. It is essential that the people need not cease to be French or German or Italian. Rather, they will simply forfeit the right to be *independent* Frenchmen, Germans, or Italians. Local autonomy would preserve a channel for territorialism and guarantee preservation of cultural distinctiveness for the individual member groups. The example of Switzerland provides ample hope . that such an approach could succeed.

In practical terms, the European federation would have to be confined to *western* Europe. The Soviet Union, at least under its present leadership, is not willing to abandon its large sphere of influence in eastern Europe. It is extremely unlikely that the Russians would permit a neutralized Europe, which almost surely would be dominated to some degree by the eighty million Germans, to take shape on their western borders.

SOURCES AND SUGGESTED READINGS

Robert Ardrey. *African Genesis.* New York: Atheneum, 1961.

Robert Ardrey. *The Territorial Imperative: A Personal Inquiry into the Animal Origins of Property and Nations.* New York: Atheneum, 1966.

Howard Bliss (ed.). *The Political Development of the European Community: A Documentary Collection.* Waltham, Mass.: Ginn/Blaisdell, 1970.

Jan O. M. Broek and John W. Webb. "Ideologies and the Political Order," Chapter 7 in *A Geography of Mankind.* New York: McGraw-Hill, 1968.

Andrew F. Burghardt. *Borderland: A Historical and Geographical Study of Burgenland, Austria.* Madison, Wis.: University of Wisconsin Press, 1962.

Sidney A. Burrell. "The Scottish Separatist Movement: A Present Assessment." *Political Science Quarterly.* Vol. 70 (1955), pp. 358–367.

Hector M. Chadwick. *The Nationalities of Europe and the Growth of National Ideologies.* London: Cambridge University Press, 1945.

Vaughan Cornish. *The Great Capitals: An Historical Geography.* London: Methuen, 1923.

G. Philip Curti. "The Isle of Man: Geographical Factors in the Evolution of a Political Enclave." *Yearbook, Association of Pacific Coast Geographers.* Vol. 23 (1961), pp. 18–27.

W. Gordon East. "The Geography of Land-Locked States." *Transactions and Papers, Institute of British Geographers.* Vol. 28 (1960), pp. 1–22.

H. J. Fleure. "Notes on the Evolution of Switzerland." *Geography.* Vol. 26 (1941), pp. 169–177.

Wolfgang Framke. *Die deutsch-dänische Grenze in ihrem Einfluss auf die Differenzierung der Kulturlandschaft.* Forschungen zur deutschen Landeskunde, Vol. 172, Bad Godesberg, West Germany: Bundesforschungsanstalt für Landeskunde und Raumordnung, 1968.

Richard Hartshorne. "The Functional Approach in Political Geography." *Annals, Association of American Geographers.* Vol. 40 (1950), pp. 95–130.

Richard Hartshorne. "The Polish Corridor." *Journal of Geography.* Vol. 36 (1937), pp. 161–176.

George W. Hoffman. "The Shatter Belt in Relation to the East–West Conflict." *Journal of Geography.* Vol. 51 (1952), pp. 266–275.

George W. Hoffman. "The Survival of an Independent Austria." *Geographical Review.* Vol. 41 (1951), pp. 606–621.

John W. House. "The Franco–Italian Boundary in the Alpes Maritimes." *Transactions and Papers, Institute of British Geographers.* Vol. 26 (1959), pp. 107–131.

Roger E. Kasperson and Julian V. Minghi (eds.). *The Structure of Political Geography.* Chicago: Aldine, 1969.

Halford J. Mackinder. *Democratic Ideals and Reality.* New York: Holt, Rinehart & Winston, 1942 (originally published 1919).

Halford J. Mackinder. "The Geographical Pivot of History." *Geographical Journal.* Vol. 23 (1904), pp. 421–437.

Douglas R. McManis. "The Core of Italy: The Case for Lombardy–Piedmont." *Professional Geographer.* Vol. 19 (1967), pp. 251–257.

A. E. Moodie. *The Italo–Yugoslav Boundary.* London: Philip, 1945.

Norman J. G. Pounds. "France and 'Les Limites Naturelles' from the Seventeenth to the Twentieth Centuries." *Annals, Association of American Geographers.* Vol. 44 (1954), pp. 51–62.

Norman J. G. Pounds. *Poland Between East and West.* New York: Van Nostrand Reinhold, 1964.

Norman J. G. Pounds and Sue Simons Ball. "Core-Areas and the Development of the European States System." *Annals, Association of American Geographers.* Vol. 54 (1964), pp. 24–40.

Richard R. Randall. "Political Geography of the Klagenfurt Basin." *Geographical Review.* Vol. 47 (1957), pp. 406–419.

G. W. S. Robinson. "Exclaves." *Annals, Association of American Geographers.* Vol. 49 (1959), pp. 283–295.

G. W. S. Robinson. "West Berlin: The Geography of an Exclave." *Geographical Review.* Vol. 43 (1953), pp. 540–557.

O. H. K. Spate. "Factors in the Development of Capital Cities." *Geographical Review.* Vol. 32 (1942), pp. 622–631.

Nicholas J. Spykman. *The Geography of the Peace.* New York: Harcourt Brace Jovanovich, 1944.

Dan Stanislawski. *The Individuality of Portugal.* Austin, Tex.: University of Texas Press, 1959.

Westermanns Grosser Atlas zur Weltgeschichte. Braunschweig, West Germany: Georg Westermann, 1956.

Derwent S. Whittlesey. *The Earth and the State: A Study of Political Geography.* New York: Holt, Rinehart & Winston, 1939.

Derwent S. Whittlesey. "The Val d'Aran: Trans-Pyrenean Spain." *Scottish Geographical Magazine.* Vol. 49 (1933), pp. 217–228.

Geography of agriculture

Economic geography is concerned with the areal variations created by man in the process of earning a living, with the structure and function of economic space. In seeking his livelihood, man is influenced not only by the physical environment, but also by the culture to which he belongs. European man has found numerous ways to obtain a living, but one of the oldest and most fundamental is the tilling of the soil and the tending of flocks and herds—in short, agriculture. For most of European history, farming was the dominant aspect of the economy, and only recently have manufacturing industries surpassed agriculture in most countries of Europe.

8.1 ORIGINS AND DISPERSALS

Agriculture is of great antiquity in Europe, though it did not originate there. Domestication of plants and animals almost certainly originated in Asia, perhaps in the seasonless humid tropics of the far southeastern reaches of that culture area. Gradual diffusion to the west and north, through India and the Fertile Crescent, where new crops and livestock were added, brought agriculture to the Mediterranean sector of Europe perhaps as early as 6500 B.C. Central Europe, including the present-day German lands, became agricultural by 3000 B.C.; Ireland, on the European periphery, by 2000 B.C.; and the remote Trondheim area of Norway, the northern outpost of farming, by 1800 B.C. Agriculture was apparently known to the earliest speakers of the Proto–Indo-European language, for their vocabulary included such words as *ox, sheep, pig, plow, wheat, barley,* and *apple.* Nearly all of the plants and animals which came to typify European agriculture were domesticated far beyond the borders of the culture area, and the Indo-Europeans inherited them from the peoples to the south. Wheat was probably derived from the northwestern area of India, Pakistan, or Afghanistan; citrus fruit from the tropics of India by way of Arabia; the white potato and corn from the American Indian; sheep and goats from southwestern Asia; the pig from Southeast Asia; cattle from northwestern India; and the horse from the slopes of the Caucasus Mountains. The same is true of various farming techniques and tools, such as the art of terracing, which probably originated in the hill lands adjacent to the Fertile Crescent; methods of irrigation, a gift of the desert and steppe peoples adjacent to Europe on the south; the hoe; and the plow. In sum, Europe was not an early center of agricultural innovation and advancement, but rather a peripheral area which received a belated impulse from higher cultures to the south and west.

8.2 MEDITERRANEAN AGRICULTURE

Europe has been shown to possess great diversity in the physical, cultural, and political sense. It is no less diverse in its agriculture, for man has developed a number of distinctive combinations of crops and livestock, each of which typifies a certain region of the European culture area. Since the southern peninsulas of Europe were the first to receive agriculture, it is appropriate to begin with a consideration of the type of farming which evolved there.

The rural peoples of southern Iberia, the Mediterranean coast of France, the southern three-quarters of Italy, the Adriatic coast of Yugoslavia, and Greece developed a most distinctive rural economy which is appropriately referred to as *Mediterranean agriculture.* In order to understand the present characteristics of this system of farming, it is helpful to view Mediterranean agriculture as it existed in the classical and preclassical periods, in the time of the ancient Greeks and Romans (Figure 8.1).

CLASSICAL MEDITERRANEAN AGRICULTURE

Classical Mediterranean agriculture was composed of three distinct, separate elements, each of which represented adaptations to the unique climate and rugged terrain of the southern part of Europe. The Mediterranean climate is typified by a long summer drought and mild, rainy winters. The first of the three facets of classical Mediterranean farming was the winter cultivation of small grains, wheat and barley. These grains thrived in the cool, wet season, and no irrigation was needed. Wheat and barley were sown with the arrival of the first autumnal rain showers, grew slowly through the winter months, and reached maturity in the warm, sunny days of spring. Harvesting was done in the late spring and early summer, before the annual drought tightened its grip on the land (Figure 8.2). The great harvest festivals of Mediterranean folk were accordingly held in the spring rather than fall, as is represented by Jewish Passover and the Feast of Booths. Typically, a two-field rotational system was employed, in which land was cultivated every other year and allowed to lie fallow half of the time to prevent soil exhaustion. In many

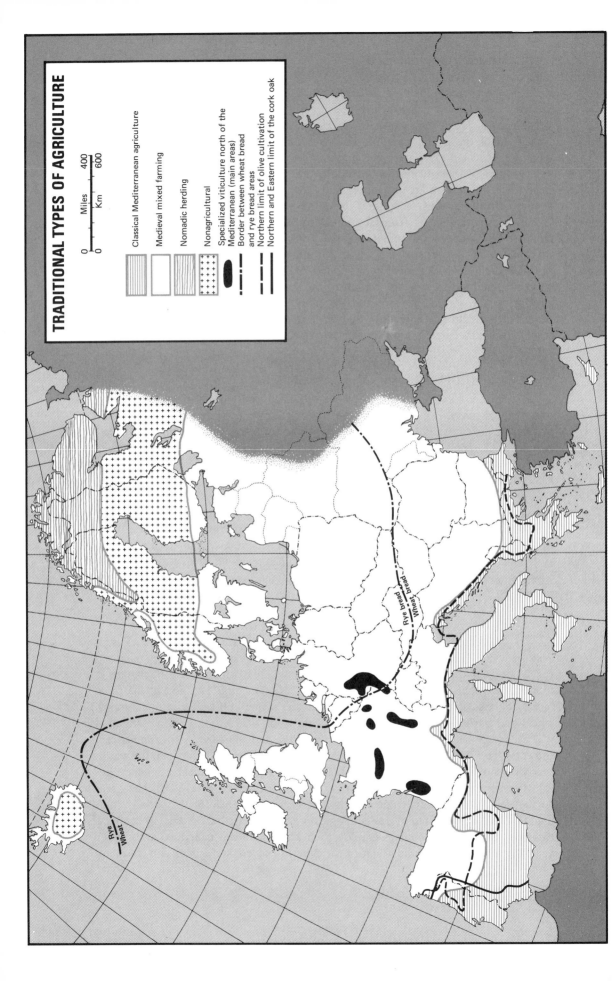

TRADITIONAL TYPES OF AGRICULTURE

Miles
0   400
0   600
Km

Classical Mediterranean agriculture

Medieval mixed farming

Nomadic herding

Nonagricultural

Specialized viticulture north of the
Mediterranean (main areas)

Border between wheat bread
and rye bread areas

Northern limit of olive cultivation

Northern and Eastern limit of the cork oak

Rye bread
Wheat bread

Rye
Wheat

Figure 8.2 Intertillage of wheat and olives in an alluvial valley in Greece. Two typical Mediterranean crops share the same field on the island of Kriti. The wheat has only recently been reaped by hand and tied into bundles to be carried in for threshing. Intertillage is common in traditional Mediterranean agriculture. The month is May, the time of grain harvest before the drought of summer. Olives from these young trees will be ready for harvest in autumn. (Photo by the author.)

districts, the grain was raised in the alluvial lowlands, while the farmers lived in villages on adjacent hilltops for defensive purposes, a siting later reinforced by a desire to avoid the malaria of the lowlands. Wheat was generally the more important of the two grain crops, for Mediterranean peoples prefer light bread. Barley achieved greater importance in marginal areas where precipitation was less abundant and soils poorer, for it is hardier than wheat. Wheat and barley still account for 40 percent of all tilled land in Italy and 50 percent in Greece.

The second member of the classical Mediterranean trinity was the culture of drought-resistant vine and tree crops, perennials which could withstand the summer drought. The grapevine belongs in this category and may well have been native to the Mediterranean climate region. Southern European farmers derived a principal beverage from it, in addition to raisins and table grapes. The grapes were harvested in the late summer or early autumn, and the raisins were dried before the first rains came. Unexpected early rains, followed by bright sunshine, can split open and ruin the grapes laid out to dry. Vineyards were found both on terraced hillsides and on alluvial valley floors. In modern Greece, about 40 percent of the grape harvest goes to the making of wine, 25 percent for raisins, and the remainder is consumed as table grapes.

The olive is a splendid, long-lived native tree, quite drought-resistant but not tolerant of a hard frost, long recognized as the single best indicator of the pres-

Figure 8.1 Traditional types of agriculture.

ence of Mediterranean climate and agriculture (Figure 8.2). It is not uncommon for these gnarled, twisted trees to survive for a thousand years or more. The principal value of the olive to the classical Mediterranean farmer was as a source of fat and cooking oil. Butter was not produced in southern Europe, and olive oil provided a needed substitute. The image of butter-eating Germanic tribesmen was most repulsive to the Roman writers who left behind descriptions of their northern neighbors. The olive tree thrives on slopes and hillsides as well as in valleys, and does well in thin soils. Other orchard trees of the classical Mediterranean included the fig, also drought-resistant, native to the area, and suited to hillsides; the chestnut, used in many areas as a food; and the cork oak.

The herding of small livestock, in particular sheep, goats, and swine, constituted the third basic trait of classical Mediterranean agriculture (Figure 8.3). These animals are able to survive on the scanty forage offered by the rugged highland pastures and mountain oak forests of southern Europe. The goats and sheep moved with agility through the rocky landscape, and the pigs thrived on the mast of the oak trees. Herders tended these animals in areas back away from the villages, though in classical times it was not typical to take the herds, flocks, and droves too far from home. Sheep, the most numerous livestock, provided wool, hides, and meat, though they were only rarely eaten, since the Mediterranean diet is heavily vegetarian. Goats were raised for mohair, milk, and hides, and to a certain extent they took the place of dairy cattle in southern Europe. The cheeses produced in Mediterranean districts are still today derived from goat's milk, or more rarely from sheep's milk, as in the case of Roquefort. Classical references such as the Homeric episode concerning the swineherd Circe suggest a fairly widespread importance, but swine are now the least important of the three small livestock, in part because the forests which provided their food have steadily diminished. Today, swine are concentrated in the remnant oak forests such as those on the rainier western slopes of Iberian mountains. Mediterranean stock-raising was divorced from the raising of crops, and stall-feeding, hay-cutting, and collection of animal manure for fertilizer were rare.

Large livestock, such as cattle, donkeys, and horses, were present in classical Mediterranean agriculture, but they were much less numerous than the small animals and had relatively little importance. It is true that cattle were highly valued and even considered sacred or semisacred in Minoan Kriti, where athletes engaged in the dangerous game of springing over bulls, and in Homeric Greece, as is suggested by a reference in the *Odyssey*. A relic of the special position once held by cattle is Spanish bullfighting. Still, the average classical Mediterranean farmer did not have many cattle, partly because the broken terrain of the area and paucity of summer forage were not well suited to large livestock.

This, then, was the agriculture of classical times. All three of the basic enterprises were generally combined on each farm, though one or another might have been emphasized. From the diverse unspecialized trinity of small grains, vine and tree crops, and small livestock, nearly all of life's necessities could be obtained, including woolen and leather clothing, bread, beverages, fruit, cheese, and even a cork for the leather wine-container. This is the agriculture described by Homer in the *Iliad* when he referred to "Epidauros full of vines," "wheat-bearing Argos," and "Iton, mother of flocks." He also mentioned a man named Tydeus, who "had wheat-bearing fields and many orchards of trees apart, and many sheep," and peasant

Figure 8.3   A shepherd with a flock of sheep near Bari in the south of Italy. The herding of small livestock such as sheep and goats is one of the three basic traits of classical Mediterranean agriculture. This shepherd is little different from his predecessors of the time of Homer. (Photo courtesy Istituto Italiano di Cultura.)

reapers who "drive their swaths through a rich man's field of wheat or barley." It is the agriculture of Palestine described in the Bible, for the eastern Mediterranean closely resembled the European sector in farming practices, with frequent references to sheep, vineyards, wine, and olives, as in the Mount of Olives.

Other characteristics of classical Mediterranean agriculture included a land-tenure system of large estates, or latifundia. On these estates, which were owned by a small wealthy minority, peasant families scratched out a living from tiny, frag-

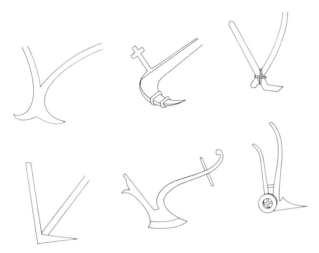

Figure 8.4 The Roman plow (*aratro* or *araire*), typical of Mediterranean agriculture and still in use in backward areas. Six different forms of this crude plow are pictured. The Roman plow did not turn a furrow, but rather simply scratched the surface. (After Meitzen.)

mented farms. The plow was rather unimportant, and the hoe constituted the chief tool of tillage, in part because of the prevalence of orchards and vineyards. Grain fields were plowed with a small, crude plow known as the aratro or araire, which simply scratched the surface and did not turn a furrow (Figure 8.4). Intertillage, vegetables or grains planted among the trees and vines, was also typical, an example of the intensity of land use.

CHANGES IN THE CLASSICAL MEDITERRANEAN AGRICULTURE

Much of this classical Mediterranean system has been passed down to the present. It is still possible in the more remote and backward parts of southern Europe to see farmers operating very much like their ancestors in Homer's day. In the intervening centuries, however, many areas have witnessed changes and additions to the classical agriculture, most of which have resulted from contacts with alien peoples.

One of the most significant changes involved irrigation. Some artificial watering had been done in classical times, but usually only for small garden plots. Homer spoke of the "field waterer [who] leads water from a dark spring along a bed through crops and garden grounds," and the Romans later developed some larger systems, but in general, irrigation was alien to the typical farmer of classical times. The crops he raised were either drought-resistant or cultivated in the rainy season, and he actually had little need for irrigation. The collapse of the Roman Empire, and with it the orderly government needed to operate irrigation systems, just about eliminated this technique.

A major expansion of irrigation resulted from contacts with the desert-dwelling Arab peoples, who invaded Iberia and other southern European areas, beginning in the eighth century A.D. The Arabs found a splendid natural setting for irrigation, with mountains where the winter precipitation was stored up as snow and carried into the lowlands in meltwater streams during the spring and summer. Arabic influence eventually spread throughout the European Mediterranean, and many alluvial lowlands which had traditionally been planted mainly to small grains blossomed with more valuable crops. The spread of irrigation was rather slow, however, and it still remained rather uncommon in the Middle Ages. One of the first projects in Mediterranean France was begun on the Durance River in Provence as late as the year 1171.

The development of irrigation allowed the introduction of a number of new crops which were not resistant to drought. Perhaps the most important were the citrus fruits, which were apparently unknown to the classical Greeks, though the mythological eleventh labor of Hercules had been to obtain the "golden apple" from the Garden of the Hesperides, a possible reference to the orange. Apparently the ancient Greeks had heard of citrus but had no firsthand experience with it. Hercules' quest supposedly took him into the warm lands to the south, where the orange was in fact present in the irrigated gardens of Arabia. The Jews of the Diaspora finally brought citrus to Europe from the Middle East, though this transplant did not survive the turmoil of the fall of the Roman Empire. The permanent introduction of citrus must be credited instead to the same Arabs who were responsible for the rise of irrigation. In the period since, citrus fruits have become very important in many European Mediterranean districts.

Rice was brought to Portugal and Italy in the Age of Discovery by explorers returning by sea and land from China and other oriental lands, or perhaps even earlier by the Moorish conquerors of Iberia, and is now raised in some localities, as is cotton, which spread from adjacent Egypt. Tobacco, of great importance as a cash crop in the eastern Mediterranean, was acquired after the Americas were discovered.

A second major change in the classical system involved transhumance, the seasonal migration with livestock from winter pastures in the lowlands to summer mountain grazing areas. Unlike the nomad, the transhumant generally occupies a permanent, well-built home during the winter season instead of moving from place to place all year round. Migration with livestock was practiced in classical times in a very limited way, although there is some evidence that the great city of Roma may have developed from settlements situated on a Bronze Age route of transhumance. Most classical flocks and herds were basically sedentary, rarely moving any great distance from the home village. In post-Roman times, however, this migratory way of life increased in importance, perhaps mainly due to the practices of numerous nomadic invader groups, such as the Vlakhs and Goths from the north and the Berbers from Africa who came to Moorish Spain. A series of transhumance routes developed in Italy between abandoned coastal marshes such as the Roman Campagna, which had reverted to wasteland after the fall of the empire, and the slopes of the Appennini Mountains. In France, many sheep and goats wintered in the Languedoc Plain and then were driven to summer pastures in the Maritime Alps.

It was in Iberia, however, that transhumance developed most fully, particularly in the Middle Ages. The *Mesta,* a Castillian association to organize and control movements of sheep, became a very powerful institution, and by the 1520s there were 3.5 million transhumant sheep in Castilla alone. In some cases, livestock were driven all the way from Andalucia in the southern part of Spain to summer pastures in the Pyrenees and the Cordillera Cantabrica. Transhumance has declined greatly in importance in recent centuries, but many sheep and goats are still driven on foot or carried by truck or railroad. The chief advantage of transhumance was that it led to more effective utilization of available forage, allowing much greater numbers of livestock than had been possible under the old system of sedentary herds and flocks.

INCREASED SPECIALIZATION

The key change to come to Mediterranean agriculture since classical times has been the recent trend toward increased commercialization and specialization. One fundamental characteristic of the classical system was its diversity, combining the largely unrelated elements of grain cultivation, orchard- and vineyard-keeping, and livestock-herding. Subsistence agriculture is typically diversified, simply because the people rely on it for most of life's necessities and must subsist on what they raise. A certain limited amount of market orientation and specialization had developed in classical times, so that Attikí, the vicinity of Athínai, was known for its olive groves, Sicilia and Thráki for their wheat fields, and certain of the Aegean islands for vineyards and wine. Later, in response to the demands of the medieval Italian and Flemish textile industry, sheep-raising became the major specialization on the Spanish Meseta, and cattle-ranching developed in Andalucia as a supplier of hides to the leatherworkers of various European lands. Nevertheless, as recently as 1800, the large majority of Mediterranean farmers retained the old, diversified system and concentrated on production for their own needs.

The industrialization and urbanization of northern and western Europe in the last century and a half created a huge demand for agricultural produce; consequently, specialization and market orientation have come to the Mediterranean. Improved transportation facilities have allowed the farmers of southern Europe to reach the markets of Germany, Britain, France, and the Low Country. As the Mediterranean farmer became commercial, he faced competition from other parts of the world. In choosing an agricultural specialty, he had to take this competition into account. He found that wheat grown on his tiny, inefficient, fragmented holding could not be produced and marketed as cheaply as grain from the huge, mechanized farms of the United States, Canada, and Australia. Accordingly, the acreage planted to grain declined dramatically in those areas evolving toward market production. Similarly, the Mediterranean farmer found that wool and mohair from his small herds and flocks could not successfully compete with the produce of large ranches in the United States, Argentina, South Africa, Australia, and New Zealand, and once the decision was made to produce for market, the number of livestock dropped rapidly.

In effect the southern European agriculturist found that two of the three facets of his traditional diversified system, grains and livestock, held little market promise. Instead, the produce of orchards, vineyards, and vegetable gardens offered the best opportunity for commercial specialization. The mild southern climate gave the Mediterranean farmer a distinct advantage: Many of his fruits and vegetables, such as citrus, could not be raised elsewhere in Europe, and he was free of overseas competition by virtue of the perishability of the produce. The result has been a great increase in the acreage of orchards, vineyards, and gardens, with a corresponding increase in irrigation.

The typical pattern has been for whole districts to follow one course of specialization. The French Mediterranean zone, for example, was converted into one huge *mer de vignes,* a "sea of vines" stretching in many places as far as the eye can see; the irrigated *huertas* of eastern coastal Spain became the scene of specialized citrus cultivation, and gave the name to the Valencia orange (Figure 8.5); while Andalucia, the Adriatic coast of Italy, and the Riviera are famous for olives. Northern Sicilia and the area around Napoli also developed citrus specialization, and the valley of the Douro River in Portugal expanded production of the famous port wines. One of the most remarkable agricultural sights in the Mediterranean lands is the view from adjacent mountain heights of the olive-clad expanse of the once-sacred Plain of Krissa, near Delfi in Greece. This plain is one solid olive orchard, to the almost complete exclusion of other trees or crops, giving an appearance from above of a gray-green embayment of the nearby Gulf of Kórinthos.

Specialization has destroyed the distinctiveness of Mediterranean agriculture, which was above all based on a combination of three diverse agricultural endeavors on each farm. The end product of specialization in southern Europe is better described as *market gardening and orchardry* (Figure 8.6). Few areas have

Figure 8.5 An orange grove with irrigation system at Carcagente, in the coastal plain near Valencia, eastern Spain. Three basic modifications of classical Mediterranean agriculture are visible in the picture, including (1) the introduction of citrus, an accomplishment of the Jews and Arabs; (2) the development of large-scale irrigation systems, attributable to the Arab conquerors of Spain; and (3) the specialized production for market, largely the result of European urbanization in the last century and a half. The coastal plain around Valencia now resembles one huge citrus orchard, a monoculture fundamentally different from the traditional diversified subsistence farming of the Mediterranean. (Courtesy Spanish National Tourist Office.)

PRESENT–DAY TYPES OF AGRICULTURE

Miles 0 — 400
Km 0 — 600

········ Northern limit of orange cultivation

–·–·– Corn / root crop–small grain border in livestock fattening

▓ Market-gardening and orchardry (including viticulture and specialty crops such as tobacco, rice, and cotton)

Places for which selected wines are named

C Champagne   R Rheinwein   S Sherry
B Burgundy   P Port   CH Chianti

Survival of traditional diversified Mediterranean agriculture (grains and small livestock dominant)

Dairying

Places of origin of dairy breeds

1 Islands of Jersey and Guernsey   5. Brown Swiss (Canton of Schwyz)
2 Ayrshire   6. Kerry
3 Friesland ⎫ Holstein–Friesian
4 Holstein   ⎭

Towns for which selected famous cheeses are named

(CA) Camembert, France   (G) Gruyère, Switzerland
(CH) Cheddar, England   (M) Muenster, Germany
(E) Edam, Netherlands   (T) Tilsit, formerly German East Prussia

Livestock fattening (including raising of sheep for wool)

Meat products named for localities in the livestock fattening area

B Bologna (Italian city)
BR Braunschweiger (German city)
F Frankfurter (German city)

T Thüringer (East German province)
W Wiener (Austrian city)
WE Westphalian ham (West German province)

Survival of diversified mixed farming

▒ Commercial grain farming (in USSR)

〰 Livestock ranching

⫴ Survival of nomadic herding

✚ Nonagricultural areas

completely escaped the trend toward specialization and commercialization, but the interior of the Mediterranean peninsulas generally retain much of the traditional diversified system. These are often areas poorly endowed with irrigation water, where small grains and livestock are more important than vines and trees. In effect, two quite different agricultural–cultural zones have developed in southern Europe, one of which preserves the traditional system and the other of which has evolved into market-gardening. Alongside methods which date back to the time of Homer, types of farming are being developed in accordance with modern scientific agriculture and commercial requirements. Here one can view two worlds—that reminiscent of the Neolithic and classical past, which still survives in the small holdings where people live their lives with few outside contacts, and that inhabited by the specialized cash-crop farmer in touch with the world markets.

Other changes associated with the disappearance of feudalism have also occurred in recent times. The large landed estates are being broken up, the wealthy rural landowning class abolished, and the individual farms turned over to peasant ownership. Some of the latifundia have survived in southern parts of Iberia and Italy, but they are decreasing in number. In Greece, the successful rebellion against Turkish rule had the beneficial side effect of destroying the landed aristocracy, which was primarily composed of Turks. Typical of present conditions is the Greek island of Kriti, where 96 percent of the farmers now own their land. At the same time, an effort is being made through land reform to do away with the ancient, inefficient practice of fragmented farms.

8.3 MIXED CROP AND LIVESTOCK AGRICULTURE

Almost the entire agricultural zone north of the Mediterranean farming was once occupied by mixed crop and livestock farming. Here it is also helpful to gain an overview of the agricultural system as it existed traditionally, a system which might best be called medieval mixed farming (Figure 8.1).

MEDIEVAL MIXED FARMING

In this traditional system, various small grains were again raised on a rotational basis. In the southern and western parts of the mixed-farming zone, wheat was the principal grain, raised either in summer or winter primarily as a food crop. In France, the British Isles, the Balkans, and the steppes of Russia, white bread was dominant, a dietary trait which has been handed down to the present day. Rye, the second great bread grain of the medieval mixed-farming area, was concentrated in the north, in Germany, Scandinavia, Poland, and forested portions of Russia, where dark bread was and is preferred. The rye-wheat dividing line was fairly sharp, though some rye was found in the south and wheat in parts of the north (Figure 8.1). Rye was better suited to the cooler climates of the northern areas. Oats were raised throughout the medieval mixed-farming area, primarily as livestock feed, though in some poorer areas such as Scotland, where wheat did not thrive, it was used for human consumption, often in the form of oatmeal. Normally, oats were raised in the summer season. The fourth major small grain was barley, primarily

Figure 8.6 Present-day types of agriculture. (After Whittlesey, Gillmor, Freeman, Siegfried, Sourdillat, Otremba, Hartshorne-Dicken, and others.)

a livestock feed, though also widely used in the brewing of beer, the northern substitute for wine.

Part of the cropland was also given over to the fiber crop flax, from which linen garments were made. European lands, including the Soviet Union, still today produce well over 90 percent of the world's flax each year.

The crops were typically rotated in the well-known three-field system, in which each piece of land was used successively for winter grain, fallow, and summer grain. In poorer areas, a one-field system was dominant, involving a small, continuously cropped area known as the "infield" (German *Esch*, Norwegian *innmark*), surrounded by a much more extensive "outfield" (Norwegian *utmark*), used only for pasture and meadow or, in areas such as Scotland, for short-term cropping. In the Scottish outfield, a shifting cultivation was practiced: two to four years of cropping followed by a decade or more of fallow. In the one-field system, typical of northwestern Germany, highland Britain, and Norway, livestock were penned on the infield from harvest to planting in order to maintain soil fertility. This permitted the "eternal rye culture" of northern Germany, in which the same bread crop was planted year after year. In parts of lowland Britain, southern France, and northern Iberia, a two-field system similar to that of the Mediterranean grain lands was characteristic, in which the fallow was observed every other year rather than the one in three of the three-field system. Both the two- and three-field rotations may have been derived from the more primitive one-field system, as increased population pressures forced the settlers to bring the outfield under more continuous cultivation, until finally a piece of land there was fallowed only once every two or three years.

An important part of the traditional system was the maintenance of a sizable kitchen garden adjacent to the farmhouse in the village, a task typically allotted to the women of the family. Here were the typical mid-latitude fruit trees, such as the apple, pear, cherry, and plum. Various summer vegetables were also grown, including lettuce, peas, turnips, and carrots.

A second basic part of medieval mixed farming was the cutting of hay from meadowland to provide additional sustenance for livestock during the winter season. In our modern urban society, the meanings of "meadow" and "pasture" have become somewhat blurred, trending toward synonymity. The fundamental difference was that livestock were allowed to graze the pasture, but not the meadow, from which hay was to be cut. As the famous nursery rhyme admonishes, "sheep's in the meadow" was a state of affairs to be corrected. During much of the winter season, the livestock were kept in stalls to consume hay and feed grains. At the opposite season, they grazed on fallow fields, pastures, and in remnant forests, which usually lay toward the periphery of the village lands.

Livestock were of much greater significance in the medieval mixed-farming area than in Mediterranean agriculture, and they supplied a larger part of the rural diet. Cattle were the dominant animals, providing meat, dairy products, manure for the fields, and power to pull the bulky plow characteristic of the Germanic lands. Until recent times, it was possible to see even milk cows being used in plowing (Figure 8.7), though oxen were more common. In much of central Europe, including Germany and Poland, swine were a more important source of meat than were cattle, and pork is still a mainstay of the diet there. The unique value of swine is their ability to convert even the least savory garbage and waste into high-quality

Figure 8.7 Cows used for plowing in West Germany. This view, taken in 1951, is becoming increasingly rare in western Europe as farm mechanization advances rapidly. It is a vestige of the practices of medieval times. (Photo courtesy G. J. Jordan.)

meat, and the mast of remnant oak and beech forests added to their diet. Horses were normally owned by only a fortunate minority of farmers and bore the disadvantage of confiscation in time of war. Few areas lacked flocks of sheep, but only in areas of poor quality, such as the Lüneburger Heath of northern Germany and the British highlands, did they attain the position of most important livestock in the medieval mixed-farming zone. Chickens, ducks, and geese were numerous on most farms.

Perhaps the key difference between the medieval mixed farming and classical Mediterranean agriculture was the close relationship in the former between crops and livestock. The Mediterranean farmer raised both plants and animals, but there was little or no tie between the two, and animal husbandry was separate from tillage. In medieval mixed farming, crops and livestock were inseparable, for the animals provided the manure used to maintain soil fertility and the power for plowing the fields. In turn, much of the produce of the cropland, particularly the barley and oats, was fed to the livestock, and extensive areas were used for meadow and pasture.

In other respects, the traditional agricultural systems of northern and southern Europe were similar. A landed aristocracy dominated a tenant peasantry in both, and the individual farms were small and fragmented. Both medieval mixed farming and classical Mediterranean agriculture were unspecialized, subsistence types of farming, with a low ceiling on ambition and scant hope for improvement in living standards. In each case, a deeply conservative peasantry developed, unlearned and completely outside the currents of innovation which swept the cities and towns.

CHANGES IN MEDIEVAL MIXED FARMING

As in the Mediterranean peninsulas, important changes occurred in the agricultural system of the mixed-farming area. New crops were introduced as a result of the Age of Discovery, which brought Europeans into contact with many new domestic plants. The "Irish" or white potato, a domesticate of the South American Indians, was brought to Europe in the 1600s and gained widespread acceptance throughout the mixed-farming zone in the eighteenth century, particularly in Ireland, Germany, and Poland. In some countries the potato became a principal food crop, and it was also found to be useful as livestock feed and as a source of alcoholic beverages. The value of the potato lay largely in its ability to provide large amounts of food from a small acreage, even in cloudy, cool climates. This can properly be regarded as the single most important crop introduction of modern European history, for reliance on the potato became so great that harvest failures in the 1840s caused the starvation of hundreds of thousands of rural Irish and the emigration of many more.

The second great American crop to be introduced into Europe was Indian corn or maize, which became a key livestock feed crop in the warm southern part of the mixed-farming area, including the Balkans, northern Iberia, the Po Valley, and parts of southern France (Figure 8.6). As a food crop, maize has been adopted only in northern Italy and Romania, though Bulgarians and Hungarians have at times relied on it as an emergency food. Maize was not widely accepted in the Mediterranean, partly because the summer drought retarded its growth, and it was equally unsuited to the cooler, cloudier parts of the marine west coast climate. It thrives, however, in the warm-summer humid continental and humid subtropical areas, and the Balkans have become Europe's version of the American Corn Belt.

Other changes were made to obtain greater intensity of land use, leading to greater productivity or output. Gradually the fallow was eliminated and the old two- and three-field rotation systems disappeared, greatly increasing the acreage and production of feed crops. The fallow had always been something of a problem, since the field quickly became choked with grass and weeds in the idle year unless the farmers continually cultivated it. In many areas, turnip crops replaced the fallow, with repeated hoeing employed to keep the weeds out. Improved, more complicated crop rotations were developed, such as the Norfolk four-course rotation, which included turnips. Improved pastures and meadows resulted from the spread of new varieties of clover, and the increased planting of turnips and sugar beets added significantly to the amount of livestock feed.

The amount of pastureland was also reduced, and many old grazing areas were planted to crops. The net result of the changes was a marked increase in the amount of feed available for livestock, and the numbers of animals rose accordingly. Stall-feeding became all important, for the stock were kept penned rather than roaming about in pastures and forests. Increased confinement of the animals also allowed a more complete collection of manure, which in turn aided the elimination of fallowing. Selective breeding of livestock was promoted, resulting in higher quality animals.

The German scientists Justus von Liebig and Albert Thaer developed chemical fertilizers in the 1800s, though many farmers still today prefer to use the organic fertilizer derived from compost or dung heaps, which remain an unforgettable olfactory aspect of most rural villages in Germany and other countries.

All of these changes taken together comprised the so-called Agricultural Revolution, of which England was the leader. The changes occurred in a spiral: the elimination of fallow → an increase in yield of feed crops → more livestock per farm → more manure per farm → increased fertility of fields → increased yields of feed crops, and so on.

As in the Mediterranean areas, significant changes occurred in land tenure, though the course of modification differed in the eastern and western parts of the mixed-farming area. In western Europe, there was a steady move toward peasant landownership between about 1650 and 1850, with a gradual elimination of the landed aristocracy. This transition occurred in various ways, but the sequence of events in the Po Valley of northern Italy is illustrative. Landlords there were obligated by law to pay outgoing peasant tenants for any improvements made during their terms as renters, and failure to do so forced the owner to renew the lease at no increase in rent. These improvements often included woodland-clearing, marsh drainage, or even irrigation development, for which the landlords were hard pressed to pay, and typically they allowed the lease to be renewed. The rent thus remained constant while inflation lowered its relative value, until eventually the peasant was able to buy the land.

In eastern Europe, beyond a line closely paralleling the present Iron Curtain, the aristocracy persisted and few farmers gained possession of the lands they worked. Many aspects of feudal bondage actually persisted in Slavic Europe and eastern Germany down to the present century. Perhaps partly for this reason, a more drastic and violent solution for the problem of tenancy was chosen—liquidation of the landed aristocracy under Communist dictatorships. Typically, the Communists won early peasant support by promising the farmers landownership. In 1946, for example, such a campaign was carried out in Russian-occupied East Germany under the slogan *"Junker Land in Bauern Hand"* ("Aristocrats' lands in farmers' hands"). After a brief period of peasant ownership, the state confiscated the land and established the collective and state farms which now dominate most countries of eastern Europe.

Collectives involve a group of farmers operating as a unit, more or less in business for themselves as a group, paying rent to the state and splitting profits. In the less common state-farm system, the farmers are simply salaried state employees who work for a fixed wage on huge superfarms and turn over all produce to the government. Collective and state farms are overwhelmingly dominant today in all Communist countries except Poland and Yugoslavia, which have allowed private family farms to remain. The rapidity with which collectivization spread is indicated by East Germany, where the percentage of farms privately owned dropped from 93 percent in 1952 to 7 percent in 1960. In contrast, the Yugoslavs, who are perhaps not so intense in their Communism, have left over 90 percent of the farms under private ownership.

Since about 1950, increased mechanization has also brought significant changes to the traditional mixed-farming system. In western Europe, the number of grain combines increased by thirteen times from 1950 to 1960, milking machines by seven times, and tractors by over three times. It is still possible to see plows pulled by oxen, or even cows, and horse-drawn farm wagons, but such reminders of the past are disappearing rapidly, at least in western Europe.

THE RISE OF SPECIALIZATION

As in the Mediterranean, the most far-reaching changes in medieval mixed farming were caused by the rise of commercialization and specialization, destroying the traditional diversified system. In some cases, small and relatively unimportant facets of medieval agriculture were magnified to become the focus of a market-oriented economy. The trend toward specialization had its beginnings in late medieval and early modern times, but the major progress in that direction has been made in the nineteenth and twentieth centuries. Small, islandlike areas of intensive market-farming first appeared in the Low Country, including Zeeland, Holland, and Flanders, in the regions near Milano and Venezia in the Po Valley of Italy, around Paris, London, and the towns of the Rhine Valley, and in some other urbanized areas. The major impetus was provided by the rise of the towns during the Industrial Revolution.

Agriculturists in the mixed-farming zone had to choose specialties which allowed them to compete with foreign suppliers. They found in time that food-grain production on a commercial basis was unprofitable in competition with the wheatlands of the Americas, Russia, and Australia, although there was a trend in some districts toward specialized food-grain production in the period before competition began. In France, the regions of Beauce and the Île de France developed into major granaries in the 1600s and 1700s, and many farmers in Germany and Denmark chose the same specialty in the 1800s. In the final analysis, however, cash grain-farming did not prove to be a viable form of rural economy, and the mixed-farming area developed in the direction of dairying, livestock-fattening, and market-gardening. In the United Kingdom, the decline of commercial grain-farming was hastened by the repeal of the so-called Corn Laws in 1846, removing import restrictions on foreign grain.

DAIRYING. In many parts of the medieval mixed-farming area, the milk cow came to dominate agriculture, and dairy products became the specialization of most farmers. The European Dairy Belt stretches around the shores of the North and Baltic seas, including most of the British Isles, coastal France, the Low Country, northern Germany, and the Scandinavian lands. An outlier is found to the south, in the Alps of Switzerland and Austria (Figure 8.6). These regions developed dairying as a specialty for several reasons, not the least of which was the Germanic dietary preference for dairy products derived from cows, a preference not found further south in the Mediterranean lands. In addition, the Dairy Belt occupies the cloudiest, coolest part of northwestern Europe, a land better suited to pasture and the raising of hay than to field crops such as wheat. Similarly, the rugged mountain terrain of the Alps is more easily adapted to the raising of grasses, and hay can be mown on the steep slopes where crop tillage would be difficult. Extensive areas of mountain pasture, the *Almen,* lie too high to be farmed but are valuable to a livestock-based economy.

In addition to the environmental factors and cultural food preference, the distribution of population influenced the location of the Dairy Belt. Farmers practicing a dairy economy deal in part with highly perishable products such as butter and fluid milk, which must have quick access to market to prevent spoilage. It is not accidental that the Dairy Belt parallels in part the great east–west corridor of dense population which stretches across north-central Europe, containing a large proportion of the more important urban centers and industrial districts (compare Figures 3.5 and 8.6).

The trend toward specialized dairying can be traced back to the Middle Ages in some parts of northern Europe. In England, the counties of Essex and adjacent East Suffolk, on the North Sea coast just to the northeast of London, were known for dairying in the late Middle Ages. In the 1600s the shires of Hertford and Buckingham north of the British capital adopted the same agricultural specialty, as did certain districts in the Midlands. Generally the more peripheral dairy areas produced cheese, which was less perishable. Also in the 1600s, the French provinces of Normandie on the English Channel and Brie near Paris became known as dairy areas, as did parts of the Low Country. In the nineteenth century, dairying spread to its present limits, displacing cash grain-farming in countries such as Denmark, a spread facilitated by the development of improved transportation facilities.

The Dairy Belt has an importance which extends far beyond the confines of Europe. Developments in dairying in the European culture area have shaped subsequent similar economies in overseas colonial settlement zones, including Anglo-America, New Zealand, and Australia. For example, every major breed of dairy cattle in the world today was derived from the European Dairy Belt, and the breeds have names indicative of their origin. The Jersey and Guernsey bear the names of two of the Channel Islands, which lie between France and England; the Ayrshire breed was developed in Scottish Ayr; the Holstein-Friesian is derived from Friesland in the northern Netherlands and the north German province of Schleswig-Holstein; the Brown Swiss was originally bred in the canton of Schwyz in central Switzerland. A lesser dairy breed, the Kerry, is named for its Irish county of origin, and the name of another minor breed, the Dutch Belted, also suggests its origin (Figure 8.6). Similarly, the famous cheeses of the world generally are named for towns and cities in the European Dairy Belt, including Edam, in the Netherlands, Münster, in northern Germany, Camembert, in French Normandie, Gruyères, in the French-speaking part of Switzerland, Tilsit (now Sovietsk), in East Prussia, Cheddar, in the western English shire of Somerset, and many others (Figure 8.6).

The economic decision to specialize in dairying brought with it some striking changes in land use. The area in pasture and meadow greatly increased, occupying the larger proportion of the farmland, and the food crops virtually disappeared (Figure 8.8). Feed grains, mainly barley and oats, exceeded wheat and rye, and some root crops such as sugar beets were raised for feed. Still, the dominant impression gained from travel through a dairy region is one of almost continuous grassy pastures and meadows.

There are some pronounced regional contrasts within the European Dairy Belt, both in type of produce and intensity of farming. Denmark, which specializes in butter production and contributes 16 percent of all butter entering international trade, is an example of highly developed dairying. The Danish farmers have banded together into local cooperatives, mainly for purposes of marketing, but also for the communal construction of creameries. Land and livestock, however, are still privately owned. Each package of butter is stamped with the code number of the

Figure 8.8 Cows at pasture in Denmark, part of the European dairy belt. The cows are of the Red Danish (rød dansk) breed, first bred in the 1840s. Just over two-thirds of all dairy cattle in Denmark today are of this breed. In the background is a typical Danish courtyard farmstead, with thatched roof and half-timbered walls (see Chapter 9). The buildings are grouped compactly around all four sides of a central courtyard. (Danish Information Office.)

cooperative and the individual farmer, so that any customer complaints concerning quality can be directed to the farmer responsible and fines levied. This system produces the highest-quality butter to be found anywhere, supplemented by fine pork and bacon derived from swine fattened on skim milk, a by-product of the butter-making process. In the Netherlands, attention is focused on milk and high-quality cheeses. The Dutch produce 21 percent of the world cheese which enters international trade and one-quarter of the condensed or evaporated milk. Another advanced dairy country is the United Kingdom, where the farmers specialize in marketing fluid milk.

Transhumant dairying has long been typical of mountainous Switzerland,

Austria, and Norway. The dairy cattle are driven into the high mountain pastures (Swiss *Almen,* Norwegian *seter*) in the summer season, where herdsmen living in small huts milk the animals and make cheese, which is collected at regular intervals and taken to market. In the meantime, fellow workers at the farmsteads in the valleys raise feed crops and cut hay for the winter, when the dairy cattle are driven back downslope to be housed in barns during the cold season. Transhumance tends to cut down the productivity of the cows, due to the great amount of walking necessary, but this has partly been overcome by an increased reliance on motor vehicles in moving the stock between summer and winter areas. In Norway, where transhumance is on the decline, many farmers traditionally left the cattle in the care of their families and worked seasonally as fishermen or lumbermen.

LIVESTOCK-FATTENING.   In most nondairy parts of the old medieval mixed-farming zone, the trend in specialization was toward livestock-fattening, which had been an important aspect of the original diversified system. Much of the area south of the Dairy Belt and north of the Mediterranean now concentrates on the feeding of cattle, hogs, and sheep—with fattened meat animals as the end product of the agricultural system (Figure 8.6). Feeder specialization began at least as early as the 1600s in parts of England, particularly in East Anglia northeast of London and Leicestershire in the Midlands. Similar developments occurred about the same time in parts of Germany and the Netherlands, but most of the progress awaited the growth of urban markets in the 1800s.

In the feeder areas, raising of livestock feed replaced production for human consumption, and a pronounced regional contrast developed in the choice of crops. South of a rather sharp line across the neck of the Balkan Peninsula, the southern edge of the Alps, and on through southern France, Indian corn or maize is the principal feed crop used to fatten livestock, as in the American Corn Belt, but to the north of the line, the small grains and root crops are dominant, including barley, oats, potatoes, and sugar beets (Figure 8.6). In Germany, 70 percent or more of the potato harvest is used as livestock feed.

Just as the European Dairy Belt gave names to many important breeds and dairy products, so the livestock-feeder area has influenced the names of meats and sausages. For example, Thüringer, Braunschweiger (a liver sausage), and Westphalian ham (which is actually beef) are all derived from the names of German provinces in the livestock-fattening area, while Frankfurter, Wiener, and Bologna bear the names of cities there (Figure 8.6).

MARKET-GARDENING.   Still another direction of specialization within the old medieval mixed-farming area was market-gardening, the same course taken by many Mediterranean agriculturists. In the diversified mixed-farming system, the kitchen garden and orchard was an important adjunct to the field crops, and from them developed in certain small areas the specialization in production of mid-latitude fruits and vegetables. Wherever large urban markets were at hand, kitchen gardens began spilling out into the fields, gradually becoming the focus of the agricultural system. Most of the areas so affected are too small to be shown on the map of modern types of agriculture, and typically narrow halos of market-gardening surround the larger cities and towns.

The products of market-gardening vary from one area to another, includ-

Figure 8.9   A flower-bulb farm in the Netherlands. Such agricultural activity is classified as market-gardening, which developed out of medieval mixed farming. It is characterized by very intensive cultivation of small acreages, involving a great deal of hand labor. Market-gardening is usually found in areas adjacent to large urban population clusters. (Photo courtesy the Netherlands Information Service.)

ing apples, important for cider production in the west of France, pears, plums, tobacco, cherries, various vegetables, and flowers for seed in parts of the Low Country. The tulip fields of the Netherlands and Belgium present a scene of unsurpassed agricultural beauty when the flowers are in blossom (Figure 8.9).

Such "islands" of intense garden cultivation began to appear in the late Middle Ages in the Po Valley of Italy, Flanders, and other areas where towns were developing, and as early as the 1600s the modern pattern was fairly well evolved in the Netherlands. Most market gardens, however, arose with the coming of the Industrial Revolution, which first affected England and later spread to the European mainland.

Acceptance of market-gardening as a specialty caused a drastic change in the agricultural character of areas involved. Livestock were greatly reduced in number or disappeared altogether from such farms, and the pasture, meadow, and small grains were eliminated. The farm simply became one large garden or orchard.

COMMERCIAL FOOD-GRAIN AGRICULTURE.   While it is true that most farmers of the mixed-crop–livestock zone found concentration on cash food grains undesirable because of overseas competition, one area of this type of specialization did develop on the periphery of the European culture area. In the Ukraine, along the northern shores of the Black Sea in the steppe grasslands, a major "wheat belt" developed (Figure 8.6). As wheat ascended to a leading position in this area, there was typically a decline in the number of livestock per farm unit and a virtual disappearance of the three-field system and other crop rotations. Pasture and meadow lands were plowed and planted to wheat, and feed grains, those raised for livestock consumption, also gave way to a monoculture of wheat. The Ukraine remains a wheat specialization area still today, but elsewhere in Europe commercial food-grain agriculture was displaced by more intensive types of farming in the late nineteenth century.

8.4 TRADITIONAL SPECIALIZED VITICULTURE NORTH OF THE MEDITERRANEAN

Grape culture was one of the basic elements of classical Mediterranean agriculture, and viticulture subsequently became the basis for specialized market-gardening in many southern districts, as in the Douro area of Portugal. Viticulture was not limited to the Mediterranean zone, however, for it had spread northward even as early as the period of the Roman Empire. By the fourth century A.D., vineyards had been established in the Rhône–Saône Corridor of eastern France, including the now-famous Côte d'Or region of Bourgogne (Burgundy), along the course of the Loire River, in the Bordeaux area of southwestern France, and in more northern regions such as the valleys of the Mosel near the present German city of Trier (Figure 8.1). In following centuries, the need of the Christian Church for sacramental wine aided an expansion of viticulture in the Rhine, Neckar, and Main river valleys of western Germany (Figure 8.1), as well as in some districts where grape cultivation failed to survive, as in Flanders, southeastern England, and northern Germany. Carolingian Frankish rulers also encouraged the establishment of viticulture in their various crown domains in an effort to acquire greater revenue from the land.

This northern viticulture differed both from its Mediterranean parent and from the medieval mixed farming of surrounding areas. In contrast to the traditional Mediterranean system, these areas totally specialized in raising grapes, most particularly wine grapes, for neither raisins nor table grapes were of any consequence. Northern viticulture has been from its very beginnings a highly specialized, market-oriented form of agriculture, involving great care and skill. Knowledge was passed from father to son or from one generation of monks to the next, and a vineyard typically remained in the same family for centuries. The vintners were often free of feudal restrictions and formed a small but prosperous middle class in the midst of a quite alien feudal society.

During the Dark Ages, northern viticulture declined somewhat, kept alive principally at the numerous monasteries of France and western Germany, but the reestablishment of major trade ties in the later Middle Ages revived the business. The wines of Champagne, Bourgogne, and of the Rhine and Mosel are world famous today, based on a heritage extending back 1500 years or more.

Another difference from Mediterranean viticulture was found in the siting of vineyards. In southern Europe, vines are found both on plains and slopes, but in the trans-Alpine lands the vineyards are almost invariably on terraced hillsides where better sun exposure is available. The German word for vineyard, *Weinberg,* literally means "wine hill" or "wine mountain," suggesting the close tie to slope location (Figure 2.3). Some of the best wines come from south-facing slopes, as the famous Rheingau near Frankfurt and Wiesbaden in West Germany. Sun exposure varies with every twist and turn of the valleys, and wines of quite different quality are often obtained from adjacent vineyards. Wine connoisseurs are familiar with the names of the better-endowed vineyards, as well as the best years of bottling. Weather conditions are never exactly the same from one year to the next, and the quality of wine in these marginal northern areas of viticulture fluctuates accordingly.

In modern times, the areas of historic viticulture north of the Mediterranean have blended well into the specialized agricultural economy of Germany and France, falling into the classification of market-gardening and orchardry (Figure 8.6). The basic difference is that these vineyard-keepers are inheritors of an ancient agricultural specialty rich in tradition, not one derived from medieval mixed farming in recent times.

The presence or absence of viticulture in various areas north of the Mediterranean is closely tied to local beverage preferences. Generally, where wine is available it is the drink of the common folk, as in France and southwestern Germany. But beyond the vineyard regions, in northern Germany, Bayern, the Low Country, Scandinavia, the British Isles, and the northern Slavic lands, beer or other alcoholic drinks prepared from small grains are preferred. It is not unusual for the common rural folk of the Northern German Plain to offer three or four different types of beer to visitors but no wine. In urban areas, the wine-beer contrast has broken down, with both accepted by the people, but in rural districts it is even today often a matter of beer *or* wine.

8.5 NOMADIC HERDING

A final traditional agricultural type is *nomadic herding*, found in the northernmost reaches of Scandinavia and Finland, as well as adjacent parts of the Soviet Union, among the group known as the Lapps (Figure 8.1). The traditional system involved seasonal wanderings with herds of domesticated reindeer, a total absence of crops and other livestock, and movable tent housing (Figure 8.10). Lapp herders acquired many of the necessities of life from the reindeer: meat for food, skins for housing and clothing, and bone for tools and instruments. Summers were spent herding the stock on the tundras of the hilly interior and northern coastal fringe of the Lappish domain, including some islands off the coast of Norway. In wintertime, the reindeer were driven into the protective coniferous forests adjacent to the tundra, which afforded shelter from the bitterly cold winds of the open, grassy tundra. Autumn and spring were spent en route to and from the summer pastures on the tundra. The Lapps had no awareness of international boundaries and wandered freely through what is today Norwegian, Swedish, Finnish, and Soviet territory.

Even this remote corner of Europe has not been immune to the far-reaching changes which affected the agricultural economy in other parts of the culture area. The Lapps and their traditional way of life have experienced far-reaching changes in recent times, which have destroyed their nomadic herding. Beginning in 1852, certain borders were closed to international migration, forcing the Lapps to accept citizenship in one or another country and disrupting many routes of seasonal movement. An agreement between Norway and Sweden allowed some Swedish Lapps to use summer tundra pastures in Norway, in exchange for the use of Swedish forests for winter refuge by a small number of Norwegian Lapps, but border crossings are generally rare. Perhaps one of the more significant changes,

Figure 8.10   Norwegian Lapps engaged in the traditional nomadic reindeer-herding. This large reindeer herd is in Finnmark, Norway's northernmost and easternmost province. Tent housing is employed during the migrations, and the principal vehicle is the sled, several of which are shown. These two herders also have skis to facilitate movement. (Norwegian National Travel Office.)

only recently begun, involves the fencing of the range, which will separate the herds of adjacent groups of Lapps and ends the traditional open-range system. One such fence parallels most of the Norwegian–Finnish border, and others have been built within the various nations. Sweden has designated a *Lappmark* border within its territory, north of which the Lapps have precedence in rural land use.

Norway has established a Reindeer Office within its Ministry of Agriculture, and the Lapp herders of that country belong to the National Association of Reindeer-Herding Lapps. The Reindeer Office requires reports of the number of livestock each year, supervises migrations, and demands that each owner mark his deer and register the mark with the government. Sanitary slaughter sheds and meat-freezing plants have been built, and some efforts at commercialization have been made.

Most significant of all, many Lapps have abandoned herding altogether, accepting employment in fishing, farming, mining, and other industries. Only part of the group known as the Mountain Lapps still engages in livestock raising, and even they have largely given up tent housing for more permanent, though rather wretched, shacks. A visitor to Lappish settlements is strongly reminded of American Indian reservations. Nomadism has all but disappeared, replaced by a transhumance in which the people are sedentary for five to six months during the year. The end product is much better described as livestock-ranching than nomadic herding, though more of the traditional system survives in Soviet areas (Figure 8.6). Europe and Asia have met in these northlands, and Europe has won.

8.6 CAUSAL FACTORS IN AGRICULTURAL DISTRIBUTIONS

The pattern of agricultural types which has developed in Europe is due to a complex interworking of environmental, cultural, and economic causes. The role of the climate, soils, and terrain has been suggested, as, for example, the tie between classical Mediterranean agriculture and the seasonality of rainfall, which led to winter grain cultivation and selection of drought-resistant trees and vines. Infertile districts are frequently given over to sheep-raising in many parts of Europe, and regions of steep slope have been left to pasture and woodland. Farmers have scarcely penetrated the inhospitable subarctic climate zone. Vineyards north of the Mediterranean thrive mainly on slopes with proper sun exposure, and the Dairy Belt corresponds locationally to the cloudiest, coolest part of the marine west coast climate. The production of raisins in Mediterranean lands depends heavily on sunny, rainless days after the grape harvest, and Swiss dairymen rely on the Alpine pastures for summer grazing.

In all of these ways and many more, man has been obliged to consider the nature of the physical environment in making his agricultural decisions. At the same time, European man has long demonstrated a great ability to modify unsuitable environments to better suit his needs. Insufficient rainfall is overcome through irrigation in the *huertas* of eastern Spain; infertile sandy soils are rendered highly productive through the addition of chemical fertilizers; and rugged terrain is tamed through the device of terracing. Some Icelandic market-gardeners are freed from the disadvantages of a cold climate by using hothouses, heated by water piped in from hot springs, for vegetable production. The search for causal factors obviously must be carried beyond a consideration of the physical environment to variations in man's culture.

VON THÜNEN'S ISOLATED STATE

Various scholars have attempted to explain the pattern of land use in economic terms, and the pioneer study of this type was written in the 1820s by a German rural landlord named Johann Heinrich von Thünen. His book, *The Isolated State,* has become a classic in the field of location theory, though his ideas are better classified as a method of analysis than a theory of location. Von Thünen was convinced that transport costs and the location of market had a great influence on land-use decisions, and he sought to set up a "model," or ideal situation, in which to express his ideas. He proposed a hypothetical, completely isolated country surrounded by a wilderness, devoid of arterial transport routes (Figure 8.11). At the center of the circular state was a single market town or city, and farmers at equal distances from the town were assumed to have equal access to it. There were no differences in soil fertility or crop yields, and the isolated state lay in a flat, featureless plain. Further, von Thünen assumed for the purposes of his study that all farmers were market-oriented and would seek the maximum profits possible from their land. In effect, von Thünen was neutralizing many potentially causal factors in order to study the effect of a few which were economic in character.

Of crucial interest to von Thünen was the difference between the price of

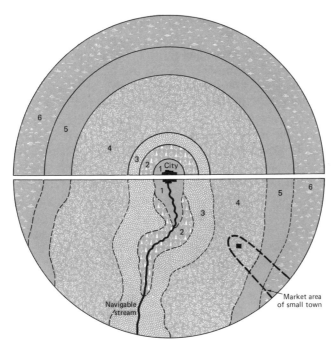

Figure 8.11   A diagram of von Thünen's Isolated State. The lower half of the illustration shows the effect of a navigable stream and a second, smaller town on the pattern of land use. Types of land use are shown to change with increasing distance from the central market city as follows:

> Zone 1—crops and livestock raised according to the character of climate and soil, as well as the demands of market; transport places little or no restrictions on land use due to adjacency of market.
>
> Zone 2—forests (assuming the widespread use of wood for fuel); nearness to the market city is required because of the bulk and weight of wood.
>
> Zone 3—rotation of root crops, clover, grains, and legumes; intensive cultivation with no fallow or pasture.
>
> Zone 4—rotation of grains, pasture, and fallow, with one year in seven fallow.
>
> Zone 5—three-field system; rotation of grains and fallow, with one year in three fallow.
>
> Zone 6—grazing of livestock, with pasture as dominant use of land.

The diagram must be evaluated in terms of economic conditions of the early 1800s, when von Thünen wrote his book. (After von Thünen.)

agricultural goods and the cost of producing and marketing them. Both costs and prices were higher near the city, because land and labor were more expensive and the demand greater. With increasing distance from the city, prices dropped off faster than did costs, in large part because the cost of transport grew greater, partially offsetting lower expenses for land and labor. Therefore, the difference between costs and prices, the farmer's profit, was greater in areas nearest to the city. Von Thünen further reasoned that more intensive forms of agriculture would be found in the areas of maximum potential profit, that is, in the areas nearest to the city, and that intensity would decline toward the periphery of the isolated state. The greater intensity of land use near the city is a result of the fact that higher potential profits allow more application of labor and capital per acre before the point of diminishing returns is reached. Furthermore, the higher value of real estate near the city, reflected in costs for purchasing or renting and in taxes, encourages a more intensive use of the land. Greater intensity may be attained either by an increased application of labor and capital per acre or by changing to the production of more valuable crops and livestock. Typically, both of these methods are employed to obtain high intensity of land use.

The map of von Thünen's hypothetical state reveals six concentric zones of land use (Figure 8.11). In the zone nearest the central town or city, crops and livestock would be raised according to the character of the climate and soil, as well as the demands of the market. Nearness to the town renders transport costs and time unimportant in determining land use, and von Thünen labeled this zone as one of "free" choice of type of agriculture. In effect, however, the intensive production of highly perishable commodities such as milk, fruits, and vegetables would be favored by the nearness of the market and high potential profits, giving rise to a belt of dairying and market-gardening. It is to be expected that the most intensive forms of agriculture, in which the greatest amounts of labor and capital are applied per unit of land, would be attracted to this first zone.

Von Thünen's second concentric belt of land use was a zone of forest. To understand his reasoning here, one must recall that wood was in widespread demand as a heating fuel in the early nineteenth century, and transport facilities were very poorly developed. The extreme weight and bulk of wood required that its source not be too far removed from the consumers in the central market town. Beyond the forest zone were three successive crop areas, differentiated from one another by decreasing intensity of land use with increasing distance from the central market town (Figure 8.11). In the belt of cropland just beyond the forest (zone 3), no pasture or fallow was present, a sign of high intensity agriculture, while the fallow was observed one year in seven in the zone 4 belt and one year in three in the outermost crop area, zone 5. The periphery of the isolated state, zone 6, was occupied by a livestock-grazing economy, one of the least intensive uses of land.

Obviously, if other causal factors are considered, then von Thünen's concentric zones become distorted as a host of forces exert diverging pulls. Differences in soil fertility, inequality of access to transportation, the presence of multiple markets, and countless other factors all come into play. The effect of several of these is shown in the lower half of the map of the isolated state (Figure 8.11).

Von Thünen's specific findings are definitely somewhat obsolete, but his general ideas and methods of analysis remain valid, offering a point of departure for more sophisticated studies of the causes of land-use patterns. There is much in the present and past distribution of types of agriculture in Europe which suggests the basic validity of von Thünen's theory, and the evidence is visible on several different scales. Around individual villages in lands as diverse as Italy, the Netherlands, Sweden, and Bulgaria, it has been noted that the fields nearest the village or farmstead are more intensively farmed, with peripheral areas often left to pasture and woodland (Table 8.1). One cannot help but be reminded of von Thünen when observing the halo of vineyards and orchards which surrounds many Italian villages, giving way to grainlands and livestock pasture at increased distances from the settlements.

On a national scale, the change in type of agriculture with increasing distance from market can be illustrated by the United Kingdom, where understanding of the causal factors in agricultural distributions has been greatly aided by the

TABLE 8.1 Decreasing Intensity of Land Use
and Productivity with Increasing Distance from Farmstead

Netherlands		Sweden	
Distance of plot from farmstead	Average man-hours applied per year on cropland plots larger than 15 hectares (37 acres)	Size of farm	Percent reduction in output per unit of land for each kilometer (0.6 mile) increase in distance from farmstead
0.5 km (0.3 mi)	400	10–20 hectares (25–50 acres)	4
1 km (0.6 mi)	360	20–40 hectares (50–100 acres)	9
2 km (1.2 mi)	300	Over 40 hectares (Over 100 acres)	26
3 km (1.9 mi)	240		
4 km (2.5 mi)	190	All farms	13
5 km (3.1 mi)	150		

Source: Chisholm, *Rural Settlement and Land Use*, London: Hutchinson and Co., 1962, used with permission.

work of the British geographer Michael Chisholm in particular. A description of farming in 1811 notes zones of dairying, hay production, and market-gardening on the periphery of London, and certain elements of this zoning have survived to the present. Garden crops which are highly perishable or require particular soil or climate types have been shown to be the most highly localized in distribution in England, and less perishable dairy products such as cheese, salted butter, and dried milk are drawn from more remote areas than is fluid milk. Sheep-raising, one of the least intensive forms of land use, is confined largely to more remote regions such as the Scottish Highlands, and the survival of a subsistence farming reminiscent of medieval times is evident only in the distant island fringe of Gaelic-speaking northern Scotland.

On a grander scale, the Thünian principles can be seen in Europe as a whole. As early as the 1920s, the Swedish geographer Olaf Jonasson expressed the belief that the industrial belt of northwestern Europe constituted one huge urban area or supercity, flanked by a Thünian inner zone of market-gardening and dairying, in much the same manner as the central market town of the isolated state. Van Valkenburgh and Held's study, dating from the early 1950s, revealed that intensity of farming, as measured by the average yields of eight major crops, declined with increasing distance from the huge urban-industrial market in northwestern Europe. There is every reason to believe that this pattern still exists at present.

RECENT ANALYSES BASED ON VON THÜNEN

The Thünian concept of commercial agricultural zoning in Europe as a whole has been further developed recently by the geographer J. R. Peet, who added an analysis of changes which have occurred through time, particularly in the nineteenth century. Obviously, population changes in von Thünen's central city, with resultant changes in demand for farm products, would have an effect on agriculture in the surrounding zones, as would the development of new and cheaper means of transporting produce. Such changes occurred in nineteenth-century northwestern Europe, where a "supercity" took shape, composed of myriad industrial centers lying in the belt of manufacturing on the coal fields of Britain, the Low Country, and Germany. The European supercity, coupled with another which arose in the northeastern United States, formed what Peet and others called the "Thünen World City." A huge increase in total population accompanied the development of the supercity, thereby greatly enlarging the market. At the same time, transportation of farm produce became easier and cheaper through the building of canals, railroads, and oceangoing steamers. Furthermore, the average income of the urban population of the Thünen World City rose markedly in the 1800s, magnifying the purchasing power and increasing the consumption of high-quality foods. The net result of the above-mentioned changes was an increase in demand for farm products and an improvement in access to market. The impact on Europe as a whole was the same that similar modifications would have on farming zones in the isolated state.

Peet argued that the increased demand for a given farm product would (1) intensify its production where it is already being raised and (2) produce an expansion of the zone of its production. Thus the increased demand for high-quality foods such as fruit, dairy products, and meat, made possible by rising incomes in the Thünen World City, led to (1) more intensive market-gardening, dairying, and livestock-fattening in areas traditionally devoted to those specialties and (2) a displacement of less intensive forms of agriculture as the zones of dairying, livestock-feeding, and truck-farming expanded. In this light, the decline and fall of commercial wheat-farming in the 1800s in countries such as Denmark, where dairying now dominates, fits neatly into Thünian perspective. Peet concluded that the von Thünen model provided a connection between the causal factor of the Industrial Revolution and the well-documented spread of commercial agriculture through Europe and other parts of the world in the 1800s. Furthermore, Thünian concepts go a long way toward explaining the zonation of dairying, livestock-fattening, and commercial food-grain farming evident in the present-day map of European agricultural regions (Figure 8.6).

Yet another geographer who sought explanations for crop and livestock distributions was the American O. E. Baker. His findings are applicable to Europe today, though they were published in the 1920s. Baker suggested (1) that agricultural products which are much in demand but restricted in climatic or other environmental requirements will have first choice of land in the areas where they can be raised; (2) that agricultural products characterized by small weight or bulk per unit of value will gain precedence in areas most suited to them environmentally; (3) that there will be a tendency toward specialization on a very small number of agricultural products in a market-oriented economy, because farmers will tend to raise whatever yields the greatest value per unit of land; and (4) that the character, experience, and skill of the farm population will have an effect on the selection of produce. The influence of von Thünen is quite apparent in Baker's work.

Quite aside from the influences of transport, market, and physical environment are factors of a cultural or political nature which have guided farmers along certain, frequently irrational, agricultural paths. For example, the absence of a dairy zone in the Mediterranean part of Europe is due in part to dietary preferences;

in particular, this area lacks a heritage of consuming dairy products derived from milk cows. Similarly, church requirements for sacramental wine aided the rise of viticulture in Germany, and contacts with alien cultures brought about a whole series of crop introductions and innovations in agricultural technology.

Tariffs and subsidies provided by various national governments or trade blocs often allow the continued production of certain crops in countries where foreign competition would otherwise cause a decline. Conversely, abolition of tariffs or import restrictions can cause sudden, far-reaching changes in domestic agriculture, as occurred when Britain's famous Corn Laws were repealed in 1846. At present, tariff restrictions on imported farm produce and the related agricultural price structures are the subject of difficult negotiations within the European Common Market.

The pattern of agricultural types, then, appears to be shaped primarily by the transportation and market factors operating in conjunction with cultural–political forces and the influence of the physical environment. Changes in all of these, but particularly in transportation and size of market, have been most influential in bringing about the transformation of the agricultural map of Europe over the past century or so.

SOURCES AND SUGGESTED READINGS

Swanzie Agnew. "The Vine in Bas Languedoc." *Geographical Review*. Vol. 36 (1946), pp. 67–79.

Robert Aitken. "Routes of Transhumance on the Spanish Meseta." *Geographical Journal*. Vol. 106 (1945), pp. 59–69.

Lelland G. Albaugh. *Crete: A Case Study of an Underdeveloped Area*. Princeton, N.J.: Princeton University Press, 1953.

Alfred Andrews. "Acclimatization of Citrus Fruits in the Mediterranean Region." *Agricultural History*. Vol. 35 (1961), pp. 35–46.

O. E. Baker. "The Potential Supply of Wheat." *Economic Geography*. Vol. 1 (1925), pp. 15–52.

Jean Boichard. "Perspectives de l'agriculture française." *Revue de Géographie de Lyon*. Vol. 41 (1966), pp. 99–127.

William E. Bull. "The Olive Industry of Spain." *Economic Geography*. Vol. 12 (1936), pp. 136–154.

C. P. Casutt and E. Rauch. "Zur Agrargeographie des Vorderrheintals." *Geographica Helvetica*. Vol. 16 (1961), pp. 153–161.

Michael Chisholm. *Rural Settlement and Land Use: An Essay in Location*. London: Hutchinson, 1962.

J. T. Coppock. "Crop, Livestock, and Enterprise Combinations in England and Wales." *Economic Geography*. Vol. 40 (1964), pp. 65–81.

John Wesley Coulter. "Stock Farming in Eire." *Economic Geography*. Vol. 25 (1949), pp. 81–93.

Elwyn Davies. "The Pattern of Transhumance in Europe." *Geography*. Vol. 26 (1941), pp. 155–168.

E. H. G. Dobby. "Economic Geography of the Port Wine Region." *Economic Geography*. Vol. 12 (1936), pp. 311–323.

Edgar S. Dunn. *The Location of Agricultural Production*. Gainesville, Fla.: University of Florida Press, 1954.

Richard T. Ely and George S. Wehrwein. *Land Economics*. New York: Macmillan, 1940.

Gyorgy Enyedi. "The Changing Face of Agriculture in Eastern Europe." *Geographical Review*. Vol. 57 (1967), pp. 358–372.

E. Estyn Evans. "The Ecology of Peasant Life in Western Europe." In *Man's Role in Changing the Face of the Earth*, ed. William L. Thomas, Jr. Chicago: University of Chicago Press, 1956, pp. 217–239.

Daniel Faucher. *Géographie Agraire, Types de Cultures*. Paris: Librairie de Medicis, 1949.

Th. Fischer. "Der Oelbaum." *Petermanns Mitteilungen Ergänzungsheft*, No. 147. Gotha, Germany: Justus Perthes, 1904.

S. H. Franklin. *The European Peasantry: The Final Phase*. London: Methuen, 1969.

Thomas W. Freeman. "Farming in Irish Life." *Geographical Journal*. Vol. 110 (1947), pp. 38–59.

Desmond A. Gillmor. "The Agricultural Regions of the Republic of Ireland." *Irish Geography*. Vol. 5 (1967), pp. 245–261.

Desmond A. Gillmor. "Spatial Distributions of Livestock in the Republic of Ireland." *Economic Geography*. Vol. 46 (1970), pp. 587–597.

Eduard Hahn. "Die Wirtschaftsformen der Erde." *Petermanns Geographische Mitteilungen*. Vol. 38 (1892), pp. 8–12.

William A. Hance. "Crofting in the Outer Hebrides." *Economic Geography*. Vol. 28 (1952), pp. 37–50.

John Fraser Hart. "The Changing Distribution of Sheep in Britain." *Economic Geography*. Vol. 32 (1956), pp. 260–274.

John Fraser Hart. "The Turnip and the Agricultural Revolution in England." *Geographical Review*. Vol. 60 (1970), pp. 568–569.

Richard Hartshorne and Samuel N. Dicken. "A Classification of the Agricultural Regions of Europe and North America on a Uniform Statistical Basis." *Annals, Association of American Geographers*. Vol. 25 (1935), pp. 99–120.

B. Hofmeister. "Wesen und Erscheinungsformen der Transhumance." *Erdkunde*. Vol. 15 (1961), pp. 121–135.

Homerus. *Chapman's Homer: The Iliad, the Odyssey, and the Lesser Homerica*. Edited by Allardyce Nicoll. Princeton, N.J.: Princeton University Press, 2nd ed., 1967.

James M. Houston. "Irrigation as a Solution to Agrarian Problems in Modern Spain." *Geographical Journal*. Vol. 116 (1950), pp. 55–63.

James M. Houston. "Land Use and Society in the Plain of Valencia." *Geographical Essays in Memory of Alan G. Ogilvie*. Edited by Ronald Miller and J. W. Watson. Edinburgh: Thomas Nelson, 1959, pp. 166–194.

W. B. Johnston and I. Crkvencic. "Examples of Changing Peasant Agriculture in Croatia, Yugoslavia." *Economic Geography*. Vol. 33 (1957), pp. 50–71.

Olof Jonasson. "The Agricultural Regions of Europe." *Economic Geography*. Vol. 1 (1925), pp. 277–314; Vol. 2 (1926), pp. 19–48.

A. H. Kampp. "The Agricultural Geography of Møn." *Erdkunde*. Vol. 16 (1962), pp. 173–190.

Jerzy Kostrowicki (ed.). "Land Utilization in East-Central Europe: Case Studies." *Geographia Polonia*. Vol. 5 (1965), pp. 7–498.

Hans Liebe. "Italiens Gartenbau: Erzeugung und Aussenhandel." *Berichte über Landwirtschaft*. No. 103 (1935), special issue.

Harold H. McCarty. "Agricultural Geography." Chapter 10 in *American Geog-*

raphy: Inventory and Prospect, ed. Preston E. James and Clarence Jones. Syracuse, N.Y.: Syracuse University Press, 1954, pp. 258–277.

Paul Marres. *La vigne et le vin en France.* Paris: Colin, 1950.

Giovanni Merlini. *Le Regioni Agrarie in Italia: Saggio di Geografia Agraria.* Bologna: Upeb un. Poligr., ed. Bolognese, 1948.

Jacqueline Murray. *The First European Agriculture.* Chicago: Aldine, 1970.

Erich Otremba. "Die deutsche Agrarlandschaft." *Geographische Zeitschrift Beiheft (Erdkundliches Wissen).* No. 3, Wiesbaden: Franz Steiner, 2nd ed., 1961.

James J. Parsons. "The Acorn-Hog Economy of the Oak Woodlands of South-western Spain." *Geographical Review.* Vol. 52 (1962), pp. 211–235.

James J. Parsons. "The Cork Oak Forests and the Evolution of the Cork Industry in Southern Spain and Portugal." *Economic Geography.* Vol. 38 (1962), pp. 195–214.

J. Richard Peet. "Influences of the British Market on Agriculture and Related Economic Development in Europe before 1860." *Institute of British Geographers, Transactions.* No. 56 (1972), pp. 1–20.

J. Richard Peet. "The Spatial Expansion of Commercial Agriculture in the Nineteenth Century: A von Thünen Interpretation." *Economic Geography.* Vol. 45 (1969), pp. 283–301.

G. Reverseau. "Les industries laitières dans les Charentes." *Annales de Géographie.* Vol. 34 (1925), pp. 210–218.

C. J. Robertson. "Agricultural Regions of the North Italian Plain." *Geographical Review.* Vol. 28 (1938), pp. 573–596.

Walter Roubitschek. "Zur Bevölkerungs- und Agrarstruktur Rumäniens." *Petermanns Geographische Mitteilungen.* Vol. 104 (1960), pp. 23–32.

Carl O. Sauer. *Agricultural Origins and Dispersals.* New York: American Geographical Society, 1952.

Douglas W. Gilchrist Shirlaw. *Agricultural Geography of Great Britain.* Elmsford, N. Y.: Pergamon, 1966.

André Siegfried. *The Mediterranean.* Translated by Doris Heming. New York: Durell, Sloan & Pearce, 1947.

E. S. Simpson. "Milk Production in England and Wales: A Study in the Influence of Collective Marketing." *Geographical Review.* Vol. 49 (1959), pp. 95–111.

Clifford T. Smith. *An Historical Geography of Western Europe Before 1800.* New York: Praeger, 1967.

Axel C. Z. Sømme. *Jordbrukets Geografi i Norge.* Bergen, Norway: J. W. Eide 2 vols., 1949, 1954.

J. M. Sourdillat. *Géographie Agricole de la France.* Paris: Presses Universitaires, 1950.

Joseph E. Spencer and Gerry A. Hale. "The Origin, Nature, and Dispersal of Agricultural Terracing." *Pacific Viewpoint.* Vol. 2 (1961), pp. 1–40.

L. Dudley Stamp. *The Land of Britain: Its Use and Misuse.* London: Longmans, 2nd ed., 1950.

L. Dudley Stamp. *The Land of Britain.* (Report of the Land Utilisation Survey of Britain). London: Geographical Publications, 1936–1946.

Dan Stanislawski. *Landscapes of Bacchus: The Vine in Portugal.* Austin, Tex.: University of Texas Press, 1970.

D. G. Symes. "Changes in the Structure and Role of Farming in the Economy of a West Norwegian Island." *Economic Geography.* Vol. 39 (1963), pp. 319–331.

Leslie Symons. *Agricultural Geography.* New York: Praeger, 1967.

Johann Heinrich von Thünen. *Von Thünen's Isolated State: An English Edition of Der Isolierte Staat.* Translated by Carla M. Wartenberg. Elmsford, N.Y.: Pergamon, 1966.

Karl Troll. "Die Landbauzonen Europas in ihrer Beziehung zur natürlichen Vegetation." *Geographische Zeitschrift.* Vol. 31 (1925), pp. 265–280.

William Van Royen. *Atlas of the World's Resources,* Vol. I. Englewood Cliffs, N.J.: Prentice-Hall, 1954.

Samuel Van Valkenburg. "An Evaluation of the Standard of Land Use in Western Europe." *Economic Geography.* Vol. 36 (1960), pp. 283–295.

Samuel Van Valkenburg and C. C. Held. *Europe.* New York: Wiley, 2nd ed., 1952.

Stanley W. E. Vince. "The Agricultural Regions of Belgium." In *London Essays in Geography,* ed. L. Dudley Stamp and S. W. Wooldridge. Cambridge, Mass.: Harvard University Press, 1951, pp. 255–288.

Ornulv Vorren and E. Manker. *Lapp Life and Customs.* Translated by K. McFarlane. New York: Oxford University Press, 1962.

Guido G. Weigend. "The Basis and Significance of Viticulture in Southwest France." *Annals, Association of American Geographers.* Vol. 44 (1954), pp. 75–101.

Derwent S. Whittlesey. "Major Agricultural Regions of the Earth." *Annals, Association of American Geographers.* Vol. 26 (1936), pp. 199–240.

CHAPTER NINE

Rural settlement geography

Settlement geography, derived from the German *Siedlungsgeographie,* involves the study of the cultural landscape, the visual imprint made by man on the countryside in the process of occupancy. This imprint varies from one culture or subculture to another and takes many forms in an area as heterogeneous as Europe. The rural landscapes of Iberia differ markedly from those of Scandinavia, and major contrasts are observable even within a country as small as Germany. Indeed, the visible, man-made rural landscapes of Europe, varying from one small district to the next, provide much of the charm for visitors from more monotonous cultural landscapes such as those of Anglo-America or Australia. Rural settlement geography focuses on three separate aspects of the cultural landscape: (1) the *settlement pattern,* or distribution of farmsteads; (2) the *field pattern,* or the form resulting from man's division of the land for productive use; and (3) *house and farmstead types,* including the building materials and folk-architecture.

9.1 SETTLEMENT PATTERN

Rural dwellings can be clustered, dispersed, or display some pattern intermediate between these. Europe offers a great variety of rural settlement patterns, from one extreme to the other.

CLUSTERED RURAL SETTLEMENT: THE FARM VILLAGE

Most European farmers live in villages rather than in homes dispersed through the countryside as in the United States, Canada, Australia, and other zones of overseas European settlement. Farmsteads are clustered in a myriad of small villages, leaving the surrounding arable land bare of structures, and the people journey out to their fields each day to work.

CAUSES OF CLUSTERED SETTLEMENT.   Numerous causal factors, primarily historic rather than modern, produced nucleation of the rural population. One was the *need for defense* prompted by the insecurity of the European countryside, where bands of outlaws and raiders once held sway. Farmers could better defend themselves against such dangers by grouping together in villages. In numerous recorded instances, villages have grown larger during periods of insecurity and war, only to shrink or disappear when peace and security were restored. European farm villages frequently occupy the most easily defended sites in their vicinity, in which case they are referred to as "strong-point" settlements.

Even more important as a cohesive force were *family and clan ties,* for the initial sedentary settlements were often made by people who were related by blood. Kinship gave rise to the desire to live in close proximity to one another, and is indicated by many place names. The common western European suffixes *-ingen, -inge, -ing, -ange,* and the like, as in Trossingen (Germany), Challerange (France), and Kolding (Denmark) are all derived from the Germanic tongue and mean literally "the people of," suggesting a cohesive group. The prefix typically was the name of the family or clan leader, so that Sigmaringen, a town in southwestern Germany, means "the people of Siegmar." Such social ties in turn were often associated with a certain degree of communalism, in which cropland, pastures, and forests were not privately owned. Cropland was typically allotted so that each villager had equal acreage, travel, and soil fertility. This was accomplished in two ways. First, the land used by any farmer was fragmented into a number of separate parcels, lying in different directions and at varying distances from the village, including a cross section of soil types. In addition, these parcels were periodically redistributed, so that a farmer in any given year might till land that had not been his the previous year. Fragmentation and redistribution of holdings also retarded settlement dispersal, because the scattered parcels of land were generally too narrow or small for the construction of houses.

Scarcity of water, especially in areas of permeable rock such as limestone, where moisture is absorbed quickly into the ground, again encouraged clusters of farmsteads where water was available. Such "wet-point" settlements can be centered on deep wells, communally dug and maintained, or at widely scattered springs. The region of Picardie in France and the south Wiltshire Downs of southwestern England are both underlain by permeable rock and typified by clustered villages. However, the concept of the wet-point village, developed in large part by the geographer Marcel Aurousseau, is subject to challenge in Picardie, for the deep wells of that area date only from the last two or three centuries, long after the village settlement form was established there.

Conversely, the superabundance of water in marshy areas and zones subject to flood can stimulate clustering on available "dry points" of higher elevation.

In the coastal Netherlands, tightly compact *"Wurt"* settlements developed on the man-made mounds, or *terpen*.

The presence of villages may also be related to the practice of *divided inheritance*, for an originally isolated farmstead will gradually become a clustered settlement as numerous generations of descendants of the initial settler build their homes on the same site. Conversely, the dispersed pattern persists in areas of undivided inheritance, as in northwestern Germany and parts of Norway.

There is also a correlation between clustering and *crop-centered economies,* as opposed to those based on the raising of livestock, mainly because less land area is needed per farmer in crop-dominated systems. Livestock-herding requires large farm units, and the larger the farm, the more difficult is village settlement, because travel time to and from the countryside is increased. In general, lowland plains areas have historically been dominated by crop agriculture, and hilly and mountainous areas have been used for herding, producing a related correlation between level terrain and village settlement in Europe. Because the environment does not absolutely govern the behavior of Europeans, exceptions do exist, as in the dispersed settlements of the plains of Flanders and northwestern Germany and the large clustered villages of mountainous southern Italy. In more recent times, dictatorial governments, particularly in Communist countries, have adopted policies aimed at even greater clustering of the rural population, in part to facilitate control and political indoctrination of the rural folk.

Of all the factors causing clustering into villages, the historic presence of clan communalism and its perpetuation under the feudal system might best be judged the most important. People bound together by such ties normally accepted clustered settlements. The gradual disappearance of communal organization, which accompanied the decline of feudalism, left behind the farm village as an economically inefficient relic of a bygone age. It persists nevertheless, partly because rural folk are resistant to change. Similarly, the day when a village provided farmers any significant measure of defense in times of warfare and raiding is long past, but its heritage persists.

TYPES OF CLUSTERED RURAL SETTLEMENTS.   The farm villages of Europe vary greatly in outward appearances from one region to another, and settlement geographers have distinguished a number of major types (Figure 9.1). German scholars have been most active in such research, and much of their terminology has been accepted by non-German geographers, particularly in the English-speaking countries. One of the most common types is the *Haufendorf,* or "irregular clustered village," found in parts of western Germany, northern France, lowland Britain, and much of southern Europe (Figure 9.1). As its name implies, the irregular clustered village presents a haphazard appearance devoid of any trace of planning, with winding streets and randomly bunched farmsteads (Figures 9.2, 9.15). Usually somewhere toward the center of the cluster, the village church is found, surrounded by the farmhouses, barns, and kitchen gardens of the villagers. The size varies greatly, ranging from perhaps 400 to 1,000 population in the Germanic lands to 10,000 or more in the hilltop agricultural settlements of southern Italy, and even as many as 20,000 or 30,000 inhabitants in the large farm "cities" of the Hungarian Basin. The latter, called *kertes varos,* represent a Magyar response to the military

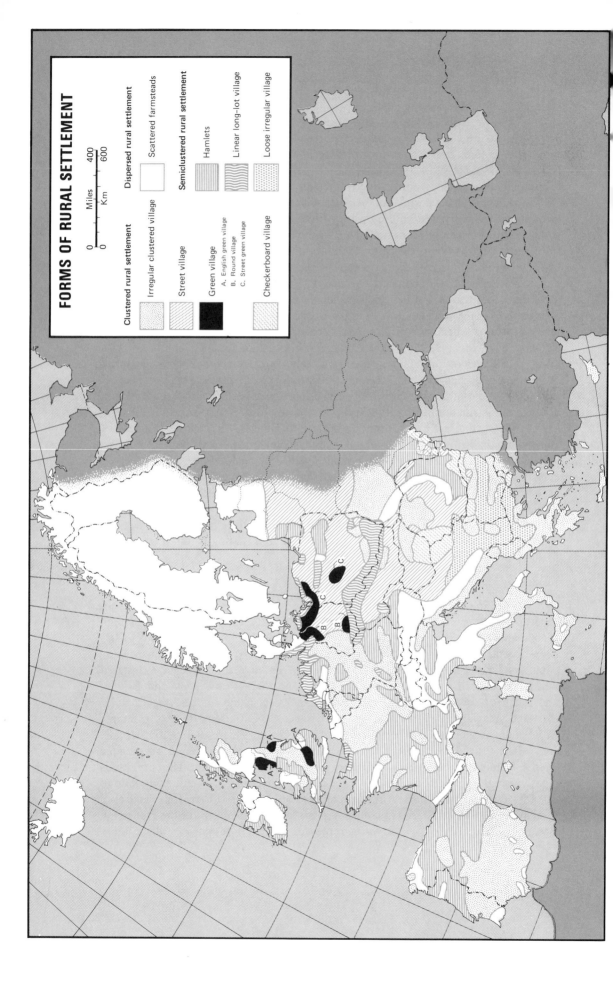

FORMS OF RURAL SETTLEMENT

0 ___ 400 Miles
0 ___ 600 Km

Clustered rural settlement

Irregular clustered village

Street village

Green village

  A. English green village
  B. Round village
  C. Street green village

Checkerboard village

Dispersed rural settlement

Scattered farmsteads

Semiclustered rural settlement

Hamlets

Linear long-lot village

Loose irregular village

Figure 9.2 An irregular clustered farm village (*Haufendorf*) in West Germany. Note the haphazard layout of the village and winding streets, suggesting spontaneous development rather than planning. (After Creutzburg.)

danger imposed by the advancing Turks. The large villages of the Italian hilltops similarly reflect the post-Roman insecurity of that part of Europe.

The key to the origin of the *Haufendorf* lies in the obvious lack of planning. In all probability, these irregular clustered villages began as a loose grouping of only a few farmsteads of related families, forming a clan hamlet. Over the centuries the population grew and new farmsteads were added, enlarging the settlement and making it more compact. What were originally paths leading out to the fields became streets. It is possible that in some areas the original settlement was a single isolated farmstead rather than a clan hamlet, with the practice of divided inheritance causing the multiplication of houses.

In much of eastern Europe, beyond the ancient German–Slav border of circa A.D. 800 (Figure 5.2), most village types exhibit in their present form a high degree of planning. West of this old Elbe–Saale–Inn–Salzach line, the irregular clustered village is dominant, but in the traditional Slavic domain to the East the settlements are quite regular in shape and layout. The most typical of these planned forms is the street village, or *Strassendorf* (Figure 9.1). Instead of the disorderly maze of streets found in the irregular clustered village, only one straight street is present, and all of the farmsteads are lined up along it, the houses and other buildings facing the street and the kitchen gardens lying out behind (Figures 9.3, 9.4).

Figure 9.1 Forms of rural settlement. (After Kuhn, Helbok, Schwarz, Houston, Boyd, Uhlig, Stamp, Smith, Cvijić, Meitzen, Stone, Radig, Schröder, Gradmann, and Thorpe.)

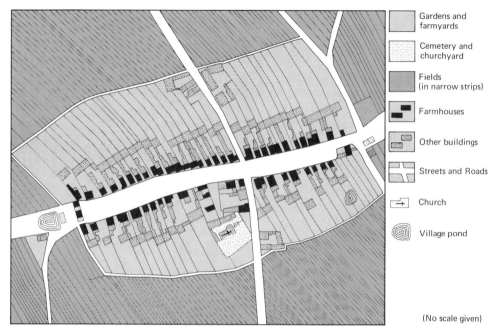

Gardens and farmyards

Cemetery and churchyard

Fields (in narrow strips)

Farmhouses

Other buildings

Streets and Roads

Church

Village pond

(No scale given)

Figure 9.3 A street village (*Strassendorf*). The farm village of Eicha in the East German province of Sachsen. The entire village is oriented along a single central street. The farmsteads are of the courtyard type typical of central Germany. (After Buschan.)

Street villages vary greatly in size, from small forms usually found on side roads or on dead-end lanes to large, long settlements on main rural highways which may house many hundreds of people.

Almost certainly the street village is of Slavic origin, linked to some particular facet of the folk culture. Even in eastern Germany, many of the street villages, particularly the smaller ones, bear Slavic names, including the suffixes *-ow, -in, -itz,* and *-zig,* as in Trebnitz. Why the Slavs, and particularly the northern Slavs, should have chosen the street village as their most common rural settlement form is something of a mystery. A certain amount of protection was afforded by the wooden fence which once surrounded the kitchen garden perimeter of the village, a first line of defense backed up some distance further by the rear walls of the farm buildings, but there are other forms which better suit the needs of self-defense. In addition, the individual houses of the typical Slavic street village are built of wood and spaced somewhat apart to lessen the danger of spreading fire, reducing the value for protection against hostile outsiders. Groups of German agricultural settlers moving eastward beyond the Elbe and Saale rivers after A.D. 800 completely abandoned the irregular clustered village form which they had known in western Germany and adopted the Slavic street village. Often the Germans simply enlarged existing Slavic villages by adding farmsteads at either end of the single, central street, but in other cases they founded completely new villages, based on the Slavic form. In time, the Slavs were assimilated in eastern Germany, but their traditional village type was perpetuated, surviving to the present day.

Another type of clustered rural settlement which displays planning, at least in its formative stage, is the so-called *green village,* distinguished by a communal

Figure 9.4 A typical East German street village (*Strassendorf*). The village of Breunsdorf, south of Leipzig. Note the single central street, along which the farm buildings are tightly clustered, and the kitchen gardens and orchards on the periphery of the village behind the buildings. (After Creutzburg.)

open place, or green, in the center of the village. The green village, in a number of subtypes, is found widely through various parts of the North European Plain, from lowland Britain to Poland (Figure 9.1). Traditionally, the green served as a festival ground, a marketplace, and a protected enclosure for livestock. The shape of the green, and with it the configuration of the entire village, varies greatly, including such diverse forms of circles, triangles, rectangles, and ovals.

Several subtypes of the green village are recognized, and they are classified on the basis of the shape of the central green. One of these is the street-green village (*Angerdorf* or *Strassenangerdorf*), found mixed in amongst the street villages of the northern Slavs and eastern Germans, differing from the street villages only in that the central street broadens toward the middle of the settlement to form a green (Figure 9.5). Street-green villages are most common in eastern Germany.

One of the visually most impressive subtypes of the green village is the *round village,* the German *Runddorf* or Danish *rundby*. In these, the core of the village is formed by a circular or roughly circular green, around which the individual farmsteads are grouped (Figures 9.6, 9.7). Round villages are limited mainly to small districts on either side of the lower Elbe River, straddling the border between East and West Germany, the east bank of the Saale River, and parts of western Czechoslovakia (Figure 9.1). Formerly they were also found in Denmark. Round villages are probably of Slavic origin, for they frequently bear names indicative of that ethnic group, such as Kremlin and Wutzow. The round villages were

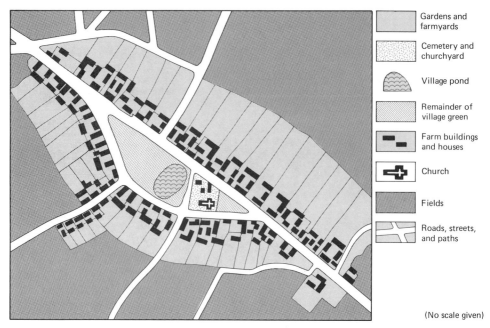

Gardens and farmyards

Cemetery and churchyard

Village pond

Remainder of village green

Farm buildings and houses

Church

Fields

Roads, streets, and paths

(No scale given)

Figure 9.5 A green village (*Angerdorf*) of the East German type. The focal point of the village is the elongated central green, upon which the church and pond are located. In other respects, the village resembles those of the *Strassendorf* type (Figure 9.3). (After Radig.)

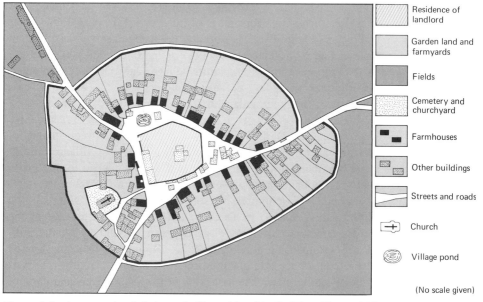

Residence of landlord

Garden land and farmyards

Fields

Cemetery and churchyard

Farmhouses

Other buildings

Streets and roads

Church

Village pond

(No scale given)

Figure 9.6 An example of the round village (*Runddorf*). The village of Lichtentanne in the province of Sachsen, East Germany. Such villages are typically of Slavic origin and lie in the old conflict zone between Slavs and Germans. (After Buschan.)

Figure 9.7   Buberow, a round village (*Runddorf* or *Rundling*) in East Germany, near Gransee, North of Berlin. Farmsteads of the courtyard type surround the central open place, which is occupied by the church. Gardens stretch out behind the farmsteads. Only one road leads into the village, an indication of an original defensive function. The *-ow* suffix on the place name indicates a Slavic origin of the village. (After Creutzburg.)

obviously planned for defense, which helps explain their concentration along the old German–Slavic border, where sporadic warfare was common. The central green served the same function as the courtyard of a castle or the interior of a circle of covered wagons—an area from which defense was directed. A circular wooden barrier around the outer edge of the gardenland made up the first line of defense, and if it was breached, the villagers withdrew to the shelter of the tightly clustered farm buildings around the courtyard. Only a dead-end street usually entered the village, leaving only one opening to be blocked off. On the green, the village well and pond provided water, and there was room to herd the livestock to protect them from the attackers. When the villagers were Christianized, the church was sometimes built in the green, while in other cases the courtyard served as a site for the manor house of a landlord, after the advent of the feudal system.

The round village also exists in varying sizes. They apparently began as very small settlements, with perhaps four or five farmsteads around the central green, a form still found in eastern Germany and perhaps best designated as a round hamlet (*Rundweiler*). Such small groupings have an unusually high frequency of Slavic place names. Through population increase the round hamlets evolved into the next-larger form, called *Rundlinge,* or "little round ones," and some of these in turn grew still more to become round villages. If the expansion involved the addition of a great many new farmsteads, the village could come to closely resemble the East German street-green village (*Angerdorf*), since the additional houses were by necessity built away from the central courtyard on the road or roads leading into the settlement. In fact, many street-green villages may be simply elongated round villages, deprived of the characteristic round shape by enlargement.

It is possible that green villages represent a modern survival of one of European man's most ancient settlement forms. Archaeologists have discovered green villages as far back as Iron Age times, and there is some evidence that they might be of even greater antiquity. Part of the difficulty in tracing their former distribution is that green villages could easily evolve into irregular clustered villages if, as often happened, later generations of farmers were allowed to build houses and barns on the green.

Still another planned settlement form of eastern Europe is the gridiron or checkerboard village (*Schachbrettdorf*), found particularly in the middle and lower valley of the Danube River in parts of Hungary, Yugoslavia, Romania, and Bulgaria (Figure 9.1). A similar type is found in some areas bordering the northern shore of the Aegean Sea in Greece. In contrast to the village types mentioned above, these of checkerboard pattern are quite recent in origin. The government of the Austro–Hungarian Empire founded many such settlements beginning about 1750, particularly in the Banat district of Yugoslavia and southern Hungary, as part of a project to repopulate areas which had been ravaged by warfare. The Greeks also established some of these checkerboard villages in districts from which Turks were expelled in the 1920s. The gridiron village is typified by a regular pattern, in which all streets meet at right angles, not unlike the layout of most American cities, towns, and hamlets, but differing in that they are peopled exclusively by farmers who work the surrounding lands.

DISPERSED RURAL SETTLEMENT: THE ISOLATED FARMSTEAD

While it is true that most European farmers live in villages, there are some districts which are dominated by isolated farmsteads, or *Einzelhöfe,* in which each rural family lives at a distance from its neighbors, as American rural families do. The factors which encourage dispersed settlement are precisely the opposite of those favoring village development, and include (1) an absence of the need for defense, prompted by peace and security; (2) colonization by individual pioneer families rather than by groups bound together by the ties of blood relationship, religion, or the like; (3) the domination by agricultural private enterprise rather than communalism; (4) unit-block farms rather than fragmented holdings; (5) a rural economy dominated by livestock-raising; (6) hilly or mountainous terrain; and (7) readily available water. In addition, dispersed settlement can result from deliberate governmental action designed to break up the villages, piece together fragmented holdings, and thereby produce a more efficient agriculture. Isolated farmsteads are dominant throughout Scandinavia, highland Britain, in the Alps and certain other mountain districts, and in various small regions scattered around Europe, such as Flanders, the Münsterland and Lake Konstanz (Bodensee) areas of West Germany, and the lower Loire valley of France (Figure 9.1).

Dispersed farmsteads fall into two categories of origin: those of great antiquity which represent a traditional form and those which have appeared in recent

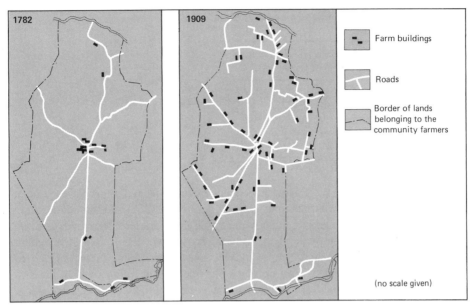

Figure 9.8 The Danish farm community of Solbjerg before and after partial dispersal of settlement. In 1782, the farmers nearly all lived in a clustered village, but by the early twentieth century, the majority had relocated in scattered farmsteads, leaving behind a partially deserted village. (After East and Vahl.)

times as a result of governmental action or economic change. In the first group would be many of the *Einzelhöfe* of northwestern Germany and the adjacent Netherlands, where individual farmers excluded from property rights in the clustered settlements through the practice of undivided inheritance went out into the surrounding bogs and marshes and reclaimed land, upon which they built their homes and began farming. These are referred to as *kamp* settlements.

More commonly, however, dispersed farmsteads are of relatively recent origin. In the Scandinavian countries, governmental decrees issued in the late 1700s and early 1800s led in time to abolition of fragmented holdings and brought about the dispersal of the large majority of the rural population (Figure 9.8, Table 9.1). In one small district of southern Germany adjacent to Lake Konstanz and the foot of the Alps, local feudal rulers began dispersing the farmers in the 1500s, a transition which continued after feudal times into the nineteenth century. The conversion from arable to sheep pasture in much of the British Isles, associated with a drastic population decline in rural areas and a replacement of fragmented holdings by unit-block farms, caused scattered farmsteads to replace many villages and hamlets, beginning in the 1400s. Landlords in Latvia and other eastern Baltic areas dispersed peasants under their control as early as the 1600s to achieve greater efficiency of production. More recently, the Italian government in the 1920s and 1930s began a program of creating scattered farmsteads in the southern part of the country, though some Mediterranean areas had dispersed settlement as an ancient tradition, as is suggested by some passages in Homer's *Odyssey*.

There is little doubt that dispersed settlement is superior to the village pattern in an economic sense. The key factor is the time required to travel from farmstead to fields in the village system. A study in the Netherlands revealed that farm-

TABLE 9.1   Dispersal of Rural Population in
Norden

Country	Percentage of rural population not living in clustered settlements
Denmark	87
Finland	97
Iceland	71
Norway	91
Sweden	79

ers made less intensive use of land which lay farthest from their villages, and a Swedish researcher reached the same conclusion (Table 8.1). At the same time, the village offers many social contacts, while the life on isolated farmsteads is often lonely, especially to people with a village heritage. Indeed, the Italian government has noted with concern the high rate of mental depression among farmers resettled out of villages into the countryside. To many Europeans, the village way of life and the companionship it provides are much to be preferred. The great French geographer, Paul Vidal de la Blache, expressed this European feeling quite well in his description of the isolated farmstead landscape of the hedgerow country in the west of France, declaring that "the impression gained from such a landscape is one of isolation, and the stranger finds himself ill at ease in the (hedgerow) labyrinth which to him seems inhospitable, even hostile." However, the current trend in non-Communist Europe is toward gradual elimination of the farm village and its replacement by scattered farmsteads, a process which may require many more centuries to complete.

SEMICLUSTERED RURAL SETTLEMENT

There are a number of rural settlement forms in Europe which do not fit well into either the clustered or dispersed categories, sharing some characteristics of both. These are best referred to as semiclustered or semidispersed, for they are intermediate between the two extremes.

HAMLETS.   Certainly the most common semiclustered type is the hamlet, referred to in German terminology as the *Weiler* or *Drubbel* (Figure 9.9), which consists of a small number of farmsteads grouped loosely together. As in farm villages, the hamlet farmsteads lie in settlement nuclei, separate from the cropland, but the hamlet differs in both its smaller size and lesser degree of compactness, for individual farmsteads are not as tightly clustered as in the villages. The number of houses varies from two or three up to as many as fifteen or twenty, though any size criterion to distinguish large hamlets from small villages would be quite arbitrary.

Hamlets are widespread in Europe, found particularly in southern France, parts of Germany, and sizable areas in Iberia and northern Italy (Figure 9.1). Many districts now characterized by dispersed farmsteads were actually former hamlet areas, as for example the Celtic highland refuges of the British Isles. In Ireland, hamlets known as *clachans* were apparently once dominant. Often, hamlets are found mixed in among dispersed farmsteads, making it difficult to map their complete distribution (Figure 9.10).

The origin of hamlets is a controversial matter among settlement geog-

Holdings of one of the three farmers (A)

Farm buildings including houses

Farmsteads, gardens, and farmyards of the three farmers

Roads and paths

0   Austrian *Klafter*   200

Figure 9.9 A hamlet (*Weiler*) composed of three farmsteads. The Austrian community of Loiferting as it appeared in the nineteenth century. (After Meitzen.)

raphers, and in all probability a number of creative processes were at work in different hamlet areas. In south Germany, as well as adjacent parts of Switzerland and France, the hamlets may well be a heritage of Roman rule, as is suggested by the frequency of occurrence of the place-name suffix *-weiler*, which in all probability is derived from the Latin word *villare*, meaning "farmstead." It has been suggested that original isolated farmsteads developed into small hamlet clusters through the Roman-law practice of divided inheritance. Among numerous examples of the *-weiler* suffix on hamlet place names in Romanized Danubian Germany are Habertsweiler in the province of Bayern, and Martinsweiler in Baden-Württemberg. The word *weiler* has come to mean "hamlet" in the German language. A French geographer, Demangeon, suggested the same origin for hamlets in the southern part of his country. Failure of the hamlets to grow still more and become villages is probably related to the low potential productivity of the areas where they are dominant. The population presumably increased until inferior lands such as the Massif Central of France could support no more. It is perhaps best, then, to regard hamlets as "stunted" villages whose growth was hindered by environmental factors.

Other scholars have argued that hamlets are the oldest settlement form,

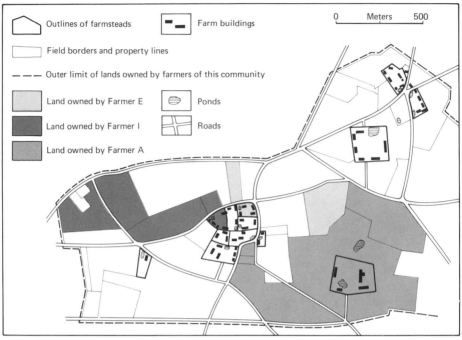

Figure 9.10   An example of partial dispersal of settlement in an area where land reform has occurred. A hamlet in France composed of eight farmsteads coexists with five dispersed farmsteads. Such mixture of settlement types is becoming increasingly common in Europe. (After Demangeon, 1946.)

dating from the earliest sedentary colonization of clan and extended-family groups, rather than derivatives of initially dispersed farmsteads. Included would be the hamlets of northern Germany, called *drubbel* to distinguish them from the *weiler* of Romanized southern Germany. They probably had much their present form when initially established, preserving both size and morphology because of Germanic undivided inheritance and the poor quality of the land.

LOOSE IRREGULAR VILLAGES.   Very similar to hamlets, but differing in one important social respect, are the *loose irregular villages* of Balkan Europe, another semiclustered form. Individual communities are often made up of three or four separate hamlet clusters, segregated on the basis of blood relationship, religion, and/or language. The collection of hamlets bears a single name, and the people all have a sense of belonging to the community, but their individual hamlet clusters are areally separated. The total population of the hamlets in a given settlement often achieves village proportions, but the compactness of the village form is absent. In some instances, the space between the separate hamlets has gradually filled in as population increased, finally producing an irregular clustered village, but this development has been confined mainly to the better soils of the plains and scattered basins of the Balkan area.

The loose irregular village is most common among the South Slavs and can perhaps be linked in origin to the traditional strength of the extended family (*zadruga*) as a social institution among this group. In all probability, the familial

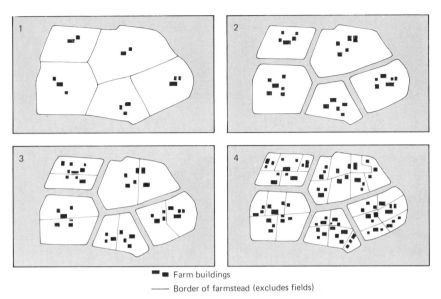

■ ■ Farm buildings
—— Border of farmstead (excludes fields)

Figure 9.11   Evolution of a loose irregular village. The loose irregular villages of the Balkans developed in the following stages:

1. Individual farmsteads of different families.
2. Buildings multiply as extended families (*Zadruga*) develop; paths or crude roads take shape in areas between farmsteads.
3. Division of original farmsteads through inheritance produces clan hamlets, which together constitute a loose irregular village.
4. Continued division through inheritance causes greater compactness of settlement, producing an irregular clustered village with clan quarters (fourth stage reached only in plains areas where soils are fertile). (After Wilhelmy.)

hamlets developed from original scattered farmsteads, as children and grandchildren built their houses near that of the family patriarch (Figure 9.11). The formation was further facilitated by the great ethnic diversity of the Balkans, which encouraged segregation of settlement. The loose, irregular villages of southeastern Europe are variously called *ibar, machali,* or *starivlah* settlements in the languages of that area.

PARTIALLY DESERTED VILLAGES.   Also in the category of semiclustered settlement are the *partially deserted villages* of areas such as Scandinavia and lowland Great Britain, where government-led reforms have caused many or most of the farmers to relocate in isolated farmsteads, leaving behind a village which contains only a fraction of its former population. In Denmark, the large majority of the rural population is now dispersed. Vestiges of villages remain, although the surviving farmsteads are more loosely clustered due to the removal of many in the dispersal process.

LINEAR LONG-LOT VILLAGES.   A final semiclustered type which is fairly widespread in Europe is the *linear long-lot village,* variously referred to in German sources as the *Reihendorf* (row village) or *Hufendorf* (long-lot village). This form is intermediate between the extremes of clustered and dispersed. The individual farmsteads are found along a single road, similar to the street villages described earlier. However, the linear long-lot village differs from the street village in that the

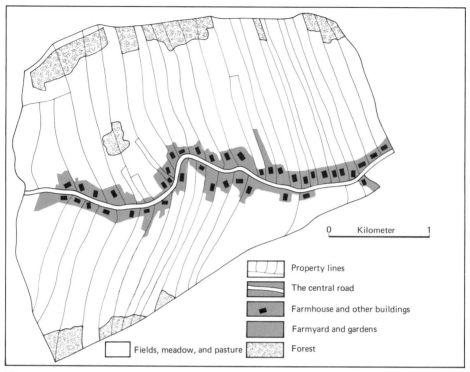

Figure 9.12   A forest-linear long-lot village (*Waldhufendorf*). Frankenau, near Mittweida in East Germany, as it appeared in the nineteenth century. The farms are in the shape of elongated lots extending back from a central road. The farm buildings are at the front of the long-lots, on or near the road. (After Meitzen.)

farmsteads are spaced some distance apart and all of the land belonging to each farmer is contained in an elongated unit block, or long-lot, extending out behind the farmstead (Figures 9.12, 9.13). In the street village, only the gardens were adjacent to the houses, and the fields lay some distance away, composed of numerous scattered parcels of land. Farmers in the linear long-lot village live on their farm, which is in a unit block rather than fragmented. In this respect, the linear long-lot settlements resemble scattered farmsteads. However, the narrowness of the long-lots and the concentration of houses on the road at the front of the farms create a certain degree of clustering not typical of average dispersed farmsteads. Moreover, the residents of such settlements generally have the feeling of belonging to a village, with the resultant social contacts.

Linear long-lot villages vary from a half-dozen member farms up to a hundred or more, and the width and depth of the lots also vary. At the narrowest, long-lots can be about 20 meters (60 to 70 feet) wide, while in some settlements their breadth reaches 200 meters (600 to 700 feet). The greater dimension, depth, can be anywhere from 300 meters to several kilometers (1000 feet to over a mile).

There are a number of distinct subtypes of the linear long-lot village. Most common is the *Waldhufendorf*, or linear long-lot village of the forest, which is found in a broken belt extending through the hill lands of central Europe, particularly in the Erzgebirge (Ore Mountains) of East Germany as well as the Sudetes

Figure 9.13 A forest linear long-lot village (*Waldhufendorf*) in Schlesien. The long-lots stretch back away from the farmsteads, which are loosely grouped along the central road. This settlement is of exceptional length, extending beyond the confines of the photograph on both sides. (After Creutzburg.)

Mountains and Carpathians of southern Poland (Figure 9.1). Scattered specimens may be seen in various hill lands of West Germany and in the North German Plain. In the *Waldhufendorf,* the road follows a stream valley, and long-lot farms extend back on either side as far as the adjacent ridges. Generally, the steeper hinter portions of the farms are left in forest. The configuration of the entire settlement is shaped by the windings of the valley, and it is rare to find perfectly straight property lines (Figures 9.12, 9.13).

A second subtype is the *Marschhufendorf,* or linear long-lot village of the marsh, which is typical of poorly drained coastal moors and marshes from northern France through the Low Country and on beyond to Denmark, Germany, and the Baltic fringe of Poland (Figure 9.1). Here the focal point is a drainage canal flanked on either side by broad man-made dikes. Roads and farm buildings are situated on the protected high ground of the dikes, and the long-lot farms stretch out behind into the drained lower land. The *Marschhufendorf* also differs from its forest counterpart in the regularity and straightness of all property lines.

The long-lot settlements were generally peopled by farmers free of feudal restrictions, and communalism was unknown: Each farmer had his own pasture, meadow, and woodland.

Considerable controversy surrounds the origin of the linear long-lot villages, though agreement has been reached on certain points. Most scholars believe that the marsh subtype appeared earliest, about A.D. 900 in the Netherlands, in an initial period of dike-building there. It is a matter of historical record that the first *Marschhufendorf* in Germany was founded soon after 1106 by six Dutchmen who were granted some wasteland on the lower Weser River near Bremen. In the centuries that followed, the marsh linear long-lot village spread both east and west, reaching the Polish river marshes in the 1500s and 1600s and the lower Seine River of France. Dutch migrants were most instrumental in the dispersal. The long-lot form was well suited to a dike landscape, and its practicality probably explains its popularity.

Much less agreement is found concerning the beginnings of the forest sub-type of the long-lot village. One group believes the *Waldhufendorf* to be a descendant of the *Marschhufendorf* and that Germans adopted it from the Dutch and carried it inland to the hills of central Europe. In support of this theory, linear long-lot villages of the marsh and forest varieties are found within 34 kilometers (21 miles) of one another in the lower Rhine River plain in West Germany. Certainly the great similarity in form of the two subtypes would suggest a common origin. However, the *Waldhufendorf* may have developed from the previously mentioned *kamp* settlements on the periphery of north German hamlets (*drubbel*), the unit-block farms established by farmers excluded by inheritance from communal rights in the hamlet. The *kamp* farms sometimes took on the long, narrow shape of long-lots. It has also been proposed that long-lots are derived from the narrow strip fields typical of most German village areas, in particular the unusually long, parallel strip fields once found in the southern part of East Germany in the area known as Sachsen, adjacent to a major concentration of forest long-lot villages in the Erzge-birge.

9.2 FIELD PATTERNS

A second basic aspect of the rural European cultural landscape is the field pattern, or the division of arable land for use by man. Most European farmers today do not have unit-block farms in the American or Australian style, but rather fragmented holdings, in which the land they own and work is scattered in many separate parcels in varying directions and at different distances from their farm-steads in the villages. Only the farm garden is in the village adjacent to the buildings. All of the cropland, pasture, and meadow can be reached only by traveling out of the village. In the modern world, where the European farmer is trying to compete to supply the demands of an urbanized population, the system of frag-mented holdings is inefficient and places him at a distinct disadvantage. Obviously, the fragmented holdings were not produced by causal factors operating today, but by ancient social forces, for the fragmented holding is just as much a cultural relic as the farm village.

THE OPEN FIELDS

The origin of fragmented holdings can be traced back to the traditional practice of open fields. Communalism was very strong under this ancient system, which has now almost vanished. An entire village community worked together in the fields, observing set dates for plowing, planting, and harvesting.

The choice of crops was made by the village elders and generally followed one or another of the rigid rotations described in the previous chapter, such as the two- or three-field system. The farmland was divided into a number of large units (*zelgen*). One particular unit might be planted to wheat in a certain year, while another lay fallow and a third was given over to oats or barley. Each farmer worked one or more small parcels within each of these large units, following the dictates of the village elders as to when to work and what to plant (Figure 9.14). The indi-

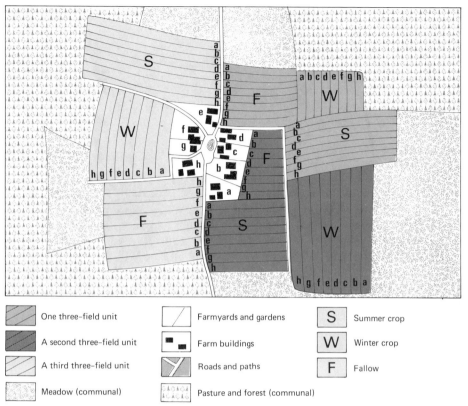

One three-field unit

A second three-field unit

A third three-field unit

Meadow (communal)

Farmyards and gardens

Farm buildings

Roads and paths

Pasture and forest (communal)

S   Summer crop

W   Winter crop

F   Fallow

Figure 9.14   Schematic plan of a farm village with open fields. Individual letters stand for different farmers. Each farmer has a farmstead in the village and nine strip fields. In this case, there are three units of land, each operated under the three-field system, with pasture and meadow toward the periphery of the village lands. The open fields no longer exist in Europe, though their influence is still seen in cadastral patterns. (After Putzger and East.)

vidual parcels were rarely fenced, leading to the term "open" fields. As mentioned previously, land was periodically redistributed so that an equality was achieved among the various farmers: Each had some good soil and some poor, some distant plots and some close at hand.

There were two basic field patterns associated with the fragmented holdings of the open-field system. In the lands north of the Alps, the individual scattered parcels worked by any given farmer were in the shape of long, extremely narrow strips (Figure 9.15). It is believed that this unusual shape was chosen to accommodate the large, unwieldy German plow. This plow, called the *charure,* was difficult to turn around due to its size and bulk and prompted the farmers to use long strip fields requiring less turning. The pattern of parcels in Mediterranean Europe, including southern France, was quite different. The individual plots were irregular in shape or roughly rectangular. In some limited areas, a rigid rectangularity was imposed on field patterns by the Roman land-survey system (Figure 9.16). The small plow used in the grain fields of Roman areas (Figure 8.4) was, in contrast to the German plow, small and easy to handle. Further, much of the productive cropland of southern Europe was planted to orchards and vineyards, where the hoe

Buildings

132

Gardens, vineyards, and orchards

0   400   800
      m

Figure 9.15   Fragmented land holdings in French Lorraine. Small strip fields surrounded the irregular clustered village of Seichamp, near Nancy in northeastern France, before land reform. The 132 separate strips belonging to one sample farm are shaded. Compare to Figure 9.17. (After Demangeon, 1946.)

rather than the plow was the principal agricultural tool. Consequently, narrow strip fields offered no advantage and were not used.

As long as communalism persisted, the awkward system of open fields and fragmented holdings possessed some degree of efficiency. Time weakened the bonds of clan membership and group cohesiveness, however, and private enterprise gradually supplanted communalism. Periodic redistribution of the land ceased, and farmers acquired permanent ownership of their scattered parcels. No longer were all plots in a given open field or *zelge* planted to the same crop, for each farmer was now free to raise whatever he chose on his land. In this manner present-day farms evolved, consisting of a farmstead and garden in the village and several tens or hundreds of scattered tiny fields in the outlying vicinity (Figure 9.15).

LAND REFORM

Fragmented holdings are, of course, extremely inefficient. In a community near Zamora, in the Spanish province of León, one farmer owned 394 separate parcels of land, averaging only 0.07 hectare (0.17 acre) each, while in the village

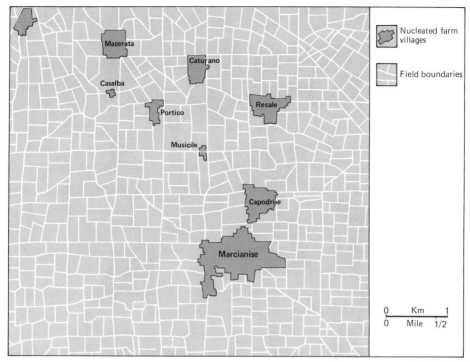

Figure 9.16 Field patterns exhibiting Roman influence, in the Campania just North of Napoli, Italy. Fields in the areas dominated by use of the small Roman plow take on rectangular rather than strip shape. In this instance, the rectangularity has been made even more pronounced by the survival of the Roman rectangular survey system. This map shows the field pattern as it was in the nineteenth century. (After Meitzen.)

of Seichamp in French Lorraine, the 325 total hectares (800 acres) belonging to the farmers was once divided into 1451 separate parcels, a little over 0.22 hectare (half an acre) per plot. Such tiny fields and the time required to travel to them obviously place European farmers at a competitive disadvantage. In recognition of this problem, most governments have taken steps to bring about land reform, in which the property lines are redrawn to reduce or eliminate the fragmentation of holdings.

Land reform actually began as early as the 1200s in England as part of the movement known as *enclosure,* which reached its peak between 1450 and 1750. Landlords abolished the fragmented holdings and replaced the open fields with unit-block farms enclosed with hedges, often as a result of their desire to convert from crop production to sheep-raising. By the time of the Protestant Reformation, almost half of the 8500 parishes in England had been enclosed. The British government joined with landlords to complete the reform in the 1700s, and today there are relatively few fragmented holdings left in the United Kingdom. The visually dominant aspect of the rural British landscape today is the rows of trees grown up along property lines and field borders where the hedges were originally planted.

In Scandinavia, where fragmentation was less severe, much progress in land reform was made during the 1700s and 1800s, though some consolidation is still in progress. The Danish government issued a decree in 1781 demanding an end

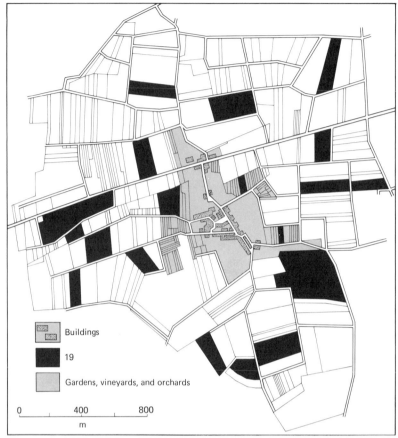

Figure 9.17   Seichamp after land reform. The same village and farmland as in Figure 9.15, but after land reform took place, greatly reducing the number of parcels. The sample farm, shown shaded, remained approximately the same size but was reduced from 132 to 19 parcels. Such incomplete reform is typical of France and West Germany. (After Demangeon, 1946.)

to the open fields and consolidation of parcels, a process largely completed by 1835.

With isolated exceptions, the remainder of non-Communist Europe has not been able to duplicate the success of Britain and Scandinavia in land reform. The farmland of Germany, France, Spain, Italy, and other countries is still plagued by fragmented holdings. Some slow progress is being made, but even when reform is carried out, complete abolition of the scattered parcels is rare (Figures 9.15, 9.17). For example, land reform was accomplished in the West German village of Nerdlen, near the city of Trier, in the year 1905, but even though the number of parcels was reduced by a factor of ten or more, considerable fragmentation remains (Table 9.2). Plans have been made, however, to accelerate land reform in Common Market countries.

In most of Communist Europe, the problem of fragmented holdings has been solved by returning to a communalism not unlike that of antiquity. Private property has been abolished and the land converted into large collective and state farms. It is entirely possible that the greater potential for efficiency produced by the

TABLE 9.2 Examples of Reduction of Fragmentation of Land-holdings in Nerdlen, West Germany, 1905

Sample farms	Number of parcels before land reform	Number of parcels after land reform
Farmer A	296	24
Farmer B	216	21
Farmer C	92	13

forced, rapid abolition of fragmentation could allow Communist eastern Europe to outstrip the western countries in farm production. One example of the potential for greater efficiency is that farm machinery is much more suited to East Germany's large collective fields than to the small, narrow strip parcels of West Germany.

9.3 HOUSE AND FARMSTEAD TYPES

In the ever-changing rural cultural landscape which meets the eye of the traveler in Europe, no single element changes more rapidly and often than the traditional house and farmstead types. Almost every small district offers its own distinctive folk architecture and building methods. Still, generalization can bring some order to what appears to be hopeless chaos and allow recognition of fairly extensive areas where certain characteristics dominate.

TRADITIONAL BUILDING MATERIALS

One trait which can classify house and farmstead types is the traditional building material (Figure 9.18). Perhaps the most primitive means of construction involves the use of earth or sod, including sun-dried bricks. This is relatively rare in Europe today, although more common in prehistoric times. Mud-brick buildings can be found in parts of the Mediterranean peninsulas, particularly on delta plains where stone is scarce, but for the most part they are confined to adjacent North Africa and the Middle East, in the desert belt from India through Morocco.

Another of the primitive methods is to pack clay around a wattle of twigs, reeds, or rushes to form the walls of the house. This is found traditionally in such varied parts of Europe as lowland Ireland, the Vendée Marshes of France, and the plains of Romania. In the grasslands of eastern Europe, extending into the Ukraine, houses made of sod bricks are still common today. In Iceland, walls were traditionally made of turf and clods of earth on which grass was planted. Only the front side of the house was boarded with driftwood. These varieties of earthen construction are generally confined to regions where more desirable materials such as stone and wood were unavailable. This is apparent in the Mediterranean area where earthen structures are found in alluvial plains, and in lowland Ireland where stone lies inaccessible beneath the bogs. Even rarer is the use of caves as dwellings, a practice generally associated with man's distant ancestors but one which can still be observed in parts of Spain and elsewhere (Figure 9.18).

Stone construction is more common and dominates most of southern Europe, extending up the Atlantic front into portions of the British Isles. For the most part, this zone is mountainous or hilly, with bare rock exposed in many places.

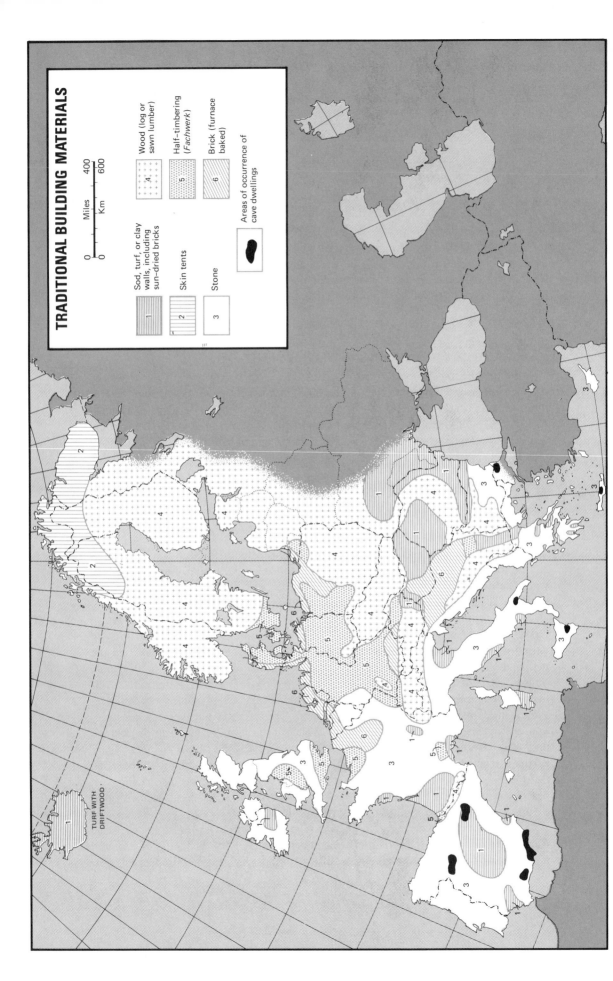

TRADITIONAL BUILDING MATERIALS

1 Sod, turf, or clay walls, including sun-dried bricks

2 Skin tents

3 Stone

4 Wood (log or sawn lumber)

5 Half-timbering (Fachwerk)

6 Brick (furnace baked)

Areas of occurrence of cave dwellings

Miles 0 400
Km 0 600

TURF WITH DRIFTWOOD

Figure 9.19 A village in the southern European zone where stone construction is dominant. These unique domed houses, called Trulli, are typical only of a portion of the southern Italian province of Puglia (Apulia). Note that the walls, roofs, fences, and streets are all built of stone. (Photograph ENIT, courtesy Italian State Tourist Office.)

Stone is readily available except in the larger river deltas and plains, and easily worked limestone is also widely distributed. Stone construction, perhaps more than anything else, lends distinctiveness to the cultural landscape of southern Europe, for nearly all man-made features are built of this material, including houses, churches, terraces, bridges, fences, windmill towers, and even the ruins of ancient civilizations (Figure 9.19). Stone construction provides, as the French geographer Vidal de la Blache suggested, "a guarantee of whatever permanence is consistent with human undertakings," though Mediterranean man has long plundered the ruins of older structures to acquire stone for new buildings. The belt of stone construction corresponds very closely to the regions of most complete deforestation, and archaeological evidence leaves no doubt that southern Europeans once preferred to build wooden structures. Only when the forests were gone was stone accepted as the dominant material. The stonemasonry skills developed in the Mediterranean were later carried north, as southern European artisans were called upon to build cathedrals and other important structures beyond the Alps.

Wooden construction long dominated the northern and eastern parts of Europe, generally the Scandinavian countries and the huge Slavic realm, as well as hilly and mountainous areas in central Europe. These are the regions of greatest forest survival, and as a general rule, wood is the dominant building material wherever timber is plentiful. Log construction was perhaps the most typical, though few such structures are any longer being built. The American log cabin was derived from Swedo–Finnish and Black Forest German colonists (Figure 9.20). Even churches in northern and eastern Europe were traditionally built of wood, and some beautiful specimens survive in Russia, Romanian Moldavia, and Norway. One of

Figure 9.18 Traditional building materials. (In part after Vidal de la Blache, Houston, Boyd, Jessen, Batsford, and Milojević.)

Figure 9.20   A log cabin in the province of Jämtland, interior central Sweden. Log construction once dominated the countries of northern and eastern Europe, and examples are still to be seen, especially in rugged, thickly forested areas such as Jämtland. Also of interest is the grass-covered roof, a frequently encountered feature of folk architecture in the colder parts of Europe. (Photo courtesy Swedish National Tourist Office.)

the landmarks of the Latvian capital, Riga, was the impressive wooden steeple of the St. Petri Church, which went up in flames in 1941 as the Germans expelled Russian troops from the city. Entire towns and cities are dominated by wooden structures in northern Europe, as in the charming frame city of Bergen in Norway or the town of Tampere in Finland, which was 84 percent wood construction as recently as 1900. The chief disadvantage of wood buildings is their susceptibility to fire, particularly when packed together in towns or farm villages. Settlements in Switzerland have been destroyed by fire even in the present century, and cities such as Bergen and Moskva were, on occasion, wiped out.

Along a narrow strip of coastal marshes and river deltas on the North and Baltic sea shore of the Low Country, Germany, and extending into northern France, brick construction predominates. This area was in part devoid of forests due to flooding, and the depth of alluvial deposits often made stone inaccessible. Bricks were a practical alternative, and their reddish hue, derived from the native clays, produces a distinctive cultural landscape. The impression of colors carried

Figure 9.21 Half-timbered farm buildings in a West German hamlet. Half-timbering (*Fachwerk*) is the dominant building method in the German lands. The scene here is from the hamlet of Öleroth in the hilly Bergisches Land just east of Köln. (Photo courtesy G. J. Jordan.)

away by the visitor to this coastal land is of bright green pastures, herds of black and white Holstein-Friesian cattle, and red-brick buildings. Another large zone of brick construction is found in the plains of northern interior Yugoslavia.

Most of the remainder of Europe, primarily Germany, Denmark, southernmost Sweden, Normandie, Alsace, and parts of lowland England, is characterized by traditional *half-timbering* (German *Fachwerk*) (Figure 9.18). A framework of heavy oaken beams is erected, typically with angular support beams, and the interstices are then filled in with a woven wattle of twigs and small branches mixed with clay (Figure 9.21). In more recent times, the wattling has often been replaced by brick or fragmented stone. Generally the interstices are plastered over and whitewashed, and the beams are stained or painted a darker color, producing a striking and distinctive appearance. While half-timbering is identified with Germany so closely as to have become part of the stereotyped image foreigners have of that country, it is quite common in the non-German districts mentioned, and there are parts of Germany where it is absent. In Germany, half-timbering is rarely seen south of the Danube or west of the Rhine, in the areas once ruled by the Romans. It is probably Germanic in origin, however, and was presumably carried to England and France by Saxon and Frankish invaders.

This method also appears to be linked to zones of moderate deforestation, where enough timber remained for the substantial framework but not for the complete walls. Half-timbering may also be viewed as an intermediate type between the timber construction to the north and the southern earthen-building zone. The German geographer Adolf Helbok identified half-timbering with the zone of oak forest, arguing that oak makes splendid beams but is inadequate for log houses

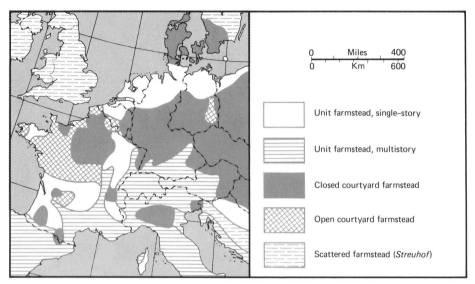

Figure 9.22   Traditional rural house and farmstead types. (In part after Demangeon, Haberlandt, Milojević, and Houston.)

because the trees are not straight enough to provide long logs. Half-timbering can also be found in parts of Yugoslav Makedonija and Srbija, as well as on the island of Corse, in the Basque lands, in parts of central Spain, and in Cévennes, a district in southern France. In Yugoslavia, the filler placed between the beams is generally mud-dried brick. In these outlying areas of half-timbering, Germanic origin seems highly unlikely.

In recent times, particularly within the past half-century, traditional building materials have been abandoned in many parts of Europe and are being replaced by modern materials, such as concrete blocks. Half-timbering, for example, is rarely used now, even in Germany. However, the traditional, older, well-constructed houses are still very much a part of the cultural landscape, and their durability guarantees their presence for many years to come.

FOLK ARCHITECTURE

The style of construction is visually as noticeable as the materials used and perhaps even more important in the classification of house and farmstead types (Figure 9.22). While the diversity of folk architecture in Europe is very great, it is possible to distinguish two broad categories: the *unit farmstead* (*Einheitshaus*), in which both human and animal quarters, as well as storage facilities, are housed in one building under a single roof; and the *multiple-structure farmstead* (*Mehrbauhof*), involving a number of separate buildings.

The unit house can be further divided into two subtypes on the basis of the number of stories. In a belt stretching across the North German Plain into the Low Country and Flanders (Figure 9.22), the single-story unit farmstead is found, in which the people and livestock occupy different parts of the same floor. Included in this group, among others, are the Saxon, Frisian, and Eiderstedt types, the former characterized by living quarters and stalls at opposite ends of an elongated

Figure 9.23   Two Saxon-type single-story unit farmsteads in the *Runddorf* (round village) of Mammoisel, near the Iron Curtain in West Germany. The livestock are housed toward the front of these half-timbered structures, while the people live toward the rear. The larger window in the side of the house on the right marks the beginning of the human quarters. Originally, the roofs of these houses were probably thatched, but in recent times various substitutes have been used, such as the corrugated metal on the right house. The view is from the central, circular village green, around which the Saxon houses are arranged like the spokes of a wheel. (Photo by the author.)

structure separated by the hearth, half-timbering with brick filler, and thatched roof (Figure 9.23). The Eiderstedt house is one of the largest single-family structures in the world and is distinguished by a huge, thatched pyramid roof covering a square house centered on a threshing floor. These single-story unit farmsteads represent ancient Low German types which have survived to the present day, though they are in retreat everywhere. The Saxons carried them to England, but by the 1500s separate animal quarters had been built in all districts except the far north of that country. A law passed in 1419 in London made it illegal to keep livestock under the same roof with people.

Much more common is the unit farmstead of multiple story construction, the dominant type in southern Europe and many mountain or hill districts such as the Alps and Black Forest. Here the people and livestock usually occupy different stories, normally with the stalls at ground level, the living quarters immediately above, and perhaps an attic for hay storage. Cellars for cheese-making are typical of the Alpine area, and in vineyard districts, where livestock are few, a wine cellar may be directly under the residence. Elsewhere, as in southern Bayern these farmsteads are often composed of a multistory house built beside an attached barn. The well-known Black Forest house of southwestern Germany and Swiss chalet are examples of multistory unit farmsteads (Figure 9.24).

The remainder of rural Europe is dominated by multistructure farmsteads of several types. The *courtyard farmstead,* in which the house, barn, and other buildings are tightly clustered around three or four sides of a central farmyard is found in a broad, wedge-shaped area of central Europe, extending from an apex in

Figure 9.24   A multistory unit farmstead of the Bernese type, found in central Switzerland. The two floors with windows are the human quarters, the livestock are housed on the ground level, and the attic is used for storage of hay. Such farmsteads, in various local forms, are typical of many of the southern German-speaking peoples of Europe. (Photo courtesy Swiss National Tourist Office.)

northern France eastward into Poland and the Balkans (Figures 9.22, 9.25). The best-known example of this type is the Frankish farmstead, which corresponds fairly well in distribution to the Middle German dialect and the ancient zone of influence of the Frankish tribe. In most cases, buildings flank three sides of the Frankish courtyard, with a fence and gate completing the enclosure. The courtyard farmstead was probably designed to provide defense on the family level.

Other multistructure farmsteads are not so tightly clustered around a farmyard. They consist instead of a loose assemblage of buildings scattered about the area near the house. The German geographers designate this type as the *Streuhof,* or "strewn farmstead," and it is more common in Anglo-America than in Europe. It is generally confined to the zone of wooden construction in northern and eastern Europe, where the spacing of buildings is a practical solution to the danger of fire. Furthermore, the *Streuhof* is related to dispersed farmsteads and unit-block farms,

Figure 9.25 A courtyard farmstead in the village of Wallern, Burgenland, Austria. The view is from the courtyard of the farmstead, looking out through the gate toward the village street. The farmhouse and other structures are lined up around the courtyard. The plastered, whitewashed walls and thatched roofs are typical of this eastern section of Austria. (Reproduced by permission of Calendaria Ltd., Immensee, Switzerland.)

where crowding of buildings is unnecessary, unlike the clustered villages further south and west where limited space is available.

*   *   *

THE CULTURAL LANDSCAPE of rural Europe reflects the antiquity of the culture area. As the German scholar August Meitzen said, "we walk to a certain degree in every village among the ruins of antiquity." The forces which produced field patterns, house types, and farm villages are often so remote in time as to be unknown to present scholars. Slowly, however, the traditional forms, relics which are ill suited to the demands of the twentieth century, are dying. The European countryside is being gradually "Americanized," with scattered farmsteads, unit-block holdings, and contemporary building materials and methods replacing the traditional forms. With their slow passing, much of the charm of the rural landscape will be lost, but such is inevitably the price of "progress."

SOURCES AND SUGGESTED READINGS

Swanzie Agnew. "Rural Settlement in the Coastal Plain of Bas Languedoc." *Geography*. Vol. 31 (1946), pp. 67–77.

Marcel Aurousseau. "The Arrangement of Rural Populations." *Geographical Review*. Vol. 10 (1920), pp. 223–240.

Harry Batsford. "Types and Materials of Houses in England." *Geography*. Vol. 12 (1923–24), pp. 42–50.

Maurice W. Beresford and J. K. S. St. Joseph. *Medieval England: An Aerial Survey*. London: Cambridge University Press, 1958.

Arnold Beuermann. "Typen ländlicher Siedlungen in Griechenland." *Petermanns Geographische Mitteilungen*. Vol. 100 (1956), pp. 278–285.

Louise A. Boyd. *Polish Countrysides: Photographs and Narrative*. New York: American Geographical Society, 1937.

Walter Christaller. "Siedlungsgeographie und Kommunalwirtschaft." *Petermanns Geographische Mitteilungen*. Vol. 84 (1938), pp. 49–53.

Comptes Rendus du Congres International de Géographie, Paris. 1931. Vol. 3. Paris: XIII Congres, 1934.

Nikolaus Creutzburg. *Kultur im Spiegel der Landschaft: das Bild der Erde in seiner Gestaltung Durch den Menschen*. Leipzig, Germany: Bibliographisches Institut, 1930.

Jovan Cvijić. *La Péninsule Balkanique: Géographie humaine*. Paris: Armand Colin, 1918.

H. Clifford Darby. "The Changing English Landscape." *Geographical Journal*. Vol. 117 (1951), pp. 377–398.

Albert Demangeon. *La France*. Vol. 6 of *Géographie Universelle*. Paris: Armand Colin, 1946.

Albert Demangeon. "Types de villages en France." *Annales de Geógraphie*. Vol. 48 (1939), pp. 1–21.

Robert E. Dickinson. "Dispersed Settlement in Southern Italy." *Erdkunde*. Vol. 10 (1956), pp. 282–297.

Robert E. Dickinson. "Land Reform in Southern Italy." *Economic Geography*. Vol. 30 (1954), pp. 157–176.

Robert E. Dickinson. "Rural Settlement in the German Lands." *Annals, Association of American Geographers*. Vol. 39 (1949), pp. 239–263.

Frans Dussart. "Geographie der ländlichen Siedlungsformen in Belgien und Luxemburg." *Geographische Rundschau*. Vol. 9 (1957), pp. 12–18.

H. Fairhurst. "Types of Settlement in Spain." *Scottish Geographical Magazine*. Vol. 51 (1935), pp. 283–296.

Robert Gradmann. "Die ländlichen Siedlungsformen Württembergs." *Petermanns Geographische Mitteilungen*. Vol. 56 (1910), part 1, pp. 183–186, 246–249.

Howard L. Gray. *English Field Systems*. Cambridge, Mass.: Harvard University Press, 1915.

A. Haberlandt. Map of house types in Central Europe. In *Illustrierte Völkerkunde*, ed. Georg Buschan. Vol. 2, Part 2. Stuttgart, Germany: Strecker and Schroeder, 1926, following p. 176.

Adolf Helbok. *Deutsche Siedlung: Wesen, Ausbreitung und Sinn*. Halle, Germany: Max Niemeyer, 1938.

S. Helmfrid (ed.). Vadstena Symposium: "Morphogenesis of the Agrarian Cultural Landscape." In *Geografiska Annaler*. Vol. 43, nos. 1–2 (1961), pp. 1–328.

George W. Hoffman. "Transformation of Rural Settlement in Bulgaria." *Geographical Review*. Vol. 54 (1964), pp. 45–64.

W. G. Hoskins. *The Making of the English Landscape*. London: Hodder & Stoughton, 1957.

James M. Houston. *A Social Geography of Europe*. London: Duckworth, 1953, chapters 4–6.

Dimitri Jaranoff. "Die Siedlungstypen in der östlichen und zentralen Balkenhalbinsel." *Zeitschrift der Gesellschaft für Erdkunde zu Berlin*, 1934, pp. 183–191.

Otto Jessen. "Höhlenwohnungen in den Mittelmeerländern." *Petermanns Geographische Mitteilungen.* Vol. 76 (1930), pp. 128–133, 180–184.

James H. Johnson. "Studies of Irish Rural Settlement." *Geographical Review.* Vol. 48 (1958), pp. 554–566.

Terry G. Jordan. "On the Nature of Settlement Geography." *Professional Geographer.* Vol. 18 (1966), pp. 26–28.

Lester E. Klimm. "The Relation Between Field Patterns and Jointing in the Aran Islands." *Geographical Review.* Vol. 25 (1935), pp. 618–624.

Fritz Klute (ed.). *Die ländlichen Siedlungen in verschiedenen Klimazonen.* Breslau, Germany: F. Hirt, 1933.

Audrey M. Lambert. "Farm Consolidation in Western Europe." *Geography.* Vol. 48 (1963), pp. 31–48.

Marguerite A. Lefèvre. *L'habitat rural en Belgique.* Liège, Belgium: H. Vaillant-Carmanne, 1926.

Olive Lodge. "Villages and Houses in Jugoslavia." *Geography.* Vol. 21 (1936), pp. 94–106.

David Lowenthal and Hugh C. Prince. "The English Landscape." *Geographical Review.* Vol. 54 (1964), pp. 309–346.

Rudolf Martiny. "Die Grundrissgestaltung der deutschen Siedlungen." *Petermanns Mitteilungen Ergänzungsheft Nr. 197.* Gotha, Germany: Justus Perthes, 1928.

August Meitzen. *Das deutsche Haus.* Berlin: Dietrich Reimer, 1882.

August Meitzen. *Siedelung und Agrarwesen der Westgermanen und Ostgermanen, der Kelten, Römer, Finnen und Slawen.* 3 vols. and atlas. Berlin: Wilhelm Hertz, 1895.

Borivoje Milojević. "Types of Villages and Village-Houses in Yugoslavia." *Professional Geographer.* Vol. 5, no. 6 (1953), pp. 13–17.

Wilhelm Müller-Wille. "Haus- und Gehöftformen in Mitteleuropa." *Geographische Zeitschrift.* Vol. 42 (1936), pp. 121–138.

John Naylon. "Land Consolidation in Spain." *Annals, Association of American Geographers.* Vol. 49 (1959), pp. 361–373. (See also his follow-up study, *ibid.,* Vol. 51 (1961), pp. 335–338.)

Georg W. Niemeier. "Frühformen der Waldhufen." *Petermanns Geographische Mitteilungen.* Vol. 93 (1949), pp. 14–27.

Georg W. Niemeier. *Siedlungsgeographie.* Braunschweig, Germany: Georg Westermann, 1967.

Gottfried Pfeifer. "The Quality of Peasant Living in Central Europe." in *Man's Role in Changing the Face of the Earth,* ed. William L. Thomas, Jr. Chicago: University of Chicago Press, 1956, pp. 240–277.

Werner Radig. *Die Siedlungstypen in Deutschland.* East Berlin: Henschel, 1955.

Karl Heinz Schröder and Gabriele Schwarz. *Die ländlichen Siedlungsformen in Mitteleuropa.* Forschungen zur deutschen Landeskunde, Vol. 175. Bad Godesberg, West Germany: Bundesforschungsanstalt für Landeskunde und Raumordnung, 1969.

Gabriele Schwarz. *Allgemeine Siedlungsgeographie.* Berlin: Walter De Gruyter, 2nd ed., 1961.

D. J. Shaw. "The Problem of Land Fragmentation in the Mediterranean Area: A Case Study." *Geographical Review.* Vol. 53 (1963), pp. 40–51.

L. Dudley Stamp. "The Common Lands and Village Greens of England and Wales." *Geographical Journal.* Vol. 130 (1964), pp. 457–469.

Kirk H. Stone. "The Development of a Focus for the Geography of Settlement," *Economic Geography.* Vol. 41 (1965), pp. 346–355.

Kirk H. Stone. "Regionalization of Spanish Units of Settlement." *Tijdschrift voor Economische en Sociale Geografie.* Vol. 61 (1970), pp. 232–241.

B. M. Swainson. "Rural Settlement in Somerset." *Geography.* Vol. 20 (1935), pp. 112–124.

Harry Thorpe. "The Green Villages of County Durham." *Institute of British Geographers, Transactions and Papers.* Vol. 13 (1949), pp. 153–180.

Harry Thorpe. "The Green Village as a Distinctive Form of Settlement on the North European Plain." *Bulletin de la Société Belge d'Études Géographiques.* Vol. 30 (1961), pp. 93–134.

Harald Uhlig. "Old Hamlets with Infield and Outfield Systems in Western and Central Europe." *Geografiska Annaler.* Vol. 43 (1961), pp. 285–312.

Paul Vidal de la Blache. *Principles of Human Geography.* Translated by M. T. Bingham. New York: Holt, Rinehart & Winston, 1926.

J. M. Wagstaff. "The Study of Greek Rural Settlements: A Review of the Literature." *Erdkunde.* Vol. 23 (1969), pp. 306–317.

J. M. Wagstaff. "Traditional Houses in Modern Greece." *Geography.* Vol. 50 (1965), pp. 58–64.

Herbert Wilhelmy. *Hochbulgarien, I: Die ländlichen Siedlungen und die bäuerliche Wirtschaft.* Kiel, Germany: Geographisches Institut der Universität, 1935.

Herbert Wilhelmy. "Völkische und koloniale Siedlungsformen der Slawen." *Geographische Zeitschrift.* Vol. 42 (1936) pp. 81–97.

Bogdan Zaborski. "Sur le forme des villages en Pologne et leur repartition." *Boletin de la Société de Géographie de Quebec.* Vol. 22 (1928), pp. 65–76.

CHAPTER TEN

Industrial geography

Complementing the agricultural side of the economy is the much more important industrial sector. The proportion of the European population involved directly or indirectly in manufacturing and other industries has risen steadily since the 1700s, far surpassing the numbers in agriculture.

The geographer is interested in the areal aspect of industry. He is concerned about where industrial activity is located and how its distribution has changed through time. Still more important, the geographer seeks to understand *why* industries are distributed as they are. In seeking the causes of industrial location, he searches for relationships between the areal pattern of industry and the distribution of other geographical phenomena, both environmental and cultural.

Both the distribution and magnitude of industrial activity have changed greatly over the centuries. In order to understand the present pattern, it is necessary at the outset to survey the more important temporal changes. Modern European industries are firmly based in a very old tradition of manufacturing.

10.1 TRADITIONAL MANUFACTURING SYSTEMS

The most widespread system of manufacturing before the 1700s was *cottage* or *household industry*. It was rural in nature, was confined mainly to European farm villages, and was generally practiced as a sideline to agriculture. A village might have a cobbler, weaver, miller, and blacksmith, who spent part of their time farming and the remainder, during slack periods in the fields, working at the household trade. The abundance of people today in English and German lands with surnames such as Smith, Schmidt, Miller, Mueller, Weaver, Weber, and the like suggest the former abundance of village craftsmen. There was little formality associated with the passing on of skills, and sons most commonly learned from fathers and daughters from mothers simply by observing the work being done. Cottage trades were nearly wiped out by the Industrial Revolution, but they do survive today in some parts of Europe, particularly if they have been able to attract buyers from beyond the village community. In certain areas of Scotland, for example, housewives still weave the famous Harris tweed on crude looms in their individual cottages.

The other, more important, traditional manufacturing system was that of the *guild,* a professional organization of artisans skilled in a particular trade. Unlike the cottagers, guild artisans engaged in their trade full-time and usually lived in towns or cities rather than farm villages. The skills involved were more advanced than those of the cottage artisan, and they were passed on through an apprenticeship system. A boy was apprenticed, for example, to a cooper, potter, mason, glassblower, silversmith, sculptor, or master weaver and served for years in the workshop as a helper. At the end of apprenticeship, the young man was obliged to demonstrate his skill before an examining board composed of members of the particular guild in question. Approval allowed the apprentice to be a member of the guild and begin practicing the trade on his own. In larger cities, each guild had a house on the main municipal square, and these may still be seen today in well-preserved towns such as Gent, Brugge, and Antwerpen in Belgium.

Many relics of the guild system can be found today, and craft shops are still surprisingly numerous, even in the more advanced countries, such as West Germany. In that nation there are still sixty-four registered crafts, represented by over 9000 local guilds, including tailors, bakers, knifesmiths, sausage-makers, and others. The same high standards for membership typical of medieval times survive to the present day. Service crafts, trade crafts, and manufacturing crafts, both registered and unregistered, employ almost 15 percent of the West German labor force, a remarkable survival in the face of the far-reaching changes brought by the Industrial Revolution.

In spite of numerous differences, there were some basic similarities between the guild system and cottage industry. Both depended on skilled hand labor and human power, though millers had harnessed the winds and waters to drive machinery. Textiles were woven on small looms operated by individual weavers, and iron was smelted using charcoal in small, shoplike forges.

10.2 THE SPREAD OF URBAN MANUFACTURING BEFORE 1700

Early manufacturing on a higher level was centered in Mediterranean Europe, particularly in Greece, where it had spread from the Fertile Crescent and Egypt. By the golden age of Greece, the cities of Athínai and Kórinthos led in manufacturing, boasting cloth-makers, dyers who perpetuated the trade of still older Phoenician towns, leather-workers, potters who left behind numerous exquisite remains of their work, weapon-makers producing spears, shields, helmets, and other weaponry, jewelers, a variety of metalworkers, stonemasons, and shipwrights, who kept the great Greek merchant fleets and navies afloat. The Hellenic leadership in artisanry passed with political leadership to Roma, and it in turn was succeeded by Constantinople.

In the Dark Ages, manufacturing declined and merchant activity generally decreased, but such industry as did survive remained centered in the Mediterranean lands. Constantinople was in time rivaled by Moorish Spain, where Toledo developed a reputation for high-quality steel and Córdoba produced fine leather goods. The single most significant development of the Middle Ages, however, was the rise of northern Italy to industrial leadership, a rise aided by (1) the reduction of hostile Arab influence in the Mediterranean, (2) the increasing power of the papacy, coupled with the Christianizing of trans-Alpine Europe, and (3) the growth of population and agricultural production in Germanic and French areas, which increased the economic hinterland of north Italy. Above all, the growth of Italian industry resulted from the dominant position achieved by its merchants, who ranged from China to England, taking full advantage of the central position of Italy in the Mediterranean.

Cities such as Genova, Milano, Firenze, and Venezia acquired widespread fame for their silks and other textiles, cloth-dying, brassware, weaponry, glass, and shipbuilding. At its peak, Venezia housed 16,000 shipwrights who turned out an average of one galleon per day, using prefabricated parts in an early-day assembly-line production. By 1307, artisans of the city of Firenze were making 100,000 pieces of cloth per year, and Milano became the chief European center of weaponry manufacture. A system of free guild craftsmen was at the core of the northern Italian achievement, representing a major departure from the classical tradition of slave artisans.

Widespread warfare, involving France, England, Spain, and southern Italy, plus the ravages of the Black Death, Turkish expansion, and the rise of the Atlantic as a primary route signaled the decline of northern Italy as a manufacturing region in the fourteenth and fifteenth centuries. The centers of Moorish industry in Iberia also diminished in importance after the Christian reconquest, and the Turks hastened the decline of Constantinople. All the major industrial areas of Mediterranean Europe suffered setbacks at this time.

The industrial-commercial leadership shifted north to Belgium, Switzerland, and southern Germany in particular, where Italian skills were in some instances transplanted. The towns affected included Nürnberg, Ulm, Augsburg, Nördlingen, Rothenburg-ob-der-Tauber, and St. Gallen. Other Italians founded the famous silk industry of Lyon, in the Rhône–Saône Corridor of France. The key industrial district of the north, however, lay in Flanders, where the first major developments occurred in the 1100s. This district was not an offspring of northern Italy, but a contemporary; in fact, migrant Flemish cloth-workers had helped found the textile industry of Italian Firenze. Flanders, like northern Italy, acquired its industrial importance partly as a result of a favorable trade location. A fortunate concentration of river, highway, and marine trade routes allowed Flanders to achieve the same dominance in northern Europe that the Italian towns had in the Mediterranean. Cloth-making was first centered at Ypres, Gent, Brugge, and Douai, which drew on the wool of England and Spain as primary raw material. In the 1400s, linen joined wool as a major product of the Flemish towns and attained an importance which persisted into the nineteenth century.

Carried by emigrant artisans, the influence of Flanders was instrumental in the industrial development of the Netherlands beginning in the 1400s. Flemish tradesmen skilled in woolen-textile manufacture also migrated to England, particularly Yorkshire, as early as the 1300s. The Netherlands rose to industrial dominance in the seventeenth century, even surpassing Flanders, while northern Germany, particularly Prussia, outstripped the southern German lands. In the 1600s and 1700s, Sweden and England developed major industries.

The gradual northward shift of industrial activity and corresponding decline in southern Europe meant that manufacturing became increasingly identified with Germanic, Protestant areas and less with Catholic, Romance language countries. Some writers have even suggested that certain social characteristics of Protestantism, including approval of change and veneration of work, were more conducive to industrial development than were those of Catholicism and Eastern Orthodoxy. There can be no doubt that persecution and expulsion of Huguenot merchants and artisans by the Catholic-backed French government and similar pressure on Protestant Flemings by the Spanish rulers contributed materially to the industrial rise of the Netherlands, Prussia, and England. In any case, the most important European manufacturing was carried on by the guildsmen of Protestant, Germanic lands by the 1700s. Industrial leadership brought political power and allowed England to defeat France, and Prussia to overwhelm Austria. It was in this areal context that the Industrial Revolution took place.

10.3 THE INDUSTRIAL REVOLUTION

The inventions and innovations of the Industrial Revolution, which began appearing in force about 1730, undermined the guild system and cottage industry. It is increasingly evident that this revolution, which is still in progress, involves the most rapid and significant technological change in the history of the human race, and it may well prove to contain the seed of eventual human destruction. For better or worse, the infant technology of this Industrial Revolution burst forth in England in the 1700s.

Two fundamental changes accompanied the revolution. First, machines replaced human hands in fashioning products, and the word "manufacturing" (made by hand) became technically obsolete. No longer would the weaver sit at his hand loom and painstakingly produce each piece of cloth; instead, huge mechanical looms were invented to do the job faster and more economically. In many industries the machine made possible the use of interchangeable parts and the assembly line, both generally absent in the old system. A second change involved the rise of inanimate power, as man harnessed water, steam, and eventually electricity, petroleum, and the atom. The new technology was not acquired overnight but in bits and pieces over many decades and even centuries. Nearly all of the interconnected developments of the formative stage of the Industrial Revolution, from about 1730 to 1850, occurred in the United Kingdom. The British gave the Industrial Revolution to the world, and for that reason alone should perhaps be judged the single most important group of people in modern history.

TEXTILES

The textiles industry was the first to feel the effects of the Industrial Revolution. Between 1733 and 1785, major advances were made in the development of mechanical looms, driven by waterpower and operated by semiskilled labor. The day of the artisan was over. New factories were built wherever waterfalls or rapids could be found to power the looms, particularly on the eastern and western flanks of the Pennines in north-central England and in the Scottish Lowlands, where streams descended from the adjacent Highlands. The district known as Lancashire, on the west side of the Pennines near the Irish Sea, was the key area in which the new textile technology arose, and its cotton cloth-makers, inheritors of a much older tradition in linens and woolens, were the first to profit from the innovations (Figure 10.1). The woolen industry dating from medieval times in nearby Yorkshire (Figure 10.1), located on the opposite Pennine flank, soon shared the new inventions, and the same streams which had long provided the soft water for cleaning wool now turned the waterwheels which drove the new machine looms.

COAL-MINING

Waterpower dominated the early textile phase of the Industrial Revolution, but it was not destined to rule for long. The Scotsman James Watt and others perfected the steam engine in the 1760s, and the first steam-powered cotton textile mill was put into operation in 1785. General acceptance followed in the 1790s. The steam engine required fuel, but Great Britain was an almost totally deforested land, and the supply of wood was inadequate. The island was gifted, however, with an even better fuel—coal. The mining of coal was, accordingly, the second major industry to be affected by the Industrial Revolution. It was not a new industry in Britain, for there is evidence that coal had been dug as far back as Roman times, to heat the public baths of conquerors from the sunny Mediterranean, who shivered in the perpetual coolness of England. It was used in medieval times to heat homes and caused air pollution in London as early as the 1200s. Still, the use of coal before about 1800 was insignificant compared to the new industrial use.

Coal had one problem: It was bulky and difficult to transport any great distance. This was especially true at the turn of the nineteenth century, before the railroad, internal-combustion engine, and bulk-carrying ships had been developed. Consequently, the industries which relied upon coal as fuel were drawn to the coalfields, just as the earlier factories were attracted to waterfalls and rapids. Both Lancashire and Yorkshire, as well as the Scottish Lowlands, were endowed with coal deposits, allowing a smooth transition from water to thermal power with a minimum of factory relocation. In addition, substantial reserves of coal were found in the Midlands, south of the Pennines in central England; along the coastal fringe of southern Wales; and in the region of Newcastle on the North Sea coast near the Scottish border (Figure 10.1).

A distinctive trait of the Industrial Revolution soon became evident: areal concentration of industries. It is true that certain towns and districts were known for a particular product under the guild system, but many such industries were dispersed through a large number of small towns over fairly large regions. In contrast, mechanized production focused on a small number of cities and districts which attracted very large populations. Gravitation to the coalfields accelerated the

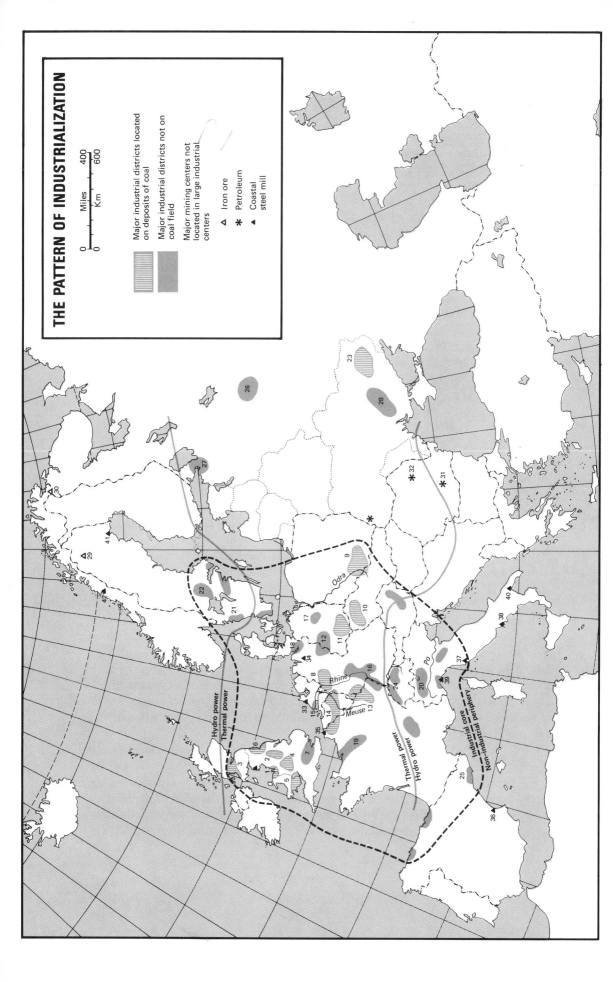

THE PATTERN OF INDUSTRIALIZATION

Miles
0   400
Km
0   600

Major industrial districts located
on deposits of coal

Major industrial districts not on
coal field

Major mining centers not
located in large industrial
centers

△ Iron ore

* Petroleum

▲ Coastal
  steel mill

Odra

Rhine

Meuse

Po

Hydro power
Thermal power

Thermal power
Hydro power

Industrial core
Non-industrial periphery

areal focalization of industry, causing great increases in population in favored districts and substantial emigration elsewhere.

IRON AND STEEL

Metallurgical industries are ancient, reaching back to the beginning of the Bronze and Iron Ages in prehistoric times. Throughout most of history, the smelting or iron was a very primitive process, and few who practiced it had any valid understanding of what happened. Iron ore was simply heated over a charcoal fire, and the charcoal's carbon combined with the ore's oxygen to free the iron. Some carbon also combined with the iron to provide hardness, for pure iron is rather malleable and easily cut. Too much carbon resulted in brittle cast iron; a proper amount resulted in steel. Different varieties of steel could be produced by accidental or purposeful addition of various *ferroalloys,* metals such as nickel or chrome.

Before the mid-1700s much superstition, ritual, and ceremony were associated with steelmaking as the keepers of the forges sought to make good steel. Those towns which became famous for high-quality steel, such as Toledo or Solingen, more often than not owed their reputation to particular local ores which spontaneously produced fine steel when smelted. Iron processing had changed little in thousands of years, and the industry in Europe was thoroughly dispersed, with small forges located wherever iron was found. The industry was more rural than urban and was often found in thinly populated hill districts.

The Industrial Revolution brought major changes to the iron and steel industry. First, coke replaced charcoal as a supplier of heat in the smelting process. Coke, which is nearly pure carbon, burns at a higher temperature than charcoal and is derived by heating high-grade coal to draw off the gaseous constituents. In timber-poor Britain, the use of coke became important in the early 1700s and increased rapidly after midcentury. By 1788, some 70 percent of all blast furnaces in England and Scotland relied on coke instead of charcoal, and by 1806 the proportion had reached 97 percent.

Acceptance of coke drastically changed the areal distribution of steelmaking. The industry abandoned the countless scattered small forges and, out of necessity, relocated in the coal districts where coke could be obtained most cheaply. Iron and steel thus contributed to the accelerating nucleation of industries in small districts; the industry had joined textiles in the march to the coalfields.

Several British districts developed important iron and steel industries. On the River Tees, near the North Sea coast, the coal of nearby Newcastle was combined with the iron ore of the Cleveland Hills to the south, while in the Midlands a fortunate juxtaposition of coal and iron deposits encouraged the rise of such steel towns as Birmingham and Sheffield. Local ores were also adjacent to the coalfields

Figure 10.1 The pattern of industrialization. The numbers stand for: 1. Lancashire, 2. Yorkshire, 3. Scottish Lowlands, 4. English Midlands, 5. South Wales, 6. Newcastle–Tyneside, 7. Greater London, 8. Ruhr, 9. Upper Silesian District, 10. Bohemian Basin, 11. Saxon Triangle, 12. Hanover–Braunschweig, 13. Saar–Lorraine, 14. Sambre–Meuse–Lys, 15. Rotterdam, 16. Upper Rhine Plain, 17. Berlin, 18. Hamburg, 19. Paris–Lower Seine, 20. Po Valley, 21. Göteborg, 22. Bergslagen, 23. Donets Basin, 24. Swiss Plateau–Jura, 25. Barcelona, 26. Greater Moskva, 27. Leningrad, 28. Krivoi Rog–Dnepr, 29. Kiruna–Gällivare, 30. Kirkenes, 31. Ploёşti, 32. Bacău, 33. IJmuiden, 34. Bremen, 35. Dunkerque, 36. Valencia, 37. Piombino, 38. Napoli, 39. Genova, 40. Taranto, 41. Luleå, 42. Mo i Rana.

in south Wales and the western end of the Scottish Lowlands around Glasgow, and steelmaking flourished there too (Figure 10.1).

Other improvements in Britain's iron and steel industry included (1) the separation of smelting and refining into two distinct processes; (2) the *puddling process* (1784), an improved means of refining pure iron from cast iron after the initial smelting; (3) the *rolling mill* (1728), which replaced the hammer and anvil in final processing; (4) the development of much larger blast furnaces in the place of small ovens; (5) the *Bessemer process* (1856), which first made use of oxygen derived from the air for refining purposes, thereby greatly increasing the scale of operation that was possible; (6) the *open hearth process* (1868), which permitted careful control over carbon content; and (7) the *Gilchrist process* (1876), which allowed the use of low-grade phosphoric iron ores. The science of metallurgy became much more sophisticated at this time, as understanding replaced superstition. Use of ferroalloys increased as a result.

Through such innovation and change, the steelmakers of Britain achieved world leadership in the nineteenth century. Victorian England became a society built of steel, and its stark monuments are still visible throughout the British Isles. Its bridges, ships, machines, railroads, and structural frameworks were steel, as was its weaponry.

SHIPBUILDING

Another industry forever changed by the Industrial Revolution was the ancient and honored craft of the shipwright. Traditionally, ships had been small, wooden, and powered by wind or oars, and England had come to rely heavily on her American colonies, particularly those in New England, for ship's timbers. In fact, the shortage of lumber in Britain had allowed colonial Boston to become a shipbuilding center of considerable magnitude.

The Industrial Revolution created demands for larger and faster ships to transport bulky raw materials and finished products; the revolution also provided the technology needed to produce such vessels. Steel replaced wood, steam power supplanted the winds, and by the 1850s, ships worthy of the new age were plying the ocean waters, linking the worldwide British Empire.

The major shipbuilding centers that developed in Great Britain arose where coalfields and steel mills approached tidewater level. One such location was the Tyneside, between Newcastle and the North Sea on the River Tyne, but the major center developed on the Clydeside near Glasgow in the Scottish Lowlands. By the 1890s, British shipyards were producing 80 percent of the world's seagoing tonnage, and Britannia ruled the waves.

OTHER INDUSTRIES

Textiles, coal-mining, steelmaking, and shipbuilding formed the core of the Industrial Revolution, but they were by no means the only industries involved. Their clustering on the coalfields attracted both population and other industries. The shift to machinery gave rise to an entire new industry specializing in the manufacture of machines and machine tools. Both the raw material of this industry—steel—and its market—other manufacturing industries—lay in the coalfields, and it was logical that the machine-makers should locate there too. As machines became more numerous and complex, the industry which supplied them grew steadily.

Another basically new industry was that devoted to the large-scale manufacture and processing of various chemicals, including dyes, paints, fertilizers, drugs, explosives, soap, and, eventually, more sophisticated products such as synthetic fibers. Many such items could be salvaged from by-products of the coking process, and, partly for this reason, many chemical factories were also drawn to the coalfields.

Other industries besides shipbuilding and machine-making used finished steel as a raw material, and these often located near the steel mills: manufacturers of cutlery, surgical instruments, locks, and weaponry. Similarly, textile-using industries, such as makers of clothing, often found it advantageous to be situated near the textile factories.

The snowballing accumulation of a great variety of industries in the coalfield districts of Great Britain caused hundreds of thousands of people to migrate to the same areas seeking factory employment. In short order, the British population was massed in a small number of clusters. These concentrations in turn attracted still other manufacturers, primarily those which needed to be close to the consumers of their products, such as bakers, brewers, meat-packers, and other food processors, as well as newspaper publishers.

THE DEVELOPMENT OF INDUSTRY IN GREATER LONDON

The importance of coal as a locational factor in the formative stages of the British Industrial Revolution was so great that all but one of the major industrial districts developed on the coalfields. The only exception was London (Figure 10.1). The city was remote from coal deposits and had no significant natural resources other than its navigable river; yet it developed into the largest single industrial center in the United Kingdom.

Its advantages were several. First, it had already accumulated a large population before the Industrial Revolution, reaching 700,000 in the late 1600s and accounting for one out of every ten Britishers. This population offered both market and labor supply when industrialization came. Secondly, London was the center for commerce and trade of the country, handling in its harbor three-quarters of the nation's overseas trade by 1700. As a result, a concentration of banks, insurance firms, and shipping brokerage houses developed, which in turn stimulated the process of growth. Industries which depended on foreign areas either as suppliers of raw materials or as consumers of finished products found advantage in locating in London. Thirdly, the large, well-to-do merchant class of the city controlled a huge amount of capital which was needed for investment in industrial activities. Consequently, London has thrived in the Industrial Revolution and today claims one of every five citizens of the country as a resident. The industries present are quite varied, ranging from clothing and food-processing to oil-refining, production of automobiles, manufacture of electrical equipment, and the building of aircraft.

10.4 DISPERSAL OF THE INDUSTRIAL REVOLUTION TO MAINLAND COALFIELDS

The British would have liked to maintain a monopoly on the Industrial Revolution, to prevent the spread of this complex of ideas to other countries. Some attempts were actually made to keep the technology secret, but such efforts had little chance of success in a free society. Had the British been able to prevent the spread of industrialization, they would in all probability still be masters of much of the world. They failed, however, and one of the first areas to imitate their success was mainland Europe, where numerous industrial districts rose in the nineteenth century. With some notable exceptions, the spread was confined to Germanic, Protestant areas, especially northern Germany, but traits associated with the Protestant faiths were not necessarily spurs of industry. A much closer correlation can be detected between industrialization and the location of coal deposits on the mainland. Through good fortune alone, the Germanic folk found parts of their land much better supplied with coal than did the French, Iberians, and Italians.

THE RUHR INDUSTRIAL DISTRICT

As in Britain, industrialization on the European mainland tended to focalize in small districts, mainly on the coalfields. One such district, the Ruhr of West Germany, was destined to become the single most important in all of Europe, far surpassing any British antecedents (Figure 10.1).

The Ruhr, bearing the name of a right-bank tributary stream of the Rhine, is found at the juncture of the North German Plain and the hilly regions to the south called the Sauerland and Siegerland. It lies in one of the many fertile loessial *Börde* which dot the southern edge of the plains, though the Ruhr River itself flows just within the hill zone and is separated from the North German Plain by a single, narrow line of hills, the Haarstrang ("hair string") (Figure 10.2). Underlying the *Börde,* from the Haarstrang northward, were huge deposits of high-grade coal, which outcropped at the surface in some places near the southern fringe of hills.

Development of the Ruhr district lagged considerably behind English or even Belgian efforts. From Neolithic times, a large agricultural population had been attracted by the fertile loessial soils, and small amounts of coal had been chipped

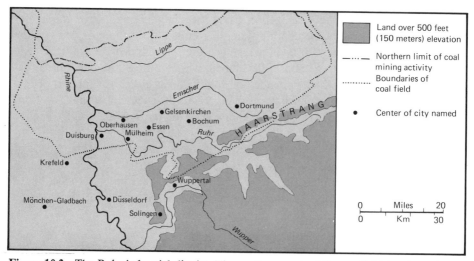

Figure 10.2   The Ruhr industrial district. The southern part of the coalfield has been largely mined out, and mining has migrated steadily northward. Steel mills remain concentrated between the Ruhr and Emscher rivers, while textiles are manufactured at Wuppertal and in the cities west of the Rhine.

away from the surface outcroppings at least as early as the 1200s A.D., mainly to provide heat for local houses. In medieval times, a significant iron and steel industry under the guild system had developed at the town of Solingen and elsewhere in the hilly Sauerland and Siegerland, based on local deposits of iron ore and the survival of large charcoal-producing forests. Linen textiles made from locally grown flax by both guildsmen and cottagers was similarly well established in the area by the time of the Hanseatic League in the late Middle Ages.

In 1800 the steelmakers continued to function in the traditional way, as did the textile-weavers who were concentrated mainly west of the Rhine. Little or no suggestion of the Industrial Revolution sweeping England was visible in the Ruhr, though steam pumps were installed in 1801 to combat water seepage in some of the small coal mines. The towns remained small, confined within medieval walls and functioning primarily as agricultural trade centers. A visitor from the thirteenth or fourteenth centuries would have been quite at home in the Ruhr at the beginning of the 1800s. The next half-century surprisingly brought very few changes, and a traveler in 1847 described the Ruhr as "poetically rural." Coal-mining was still carried on in hundreds of small rural mines, employing in total only some 13,000 men. Urban growth had not been rapid, and the guilds still dominated the manufacture of steel at Solingen.

Nevertheless, the first mark of the Industrial Revolution had been placed on this pastoral setting: Mechanized, steam-powered textile mills arose by 1850 in Krefeld, the twin cities of Mönchen-Gladbach, and others west of the Rhine. The textile guilds and cottage weavers were rapidly being displaced by the new technology. As in Britain, the textile industry was the first to be affected.

In the last half of the nineteenth century, coincident with the unification of Germany, the Ruhr underwent almost complete change, emerging by the end of the 1800s as the most important European industrial center. Annual coal production had risen sevenfold between 1800 and 1850 and increased by thirty-three times in the last half of the century. The mines were no longer small rural enterprises scratching at the surface, but large urban establishments employing hundreds of thousands of workers and utilizing sophisticated mining machinery. Many of the mines were now owned by large steel companies. The manufacture of iron and steel had shifted primarily to the coalfield, and large plants using coke had supplanted the charcoal-burning guilds of Solingen. The small local iron-ore deposits were not adequate to supply the demand, and the Ruhr reached out to Sweden, Spain, and the newly annexed German Lorraine for additional ore, exporting in exchange large amounts of coking coal. The Rhine River forfeited much of its romantic character, steeped in German mythology, to become the major transport route linking the Ruhr to the rest of the world. Barges bearing coal and ore came to dominate the riverine scene at the foot of the Lorelei Cliffs, as progress shoved aside poetry. Industrial names such as Krupp and Thyssen joined Heine and Goethe in the German pantheon.

The population of the Ruhr exploded, as towns became sprawling industrial cities. Along the northern side of the Haarstrang, a line of urban centers developed, from Dortmund in the east through Bochum, Essen, and Oberhausen to Duisburg on the Rhine in the west. Essen, which had a population of only 4,000 within its medieval town walls in 1800 and still only 10,000 at midcentury, was a city of 200,000 by 1900. The local agricultural population had proven inadequate

Figure 10.3   Industrial landscape of the Ruhr district, West Germany. The scene is in Gelsen-kirchen, one of the principal cities of the Ruhr, Europe's single most important industrial district. Here, as in many other European manufacturing districts, industrialization has demanded an ugly, polluted landscape as the price of prosperity. (Courtesy German Information Center.)

as a labor supply, and workers were being drawn in from other parts of Germany, as well as from Belgium, the Netherlands, Italy, and the Slavic lands of the east. A melting pot of peoples was assembled, giving the Ruhr a distinctly different ethnic character from the rest of Germany.

A gray pall of smoke settled over the Ruhr, blackening buildings and human lungs and blotting out the sun. With the smoke came a prosperous, powerful Germany, which assumed its place among the leading nations of the world (Figure 10.3).

The years since 1900 have been eventful and at times tragic for the people of the Ruhr. Twice the district was called upon to supply arms for the German military, and twice it suffered dire consequences. The loss of World War I did not bring any physical damage to the Ruhr, for the front still lay far into France when the Germans surrendered. Unfortunately, absurdly high "reparations payments" were demanded of Germany, and failure to meet these financial obligations caused the French, who clearly recognized that the Ruhr was the economic key to Germany, to invade and occupy the district in 1923–1924. World War II left the district a bombed-out shell, and it is said with considerable exaggeration that in the absence of air pollution the sun shone on the Ruhr for the first time in seventy-five years in 1945. Men with proud names such as Krupp stood condemned as war criminals before the tribunal at Nürnberg and were sent to prison. Some foreign-policy advisers in the United States suggested that the Ruhr be returned to its original agrarian condition, that the greatest industrial center of Europe be converted to a "goat pasture" to prevent any future revival of German power. Instead, precisely the opposite course of action was taken as the Americans, through the Marshall Plan, helped rebuild the Ruhr. In only a few years, production levels had equaled and surpassed those of the prewar period.

The Ruhr today is the throbbing industrial heart of the Common Market. Its core, the inner Ruhr—only about 56 kilometers east-to-west by 24 kilometers north-to-south (35 miles by 15 miles)—has traditionally been divided between the southern concentration of steel mills and the northern zone of coal-mining. Mining has migrated steadily to the north through the years as the deposits nearer the surface in the south were exhausted. The outer Ruhr contains the textile centers in Wuppertal and the trans-Rhine cities, as well as many other industries, including those which use steel as raw material.

THE UPPER SILESIAN INDUSTRIAL DISTRICT

At the headwaters of the Wisla and Odra (Oder) rivers in southern Poland, where the North European Plain joins the Carpathian and Sudetes mountains in another of the loessial *Börde,* lies the Upper Silesian industrial district (Figure 10.1). Its origin and development were German, but its ownership has been Polish since 1945.

A tradition of guild-type iron-smelting was well established here by the 1700s, reliant on abundant local forests for charcoal and on small amounts of iron ore found in the region. The large coal deposits were very nearly left untouched. Upper Silesia (Oberschlesien), part of the Prussian province of Schlesien which had been seized from the Austrians in the mid-1700s, was hindered in industrial development by several disadvantages. First, it lay on a remote frontier, the outermost tip of Prussian, and later German, territory, in an area far removed from markets and sparsely populated. In addition, the Odra River at its source offered fewer possibilities for transport than did the mighty Rhine, and the distance to the sea was great. Furthermore, the coal deposits were not as large as those of the Ruhr.

In spite of these shortcomings, Upper Silesia underwent industrialization in the nineteenth century, in large part because the Prussian government desired it. Financial encouragements, including subsidies, were offered to the wealthy land-lords who owned most of the area, and they responded with investments in industry.

Because coking coal was less abundant than in the Ruhr and the quantity of timber very great, the use of charcoal persisted much longer in Upper Silesia, even into the 1860s. Local iron ores were soon exhausted, and imports from Austria via the Moravian Gate rail route became necessary. After major improvements in the Odra waterway were made in 1895, allowing easier access to the Baltic Sea, Sweden became the dominant supplier of ore. The district never rivaled the Ruhr, but it did produce about 10 percent of Germany's iron by 1900.

Unlike the Ruhr, the Upper Silesian district has been involved in two major changes in political boundaries. Before World War I, almost the entire district lay in Germany, with only a small part across the border in Austria–Hungary; after the war, half of the region was awarded to the new Polish state on the basis of a plebiscite. In 1945 the remainder was taken by the Poles, and most resident Germans were expelled. Poland, which had been quite backward and rural, thereby acquired an important industrial base.

THE SAAR–LORRAINE INDUSTRIAL DISTRICT

Another of the coalfield industrial districts developed largely by the Germans straddles the present border between West Germany and France, including parts of southern Luxembourg (Figure 10.1). The German Saar contains the greater part of the coal, while French Lorraine is one of the major centers of iron-ore mining in Europe. Here, too, industrialization occurred rather late, lagging considerably behind the British districts. Coke was first used in 1838 and only gradually replaced charcoal. Major steel plants with blast furnaces were not introduced until the 1850s. In fact, the major development of the district did not occur until after newly united Germany annexed the Lorraine in 1871. The principal hindrance to expansion is that most of the Saarland coal is not suited for coking, which necessitates the import of Ruhr coals. This movement, complemented by a less important export of Lorraine iron ore to the Ruhr, has been greatly facilitated by the recent canalization of the Mosel (Moselle) River, a tributary of the Rhine.

The industrial value of the Saar–Lorraine areas has prompted numerous boundary changes in the past century. Germany has twice seized and lost part of the iron-ore deposits, and France has twice unsuccessfully sought to permanently detach the Saarland from Germany. The Germans under Hitler also temporarily annexed Luxembourg.

THE SAMBRE–MEUSE–LYS INDUSTRIAL DISTRICT

Long before the Industrial Revolution, textile manufacture was well established in the basin of the Lys River along the Franco–Belgian border, while metalworking industries were concentrated in towns along the Sambre and Meuse (Maas) rivers in central Belgium (Figure 10.1). In the Middle Ages, copper, brass, and iron were produced by craftsmen in towns such as Dinant, Namur, and Huy. Around Namur in the mid-1500s, there were 120 forges and furnaces supporting the activities of 7000 charcoal-burners in the surrounding forests. As previously mentioned, the major forest district of Brabant was known as the Silva Carbonnaria, or forest of the charcoal-makers.

Coal in the Sambre–Meuse area is found, as in the Ruhr and the Upper Silesian districts, on the North European Plain at the foot of the belt of hills and low mountains, in this case the Ardennes. Metalworkers made some use of the coal as early as the 1500s, and it was an export commodity; but major mining activities awaited the nineteenth century. The first major use of coke on the European mainland occurred in the Walloon section of the Sambre–Meuse area: A coke-fired blast furnace was in operation at Liège in 1823. By 1842, 45 of 120 furnaces used coke, and by 1860 the expansion rate of coke production outstripped that in any other mainland industrial district. The Sambre–Meuse craftsmen were leaders in adopting new British techniques and were not surpassed by the better-endowed Ruhr until the mid-1860s. The advantages of the district included the navigable Meuse (Maas) River, adequate supplies of coking coal, and local iron-ore deposits, though some coal and considerable amounts of ore are now imported. Exhaustion of local coal supplies and problems of modernization plague the district at present.

Iron and steel remains a very important industry in the Sambre–Meuse area today, allowing Belgium to rank fifth among European nations in steel production. Nitrogenous chemicals are also produced from coal. Textile production is centered in Lille, France, known for cottons, linens, and woolens, in Verviers, Belgium, where woolens are dominant, and in a host of smaller centers in the Lys basin.

The Sambre–Meuse–Lys district departed from the nineteenth-century European industrial norm in that it was only partially Germanic, although it included a small northern projection into Flemish, Dutch, and German territory, and was almost wholly Catholic-populated. Some small Protestant enclaves were found, as around Dour in Belgium.

BOHEMIAN BASIN INDUSTRIAL DISTRICT

Another Catholic area of industrialization in nineteenth-century Europe lay in the northern part of the province of Cěské (Bohemia), until 1918 a part of German-ruled Austria but today in Czechoslovakia (Figure 10.1). Under encouragement from the Austro–Hungarian government, a well-rounded industrial district had developed by the 1870s, though the Bohemian Basin faced the same problems of remoteness and poor water-transport facilities that plagued the nearby Upper Silesian district. The coal deposits were also much smaller than in the more important industrial regions of Germany, Belgium, and Britain.

Iron and steel manufacture, based on coal deposits northwest of Praha and ore from the nearby Ore Mountains (Erzgebirge) on the north, is centered in the cities of Kladno and Plzen, contributing to the world-famous Skoda armaments works in Plzen. Heavy machinery, including automobiles and railroad rolling stock, is made at Praha. Other diverse industries of this district include cotton and linen textiles, especially around Liberec; clothing manufacture at Praha; world-famous ceramics and glassware from Karlovy Vary and Plzen; chemicals; and food-processing, including brewing at Plzen, which gave its name to the well-known Pilsner beers. Many of these industries were derived from guild artisans of the late Middle Ages.

THE SAXON TRIANGLE

Another German industrial region of importance in the nineteenth century lay in a triangular area in what is today East Germany, with apexes at the cities of Plauen, Halle, and Dresden, an area traditionally part of the Kingdom of Sachsen (Saxony) (Figure 10.1). In this case, a coalfield existed but included only small, scattered deposits of a lower quality.

Privileges and subsidies offered by the Saxon government, coupled with the presence of iron ore in the mountains to the south, stimulated major industrial growth here as early as the 1600s. Immigrant artisans, mainly French Huguenot refugees and Dutch, greatly aided the establishment of porcelain, textile, and armament manufacture. Today textiles are centered at Plauen and Karl-Marx-Stadt (formerly Chemnitz), where original use of waterpower gave way to coal as a fuel; chemicals are produced at Halle and elsewhere, based in part on potash deposits;

the tradition of fine chinaware is perpetuated by Communist-ruled craftsmen in the Dresden area; and printing and publishing are concentrated in Leipzig. Considerable manufacture of precision machinery is carried on, and Leipzig is home to a traditional and famous trade fair.

10.5 NINETEENTH-CENTURY MAINLAND INDUSTRIALIZATION OUTSIDE THE COALFIELDS

In most areas not gifted with coal deposits, the nineteenth century was one of very slow industrial growth, or even decline in the face of competition from the coal areas. Some urban centers which had acquired sizable populations in the pre-Industrial Revolution period were able to imitate the success of London in attracting industries on the basis of a large, ready-made labor force and market. In this category were such centers as Berlin, Paris, Hamburg, Wien, and Rotterdam (Figure 10.1).

Paris came to specialize in two basic industries: (1) high-quality luxury items such as fashion clothing, cosmetics, and jewelry, distributed in small workshop factories around the city; and (2) engineering industries, dominated in the present century by automobile manufacture and concentrated in the suburb towns. Most of remaining France lagged behind industrially, not only because coal was absent, but also due to (1) the slow French population growth rate, which decreased both labor supply and market; (2) a transport system so highly centered in Paris that outlying districts had difficult access to raw materials and market; and (3) a notable lag in governmental encouragement of non-Parisian industrialization in the 1800s.

One major district which developed in the nineteenth century lay in the Upper Rhine Plain of southwestern Germany, including cities such as Mannheim and Frankfurt-am-Main (Figure 10.1). This area was on an ancient routeway between the Mediterranean coast and the North European Plain, and many cities had a heritage of guild industries. In the 1800s, new industries located here, especially those producing chemicals. Ludwigshafen, a city founded in the nineteenth century on the Rhine River adjacent to Mannheim, became the site of the famous I. G. Farben chemical works, and the Frankfurt suburb of Höchst developed a similar industry. In the present century, the Upper Rhine and nearby Neckar River Valley have acquired important automobile factories, including the Daimler-Benz works at Stuttgart and the Opel plant at Rüsselsheim near Frankfurt.

10.6 DISPERSAL OF INDUSTRIES SINCE 1900

By the year 1900, the industrial zone of Europe was highly concentrated in the Germanic lands, mainly the United Kingdom and Germany, while southern and eastern Europe had been little affected by the Industrial Revolution. However, the trend since the turn of the century has been toward dispersal of manufacturing into new areas, and the rise of such countries as Italy and Sweden to positions of industrial importance. In no small part, the keys to this dispersal have been (1) the development of new sources of power, in particular hydroelectricity; (2) the perfection of new and better transport systems, which permit greater mobility of raw materials and finished products; and (3) improvements in iron and steel technol-

TABLE 10.1   The Decline of Coal as a Source of Energy Consumed in Selected European Countries

Country	Percent derived from coal and lignite			Percent derived from petroleum and natural gas			Percent derived from hydroelectricity		
	1929	1962	1969	1929	1962	1969	1929	1962	1969
United Kingdom	96	71	48	4	27	47	—	2	5
Belgium and Luxembourg	99	71	40	1	29	59	—	—	1
Norway	35	4	5	4	18	31	61	78	64
Sweden	65	7	5	7	44	66	28	49	29

Sources: Estall and Buchanan, *Industrial Activity and Economic Geography*, London: Hutchinson & Co., 2nd ed., 1966, p. 61, used by permission; Statistical Office of the European Communities, *Basic Statistics of the Community*, 1970, p. 42.

ogy, permitting smaller amounts of coal to be used in the manufacturing process.

Europe now falls into three distinct power zones in the industrial sense (Figure 10.1). In the center, in the old manufacturing belt of the nineteenth century, *thermal power* remains dominant, power derived from fossil fuels such as coal. However, a major changeover is in process from coal to petroleum and natural-gas products, most of which are imported from the Middle East (Table 10.1). The province of Groningen in the northeastern Netherlands supplies large quantities of natural gas, and recent discoveries suggest that the continental shelf covered by the North Sea may provide much of Europe's oil and gas in the future, decreasing the dependence of foreign sources. By 1969, countries of the Common Market, mainly in the thermal-power zone, derived 57 percent of their energy needs from oil, and only 30 percent from coal. Flanking the thermal-power zone on north and south are two hydropower areas, where high mountains have facilitated the production of hydroelectricity. Even there, however, oil and gas are rising to a position of dominance as the demands for power exceed the hydroelectric potential (Table 10.1).

THE PO VALLEY INDUSTRIAL DISTRICT

Hydropower, in the twentieth century, helped revive the former industrial greatness of northern Italy, particularly in the area between Milano and Torino in the upper reaches of the Po Valley (Figure 10.1). Milano was the first European city to have electric lights, in 1883. The Mussolini government provided added subsidies and incentives to industrialization, and a sizable work force of cheap labor was assembled from among the peasantry of the adjacent Alpine fringe and southern Italy. Sinch 1945 the rise of Po Valley industries has been rapid and the area now ranks behind only the Ruhr among all of the industrial districts of Europe. Most of the electricity consumed in the Po Valley today is generated by burning gas and petroleum.

The diverse industries include iron and steel, based on imported raw materials; automobile manufacture, including the Fiat plant at Torino; and textiles. The district is served by the port of Genova, across the Appennini Mountains on the Mediterranean coast, a city which functions as part of the Po Valley industrial area and boasts sizable iron and steel mills and shipbuilding yards. Once-proud Venezia has profited relatively little from the rise of the Po Valley industries, for the Adriatic Sea remains somewhat of a backwater, leading away from the major markets and suppliers of raw materials.

SWISS PLATEAU–JURA DISTRICT

The industrial portion of Switzerland, lying to the north of the Alps on the plateau and the hilly Jura, has long been characterized by industries adapted to a scarcity of raw materials (Figure 10.1). The Swiss rely on highly skilled labor to produce quality goods with a high value added in the manufacturing process. Guild type craftsmen were able to survive the nineteenth-century Industrial Revolution, and hydroelectric power brought a major expansion of industry in the twentieth century. Watchmaking, concentrated in numerous small towns and cities of the Jura, is a typical Swiss industry, retaining a pre–Industrial Revolution areal dispersal and veneration for craftsmen. St. Gallen in the east is the major textile center, producing such items as luxury silks, laces, and ribbons, while Basel in northwestern Switzerland is an important chemical center and head of barge navigation on the Rhine River. Other industries specialize in the production of various kinds of machinery or food processing, including milk-chocolate candies.

NORTHERN SPAIN

Several small areas in the northern part of Spain have been touched by the Industrial Revolution in the hydropower phase, particularly the Barcelona area on the Mediterranean shore and the Basque Biscay coast around Bilbao and San Sebastián (Figure 10.1). In the latter area, major iron-ore deposits and minor coalfields support a local steel industry, which in turn provides raw material for shipbuilders. Barcelona, whose rising industrial capacity is an additional challenge to the urban primacy of inland Madrid, is the scene of diverse manufacturing, including textiles.

CENTRAL AND SOUTHERN SWEDEN

In the 1600s and 1700s, Sweden was lord of the Baltic and one of the more powerful European countries. The country had begun its industrial rise toward the end of the Middle Ages, particularly in the mining of copper and iron ore, the latter processed before export at Swedish forges. By 1500, large amounts of iron were being exported annually, blast furnaces had replaced crude forges, and the smelting and refining processes had been separated. Most of the iron production was concentrated near the ores in the Bergslagen area of interior central Sweden (Figure 10.1), where 324 small iron-works were in operation by 1695. The absence of local coking coal obliged the Swedish craftsmen to continue using charcoal into the modern period, though most no longer do. They have acquired a reputation for extremely high-quality steel. The quantity of steel produced is not great in comparison to Germany or Britain, but the Swedes rely instead on smaller amounts of high-value produce, including various steel alloys. A variety of local engineering industries rely on this steel, including manufacturers of machines, automobiles, ball bearings, electrical equipment, aircraft engines, bicycles, diesel motors, armaments, and ships of exceptionally high quality. Steel production is concentrated still today in the Bergslagen area, but the engineering industries are widely distributed nearby in central and southern Sweden, including the Volvo automobile factory and a ball-bearing plant at Göteborg, shipyards at Malmö, and bicycle and household-appliance factories at Huskvarna, the latter city located inland on the shore of Lake Vättern (Figure 10.1).

Adoption of hydroelectric power has permitted Swedish industry to emerge from a nineteenth-century decline and create an economic well-being that has raised the standard of living to the highest level in all Europe. The use of hydropower is seen, for example, in such items as the electric furnaces employed in the steelmaking process.

The huge iron-ore deposits of far northern Sweden are mined principally for export as ores. The principal mining centers in the north are Kiruna and Gällivare (Figure 10.1).

COASTAL STEEL MILLS

The dispersal of industry in twentieth-century Europe has also affected the iron and steel industries, traditionally concentrated near sources of iron ore, coking coal, or timber for charcoal. Ties to raw material sites have been lessened by improved bulk transport, including ships which can carry 64,000,000 kilograms (70,000 tons) or more of coking coal in a single load. Coastal sites serve as the cheapest assembly points for ore, coal, and other raw materials shipped by sea, and major steel mills have appeared at IJmuiden, on the North Sea near Amsterdam; the German port of Bremen; historic Dunkerque on the French side of the Strait of Dover; Valencia, in eastern Spain; and at Piombino, Genova, Taranto, and Napoli on the Italian coast (Figure 10.1). A sizable part of European steel production is now in these coastal plants, and the trend appears to be continued dispersal.

10.7 THE INDUSTRIAL CORE OF EUROPE

In spite of the spread of industry beyond the confines of the thermal-power zone in the twentieth century, the greater part of the European industrial capacity remains rather confined in an areal sense. A heavily industrial core is evident on the map of industrial regions (Figure 10.1). The manufacturing belt of 1900 has in effect been expanded into northern Italy, northern Spain, Switzerland, and southern-central Sweden, leaving peripheral European lands still outside the industrial pale. This outer periphery, including Iceland, the Scottish Highlands, the Republic of Ireland, southern Iberia, southern Italy, the Balkans, eastern Poland, northern Scandinavia, and Finland, is much less industrialized than the core, though in some cases industrialization is either in progress or at least envisioned. The core-periphery contrast is another pattern which fits the concept of Europe as a cultural entity, concentrated in a nucleus and fading away through a peripheral zone into Africa and Asia, for industrialism is a hallmark of the culture area.

Within the industrial core, it is possible to discern one section which surpasses all others in importance. It stretches from the Rotterdam–Antwerpen port areas in the Low Country inward along the axis of the Rhine, Maas (Meuse), and Schelde rivers to the interior of western Europe, including the Ruhr, Saar–Lorraine, Sambre–Meuse–Lys, upper Rhine, and Swiss Plateau industrial districts. To the west across the North Sea, it continues into the Midlands of lowland England. This "core of the industrial core" appears to be expanding southward, so that by the end of the twentieth century it may well include the Rhône–Saône Valley in France and the Po Valley and Genova in northern Italy. This evolving, growing industrial heart of Europe, confined largely to the Common Market countries, has been called the *Lotharingian Axis* because it occupies almost exactly the same area as was ruled briefly in the Middle Ages by Lothar, one of the grandsons of Charlemagne.

10.8 OTHER INDUSTRIES

In addition to the extractive and manufacturing industries already discussed, there are a number of other industries worthy of mention. Of these, the most important are fishing and tourism.

THE FISHING INDUSTRY

In the seas which flank Europe on the south, west, and north, a great variety of commercially valuable fish is found. These are exploited in part by peoples of the less-industralized periphery of Europe, particularly Norwegians, Icelanders, Færoese, Frisians, Portuguese, Greeks, Dalmatian Yugoslavs, and Basques. Norway, with one of the smallest populations in Europe, accounts for nearly 5 percent of the total world catch of fish each year and 18 percent of the whales taken. Fishing occupies one of every five members of the labor force in Iceland, one of ten in Norway, and nine of ten in the Færoe Islands. It is also an important industry in major countries such as West Germany and the United Kingdom.

Curiously, some coastal folk have traditionally rejected fishing as a major employment. Hundreds of thousands of Irishmen starved to death in the 1840s while the seas surrounding their island teemed with fish. The great fisher folk have generally been those occupying lands poorly suited for agriculture; in Norway, for example, only 3 percent of the national territory is arable.

The types of fisheries vary from one peripheral sea to another in Europe. Mediterranean fishermen go after tuna, sardines—which are named for the Italian island of Sardegna—and sponges, which are found particularly in the Aegean. The Black and Caspian seas yield sturgeon, from which caviar is obtained, while the North Sea, Arctic Ocean, and Norwegian Sea fishermen specialize in cod, herring, mackerel, and haddock. The less saline Baltic Sea is important for flounder and eels, in addition to cod and herring. Oysters and sardines are the principal take in the Bay of Biscay and the Iberian Atlantic waters.

TOURISM

A major tourist boom occurred in Europe in the twentieth century, producing an industry which rivals manufacturing as a source of national income in many countries. In a way the tourist industry is also a product of the Industrial Revolution. Improved transportation technology, including development of railroads, motor vehicles, ocean steamships, and airplanes, greatly reduced the amount of time involved in travel, and allowed greater access to and within Europe. Furthermore, the Industrial Revolution produced in time a sizable economic middle class, in both Europe and the United States, with the financial resources to travel. Prior to about 1920 the upper class supported tourism, but since then, and particularly since 1945, the masses of the middle class have added their growing numbers to this industry.

Americans have contributed massively to the development of European tourism, a phenomenon which can be explained by a variety of causal factors.

Europe's appeal to Caucasian Americans is multiple. First, for the educated, cultured American, Europe represents the past. The United States is a new country, whose "European" history reaches back only a trifling 350 years, and the American with intellectual curiosity about his cultural origins necessarily turns his steps toward Europe. The history of white Americans permeates Europe. The ruins of classical Greece, the cathedral of Charlemagne at Aachen, the meadow at Runnymede where the Magna Carta was signed, preserved medieval towns such as Rothenburg in Germany or Carcassonne in France, and the faded splendor of Venèzia are all part of Caucasian America's past. One lonely painting by Leonardo da Vinci can be viewed in the United States. The remainder hang in European galleries.

A second appeal is Europe's uniqueness, which usually finds expression in such shopworn adjectives as "quaint" and "old-world." In spite of the fact that Europe is the cultural mother of America, it is different, a difference related principally to greater age. The cultural landscape of Europe exudes a feeling of stability, of permanence, of neatness and harmony which is absent in America, an unfinished land. Europe is satisfying to the American eye because it appears finished and completed, possessing a stability and continuity.

Furthermore, Europe is appealing because of its diversity. Over short distances, the tourist sees a great variety of cultural landscapes, hears a Babel of spoken tongues, and experiences a variety of customs. The frequent crossing of international borders adds additional spice to the journey. In Anglo-America, by contrast, it is principally the physical landscape which changes with distance, for the culture exhibits what to many seems a rather depressing degree of uniformity from one place to another in the United States.

Intra-European tourism, of rapidly increasing importance, is in part based on climatic contrasts. Swedes, Germans, and Britishers have long escaped temporarily from the cloudy, cool lands of the north by seeking refuge in the sunny lands of the Mediterranean. Individual nationality groups often dominate certain resort areas. For example, Adriatic coastal Yugoslavia is frequented mainly by tourists from West Germany, while Swedes and Britishers are the groups most common on the Greek island of Ródos.

The European reaction to the growing number of tourists, both American and fellow European, has been the establishment of an elaborate network of hotels, resorts, and inns, managed by skilled individuals proficient in several languages. There are countless guided tours aimed at all types of visitors, ranging from the "sixteen countries in fourteen days" bus tours for those who are in a hurry (known as "rat runs" to the tour directors) to the pleasingly "dangerous" two-hour tour of East Berlin, complete with propaganda lecture. From gambling casinos to ski resorts, the European tourist industry earns hundreds of millions of dollars annually and provides the economic backbone for some smaller nations.

10.9 LOCATIONAL FACTORS IN INDUSTRY

A variety of factors influence the location of any particular industry and together produce the distribution of industrialization shown in Figure 10.1. These locational forces include market, raw materials, transportation, labor supply, energy source, and political decisions.

THE ATTRACTION OF MARKET

A market is that area in which a product may be sold in a volume profitable to the manufacturer, and the size and quality of a market is perhaps the single most important factor in shaping the overall distribution of industries in Europe. Many students of industrial location consider the attractions of market to be so great that they regard a market location as the "norm" for modern industry. Certain industries, in an economic sense, *must* locate at the market; that is, certain manufacturers must situate their factories among the consumers if they are to minimize their costs and maximize profits. Such industries include those manufacturing a *weight-gaining* finished product, such as bottled beverages, or a *bulk-gaining* finished product, such as metal containers or bottles. In other words, if weight or bulk is added to the raw materials in the manufacturing process, location near consumers is economically desirable due to the transport-cost factor. Similarly, if the finished product is *more perishable* than the raw materials, as is the case with bakery goods, ice manufacture, and some other food products, a location near market is also required. Local newspapers, which have little or no commercial value outside their home area or after their date of publication, may likewise be regarded as highly perishable. In addition, if the product is *more fragile* than the materials which go into its manufacture, as in the making of glass, the industry will be attracted to market. In general, the degree of importance of market as a locational factor increases with the level of economic development of a country, reaching a peak in the wealthier, highly urbanized societies, where population is more clustered.

Numerous "unfettered" industries are not economically obliged to locate in market areas. However, it is obvious that such a footloose industry will consider the market situation in choosing a site for location, and one economist has suggested that the areal extent of a firm's market is the best indicator of the degree of wisdom employed in the selection of plant location.

The definition of "market" can also affect location. Some manufacturers supply highly clustered markets in major urban centers, while others, including the makers of agricultural machinery, cater to a much more dispersed body of consumers. The location of a factory in the former category is more influenced by market considerations than are those serving dispersed markets. The greatest market potential in Europe lies along the ridge of greatest population density from London through the Low Country and along the southern edge of the North European Plain into East Germany. This coincides with the location of many of the major industrial districts of Europe, suggesting the importance of market accessibility in location, though the population clusters were often a result rather than a cause of industrialization. As an added advantage, such a location often places an industry near other factories which produce components, such as steel, needed in the manufacturing process. Other benefits include (1) an ability to respond quickly to changes in demand, and (2) a greater capability to gauge the size and composition of the market and evaluate its changes.

Even industries tied to raw-material sources are much affected by the market factor. For example, the iron and steel industry at Luleå in northern Sweden is not as important as those of the Ruhr, England, or Belgium, in part because it is a thinly settled region far removed from markets. Remote raw materials may not be exploited at all unless they are scarce and valuable enough to offset the lack of a local market.

The influence of market on industrial location is also evident in the "multiplier effect" phenomenon. Once an industry locates in a particular area, it provides additional jobs, attracting people who in turn enlarge the market and make the location even more favorable for other industries. The multiplier effect created the concentrated industrial districts formed in the waterpower and coal phases of the Industrial Revolution, particularly in England. Large markets thus tend to hinder industrial decentralization.

THE ATTRACTION OF RAW MATERIALS

Every industry engaged in manufacturing depends on raw materials for processing. The attraction of raw materials varies greatly according to their character, the processes employed to make use of them, and the techniques available for their movement from place to place. It is important to recognize that not all manufacturers use only one raw material and that many rely on the produce of other manufacturers rather than the output of extractive industries, such as mining, for some "raw" materials.

Some industries locate at the source of these raw materials out of physical necessity. Mining and lumbering are obvious examples. Others bound to raw material sources include manufacturers turning out finished products (1) which *lose considerable weight or bulk* in processing, as in refining of minerals or manufacture of pulp and paper production, in which a loss of 40 percent of the weight of the wood pulp is typical; (2) which involve consumption of large amounts of *heavy or bulky fuel,* particularly coal; or (3) which are *less perishable* than the raw materials, as in the making of butter, cheese, and powdered milk from fluid milk and the canning of fruits and vegetables. When location is determined by the source of raw materials, there is usually little relationship to population or market distribution.

cause of transportation

In general the attractive force of raw materials declined as the Industrial Revolution progressed. The initial development of British industrial districts preceded the invention and construction of railroads, motorized highway transport, and oceangoing steamers. Steel, for example, could not be moved economically over any significant distance, and industries using steel located near the steel mills on the coalfields.

Much of the recent dispersal of industry in Europe, in particular the spectacular rise of tidewater steel mills, reflects rapidly weakening ties to raw-material sites. At the same time, locational decisions made as long as 200 years ago, which were based on the necessity of being near raw materials, continue to shape industrial location today, simply because established industrial districts have a great deal of "staying power." The industry will probably remain, even if the raw material which originally attracted it is completely used up. The large capital investment, existing marketing patterns, the presence of a labor force, and transport facilities all strongly discourage locational change.

THE ROLE OF TRANSPORTATION

In theory, if all other locational factors are neutral, industries will tend to locate at the site offering the smallest total transport costs, considering the movement of both raw materials and finished products. In reality, of course, transport costs are but one element in total manufacturing expenses. Those industries for which the cost of transportation is a large or dominant share of overall expenses will be most influenced by the transport locational factor. According to the location theory of Alfred Weber, industrial production is "naturally" pulled to the most advantageous points of transport costs, which of course are closely tied to the raw materials, market, and nature of the items manufactured. All other locational factors are secondary and simply distort the "natural" pattern determined by transport costs.

Transport costs consist of two basic parts: (1) terminal or handling charges, involving the loading and unloading of goods; and (2) a "line" charge, the expense of actually moving the commodities, which increases with distance. Depending upon the type of industry, minimization of transport costs can be achieved at the source(s) of raw materials or at the market, but only rarely in between, such as at "breaking points," where goods must be transshipped from one mode of transport to another. As mentioned previously, manufactured goods which cost *less* to transport than the raw materials, by reason of lesser bulk, weight, perishability, or fragility, will be produced most economically near raw-material sources, and vice versa. If raw materials must be brought from two widely divergent points, the most efficient location may be an intermediate transshipment point, particularly seaports. Again the coastal steel mills of Italy and other western European countries offer an example.

Other factors which influence transport costs are the *distance* to be covered and the expense of building and maintaining the transport facility. Great distance can render natural resources valueless and prevent their exploitation.

The locational role of transport facilities perhaps exercises a greater influence on specific site than on general location. For example, some experts feel that the possibility of obtaining a railroad spur line (switch track facility) is the most important factor in determining the value of industrial real estate, often doubling the price. In Europe, where much greater use is made of rivers and canals for transport, access to waterways is also of crucial importance. The industrial development of the Upper Silesian district was considerably hindered until the 1890s, when navigation improvements were made in the Odra River.

THE ROLE OF LABOR

A change of location away from the point of minimum transport costs could occur if the savings in cost of labor are greater than the additional transport costs involved. In general, labor costs are a factor of some locational consequence in many industries, but the decisive factor in only a few. Those most affected will be industries for which labor costs form a substantial or dominant part of total costs, particularly industries depending on highly skilled workers who produce small objects of high value, such as watches, cameras, transistor radios, and the like.

Manufacturers consider several characteristics of labor in deciding where to locate factories: availability of workers, average wages, necessary skills, and overall productivity. Traditionally, workers possessing certain skills have tended to focalize in a small number of places, partly as a result of the need for person-to-person training in the perpetuation of any particular skill. Consequently, manufacturers often seek out locations of workers possessing the desired skills. It was no accident that the first mechanized textile factories of England and Germany were situated in areas which had long traditions of textile manufacture. Similarly, the presence of skilled labor attracted manufacturers of cotton textiles and synthetic fabrics to districts already established as producers of linen, woolen, and silk textiles.

In recent decades, the increasing mobility of European labor has somewhat lessened the locational influence of the labor force. To be sure, international migration of workers was evident as early as the development of the Ruhr district in the nineteenth century, but it has accelerated since World War II, aided by various international agreements which permit and even encourage such migration. German and French industries, as well as those in smaller countries such as Switzerland, now rely heavily on southern European and even North African laborers. Greeks, Yugoslavs, Spaniards, and Algerians have moved north to the industrial areas, usually on a temporary basis. Resident foreigners became so numerous in Switzerland that a national vote was taken in 1970 to determine whether the Swiss wanted to place an upper limit on the proportion of aliens in the total population. Some felt that the national character was endangered by the massive influx of foreigners, but the people voted not to institute any restrictions. Immigrant workers typically form ghettos in the cities, as the Algerians have done in Paris.

Migration within countries is also increasing. In Italy, a very close correlation has existed since 1952 between the level of out-migration from the Mezzogiorno, or south, and the amount of industrial investment in the upper Po Valley–Genova area of the northwestern part of the country.

THE ATTRACTION OF POWER SOURCE

The Industrial Revolution is based on harnessed inanimate power; consequently, the source of energy often influenced factory location. This was particularly true in the formative stages of the Revolution, when the use of waterpower tied manufacturers to the banks of streams, particularly at rapids and waterfalls. Some few old British textile factories still use waterpower and have thus remained fixed in location since the 1700s. When coal-powered steam engines replaced waterwheels, the locational tie between power source and factory persisted, but it weakened steadily with advances in transportation technology. Still, the industrial development of countries without major coal deposits remained retarded into the present century, when the use of hydroelectric power, petroleum, and natural gas largely replaced coal.

At the same time, it should be recognized that precoal industrial concentrations were present in almost every coalfield of Great Britain and mainland Europe. In Lancashire, Yorkshire, the Ruhr, the Upper Silesian district, the Sambre–Meuse area, and the East German province of Sachsen, important clusterings of guild-type industries were in existence long before coal was of any great commercial consequence. In these areas the presence of coal deposits simply facilitated acceptance of the technology of the Industrial Revolution by manufacturers already well established.

Replacement of coal by oil and hydroelectricity (Table 10.1) has still further weakened the tie to energy sources, for both of these can be transported much more economically than coal. Electricity exchange between nations in Europe is becoming quite common, and impressive pipeline construction and development after 1956 of supertankers with greatly increased capacity have facilitated the movement of petroleum.

Nevertheless, much of the present distribution of manufacturing was determined in the period when proximity to power supply was a necessity. In addition, some industries, including the factories engaged in primary aluminum processing, have cost structures dominated by energy expenditures, and these are still much influenced by power sources in choice of location.

POLITICAL CONSIDERATIONS

The severe political fragmentation of Europe has had a profound influence on industrial location. In effect, many of the "laws" of location can be repealed by the mere presence of an international border. Governmental intervention typically results from a desire (1) to assist industries engaged in competition with foreign producers, (2) to develop strategically important industries, (3) to have strategic industries safely located, (4) to diversify the industrial economy of overspecialized areas, (5) to limit further growth of huge conurbations, or (6) to bring a higher standard of living to underdeveloped regions. Borders often represent tariff barriers, import-export quotas, obstacles to the movement of labor and capital, or transport hindrances.

Tariffs are less influential in industrial location than formerly in Europe due to the creation of three major international trade blocs, whose members have worked toward eliminating restrictions on exchange of goods. These are the *Common Market,* composed originally of West Germany, France, Italy, Netherlands, Belgium, and Luxembourg, and founded in 1952; the *European Free Trade Association,* EFTA or the "Outer Seven," including as charter members the United Kingdom, Norway, Sweden, Denmark, Portugal, Switzerland, and Austria, dating from 1960; and the *Council for Economic Mutual Aid,* or COMECON, including the Soviet Union and all Communist nations of eastern Europe except Yugoslavia, which was denied membership, and Albania, which has withdrawn (Figure 10.4). A major series of changes in alignment of these blocs is under way. Finland and Iceland have joined the EFTA, and the United Kingdom and Denmark will probably transfer to the Common Market. However, tariffs remain in effect between these trade blocs and among most nonmember nations. Tariffs cause political borders to decrease the accessibility of foreign raw materials and markets, thereby emphasizing domestic materials and markets. Production points near tariff-protected borders will usually suffer from greater average distribution costs, smaller-scale production, or both. The market area becomes lopsided, with the greatest consumer potential in one direction from the factory (Figure 10.5). An extreme example is the Volkswagen plant at Wolfsburg, West Germany. When the site for this factory was chosen in the Nazi period, it was roughly central in Germany and had immediate access to the Mittelland Canal, a major water artery running east–west across the country. When the Volkswagen plant was reopened after World War II, the Iron Curtain lay 11 kilometers (7 miles) to the east. The hope for political reunification fixed the postwar factory in its unfavorable location, and soon too much capital had been invested for relocation to be economically practical. Only the limited market in West Berlin provides any significant eastern sales.

Figure 10.4   Trade groups.

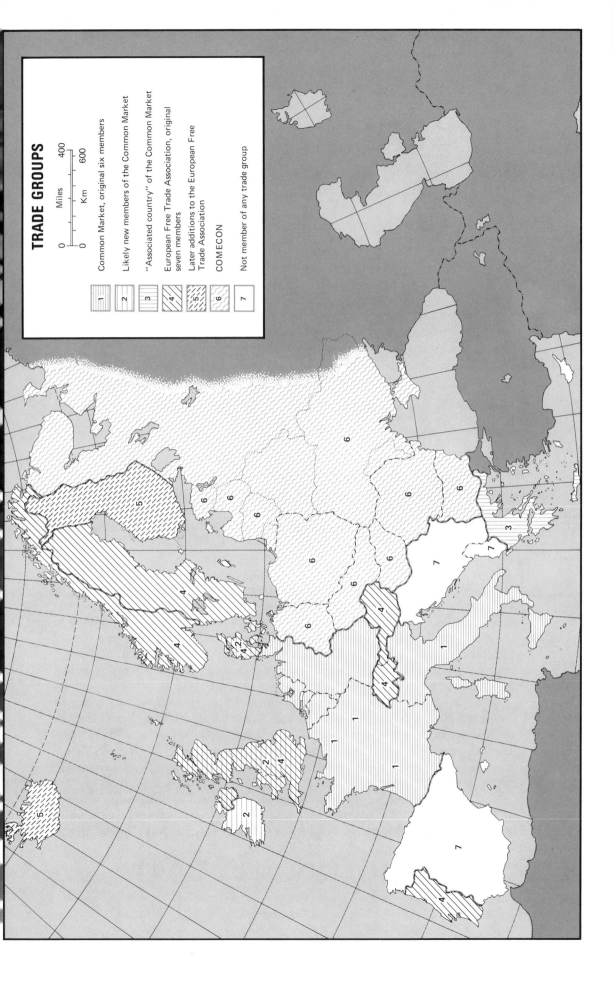

TRADE GROUPS

Miles
0   400
Km
0   600

1   Common Market, original six members

2   Likely new members of the Common Market

3   "Associated country" of the Common Market

4   European Free Trade Association, original seven members

5   Later additions to the European Free Trade Association

6   COMECON

7   Not member of any trade group

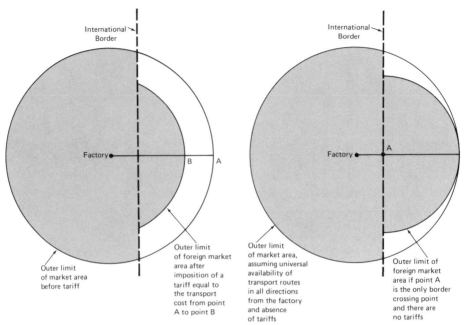

Figure 10.5 Reduction of market area resulting from tariffs and restriction of number of border crossings. In either case, the market area available to the factory is reduced by the presence of an international border. (After Giersch.)

Even if a tariff does not exist, trade across international borders is usually slow. This is due in part to the time required in customs inspections, but more so to the less-complete transport network typical of border zones (Figure 10.5). The number of crossing points is usually held to a minimum to facilitate inspection, and even where customs have been abolished, the network still reflects the earlier period of required inspection.

The presence of differing laws, tax structures, or minimum wages on either side of an international border can influence industrial location by preventing or encouraging the migration of capital and labor. Fluctuations in the monetary exchange rate can also hamper the mobility of international investment by adding to the risk factor. Similarly, the lack of a stable government on one side of a boundary can restrict investment and labor migration. The political borders of Europe typically parallel language boundaries, and this in turn reduces markets by adding bilingualism to advertising costs.

Finally, the political factor is important when governments take action to locate industries for strategic reasons. Nations threatened with war often attempt to disperse factories to lessen the possibility of a catastrophic attack aimed at destroying their strategic industries or industrial capacity. Lancashire, in relatively "safe" western England, acquired numerous munitions factories as a result of government action in the World War II period.

More frequently, governments act to industrialize backward, poverty-stricken sections of their countries, such as Italy's continuing effort to bring factories to the south. The iron and steel plant at Taranto (Figure 10.1) in the Italian province of Puglia and the petrochemical factory at Gela on the island of Sicilia are impressive results of governmental action, as is the steel mill at Mo-I-Rana, Norway. The effort of the Prussian government in the initial development of the Upper Silesian district has already been mentioned. At the opposite extreme, the British government has actively discouraged further development of industries in London and Birmingham, the two principal manufacturing centers of the nation.

It is evident, then, that international borders tend to retard industries in the boundary zone, to push them toward the interior of national territory. Tariffs act to deglomerate industry, allowing the presence of certain factories where they otherwise could not exist. Dispersal by governmental decree for reasons of national security or regional underdevelopment serves the same deglomerative process. Some industrial-location experts actually fear that the removal of all governmental restrictions on factory location in Europe would produce a boom in a small number of centrally located districts, such as the Ruhr, while causing stagnation and decline in peripheral lands.

Other borders also influence industrial location, including provincial, district, and municipal lines. City limits often are associated with major changes in taxes and availability of utilities, while zoning restrictions eliminate factories from many otherwise desirable sites. The *Greenbelt*, a nonindustrialized area surrounding London, is a good example of the effect of regional planning on industrial location. There have long been legal restrictions on establishment of industries in the Greenbelt zone.

*   *   *

A GREAT VARIETY of factors, then, have guided the course of European industrialization. The far-reaching areal changes which began with the Industrial Revolution continue, as manufacturing is diffused to the peripheries of Europe.

Among the most important of the changes which accompanied the Industrial Revolution was the reshaping of the cities of Europe. Appropriately, the following chapter will focus on the urban geography of the European culture area.

SOURCES AND SUGGESTED READINGS

Gunnar Alexandersson. *Geography of Manufacturing.* Englewood Cliffs, N.J.: Prentice-Hall, 1967.

Thomas S. Ashton. *The Industrial Revolution, 1760–1830.* London: Oxford University Press, 1950.

Stanley H. Beaver. "The Location of Industry." *Geography.* Vol. 20 (1935), pp. 191–196.

W. S. Buckingham, Jr. "Problems of Industrial Location in Great Britain." *American Journal of Economics and Sociology.* Vol. 13 (1954), pp. 247–254.

Ronald H. Chilcote. "Spain's Iron and Steel: Renovation of an Old Industry." *Geographical Review.* Vol. 53 (1963), pp. 247–262.

K. C. Edwards. "Historical Geography of the Luxembourg Iron and Steel Industry." *Institute of British Geographers, Transactions and Papers.* Vol. 29 (1961), pp. 1–16.

F. E. Elliott. "Locational Factors Affecting Industrial Plants." *Economic Geography.* Vol. 24 (1948), pp. 283–285.

R. C. Estall and R. Ogilvie Buchanan. *Industrial Activity and Economic Geography: A Study of the Forces Behind the Geographical Location of Productive Activity in Manufacturing Industry*. London: Hutchinson & Co., 2nd ed., 1966.

Douglas K. Fleming. "Coastal Steelworks in the Common Market Countries." *Geographical Review*. Vol. 57 (1967), pp. 48–72.

Herbert Giersch. "Economic Union Between Nations and the Location of Industries." *Review of Economic Studies*. Vol. 17 (1949–50), pp. 87–97.

Marvin L. Greenhut. *Plant Location in Theory and Practice*. Chapel Hill, N.C.: University of North Carolina Press, 1956.

Peter G. Hall. *The Industries of London Since 1861*. London: Hutchinson, 1962.

F. E. I. Hamilton. "Location Factors in the Yugoslav Iron and Steel Industry." *Economic Geography*. Vol. 40 (1964), pp. 46–64.

Chauncy D. Harris. "The Market as a Factor in the Location of Industry in the United States." *Annals, Association of American Geographers*. Vol. 44 (1954), pp. 315–348.

Noland R. Heiden. "Odda and Rjukan: Two Industrialized Areas of Norway." *Annals, Association of American Geographers*. Vol. 42 (1952), pp. 109–128.

Edgar M. Hoover. *The Location of Economic Activity*. New York: McGraw-Hill, 1948.

Walter Isard. *Location and Space-Economy: A General Theory Relating to Industrial Location, Market Areas, Land Use, Trade and Urban Structure*. New York: Wiley, 1956.

Tage Kahlin. "Developments in the Location of Industry and Government Location Policy." *Skandinaviska Banken*. Vol. 38 (April 1957), pp. 40–46.

Gerald J. Karaska and David F. Bramhall. *Locational Analysis for Manufacturing: A Selection of Readings*. Cambridge, Mass.: The M.I.T. Press, 1969.

Evan D. Lewis. *The Rhondda Valleys: A Study in Industrial Development, 1800 to the Present Day*. London: Phoenix, 1959.

Trevor Lloyd. "Iron Ore Production at Kirkenes, Norway." *Economic Geography*. Vol. 31 (1955), pp. 211–233.

August Lösch. *The Economics of Location*. Translated by W. W. Woglom and W. F. Stolper. New Haven, Conn.: Yale University Press, 1954.

James R. McDonald. "Labor Immigration in France, 1946–1965." *Annals, Association of American Geographers*. Vol. 59 (1969), pp. 116–134.

J. E. Martin. "Location Factors in Lorraine Iron and Steel Industry." *Institute of British Geographers, Transactions and Papers*. Vol. 23 (1957), pp. 191–212.

Francis J. Monkhouse. *The Belgian Kempenland*. Liverpool: University Press, 1949.

Francis J. Monkhouse. "The South Limburg Coal Field." *Economic Geography*. Vol. 31 (1955), pp. 126–137.

Alice F. A. Mutton. "Hydro-Electric Power in Western Europe." *Geographical Journal*. Vol. 117 (1951), pp. 328–342.

Geoffrey Parker. *An Economic Geography of the Common Market*. London: Longmans, 1968.

Norman J. G. Pounds. "Historical Geography of the Iron and Steel Industry of France." *Annals, Association of American Geographers*. Vol. 47 (1957), pp. 3–14.

Norman J. G. Pounds and William N. Parker. *Coal and Steel in Western Europe: The Influence of Resources and Techniques on Production*. Bloomington, Ind.: Indiana University Press, 1957.

Norman J. G. Pounds. *The Ruhr: A Study in Historical and Economic Geography*. London: Faber, 1952.

Norman J. G. Pounds. *The Upper Silesian Industrial Region*. Bloomington, Ind.: Indiana University Press, 1958.

Allan L. Rodgers. "Migration and Industrial Development: The Southern Italian Experience." *Economic Geography*. Vol. 46 (1970), pp. 111–135.

Allan L. Rodgers. "Naples: A Case Study of Government Subsidization of Industrial Development in an Underdeveloped Region." *Tijdschrift voor Economische en Sociale Geografie*. Vol. 57 (1966), pp. 20–32.

Allan L. Rodgers. *The Industrial Geography of the Port of Genova*. Chicago: University of Chicago, Dept. of Geography, Research Paper No. 66, 1960.

H. B. Rodgers. "The Lancashire Cotton Industry in 1840." *Institute of British Geographers, Transactions and Papers*. Vol. 28 (1960), pp. 135–153.

Frank M. Russell. *The Saar: Battleground and Pawn*. Stanford, Calif.: Stanford University Press, 1951.

Clifford T. Smith. *An Historical Geography of Western Europe Before 1800*. New York: Praeger, 1967, chapters 7, 8, 10.

David M. Smith. *Industrial Location: An Economic Geographical Analysis*. New York: Wiley, 1971.

Wilfred Smith. *An Economic Geography of Great Britain*. London: Methuen, 1949.

Wilfred Smith. *Geography and the Location of Industry*. Liverpool: University Press, 1952.

Wilfred Smith. "The Location of Industry," *Institute of British Geographers, Transactions and Papers*. Vol. 21 (1955), pp. 1–18.

Henri Smotkine. "Un type de complexe industriel: le district de Karl-Marx-Stadt en République Démocratique Allemande," *Annales de Géographie*. Vol. 76 (1967), pp. 152–167.

J. A. Sporck. *L'activité industrielle dans la région liègeoise: étude de géographie économique*. Liège, Belgium: Thone, 1957, 1959.

Statistical Office of the European Communities. *Basic Statistics of the Community . . . 1970*. Brussels: S.O.E.C., 1971.

Margaret C. Storrie. "The Scotch Whisky Industry." *Institute of British Geographers, Transactions and Papers*. Vol. 31 (1962), pp. 97–114.

J. R. Tarrant. "Recent Industrial Development in Ireland." *Geography*. Vol. 52 (1967), pp. 403–408.

Trevor M. Thomas. "The North Sea and Its Environs: Future Reservoir of Fuel?" *Geographical Review*. Vol. 56 (1966), pp. 12–39.

Trevor M. Thomas. "Wales: Land of Mines and Quarries." *Geographical Review*. Vol. 46 (1956), pp. 59–81.

W. H. K. Turner. "The Significance of Water Power in Industrial Location: Some Perthshire Examples." *Scottish Geographical Magazine*. Vol. 74 (1958), pp. 98–115.

David Turnock. "The Pattern of Industrialization in Romania." *Annals, Association of American Geographers*. Vol. 60 (1970), pp. 540–559.

Kenneth Warren. "The Changing Steel Industry of the European Common Market." *Economic Geography*. Vol. 43 (1967), pp. 314–332.

Kenneth Warren. *The British Iron & Steel Industry Since 1840: An Economic Geography*. London: Bell, 1970.

Alfred Weber. *Theory of the Location of Industries*. Edited by Carl J. Friedrich. Chicago: University of Chicago Press, 1929.

M. J. Wise. "The Role of London in the Industrial Geography of Great Britain." *Geography*. Vol. 41 (1956), pp. 219–232.

Leonard C. Yaseen. *Plant Location*. New York: American Research Council, 1956.

Alfred Zauberman. *Industrial Progress in Poland, Czechoslovakia, and East Germany, 1937–1962*. London: Oxford University Press, 1964.

Erich W. Zimmermann. *World Resources and Industries*. New York: Harper & Row, 2nd edition, 1951.

CHAPTER ELEVEN

Urban geography

The rise of manufacturing has in the past one hundred years made Europeans a dominantly urban people. In some of the highly industrialized countries, four-fifths or more of the population now live in cities and towns. The city is an ancient institution in Europe, however, with preclassical origins, and these origins are necessary to an understanding of the present urban structure.

11.1 URBAN DEVELOPMENT BEFORE THE INDUSTRIAL REVOLUTION

THE GREEK AND PHOENICIAN CITIES

Western man's first cities were in the Fertile Crescent, perhaps copied from still earlier examples in the Indus Plain of present Pakistan. A food surplus produced by irrigation agriculture had freed a sizable part of the Tigris–Euphrates population from the task of food production, while at the same time providing commodities for trade. The need for central authority to administer the irrigation projects had given rise to higher governments. This infant urbanism crept westward, first reaching European shores on the Greek island of Kriti in the third millennium B.C., an island admirably situated to command much of the trade of the eastern Mediterranean, including Asia Minor.

The population freed from food production engaged in a variety of activities, but the merchants were the most important group. The pre–Industrial Revolution urban center is typically referred to as the *mercantile* city, though farmers remained by far the numerically largest element in most early cities. The merchant in turn enlarged the livelihood of the artisan, who fashioned finished products from various local raw materials and from those transported by the traders.

A small part of the urban population always remained unproductive in an economic sense, devoting attention instead to cultural advancement. The city accordingly became the center of learning, and the accumulation of man's storehouse of knowledge began. Administrators also found cities convenient bases. From there they governed surrounding rural districts and presided over the defense and protection of the merchants, artisans, scholars, administrators, and farmers housed within the city.

Urban civilization spread from Kriti to the Greek mainland shortly after 2000 B.C.; by 1400 B.C. the mainland peoples centered in urban Mycenae in the Pelopónnisos—perhaps aided by a volcanic disaster which befell the Minoans on Kriti—were in the dominant position. Cities multiplied in the Greek lands in the following centuries, numbering 600 or more in peninsular Greece and other Aegean lands by the fifth century B.C. In addition, foreign colonial towns were established by Greek traders on the European shores of the Mediterranean, in Asia Minor, and in the lands around the Black Sea between 750 and 550 B.C. Many of the Greek overseas trading colonies still survive as cities today, including Siracusa on the island of Sicilia and the French port of Marseille.

The Phoenicians, a great trading people on the eastern Mediterranean shore at the edge of the Fertile Crescent, also founded some cities in Europe. The Phoenicians were active in western Sicilia and southern Iberia, but their most famous colony was Carthage in North Africa. Carthage in turn founded some colonies, including its namesake, the modern Spanish Mediterranean port of Cartagena ("little Carthage").

Most Greek and Phoenician cities were not impressive in appearance or size. Greek towns usually were enclosed by walls and included a fortress on high ground; narrow, winding streets, often unpaved, betraying a haphazard, spontaneous growth; mud-brick or wooden houses; a public square; and a few public buildings, such as temples and theaters. Many had developed from a union of several farm villages and remained dominantly agricultural in function and population. The only difference between "cities" and large farm villages was often cultural rather than economic: The cities invested in nonproductive public buildings and in beautification. Rarely did Greek cities exceed 5,000 in population, though Athínai may have had as many as 300,000 residents in the peak of its classical glory and Kórinthos perhaps 90,000. Only the larger acquired resident merchants, sizable artisan populations, and importance beyond their local areas. Even at the apex of classical urban development, as little as one-quarter of the Greek population lived in the cities.

Some of the Greek overseas colonial towns and a few places in the Aegean were planned settlements with regular street patterns. Piraíeus, the port town of Athínai, and Napoli in southern Italy are examples.

Many of the Greek cities became city-states, self-governing entities composed of the urban center and a surrounding tributary area. This institution had

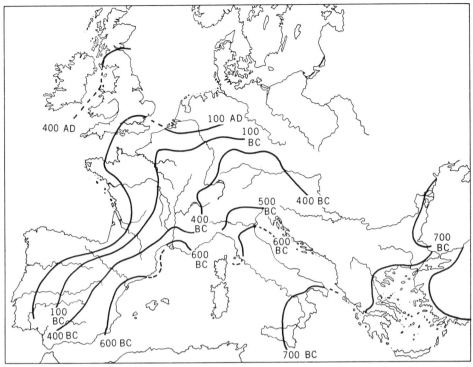

Figure 11.1 Early spread of urban development. The urban nucleus in the Greek lands was well established by 700 B.C. Urbanization spread to the west and north in the centuries that followed. (Reproduced by permission from the *Annals* of the Association of American Geographers, Volume 59, 1969, from an article by Norman J. G. Pounds.)

taken shape by the eighth century B.C., and there were some 200 city-states in existence by 600 B.C. Greek city-states eventually gave rise to major cultural activity, culminating in the golden age and a democratic form of government.

THE ETRUSCAN AND ROMAN CITIES

The urban focus of Europe shifted gradually from Greece to Italy, where Etruscans added a number of cities to earlier Greek and Phoenician colonial beginnings between 700 and 500 B.C. (Figure 11.1). Their domain was the northern peninsular part of Italy, to the west of the arc of the Appennini, but Etruscan influence in urbanization was felt as far away as northern Switzerland and the Danubian lands of southern Germany, where local tribes began building fortified cities by about 400 B.C., perhaps in emulation of the Etruscans.

The Romans derived their urban impetus from both Greeks and Etruscans. At the dawn of Roman greatness, the imperial core districts of Lazio and Toscana contained some forty-two cities; by midpoint in the empire's life-span under Augustus, 430 new cities had been founded in Italy alone. The greatest urban achievement of the Romans was the development of their capital city. In its classical grandeur, Roma may have boasted a population of one million, packed into an area of barely 23 square kilometers (9 square miles). Water was piped into homes; a sewage system, parks, and public baths were built; and a police force maintained order, no small feat considering that half the population were slaves.

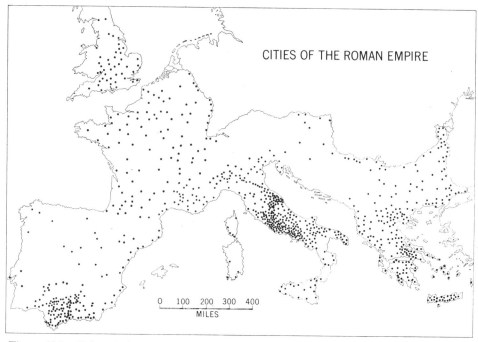

Figure 11.2 Cities of the Roman Empire by the second and third centuries A.D. Note the clusterings in central Italy, southern Spain, and Greece. (Reproduced by permission from the *Annals* of the Association of American Geographers, Volume 59, 1969, from an article by Norman J. G. Pounds.)

The Romans speeded the diffusion of urban life through Europe by founding new cities in France, Germany, Britain, interior Iberia, and other areas which had not previously known significant urbanization (Figure 11.2). Some new towns grew around military barracks or camps, an origin suggested by the British town suffixes *-caster* and *-chester,* as in Lancaster or Winchester, derived from the Latin word *castra,* or "army camp." Traders and craftsmen settled near the camps to provide for various needs of the soldiers, and so established an urban nucleus. More often, though, the Romans simply took over and enlarged the fortified tribal towns of the peoples they conquered. Other towns grew spontaneously and haphazardly at focal points of trade routes.

Most impressive, however, were the *coloniae,* new towns founded by an act of state, laid out by surveyors and, for the most part, built in Italy rather than in outlying provinces. These, typically, had a gridiron pattern of streets focused on two major avenues meeting at right angles at the center of the city, where the forum and public buildings were situated. Lesser streets ran parallel to the axial avenues at regular intervals (Figure 11.3). The checkerboard street pattern, which had appeared earlier in some Greek towns, was perhaps originally inherited from the city-builders of the prehistoric Indus Valley region of Pakistan. Like the Greek examples, the large majority of Roman cities were small and relatively unimportant, serving mainly as local market centers. In France the Roman towns ranged from about 600 to 35,000 in population, while in the English periphery of the empire the size varied from 500 or less up to the 17,000 inhabitants of London.

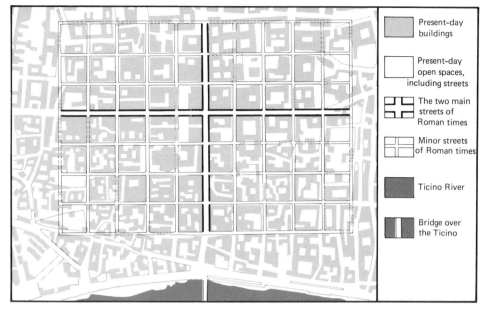

▓	Present-day buildings
☐	Present-day open spaces, including streets
	The two main streets of Roman times
	Minor streets of Roman times
▓	Ticino River
▓	Bridge over the Ticino

Figure 11.3   Survival of the Roman grid pattern in Pavia, Italy. To walk in the central section of modern Pavia (Roman Ticinum) is to be guided in the footsteps of the ancient Romans. The degree of survival of the Roman checkerboard pattern is quite remarkable, for most of the original streets are still in use after twenty centuries. The two main intersecting streets of Roman times have even maintained their dominance. Note how much less regular the streets are outside the old Roman core. Pavia is on the Ticino River south of Milano in the Po Valley. (After Gutkind.)

The heritage of Roman urbanization is considerable. Many sites have been continuously occupied since Roman times, as, for example, the city of Trier in West Germany, and other sites were reoccupied after a period of abandonment. Vestiges of Roman gridiron street patterns survive in such widely spaced places as Pavia in the Po Valley of Italy, Zaragoza in northeastern Spain, Köln in Germany, and Chester in England (Figure 11.3). Even names are often corruptions of the original Latin form, as for example Köln (Colonia Agrippinensis), Reims (Remi), York (Eboracum), Bordeaux (Burdigala), and London (Londinium). One of the most interesting is Zaragoza, which began as the Roman Caesarea Augusta and was corrupted by the Arabic Moorish conquerors to Zarakusta and again by the Christian liberators of Spain to its present form.

The larger Roman cities, like their Greek predecessors, were dominantly mercantile in function. Maintaining an empire, however, magnified the administrative and military functions, and soldiers often formed a sizable part of the population. Acceptance of Christianity in the empire provided an increased religious function for those places which became the location of monasteries or the seat of some ecclesiastical authority.

URBAN DECLINE IN THE DARK AGES

A period of urban decline began when barbarian raids on Roman towns first occurred in about A.D. 250. Conditions worsened with the fall of the empire, and the subsequent depradations of the Moors and Vikings brought urbanism to a low point. The military security upon which trade is based, a security so splendidly provided during the *Pax Romana,* had vanished; consequently, mercantile activity, the *raison d'être* of preindustrial urbanism, declined severely.

Some towns, particularly in western Europe, reverted completely to the status of farm villages or were abandoned. Others retained only their fortified citadel. Perhaps the best chance for survival was offered by religion, for the Christian Church proved remarkably viable in these times of trouble. The presence of the seat of a bishopric or a monastery often provided the only vestige of urban continuity through the Dark Ages. Only a few favored towns, such as Trier, were able to keep an assemblage of merchants and artisans. The urban decline generally was greatest in peripheral parts of the former empire, including southern Germany, England, northern France, Switzerland, and Austria. In Iberia, Italy, Greece, and southern France, the towns shrank in population but usually retained an urban character.

URBAN REBIRTH IN THE MIDDLE AGES

Urban decline and stagnation persisted into the eleventh century, until order was restored under the feudal system and trade flourished once again. During the Middle Ages, numerous Roman towns were rejuvenated and new ones founded beyond the borders of the old empire, in northern Germany, Scandinavia, and the Slavic lands.

Medieval towns probably originated in several ways. Some were simply enlargements of places which had achieved continuity and maintained mercantile activity through the period of decline. Others apparently developed when a number of artisans settled in the larger farm villages to serve the surrounding area with manufactured goods. This origin is suggested by place names ending in *-dorf* (village), *-heim, -ingen, -ingham, -hausen,* and *-house* as in Mulhouse (France), Nördlingen (West Germany), Birmingham (England), Nordhausen (East Germany), Hildesheim (West Germany), and Düsseldorf (West Germany).

Most towns, however, grew from fortified *preurban cores,* sites dominated by the stronghold of a feudal lord or ecclesiastical authority. The 800s and 900s A.D. had been a major period of castle construction by feudal landowners as they sought to secure the surrounding countryside. The catalysts in changing most preurban cores to towns were itinerant traders, who initially made use of secure marketplaces adjacent to strongholds along transport routes. In time, the desire for safe winter quarters led the traders to establish permanent residence at the preurban cores, creating merchant colonies. In an early stage of development, a "town" often consisted of several distinct nuclei: the feudal fortress; one or more marketplaces; scattered, fortified houses of merchants; a church; and some farmhouses. The German city of Braunschweig, for example, was formed in 1269 by the union of five distinct nuclei, each of which had its own name. Artisans were attracted by the presence of merchants, and the town population grew steadily.

A fourth origin was the planned establishment of new cities in colonial areas by central authority, in the manner of the earlier Roman *coloniae.* These are typical of eastern German lands and generally exhibit a regular checkerboard street pattern.

The three essential attributes of the medieval European city were the charter, the town wall, and the marketplace. The charter was a governmental decree from an emperor or lesser monarch granting political autonomy to the town, or papal authority freeing its populace from the feudal restrictions of the rural areas. The city was self-governing and responsible for its own defense. Charters were typically requested by colonies of well-to-do merchants, who found that feudal restrictions hindered the mobility and exercise of personal initiative so vital in trading activities. The petition for charter was supported by the increasingly important artisan group, who developed a variety of specialized skilled trades beginning in the eleventh and twelfth centuries. Many cities date their founding from the granting of a charter, though most existed prior to that time. City-states similar to those of classical Greece were created by charter and appeared throughout most of western Europe.

The charter gave rise to two different worlds in medieval Europe: self-governing towns, where the classical Greek urban phenomena of democratic government and rapid advances in learning and the arts reappeared; and the rural countryside, beyond the confines of the towns, where feudal tyranny flourished and the people remained backward. The university first developed in the medieval city, spreading from a nucleus in the towns of northern Italy (Figure 3.16), and the cultural attainments of urban people led in time to the Renaissance and the Age of Discovery.

Self-government demanded self-defense, and the castles and fortified houses gave way to city walls (Figure 11.4). All important parts of the city were enclosed by the wall, including the mercantile and manufacturing establishments, the fortress, the church, and the homes of the majority of the population. Suburbs often de-

Figure 11.4 The walls of Rothenburg-ob-der-Tauber, West Germany. Rothenburg, in southern Germany, is an almost perfectly preserved medieval town, with its walls still intact. The view is of the inside of the walls. (Photo courtesy G. J. Jordan.)

Suburbs
↓

veloped outside the walls, but these included mainly the homes of the poor. Urban expansion often required the construction of new, more inclusive walls, and some larger cities eventually required three or four rebuildings. In the period before gunpowder came into widespread use, city walls adequately repelled invaders.

The marketplace, often supplemented by a bourse or trading hall, was the focus of economic activity in the town, for the mercantile function remained dominant throughout the medieval period. Larger places held annual trade fairs, some of which actually began in the days of itinerant traders before permanent settlement had transformed the preurban cores into towns. Some of the more famous of these fairs survive to the present day, as at Leipzig, Frankfurt-am-Main, Milano, and Lyon.

In size, the towns of the Middle Ages closely resembled their classical ancestors: Few exceeded 100,000 in population. Gent, the famous textile center of Flanders, had only 56,000 inhabitants in the mid-1300s. Paris, the largest European city, and Napoli were the only two with more than 100,000 by the year 1400.

BAROQUE-RENAISSANCE URBAN DEVELOPMENT, 1500–1800

A number of noteworthy developments in the urban structure of Europe occurred from about 1500 to the spread of the Industrial Revolution. The estab-

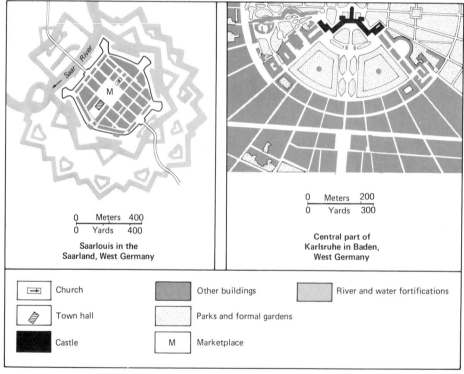

Figure 11.5 Examples of baroque towns. The layout of baroque towns displays great regularity, often with a flair for the spectacular. Typical are Saarlouis, with its impressive water defenses, founded in 1681 by Louis XIV of France as a fortress on his eastern frontier, and Karlsruhe, the capital of Baden, distinguished by the succession of avenues radiating from the royal palace in the center. (After Dickinson, in part.)

Figure 11.6 The Champs d'Elysée, Paris, looking toward the Arch of Triumph. Such broad, straight avenues are rare in European cities. Most, including the Champs d'Elysée, were imposed on the earlier irregular street patterns of national capitals by royal decree in the eighteenth or nineteenth centuries. Many older buildings had to be torn down to permit such a revision. (Photo courtesy French Government Tourist Office.)

lishment of new towns all but ceased, though some were founded as highly planned political centers or resorts, usually laid out with impressive radial street patterns and elaborate structures (Figure 11.5). Existing towns generally grew larger, except in areas such as northern Italy, where disruption of trade ties caused an urban decline.

City-states declined rapidly as towns forfeited their independent political status to be annexed, often unwillingly, into larger empires and states. Only in disunited Germany, within the structure of the Holy Roman Empire, did imperial cities retain self-government. Over thirty German cities were independent as late as 1790, most of them in the southwestern part of the country. Today, however, only a few vestiges of the medieval city-states remain, including Hamburg and Bremen, which have retained the status of statehood within the Federal Republic of Germany, and tiny San Marino, a fully independent city which has survived atop a mountain in the Italian peninsula.

Decline of the city-states was paralleled by the rise of national capital cities to urban primacy and great size. In the year 1400, London had only 50,000 inhabitants and Bristol, its major rival English port, 30,000. Three centuries later, however, London had grown to 700,000, while Bristol remained at 30,000. National capitals often underwent drastic modification to improve their appearance, with grand wide avenues cut through to provide distant vistas, as in the Champs d'Elysee in Paris (Figure 11.6), or Unter den Linden in Berlin.

Even in the heart of the Baroque-Renaissance period, however, urbanization affected only a small part of the European population. In 1600 only four million of the eighty-five million Europeans lived in towns of 15,000 population or more, about 5 percent of the total. The Netherlands and Italy, which were the most highly urbanized countries, could claim only about 12 or 13 percent of their populations as urban, while only 2 percent of the Germans, French, and English lived in large towns by 1600.

11.2 THE INDUSTRIAL PHASE, 1800–PRESENT

European cities have changed rapidly in the past two centuries, primarily as a result of the Industrial Revolution. Manufacturing has become the dominant function of many, if not most, urban centers, putting an end to the age of mercantile cities. The hallmark of the industrial phase has been the great increase in city size, prompted by the gravitation of the majority of the European population to urban, industrial areas. England and Wales were the first areas to urbanize over half of the population, a level reached in the 1850s. By the turn of the century, over three-quarters of the English and Welsh were city-dwellers, and Germany had become the second nation to find over half of its population urban. Many other states, especially in northwestern Europe, reached this level by 1930, and the trend is presently spreading toward the peripheries of the culture area. The most highly urbanized countries are the Netherlands and Belgium, where over four-fifths of the total population live in towns and cities of 2000 or more inhabitants (Figure 11.7). The least urbanized lands are Portugal and Albania, where industry is poorly developed.

The Industrial Revolution produced the first European cities since imperial Roma to have over a million inhabitants. London, which had about 950,000 in 1800, passed the million mark in the first decade of the nineteenth century and reached past 2 million by 1850. Paris claimed more than a million by the middle of the 1800s, and by the turn of the century, Berlin, Wien, Leningrad, and Moskva were also at this level. All except Moskva combined an industrial function with the status of national capital. By 1970, twenty other cities had reached and surpassed a million in population, not counting those in the Soviet Union and "European" Turkey (Figure 3.5).

Very few new cities were produced by the Industrial Revolution. Pre-existing mercantile towns were simply enlarged, with factories and housing tracts spilling out far beyond the original confines of the medieval walls. A few exceptions which were founded in the modern industrial period can be found, including Ludwigshafen and Wolfsburg in West Germany, but they are rare.

11.3 URBAN SITE

In spite of the far-reaching modifications resulting from the Industrial Revolution, the European city displays the heritage of medieval or even classical times to a remarkable degree. This debt is revealed in specific location or site, in morphology, and in areal spacing.

Decisions which determined the specific sites of most European cities were

Figure 11.7 Percentage of population living in urban areas, 1968. The percentages refer to that part of the population living in towns and cities of 2000 or more inhabitants.

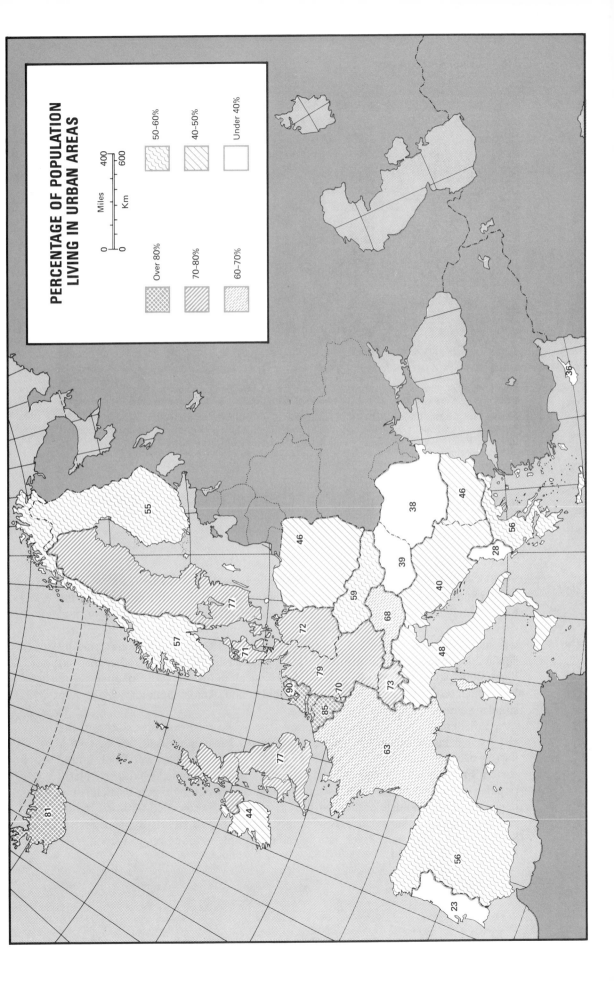

PERCENTAGE OF POPULATION LIVING IN URBAN AREAS

Over 80%

70–80%

60–70%

50–60%

40–50%

Under 40%

Miles 400

Km 600

Figure 11.8 Bern, the capital city of Switzerland, an example of a river-meander urban site. The original settlement, now the core of the city, lay inside the loop of the incised meander of the Aare River. Such a location provided natural defense on three sides. As the city expanded in modern times, it came to include the opposite bank of the river. (Photo courtesy Swiss National Tourist Office.)

made long ago by Greeks, Romans, and medieval feudal lords. These decisions were based on the *function* of infant towns or preurban cores, which was generally related to defense or trade routes.

DEFENSIVE URBAN SITES

An easily defended site was particularly important to the feudal lords, both secular and ecclesiastical, who built strongholds during the insecure period after the fall of the Roman Empire. The Romans themselves had rarely chosen protected sites for their army camps and other settlements, simply because their military force was more powerful than that of neighboring tribes. Roman camps were typically situated for *offensive* advantage, along roads and navigable streams rather than on high points. Still, episodes of piracy in the classical and preclassical Mediterranean had influenced the defensive siting of Athínai and Roma, both of which were situated some miles inland from the coast.

There are many types of defensive sites. The *river-meander site,* with the city located inside a loop where the stream turns back upon itself, leaves only a narrow neck of land unprotected by the waters. Besançon on the river Doubs in far eastern France is an example of a meander site. *Incised* meanders were particularly popular because the river loop became permanent by cutting down into alluvium deposited in the geologic past. Such sites combined the protection afforded by the river with steep banks which were difficult to ascend. The city of Bern, capital of Switzerland, on the Aare River, is a splendid example of siting on an incised river meander (Figure 11.8).

Figure 11.9 The town and abbey of Mont-Saint-Michel, France, an example of the offshore-island urban site. At low tide, as in this picture, the town is connected to the nearby Normandie mainland by an expanse of sand, but at high tide it is an island. In modern times, a causeway was built to the mainland. Such a site offered obvious defensive advantages. (Photo courtesy French Government Tourist Office.)

Similar to the meander site but even more advantageous was the *river-island site,* which often combined a natural moat with an easier river crossing, the latter an advantage for the merchant trade. Paris began as a town on the Île de la Cité, or "island of the city," in the middle of the Seine River, and the same was true of Polish Wroclaw on the Odra and others. Stockholm, the capital of Sweden, occupies a *lake-island site,* spread over a dozen or so small islands in the area where Lake Mälaren joins the Baltic Sea. Perhaps even more satisfactory was the *offshore-island site,* for it combined defense with a port facility. The classic example is Venèzia, built on wooden pilings driven into an offshore sandbar which separated a coastal lagoon from the open Adriatic Sea. Marauding bands were thus denied access to the city unless they acquired boats. In the same category would be the famous town and abbey of Mont-Saint-Michel, situated on a rock off the coast of Normandie in France (Figure 11.9). At high tide the rock and town are insular, while at low tide, tidal flats make access difficult. A causeway has changed this situation in modern times.

Marshes also afforded protection for some European cities in their early stages. The river ports of Hamburg on the Elbe, Warszawá on the Wisla, and Rotterdam on the Rhine were all very difficult to approach until flanking riverine marshes were drained. Such *dry-point sites* were also typical of many farm villages.

Danger from the direction of the sea often prompted *sheltered-harbor sites,*

Figure 11.10 The city of Salzburg in Austria, an example of the acropolis urban site. Salzburg developed at the foot of the fortified high point, or acropolis. The beautifully preserved fortress, or burg, still dominates the skyline of the city. Merchants who were responsible for creating the original urban nucleus chose to locate adjacent to the fortress for reasons of security. (Photo courtesy Austrian National Tourist Office.)

where narrow entrances to the harbor could be easily defended. Oslo, at the head of a fjord in Norway, and the Portuguese capital of Lisboa both occupy sheltered harbors.

High points also were sought out for defensive reasons. Most common is the *acropolis site,* in which a fortress or stronghold was erected on high ground and the city developed at the foot of the hill. Greek Athínai is one of the prototypes of acropolis siting, but examples are scattered throughout Europe. In areas influenced by Germanic and Slavic peoples, such towns were often named for the stronghold on the high ground, as is indicated by place names ending in *-burg, -burgh, -bourg,* and *-grad,* all of which mean "fortress." Scottish Edinburgh ("Edwin's fort"), dominated by the impressive Castle Rock, is an example of an acropolis-site city, as are Salzburg, Budapest, Praha, Heidelberg, Würzburg, and many others (Figure 11.10).

Closely akin to the acropolis are those towns and cities which, in their formative stage at least, lay entirely on the high ground, often adjacent to the stronghold. Examples are Beograd ("white fortress"), on a high bluff overlooking the confluence of the Yugoslavian Danube and the Sava; Segovia in Spain, and San Marino in the Appennini Mountains. Often such hill towns in Romance language lands bear the place name prefix *Mont-* or *Monte-,* as in Monte Corno, Italy.

TRADE-ROUTE URBAN SITES

Merchants, who were largely responsible for the development of cities from preurban cores, generally selected those stronghold sites which lay on trade routes. Numerous types of sites possessed advantages for the merchants.

In the early medieval period, before bridges were common, great value was placed on *river-ford sites*, where streams were shallow and the bed was firm. Some cities bear names which indicate the former importance of fords, including the German and English suffixes *-furt* and *-ford*. Frankfurt-am-Main in West Germany is situated at an easy crossing of the Main River, where the ancient trade route from the Upper Rhine Plain passes northward into the Wetterau district and on beyond to the North German Plain. Upstream on the Main from Frankfurt lie the towns of Ochsenfurt ("ford for oxen"), Schweinfurt ("swine-ford"), Hassfurt, Trennfurt, and Lengfurt. The English cities of Oxford on the Thames, Hertford on the Lea, and Bedford on the Ouse again suggest the former importance of river shallows in urban siting. The Latin word for ford, *trajectus*, also survives in modified form in the town names Utrecht (*trajectus ad Rhenum* or "ford on the Rhine") and Maastricht (*trajectus ad Mosam* or "ford on the Maas") in the Netherlands.

A similar function was served by bridge-point sites, where streams were narrow and possessed firm banks and beds. Town names including *pont, bridge, brück,* and the like indicate that the site was originally chosen for bridge construction. The Romans were great bridge-builders, and many towns derive both their site and name from the Roman structure, as for example Les-Ponts-de-Cé ("bridges of Caesar") on the Loire River in France, and Paunton (from the Latin *Adpontem* or "at the bridge") in Lincolnshire, England. Historic London Bridge, of which there have been several through history, was originally built at a point on the Thames just upstream from the marsh-flanked estuary, at a site where the banks were firm and the stream narrow. It served as an important river crossing on the Roman route from the Strait of Dover to the interior of England. Examples of other bridge-point cities which were named for their function include Cambridge ("bridge on the Cam River") and Brigham ("bridge town") in England, Pontoise ("bridge on the Oise River") near Paris, Bersenbrück ("broken bridge") in northwestern Germany, and Bruchsal ("bridge over the Salzbach") in the German province of Baden, Innsbruck ("bridge on the Inn River") in Austria, and Puente-la-Reina ("queen's bridge") in Spain.

Many city sites are riverine in northern Europe, where navigable streams have long been important as trade routes. *Confluence sites*, where two rivers meet, are quite common. The German city of Koblenz, at the juncture of the Rhine and Mosel, actually derived its name from the Latin word for confluence, while Passau in the West German province of Bayern may be the only city where three rivers—the Danube, Inn, and Ilz—meet at precisely the same point. The rise of Paris was facilitated by the convergence of the Marne, Oise, and Seine rivers in the general vicinity of the city, and Lyon profited from its position at the confluence of Rhône and Saône. *Head-of-navigation sites* are also fairly common and serve as transshipment points, as does Basel on the upper reaches of the navigable sector of the Rhine River in Switzerland.

Crossroad sites occur throughout Europe. One of the more famous is Wien, the Austrian capital, located where an east–west route connecting the Hungarian Plain with southern Germany along the Danube Valley met the ancient north–south route which skirted the eastern foot of the Alps and passed through the Moravian Gate to the North European Plain. Hannover in West Germany stands at the juncture of an old route which runs along the southern edge of the North German Plain and the road which follows the course of the Leine River through the hills south of the city.

Seaport sites can be divided into two basic types. Those at or near the juncture of navigable rivers or estuaries and the coast are quite common and include such cities as London, Hamburg, Bordeaux, and Gdańsk. In southern Europe, however, the seasonality of precipitation and short length of many streams rendered rivers less useful for transportation. The great ports usually developed at the juncture of highways and the coast rather than at the marshy river mouths. Cádiz lies some thirty kilometers (twenty miles) south of the mouth of the Guadalquivir, and few human eyes witness the joining of the Ebro River and the Mediterranean Sea in northern Spain. Marseille is well to the east of the Rhône delta marshes in southern France, and other Mediterranean rivers such as the Po and Tevere also have no major ports at their mouths, in part because of silting.

OTHER ECONOMIC SITES
Mercantile activity was by far the most significant of the economic functions served by the preindustrial city. However, other economic factors were occasionally determinant in siting, in particular mining and the operation of resorts.

Extraction of iron ore, copper, salt, silver, and other minerals or metals often gave rise to mining towns. In Germany and Austria, place names including *salz* ("salt"), *hall* ("salt"), *eisen* ("iron"), *gold,* and *kupfer* ("copper"), as in Salzungen (East Germany), and Kupferberg (Bayern, West Germany), indicate the present or former importance of mining.

Resorts often date back to Roman times, in particular those offering health baths in mineral or hot springs. These towns and cities typically bear names indicative of their function, including elements such as *bains, bad(en)*, or *bagni,* all of which mean "bath." Examples are Bad Pyrmont and Wiesbaden in West Germany, Bagnoli ("bath") near Napoli in Italy, and Luxeuil-les-Bains in eastern France. The English city of Bath, known to the Romans as "Aquae Sulis," has an ancient resort tradition.

11.4 URBAN MORPHOLOGY — Study of form or structure
European cities differ strikingly in physical appearance from those of Anglo-America, Australia, New Zealand, South Africa, and other zones of major overseas European colonization. In large measure, the uniqueness of the urban cultural landscape of Europe is the result of age. In addition, inhabitants are reluctant to permit far-reaching modifications, which amounts to little less than a deliberate sabotage of efficiency, an admirable disregard for the coarse demands of the Industrial Revolution.

STREET PATTERN
In most European cities the street pattern is quite irregular, particularly in the central districts. Streets meet at odd angles with no apparent planning, and square or rectangular blocks are rare (Figure 11.11). Thoroughfares are uncommon, and the flow of traffic from one part of the city to another is seriously disrupted. The haphazard network is strongly reminiscent of the pattern in irregular clustered farm villages, some of which did form the nuclei of cities. Even modern suburbs, laid out on the periphery of old medieval cores, sometimes share this disorder. The streets often followed the irregular outline of preexisting field patterns, as when the English city of Leeds in Yorkshire expanded to accommodate the growth of the Industrial Revolution.

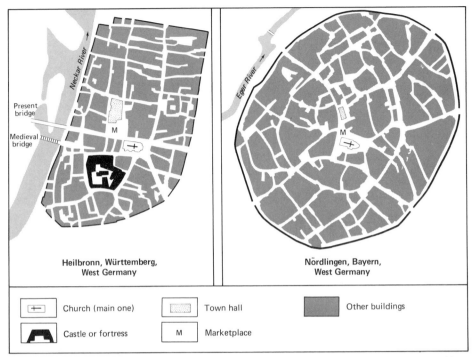

Heilbronn, Württemberg,
West Germany

Nördlingen, Bayern,
West Germany

Church (main one)		Town hall		Other buildings	
Castle or fortress		M Marketplace			

Figure 11.11 Examples of medieval towns. In Heilbronn, the castle-fortress (Deutschher-renhof) was the successor to an ancient Frankish fortress. The church, town hall, and market-place shared the center of the city with the fortress. Heilbronn was heavily damaged in World War II. Nördlingen, where the old outer wall is still intact, has the maze of streets typical of medieval towns. An earlier wall which was outgrown is clearly traced by the circular street. The overall street pattern is of the type referred to as *radial-concentric*. (After Gutkind.)

Further complicating the irregularity of street pattern is the European tendency to give several different names to an avenue or street along its short, sinuous course. Often the name changes at almost every intersection. Over a length of only six blocks in München, West Germany, for example, one reasonably straight street bears the names Maxburgstrasse, Löwengrube, Schäfflstrasse, Schrammer-strasse, and Hofgraben. Confusion is often further added by unsystematic and un-predictable numbering of the houses and buildings.

Exceptions to the disorderly street patterns are relatively rare. A few Greek towns and Roman *coloniae* were laid out in a regular checkerboard or gridiron pattern, and occasionally this survives (Figure 11.3). But considerable irregularity has crept in even in places such as Köln in Germany or Verona in Italy, where the Roman layout of streets persists. Greater regularity is displayed by the planned colonial towns built through eastern Germany, Poland, and western Czechoslovakia in the late Middle Ages. Both Neubrandenburg in East Germany and Koszalin in coastal Poland (formerly German Köslin), for example, have quite regular, square blocks in their central cores, though more irregular patterns are found in the suburbs.

Most regular of all are the strikingly geometric street layouts in the few towns founded in the Renaissance-Baroque period, from 1500 to 1800. Many of these were established as showplace residences by members of European royalty, and typically have grand radial avenues converging on spacious plazas and squares

Figure 11.12 A portion of the center of Wien, capital of Austria, showing one section of the *Ringstrasse*. The Ringstrasse, literally "circle street," follows the course of one of the former city walls of Wien, providing a much-needed boulevard and parkway around the compact urban core. Many European cities have such circular or semicircular "beltlines" marking the location of old walls. Only rarely did the walls survive into the modern period. Most were torn down during the era of state-building in Europe, when autonomous city-states were absorbed into larger political units. (Copyright Rotkin, Photography for Industry.)

(Figure 11.5). Examples include Neustrelitz in East Germany, Versailles on the outskirts of Paris, and Karlsruhe near the Rhine River in southwestern Germany.

In addition, the irregular street pattern of some medieval cities was modified in the Renaissance-Baroque period and even the nineteenth century by the cutting of new, straight avenues, superimposing a regular layout of thoroughfares on the older haphazard maze. Paris was drastically modified in this manner (Figure 11.6), as were Berlin and Wien. Even more spectacular were the great circular boulevards which replaced the medieval walls. The decline of the independent city-state through annexation into larger national political units, and advances in methods of warfare, led most towns to destroy their fortifications in an effort to facilitate movement of traffic. Some replaced the walls with circular or semicircular boulevards, as in Wien (Figure 11.12), Köln, Budapest, and Antwerpen. In Frankfurt-am-Main, West Germany, a belt of streets and parks now precisely preserves the zigzag outline of the original medieval battlements. English cities, in contrast, lack such impressive avenues and boulevards because the security of political unity led to the removal of walls much earlier.

In general, however, Europeans have resisted changes in their cities, including modifications of the street pattern. Wartime destruction leveled as much as

80 percent of the buildings in some German cities, providing a splendid, though costly, opportunity to revise street patterns in the central portions. Urban-planners wanted to lay out broader and straighter streets, ample parking space, and freeways, but their advice was generally ignored and the cities rebuilt in the old pattern. Very few German cities were even provided with much-needed thoroughfares in the process of rebuilding. In contrast, the Dutch and British reconstruction of Rotterdam and Coventry produced cities much better adapted to the needs of modern man. Perhaps the sense of loss was so much greater in Germany that the responsible officials felt more compelled to reproduce than to re-form the vanished cities.

The traffic problems created by the irregularity of street patterns is made even more critical by the narrowness of the thoroughfares and scarcity of parking space. In the West German city of Bremen, 84 percent of the total street mileage is less than 7 meters (23 feet) wide, a width recommended as the minimum for handling heavy two-way traffic. Even so, Bremen is much better off than the West German cities of Lübeck, where 91 percent is less than 7 meters (23 feet) and Oldenburg, in which only *1 percent* of all street mileage is wider than that. In Italian Verona, the streets, inherited from the Romans, are precisely 6 meters (20 feet) wide. Averages for 141 West German cities indicate that 77 percent of the total urban street mileage is too narrow for safe and efficient two-way traffic of any considerable volume.

Parking space also is at a premium. The harried visitor to European cities frequently looks in vain for the blue placards bearing the letter *P* which denotes a parking facility. München, one of the largest cities of western Europe, has over 300,000 registered automobiles but parking space for only 8,300. Only 70 percent of München's total parking area of 18.6 hectares (46 acres) is developed as parking lots, providing for 5,800 automobiles. The remainder is curb space.

In effect, the Europeans have accepted the automobile but refused to carry out the drastic modifications of their cities that adoption requires. The cities retain character and charm, but are next to impossible to move about in. Many, such as Amsterdam and København, are best negotiated by bicycle; in many other places the hopeless tangle of narrow streets has been bypassed by a splendid subway system, as in Paris.

COMPACTNESS

The European city covers much less total area than an American, Australian, or South African urban center of comparable population. Indeed, the foreign visitor is quite often struck with the impression that European cities seem smaller than they actually are in terms of population.

Europeans have achieved greater compactness by tightly packing buildings together and preferring apartments and duplexes to separate one-family residences. Indicative of the different life-style is the fact that only 16 percent of all urban residential structures in West Germany in 1965 were single-family homes, as contrasted to 76 percent in the United States in 1960. In the United Kingdom, single-family homes are more common than on the European mainland, but even there the houses are typically built in long rows abutting one another along common walls. Spacious suburban yards are quite rare. Europeans prefer to live close to the center of the city, for the old medieval core serves as the "living room," a place to gather after work, to stroll about, shop, and dine. Tightly compacted apartment housing provides proximity to the central city for a large part of the population. The flight to the suburbs so typical of American cities is largely absent, and urban cores are not blighted by decay and slum dwellings. However, an increasing number of factory workers, who also farm part-time, commute from surrounding agricultural villages. The satisfaction of having a garden to work is provided by the small plots owned by many apartment-dwellers on the outskirts of the towns. Known in Germany as *Laubengärten* (literally, "summer-house gardens"), these often contain a crude shelter, and the city folk spend many weekends there.

In the cities the medieval custom of combining residence and place of work survives to a surprising degree. It is not uncommon, even in larger cities, to find bakers, butchers, or restaurant-owners living above their shops, a practice especially common in southern Europe. Most city-dwellers live at least within walking or cycling range of their place of employment, though commuting is rapidly increasing in western Europe.

The tight packing of buildings in the city cores is in part a result of the limited technology of the medieval architects and builders, who found it impossible to erect structures of any great height. Skyscrapers, so typical of American cities, are usually absent; the urban skyline is commonly dominated by church spires, a hilltop medieval fortress or classical ruin, or some special structure such as the Eiffel Tower. Even in the central business districts, buildings more than five or six stories tall are unusual. The resistance of urban Europeans to change has prevented taller structures from invading the cities in recent times.

Further, almost invariably the old, low buildings destroyed in World War II were replaced by new structures of the same architecture. A comparison of photographs of prewar and postwar München—80 percent of which was destroyed by bombing—reveals a striking similarity. As in the reestablishment of the old, inefficient street patterns, the Europeans simply revived the vanished cities of prewar times. Perhaps the most remarkable re-creation took place in the former German Baltic port city of Danzig, present-day Gdańsk, which was taken over by Poland in 1945. The German population of the severely damaged city was expelled, along with that of all eastern German territories, but the Poles then proceeded to spend huge sums of money to produce a duplicate of the old German medieval Hanseatic city. Their attention to detail in reconstruction was simply astounding. The end product is a rather unlivable museum-town from another age, but Poland has at least solidified, with time, effort, and money, a valid claim to a city which Germans and Russians destroyed.

URBAN ZONES

At the heart of the typical European city lies the old *medieval core,* often ringed by the circular street or boulevard which follows the former course of the town walls. Here and there around this periphery, old gates, the only remnants of the walls, can often be found, sometimes dating from classical times. The famous Porta Nigra ("Black Gate") in the German city of Trier is a Roman survival, while the Holstentor ("Holstein Gate") at Lübeck is a remnant of medieval walls. The Brandenburger Gate, at the west end of the core of old Berlin and now a well-known landmark along the border between Western and Communist sectors of the city, was erected in the eighteenth century for ornamental purposes and never really served the function of city gate.

Within the medieval core section, a number of distinctive buildings are usually found, including an impressive cathedral, whose spire dominates the urban skyline and bears witness to the extraordinary importance and vitality of Christianity in the Middle Ages. Huge capital outlays were required to erect such churches, and their maintenance costs are enormous, increasing with age. Even as early as the era of classical Greece, municipal pride in public buildings and religious edifices was one of the principal traits which distinguished townsfolk from residents of farm villages, and the large expense involved in cathedral construction was borne with little complaint. Many of these churches are tourist attractions in their own right, such as Notre Dame on the Île de la Cité in Paris, San Marco in Venezia, the Köln Cathedral, St. Stephans in Wien, and the magnificent cathedral at Chartres, southwest of Paris.

If the city was fortunate enough to be the residence of a royal family, the medieval core usually includes a palace. Examples are the Louvre in Paris (now a museum), the Hofburg in Wien, the Kremlin in Moskva, Edinburgh Castle, and the Palazzo Ducale in Venezia. In some cases, the royal residence in the medieval core was identical with the feudal stronghold on high ground which had originally attracted urban settlement. In many instances, however, royalty abandoned these residences in the medieval core to build splendid new palaces in the suburbs during the Renaissance-Baroque period. Versailles supplanted the Louvre in Paris and was widely copied by other rulers; thus the Hapsburgs of Austria built the Schönbrunn Palace on the outer fringe of Wien and the Wittelsbachs of Bayern in southern Germany ordered the construction of the beautiful Nymphenburg Palace on the western outskirts of München.

The urban core area is almost invariably centered on the old marketplace, which often lies in front of the cathedral. Even now market day is held as it was 500 years ago, though the wealthy merchants and manufacturers have surrendered the square to farmers selling produce. Also in the core, and usually near the marketplace, is the old town hall (German *Rathaus,* French *hôtel de ville*), which once housed the administration of the self-governing city-state. In some towns, *guild houses* also survive, particularly in the Belgian cities of Gent, Brugge, and Antwerpen.

In an economic sense, the core serves a great number of purposes, preserving the multifunctional character of medieval times. It houses a great variety of small retail stores, multifamily residences, and workshoplike factories of craftsmen. In the entire city the distinction between residential, industrial, and commercial zones is rather weak, and there is a great deal of areal interweaving. The urban core typically contains all three functions, though the factories are usually small craft workshops.

Surrounding the core is often a zone of *preindustrial suburbs,* less-compact housing areas built outside the walls of the old town, sometimes after the walls had been removed. This zone frequently contains the railroad stations, which ring the periphery of the old medieval core. The tight clustering of venerated old structures made it impossible for the railroad lines to penetrate the interior. Such large cities as Paris and London have a circle of rail terminals, and the stations are typically named for the major city which lies on their rail route: in Paris one finds the Gare de Lyon, the "station of Lyon," at the terminus of the rail line leading out to that city in the Rhône–Saône Valley, the Gare St. Lazare, the Gare d'Orléans, and so on. In many instances, one suburban railroad station serves as the main one, where trains for all destinations may be taken, but often the traveler must choose correctly among ten or twenty stations to find the right train. Only rarely did the railroads succeed in pushing into the central city, as in Köln, where a depressingly ugly station stands almost in the shadow of the magnificent Gothic cathedral.

The Industrial Revolution added a series of dingy outer halos to the traditional European cities: belts of barracklike laborer apartments dating from the 1800s and early 1900s, modern large factories, and the somewhat more pleasing residential districts developed in recent decades. On the outskirts of the city are the small weekend gardens of city-dwellers. In some instances, urban-planners have set aside peripheral rural areas as permanent greenbelts, where urban expansion is forbidden. The most famous of these rings greater London, where an undeveloped zone first proposed by Queen Elizabeth I in the 1580s has finally been brought to reality in the twentieth century.

11.5 HUMAN PATTERNS WITHIN THE EUROPEAN CITY

Site and morphology constitute but the urban skeleton and, while interesting and reflective of the culture of the inhabitants, cannot alone convey an adequate image of the European city. Above all, it is essential to recognize that the most vital element in European cities is people.

The city, in Europe and elsewhere, is decidedly heterogeneous in the human sense. Urban people differ from one another in a great variety of cultural and economic ways. They have created within the cities distinct neighborhoods and localities, each with its own set of social characteristics. In almost every part of the world where urbanization has occurred, in ancient times or modern, there has been a tendency for people to be segregated residentially on the basis of social traits. Often, at least historically, there were legal restrictions concerning place of residence, but the development of neighborhoods occurs with or without the backing of law. It appears to be an innate human behavior pattern.

Religion has been one of the most powerful forces separating people within the cities of Europe. Most medieval towns had a Jewish ghetto, reminders of which are still seen in street names such as the German *Judengasse* (Street of the Jews). Even now, residential segregation along religious lines can be seen in cities such as Belfast, Northern Ireland, where there are distinct Catholic and Protestant neighborhoods. In Belfast, the degree of segregation increases in times of violence.

Linguistic differences have also separated people within European cities. This practice was most common in areas of speech diversity. Brno, in the Czechoslovakian province of Morava, had a medieval residential pattern in which Germans were confined to the northern part of the city and Czechs to the south. Towns such as Armagh and Downpatrick in Northern Ireland developed distinct quarters in the seventeenth century, as is indicated by the survival of English Street, Irish Street, and Scotch Street. In medieval Caernarvon, Wales, the portion of the town enclosed by walls housed the immigrant English, while the native Welsh clustered just outside the walls. Modern equivalents are the concentrations of alien immigrant workers in many cities of western Europe. Greeks, Yugoslavs, Italians, and other groups often focalize in separate parts of cities in West Germany, Switzerland, France, and elsewhere.

Race has rarely been an important segregating factor, for the simple reason that European cities have few non-Caucasians in their population. West Indian Negroes do tend to be concentrated in certain parts of London and other British cities, but there is no true segregation along South African or American lines. The Asian Indians and Pakistanis, most of whom are "Mediterranean" type Caucasians, are distinctive enough in Britain to occasion a mild segregation similar to that directed against West Indian blacks.

Certainly the chief force at work in European residential segregation is social class, which is generally determined by type of employment. In the Middle Ages it was common for merchants and various artisans to have their own quarters of town. Here again, surviving street names suggest such segregation. In München, for example, one finds the Ledererstrasse ("Street of the Leather-Workers"), Färbergraben ("Street of the Cloth-Dyers"), Sattlerstrasse ("Street of the Saddlers"), and others. Such names referred to the artisans' places of work, but were often also their residences. In medieval Lübeck, merchants lived to the west of a main north–south street, while artisans resided to the east.

Patterns of residential segregation based on type of employment are still quite evident today. A study in Liverpool, England, for example, showed that men who were administrators, shopkeepers, small employers, or engaged in the professions formed a much larger proportion of the population in residential areas farthest from the city core than in those near the center. In contrast, semiskilled and unskilled workers were far more common in the central part of the city. In Britain and most other European countries, there is a direct correlation between social class and desirability of neighborhood. No visitor to the large industrial towns and cities of the United Kingdom can avoid seeing districts of depressing tenement housing occupied by the lower classes.

Some European cities have begun developing the pattern of affluent suburbs and decaying cores so typical of American urban centers, but in many, it is the peripheral areas which are occupied by the lower classes. Before systems of mass transit were developed, almost all European town cores were dominated by the wealthier people, and this original pattern has not entirely disappeared in many countries. Later adoption of the automobile also retarded the flight of the middle and upper classes to suburbia.

The neighborhoods based on religion, language, race, and social class are made still more distinctive by a number of other social traits which display the same areal patterns. Lower-class neighborhoods typically have denser populations, while differences in religion are sometimes, as in Belfast, linked to differences in birth rates. Catholic neighborhoods in Belfast have more children and thus a lower average age for the population. In short, there are often many close interrelationships between density of population, age, occupation, class, religion, race, and nationality, producing neighborhoods which differ in many ways.

11.6 URBAN FUNCTION AND THE SPACING OF CITIES

In recent decades, urban geographers have devoted a great deal of attention to the distribution or spacing of towns and cities, in order to determine the causal factors shaping the urban locational pattern. Not surprisingly, they have found that urban economic functions are crucial in determining location, for the basic reason for the existence of cities and towns lies in the economic activities they provide. Three distinct stages of the productive process, types of economic activity, can be distinguished: (1) the *extractive stage,* or primary production, such as agriculture, fishing, mining, and lumbering; (2) the *processing* or *secondary stage,* mainly manufacturing, the processing of raw materials produced in the primary or extractive stage; and (3) the *tertiary stage,* the distribution of manufactured goods and the provision of a great variety of political, educational, medical, and transportational services, as well as wholesaling and retailing of goods. The location of cities and towns specializing in one or another of these functions will be influenced by a certain set of causal factors.

CITIES ENGAGED IN PRIMARY PRODUCTION

Some urban centers have developed mainly as resource towns, engaged directly in the use or extraction of natural resources and raw materials. Usually a certain amount of preliminary processing of the resource is also carried on in such towns. Examples include mining towns such as Kiruna in Sweden, where iron ore is mined; the fishing villages of coastal Portugal, including canneries; the sawmill and pulpmill towns which line the Bothnian coast of Sweden; centers engaged in the processing of agricultural goods, focused on creameries, grain mills, sugar-beet refineries, and the like.

The presence or absence of urban development on the site of resources and raw materials is determined by several characteristics of the resource: its scarcity, quality or quantity, and location relative to the market. Iron ore is in rather short supply in Europe, and remote deposits such as those in northern Sweden and Norway are exploited, leading to the development of mining towns. Coal, on the other hand, is much more abundant, and few permanent residents have been attracted to the deposits on the remote Norwegian Arctic island group of Svalbard.

CITIES ENGAGED IN SECONDARY PRODUCTION

Cities dominated by the secondary, or manufacturing, stage of production will be located according to the principles of industrial location discussed in the previous chapter. The causal distributional factors include the weight, bulk, and perishability of the raw materials and finished product; proximity to market; availability and price of transportation; supply and quality of labor; presence of a power supply; influence of governmental decisions; and a number of others.

CITIES AND TOWNS ENGAGED IN TERTIARY PRODUCTION

Most urban centers are engaged mainly in the third stage of production, the provision of goods and services for the consumers. These exist mainly to facilitate the distribution of manufactured goods to the people living in their vicinity and to provide political, medical, educational, and other services. Such towns and cities have attracted the lion's share of attention from geographers interested in analyzing the distribution of urban centers.

In the 1930s, the German geographer Walter Christaller formulated a theory of tertiary urban location which he called *central-place theory*. He defined a central place as any clustering of settlement which served as the center of its rural hinterland and the economic mediator between its surroundings and the outside world. Crucial to the theory is the fact that different goods and services vary (1) in range, the maximum distance or radius from the supply center at which the goods and services can reach the consumers, and (2) in the size of population required to make provision of services economically feasible. For example, it requires a larger number of people to support a hospital, university, or department store than to support a gasoline station, post office, or grocery store. Similarly, consumers are willing to travel a greater distance to consult a heart specialist, record a land title, or purchase an automobile than they are to buy a loaf of bread, mail a letter, or fill their automobile with gasoline. People will spend as little time and effort as possible in making use of the services of central places, but they will be obliged to travel further to use services which require a large market.

The consequence of the range variance of different central goods and services is a hierarchy of central places in terms of the size of population and the number of goods and services available. At the top of the hierarchy are regional metropolises, which offer all services associated with central places and have very large tributary hinterlands. These are often national capitals, or at least the political centers of sizable regions. At the opposite extreme is the small market village or hamlet, which may contain nothing more than a post office, café, or service station. Between the two extremes is a continuum of central places of various degrees of importance. Ascending the hierarchy, one finds that each higher order of central place provides all of the goods and services available at centers next lowest in the hierarchy *plus* one or more which are not provided. Central places of a lower order greatly outnumber the few at the higher levels of the hierarchy. One regional metropolis may contain thousands of smaller central places in its tributary area. The size of the market area of a central place is fundamentally determined by the distance range of the goods and services it offers.

With this background, Christaller listed three principles or causal forces which determine the spacing and location of central places. Most basic is the *market principle,* the assumption that any region will be supplied with goods and services from the minimum number of functioning central places, all other factors being equal. Ideally, the market area of a central place would be circular, drawn on the radius of the range of central goods, but adjacent centers of the same hierarchial rank necessitate the paring of the circle to a hexagon, the geometric figure closest to the shape of a circle which permits a complete network of market areas without the overlapping or underlapping produced by circles (Figure 11.13). The pattern of interlocking hexagons is the ideal distribution of tertiary towns and cities. Any variations from that pattern must be explained in terms of other, disruptive locational factors, a process regarded as "verifying the theory." The more important are included in Christaller's second and third locational principles.

The *traffic principle* holds that as many demands for transportation facilities as possible will be provided within a minimum capital expenditure for construction and maintenance of the facilities. The distribution of central places according to this principle is most favorable when as many high-ranking places as possible lie on one transport route between two important central places, the route being as straight as possible. If the traffic principle determined rather than simply modified the distribution of central places, the tertiary towns and cities would be lined up on straight routes fanning out like spokes from the larger, more important places (Figure 11.14).

The basic conflict between the market and traffic principles lies in the fact

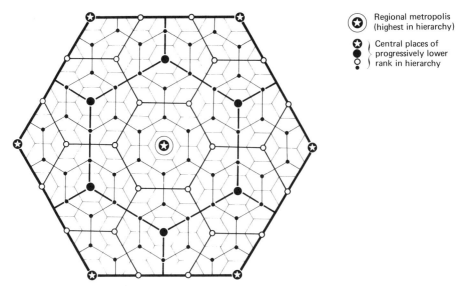

Figure 11.13 Distribution of central places according to Christaller's market principle. (Carlisle W. Baskin, translator, *Central Places in Southern Germany*, by Walter Christaller, © 1966 by Prentice-Hall, Inc., Englewood Cliffs, N. J., p. 66. By permission of the publisher.)

that direct routes between adjacent first-order central places in the hierarchy, located according to the market principle, do not pass through places of the next lowest order (Figure 11.13). Zigzag routes, which violate the traffic principle, or disruption of the hexagonal pattern, which violates the market principle, must occur. In essence, the traffic principle is *linear* while that of market is *spatial*.

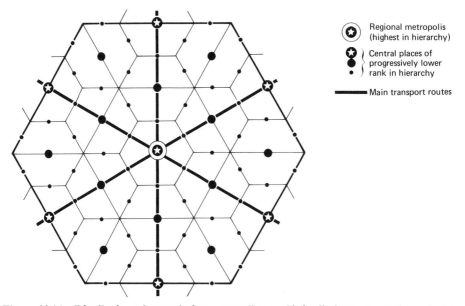

Figure 11.14 Distribution of central places according to Christaller's transportation principle. (After Christaller.)

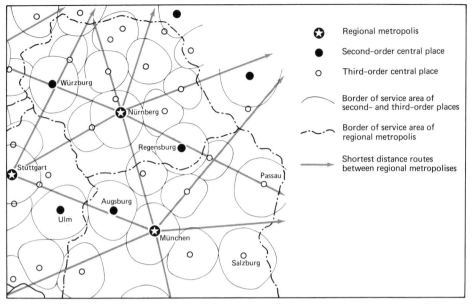

Figure 11.15   Distribution of major central places in the province of Bayern, West Germany. Even with a multitude of distorting causal forces at work, the distribution of the three highest orders of central places in southeastern Germany bears a clear relationship to Christaller's market, transport, and political principles (compare to Figures 11.13 and 11.14). Note the location of Würzburg midway between larger centers on the most direct routes, in accordance with the transport principle. The wreath of second- and third-order central places around München and Nürnberg is quite suggestive of the ideal market-principle pattern. The political border between West Germany and Austria caused central places along the boundary, such as Passau and Salzburg, to be of a lower order than would otherwise be the case. (After Christaller, 1933.)

Christaller felt that the traffic principle would gain the upper hand in densely settled industrialized countries where there were greater numbers of central places and a considerable demand for long-distance transportation. Self-sufficient lands, dominated by agriculture and more thinly settled, would tend to favor the market principle. Constriction of transport routes to narrow valleys in mountain areas favors the traffic principle, as is suggested by the distribution of central places in the Alpine valleys of Switzerland and Austria.

The *separation principle,* which might better be called the political principle, was formulated in recognition of the fact that national, regional, county, and other boundaries of administrative units tended to separate human communities, to isolate them, and to shield them from outside influences. The separation principle is disruptive because the political borders will tend to follow the hexagonal limits of the tributary area of the administrative central place of the political unit in question. Such a border, however, cuts through the "natural" trade area of lower-order central places in the border zone, disrupting the flow of goods and services (Figure 11.15).

The same disturbance results when political borders are arbitrarily imposed, without any consideration of the central-place hierarchy. The cities of Wien and Berlin, once central places of the highest order, declined when newly drawn borders cut them off from much of their former tributary territory. The amputation was especially severe for West Berlin, since the new border paralleled the outer western city limits. The Italian city of Trieste has been similarly affected, first by the loss of its extensive hinterland in Austria–Hungary in 1919, and more recently by the 1945 removal of its immediate tributary area in the Yugoslavian province of Istra. Central places in border regions generally tend to diminish in importance and size unless there is complete freedom of movement of people and goods across the line.

Further complications are caused by changes in local phenomena associated with the three basic principles. Modifications of the transport network, such as building new railroads or highways, as well as the abandonment of old routes, can change the number, distribution, and ranking of central places. Indeed, any innovation which alters the range of central goods and services will be significant in the spacing of tertiary towns and cities. A dynamic political situation can affect the separation principle. Christaller noted that the political union of southern Germany, which was begun in 1805 and completed in 1871, led to a more "rational" network of central places—that is, one in greater accordance with the market principle as the separation principle declined.

The central-place theory was applied by Christaller to the distribution of tertiary settlements in south Germany. He concluded that the three principles described with "astonishing exactness" the actual location of central places (Figure 11.15). Subsequent studies by other scholars of urban distribution elsewhere in Europe and in many overseas areas have essentially verified Christaller's proposal.

If Christaller erred, it was in overestimating dynamic forces. Even his area of special study, south Germany, has an urban heritage based to a remarkable degree in the Middle Ages. Towns such as Nördlingen, Dinkelsbühl, and Rothenburg-ob-der-Tauber are so perfectly preserved from medieval times that they actually function as tourist attractions as well as central places. Miraculously spared by war, they stand within their walls as museum pieces. Their spacing more nearly reflects the range of central goods typical of the fifteenth century than the modern era. The historical geographer C. T. Smith noted that the towns with charters in late medieval south Germany lay, on the average, about four or five hours' journey from one another and served a hinterland of 100 to 130 square kilometers (40 to 50 square miles). The ability of a medieval peasant to walk from his home to town and back in a single day was apparently a more important criterion in the spacing of European central places than the mobility provided later by railroads and motor vehicles.

In short, Christaller appears to have underestimated the remarkable persistence of the archaic in Europe, a persistence related not only to towns and cities, but also to institutions such as the farm village and fragmented holding. His theory is not less valid, but requires greater consideration of those historical causal factors now vanished.

*   *   *

JUST AS AN UNDERSTANDING of the rural landscape of Europe requires a knowledge of archaic, often prehistoric, causal factors, so the urban geography must be interpreted mainly in terms of the past. Almost every facet of the structure of European towns, including the morphology, siting, and spacing, is derived from medieval or even classical times. The urban European has proven almost as resistant to physical change as has his rural counterpart. He lives in cities which occupy defensive sites rendered obsolete by the acceptance of gunpowder six centuries ago, in cities better suited to oxcarts than to automobiles, in cities spaced to the advantage of the medieval peasant farmer rather than to the modern motorized European. If by chance the city is destroyed or badly damaged by warfare, fire, or natural disaster, the Europeans generally reconstruct the vanished relic to the best of their ability.

The resulting cities may be inefficient, but their character reflects the antiquity of European culture, rather than simply the demands of an industrial age. American cities suffer by comparison to their European counterparts in the all-important aesthetic sense.

SOURCES AND SUGGESTED READINGS

Jean Bastié. *La croissance de la banlieue parisienne*. Paris: Presses Universitaires de France, 1964.

J. Beaujeu-Garnier and G. Chabot. *Urban Geography*. New York: Wiley, 1967.

Maurice W. Beresford. *New Towns of the Middle Ages: Town Plantation in England, Wales, and Gascony*. London: Butterworth Press, 1967.

Brian J. L. Berry. *Geography of Market Centers and Retail Distribution*. Englewood Cliffs, N.J.: Prentice-Hall, 1967.

Brian J. L. Berry. *Theories of Urban Location: An Introductory Essay*. Washington, D.C.: Association of American Geographers, Commission on College Geography, Resource Paper No. 1, 1968.

Erdmann D. Beynon. "Budapest: An Ecological Study." *Geographical Review*. Vol. 33 (1943), pp. 256–275.

André Blanc. "Problème de géographie urbaine en Roumanie." *Revue géographique de l'est*. Vol. 3 (1963), pp. 307–331.

Hans Bobek and Elisabeth Lichtenberger. *Wien: Bauliche Gestalt und Entwicklung seit der Mitte des 19. Jahrhunderts*. Graz, Austria, and Köln, Germany: Hermann Böhlaus, 1966.

Dieter Böhn. *Kitzingen am Main: Stadtgeographie und zentralörtliche Beziehungen*. Würzburg, Germany: Würzburger Geographische Arbeiten, No. 28, 1969.

Gerald L. Burke. *The Making of Dutch Towns: A Study in Urban Development from the Tenth to the Seventeenth Centuries*. London: Cleaver-Hume, 1956.

W. I. Carruthers. "A Classification of Service Centres in England and Wales." *Geographical Journal*. Vol. 123 (1957), pp. 371–385.

H. Carter. "Aberystwyth: The Modern Development of a Medieval Castle Town in Wales." *Institute of British Geographers, Transactions and Papers*. Vol. 25 (1958), pp. 239–253.

Walter Christaller. *The Central Places of Southern Germany*. Translated by Carlisle W. Baskin. Englewood Cliffs, N.J.: Prentice-Hall, 1966 (originally published 1933).

J. T. Coppock and Hugh C. Prince (eds.). *Greater London*. London: Faber, 1964.

Jean Coppolani. *Toulouse: étude de géographie urbaine*. Toulouse: privately printed, 1954.

Vaughan Cornish. *The Great Capitals: An Historical Geography*. London: Methuen, 1923.

Wayne D. K. Davies. "The Morphology of Central Places: A Case Study." *Annals, Association of American Geographers*. Vol. 58 (1968), pp. 91–110.

Robert E. Dickinson. "The Morphology of the Medieval German Town." *Geographical Review*. Vol. 35 (1945), pp. 74–97.

Robert E. Dickinson. *The West European City: A Geographical Interpretation*. London: Routledge & Kegan Paul, 2nd ed., 1964.

Robert E. Dickinson. "Town Plans of East Anglia." *Geography*. Vol. 19 (1934), pp. 37–50.

Jack C. Fisher. "Urban Analysis: A Case Study of Zagreb, Yugoslavia." *Annals, Association of American Geographers*. Vol. 53 (1963), pp. 266–284.

Thomas W. Freeman. *The Conurbations of Great Britain*. Manchester: University Press, 1959.

Lucien Gallois. "The Origin and Growth of Paris." *Geographical Review*. Vol. 13 (1923), pp. 345–367.

W. Geisler. *Die deutsche Stadt*. Stuttgart, Germany: Forschungen zur deutschen Landes- und Volkskunde, No. 22, 1924.

Pierre George, Pierre Randet, and Jean Bastié. *La région parisienne*. Paris: Presses Universitaires de France, 1959.

Pierre George. "Problèmes géographiques de la reconstruction et l'aménagement des villes en Europe occidentale depuis 1945." *Annales de Géographie*. Vol. 69 (1960), pp. 2–14.

Erwin A. Gutkind. *International History of City Development*. New York: Free Press, Vols. 1–4, 1964–1969.

Peter Hall. *London 2000*. London: Faber, 1963.

Hugo Hassinger. "Boden und Lage Wiens." *Mitteilungen der Geographischen Gesellschaft in Wien*. Vol. 84 (1941), pp. 359–384.

Lutz Holzner. "The Role of History and Tradition in the Urban Geography of West Germany." *Annals, Association of American Geographers*. Vol. 60 (1970), pp. 315–339.

James M. Houston. *A Social Geography of Europe*. London: Duckworth, 1953, chs. 7–9.

James H. Johnson. *Urban Geography: An Introductory Analysis*. Elmsford, N.Y.: Pergamon, 1967.

Emrys Jones. *A Social Geography of Belfast*. London: Oxford University Press, 1960.

Emrys Jones. *Towns and Cities*. London: Oxford University Press, 1966.

F. Leyden. *Die Städte des flämischen Landes*. Stuttgart, Germany: Forschungen zur deutschen Landes- und Volkskunde, No. 23, 1925.

Richard L. Morrill. "The Development of Spatial Distributions of Towns in Sweden: An Historical-Predictive Approach." *Annals, Association of American Geographers*. Vol. 53 (1963), pp. 1–14.

Rhoads Murphey. "The City as a Center of Change: Western Europe and China." *Annals, Association of American Geographers*. Vol. 44 (1954), pp. 349–362.

Norman J. G. Pounds. "The Urbanization of the Classical World." *Annals, Association of American Geographers*. Vol. 59 (1969), pp. 135–157.

Roland Pourtier. "Munich: croissance démographique et développement industriel." *Annales de Géographie*. Vol. 76 (1967), pp. 129–151.

Allan R. Pred. *The External Relations of Cities During "Industrial Revolution," with a Case Study of Göteborg, Sweden, 1868–1890*. Chicago: University of Chicago, Department of Geography Research Paper No. 76, 1962.

Edward T. Price. "Viterbo: Landscape of an Italian City." *Annals, Association of American Geographers*. Vol. 54 (1964), pp. 242–275.

G. Sidenbladh. "Stockholm: A Planned City." *Scientific American*. Vol. 213 (September 1965), pp. 107–118.

A. E. Smailes. *The Geography of Towns*. London: Hutchinson, 1966.

Clifford T. Smith. *An Historical Geography of Western Europe Before 1800*. New York: Praeger, 1967, chs. 2, 6.

Dan Stanislawski. "The Origin and Spread of the Grid-Pattern Town." *Geographical Review*. Vol. 36 (1946), pp. 105–120.

M. B. Stedman. "The Townscape of Birmingham in 1956." *Institute of British Geographers, Transactions and Papers*. Vol. 25 (1958), pp. 225–238.

W. Steigenga. "The Urbanization of the Netherlands." *Tijdschrift voor Economische en Sociale Geografie*. Vol. 54 (1963), pp. 46–52.

David Thomas. "London's Green Belt: The Evolution of an Idea." *Geographical Journal*. Vol. 129 (1963), pp. 14–24.

Huguette Vivian. "La zone d'influence régionale de Grenoble." *Revue de Géographie Alpine*. Vol. 47 (1959), pp. 539–583.

David Ward. "The Pre-Urban Cadaster and the Urban Pattern of Leeds." *Annals, Association of American Geographers*. Vol. 52 (1962), pp. 150–166.

W. William-Olsson. "Stockholm: Its Structure and Development." *Geographical Review*. Vol. 30 (1940), pp. 420–438.

Michael J. Woldenberg. "The Identification of Mixed Hexagonal Central Place Hierarchies with Examples from Finland, Germany, Ghana, and Nigeria." *Harvard Papers in Theoretical Geography*, No. 5 (October 1967).

CHAPTER TWELVE

Transportation and trade

The highly developed economy of Europe requires efficient systems of transportation and communication to handle the exchange of commodities. Trade, and hence transportation, between any two areas is based on several elementary economic prerequisites: (1) the existence of surplus products in at least one of the two areas, (2) a desire of one area to obtain the surplus produce of the other area, (3) a competitive advantage for the potential supplying area in the production of the desired surplus, (4) an ability of the people in the potential importing area to pay for the desired product, (5) an absence of intervening, more attractive, opportunities for the sale of the surplus at some place nearer than the potential importing area, and (6) a transport cost sufficiently low that the ability of the people in the importing area to purchase the product is not greatly impaired. Europe abounds with situations which meet all of these requirements.

Many factors other than economic ones influence transport and trade. Among them, political fragmentation is particularly important in Europe. Political boundaries have traditionally been reinforced by tariffs which restricted trade, and limits placed on the number of border crossing points retarded development of an effective international transport network. Borders have at times been closed for military or strategic reasons. Perhaps the most impressive political impact on trade and transportation in modern Europe has been the drastic decline in exchange of goods between East and West Germany after World War II, the result of a new boundary drawn through the middle of what had been a unified country. Highway, airline, and waterway connections were severed or greatly restricted at this new boundary. The political factor has also operated in a positive way in Europe, to facilitate trade and transportation. From the time of the caesars and earlier, political organization into states and empires has led to the building of roads to serve the purposes of internal administration and troop movement.

The economic and political factors are joined by a host of other cultural influences which shape the transport system and the movement of goods. Among these, religion plays a major role. The movement of products such as wine and dried fish within Europe was long a reflection of Christian religious dietary requirements, and many routes were originally designed principally for pilgrim movement. Other regional food and beverage preferences, not associated with religion, have also stimulated trade. For example, the British fondness for tea has led to an old and profitable trade with lands of South Asia.

These and many other factors, operating both today and in the past, have determined the character of the European transport system.

12.1 THE TRANSPORTATION SYSTEM

The most important

Europeans have devised a number of ways to move commodities from one area to another. Of these, the most ancient and basic is transportation overland on roads, by foot, domestic animal, or wheeled vehicle.

ROADS

Roads almost invariably started out as crude tracks or trails, acquiring such improvements as bridges and pavement relatively late in their development. These early routes were much influenced by the physical environment, as travelers sought low mountain passes, shallow river fords, and level valley corridors. The first significant road improvements were accomplished by the Romans.

built for troop mobility & used by poor

THE ROMAN ROADS. Even though the Roman Empire was centered on the Mediterranean Sea, the need and desire to move overland was great. The rivers which emptied into the Mediterranean were short and of irregular flow, a consequence of the pronounced seasonality of precipitation; such streams were not satisfactory routes to the interior of Iberia, the Balkans, or even the narrow peninsula of Italy. Unlike the Greeks, the Romans desired to be masters of more than a thin coastal strip around the Mediterranean shore, and this wish to penetrate and hold interior lands led them to build a truly astounding network of roads (Figure 12.1).

Control of their lands

The Roman roads connected all parts of the empire in Europe and even included extensive development in peripheral provinces such as Britain. In the empire as a whole, they constructed some 320,000 kilometers (200,000 miles) of paved highway, some of which is still in use now (Figure 12.2). Oldest of the Roman roads was the famous Via Appia, or Appian Way, begun in 312 B.C. under the direction of Appius Claudius Caecus, whose name was given to the road. The Via Appia originally reached southeastward from Roma some 212 kilometers (132 miles) to Capua and was later extended on to Tarentum (modern Taranto) and Brundisium (modern Brìndisi) on the Adriatic coast of southern Italy.

The routes of Roman roads were laid out by surveyors, resulting in long,

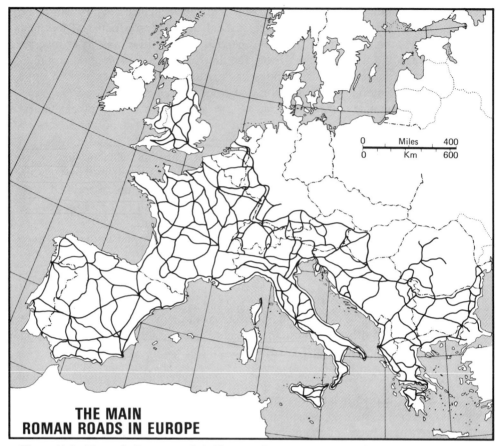

Figure 12.1   The main Roman roads in Europe. (Source: Westermann.)

perfectly straight stretches, with some accommodation made for terrain features. The preparatory excavation typically extended to a depth of one to two meters (four to six feet), into which were placed successive layers of rubble, flat slab-stones set in mortar, concrete mixed with crushed stone, and flat paving stones fitted closely together and fringed by curbstones. A slight arch to the pavement served to shed rainwater into drainage ditches on either side. The paved highways were mainly built by and for the Roman army and provided a troop mobility hitherto unknown. They were also used by merchants and the common folk, most of whom traveled the Roman highway system on foot because they owned no wheeled vehicles, though the pavement was admirably suited for carriages and chariots.

Even more visually impressive than the stretches of solid pavement were the bridges. The Romans did not shrink from the task of spanning even major streams such as the Rhône. Some of these splendid stone structures are still in use, even after 2000 years of traffic, flood, and warfare. Among them is one over the Tajo River in Alcántara, Spain, built without the use of mortar.

Contrary to the popular saying, not all roads led to Roma (Figure 12.1). A fine network with few major focal points was laid out, indicative of the military

Figure 12.2   A section of the Roman Via Appia, or Appian Way, which led southward from the imperial capital. Roman highways such as this were so well constructed that some survive and are still in use today. Even the curbstones are still in place. (Photograph ENIT, courtesy Italian Government Travel Office.)

rather than economic outlook of the highway-planners. Those few towns which had numerous roads radiating out from them were usually *not* the places which have developed as major transport centers in more recent times, in part because the modern flow of goods and people is different from that of Roman times. In France, for example, the main road junctions were at Reims (Durocortorum) and Arles (Arelate) rather than Paris, though the latter was located at the point where a Roman road crossed the Seine. Similarly, the main junction in Spain, Zaragoza (Caesarea Augusta), is of little importance today.

The Romans were so far ahead of their time in highway-building that most European countries equaled their achievements only within the last century or so. For the better part of a thousand years following the fall of the empire, the surviving Roman roads continued to be the best in Europe, a tribute to the care and precision with which they were built. Abandonment of Roman highways was generally due to changes in the directional flow of commodities and altered administrative needs rather than deterioration of the pavement. Considerable mileage remains structurally sound to the present day.

The decline of trade and urbanism during the Dark Ages greatly curtailed the use of roads, as did excessive political fragmentation. A rebirth of major mercantile activity in medieval times, coupled with the internal security provided by the feudal system, renewed the use of roads, including those in areas which had been beyond the frontiers of imperial Roma. The new roads were hardly the equals of their Roman predecessors. As a rule, they were completely unsurfaced; pavement was a rarity. Numerous streams were not bridged and, as a consequence, river-ford sites typified many newly emerging towns. Southern Europe, where Roman highways were still much in use, was in a superior position to areas such as Germany or Scandinavia.

EMERGENCE OF NEW ROAD PATTERNS. In time, new road patterns emerged bearing the stamp of economy and politics. Regions which had undergone political unification, such as France and the United Kingdom, displayed highly centralized road patterns by the eighteenth or nineteenth centuries, with the major routes radiating out from the national capital (Figure 12.3). Paris was the all-important hub of French roads, and Dublin served a similar function within Ireland. On the other hand, no transport focal point was found within the network of politically fragmented Germany, reflecting the lack of governmental organization.

For trade purposes, some new routes unused in earlier times were opened. The St. Gotthard Pass through the Swiss Alps, ignored by the Romans, became the great north–south route between Italy and the Rhine Valley in the Middle Ages, supplanting the Splügen Pass just to the east, which had been a Roman route. The dominance of the St. Gotthard Pass was facilitated by the construction of a bridge and road on its northern approach in the 1200s. The importance of this route has survived to the present.

Improvements in the post-Roman roads came very slowly. The first major advance in surfacing was achieved by the Scotsman John McAdam, for whom *macadam* roads are named. He built all-weather highways in England in the early 1800s, paved with several thin layers of tightly packed crushed rock set firmly in place by the application of water. The dawn of the modern era of bridge-building

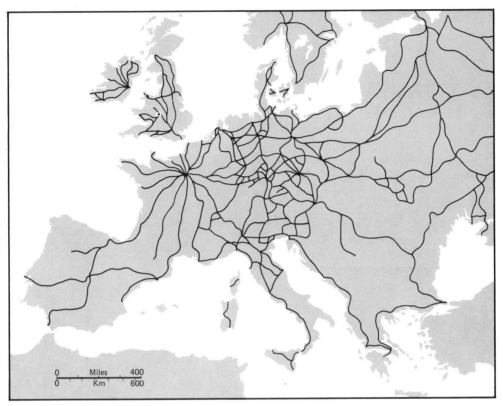

Figure 12.3 Main post roads in Europe, 1850. Note the highly centralized patterns in France and the United Kingdom and the lack of a dominant focal point in central Europe. (After Hoffman and Houston.)

occurred in 1826, when the British constructed a steel suspension bridge across the Menai Strait, linking the island of Anglesey to the coast of Wales.

THE AGE OF THE AUTOMOBILE.   Continued improvement of Europe's highway system has come about principally as a result of the automobile. Europeans accepted cars somewhat later than the Americans; the middle class gained the financial ability to purchase cars only in the 1950s and 1960s. Automobile ownership still remains uncommon in many countries of eastern and southern Europe, and the number of cars per unit of population is nowhere as high as in the United States (Figure 12.4). France led in total number of automobiles in 1968, with 11,500,000, followed closely by the United Kingdom and West Germany. Swedes have more completely accepted the automobile than any other European group, boasting a ratio of one car for every four persons in the mid-1960s. The numbers are rising very rapidly, as illustrated by the increase in Italy from 3,864,000 to 7,300,000 automobiles between 1963 and 1968. Dutch ownership of cars rose from 866,000 to 1,725,000 in the same period, and West Germany showed an increase from 2,500,000 to 11,300,000 between 1957 and 1968. The major manufacturers of automobiles are in West Germany, Italy, the United Kingdom, France, Sweden, and Belgium, countries where the middle class is affluent enough to purchase cars.

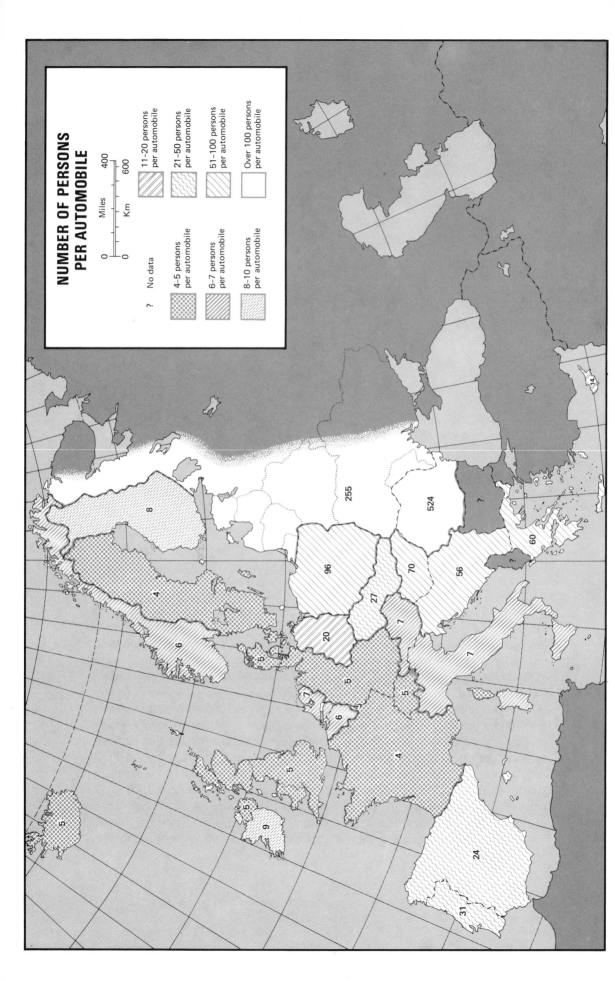

NUMBER OF PERSONS
PER AUTOMOBILE

?   No data

4–5 persons
per automobile

6–7 persons
per automobile

8–10 persons
per automobile

11–20 persons
per automobile

21–50 persons
per automobile

51–100 persons
per automobile

Over 100 persons
per automobile

Miles   0   400

Km   0   600

The European road system is generally ill-suited to the automobile age. Highways are often little more than paved-over wagon and coach roads of the nineteenth century, characterized by narrowness, sharp curves, and a gauntlet of trees planted only a foot or two away from the edge of pavement. They wind through farm villages, where metal mirrors are sometimes installed at blind corners to warn drivers of oncoming traffic. Furthermore, unpaved roads remain extremely common in eastern and parts of southern Europe, as well as in Iceland. It is true that very few points in the European culture area lie more than 40 kilometers (25 miles) from a motorable road—a condition limited to parts of interior northern Scandinavia, Iceland, and some small areas in the Balkans—but the condition of the roads leaves much to be desired.

Western Europeans have, in effect, accepted the automobile without fully accepting the burden of creating a first-rate highway system. There are some exceptions. The Netherlands had fine four-lane, divided highways in operation as early as the 1950s, and West Germany has continually lengthened and improved the *Autobahn* system bequeathed by the military planners of the Nazi period. Still, even a city as large as München (1,250,000) until very recently had *Autobahnen* leading only to the city limits, where all of the traffic was funneled into the narrow city streets. No outer-belt expressway existed to handle through traffic until the demands of handling the 1972 Olympic games spurred construction. Italy has actively pushed construction of its *Autostrada* expressway system, but progress lags considerably behind the need, as is the case in France. Roads are being improved throughout most of Europe, but the number of drivers is increasing so rapidly as to overwhelm most of the progress.

All European countries have excellent government-operated bus lines. These are particularly important in the south and east, where they are much used by the rural population.

The condition of the roads is partly responsible for a terribly high accident rate. For example, in West Germany, a nation of 60 million, 17,000 persons died on the highways in 1967 and an additional 461,000 were injured. Germany experienced one traffic death for about every 650 automobiles registered in 1967, as contrasted to only one death for every 1,500 cars in the United States. Perhaps also contributing to the higher accident rate is the absence of speed limits on highways, though several countries, including Belgium, have recently set limits. The British custom of driving on the left, a practice they abandon with varying degrees of success when vacationing on the mainland, further complicates the traffic problem. Sweden recently enforced a legal changeover from left- to right-side traffic with a minimum of negative consequences.

RAILROADS

While highways represent an ancient transport system and are increasing in importance, railroads are relatively new and of declining significance.

The railroad is a European invention, and almost one-third of the total rail mileage in the world is found in Europe. Some 400,000 kilometers (250,000 miles) of right-of-way is woven into a splendid rail network which covers nearly

Figure 12.4 Number of persons per automobile. (Source: United Nations, *Statistical Yearbook*, 1968.)

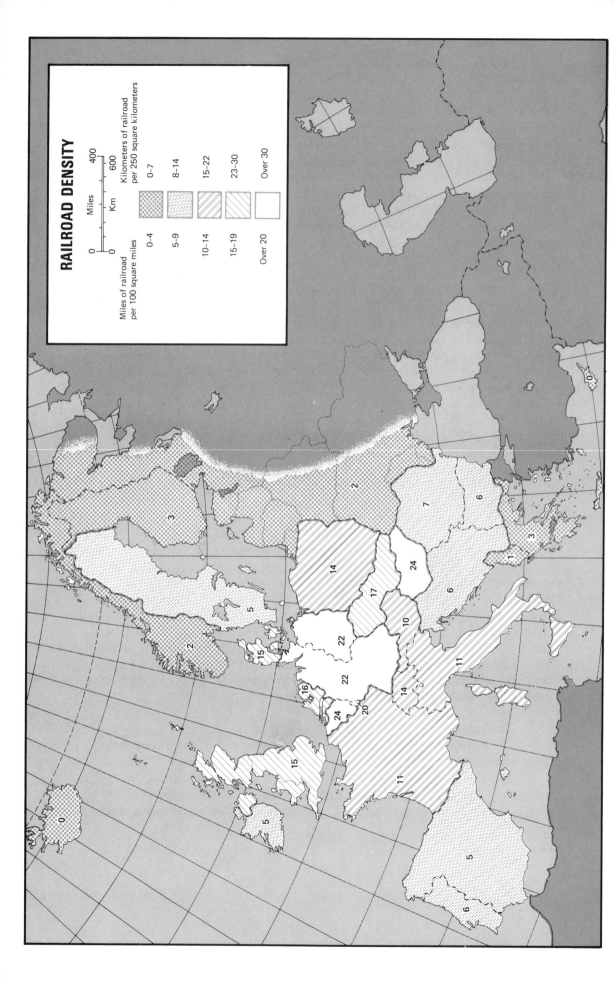

RAILROAD DENSITY

Miles of railroad
per 100 square miles

	0–4
	5–9
	10–14
	15–19
	Over 20

Kilometers of railroad
per 250 square kilometers

0–7
8–14
15–22
23–30
Over 30

Miles

0   400

Km

0   600

all parts of the culture area. Effectiveness of the network is somewhat diminished by a difference in track gauge between western and eastern Europe. The concentration of lines is densest in northwestern Europe, reaching a peak in Belgium, which has 15 kilometers of track per 100 square kilometers of territory (24 miles per 100 square miles) (Figure 12.5). Peripheral parts of Europe have less rail mileage; Iceland and Cyprus have no railroads at all. On the mainland, Albania ranks lowest with only 0.56 kilometer of rail per 100 square kilometers (0.9 mile per 100 square miles). In total mileage of right-of-way, France ranks highest with 40,000 kilometers (25,000 miles), followed by the United Kingdom and West Germany. Europeans rely to a greater extent on railroads for transport than do Americans, Australians, or other overseas peoples.

The European railroad system is a product of the technology developed in Britain in the Industrial Revolution. In 1767 an English iron works cast the first all-iron rails, followed two years later by the patenting of the first efficient steam engine by James Watt. For a time, horse-drawn trams were used on the newly developed rails, but a crude steam locomotive was invented by 1804. Ten years later George Stephenson carried out a successful experiment in which a locomotive pulled a train. By 1825 the British opened the first regularly operated railroad service, connecting the industrial towns of Darlington and Stockton on the River Tees in northeastern England. The British invention, which had been prompted by increased demands for bulk transport associated with the Industrial Revolution, spread rapidly to mainland Europe, reaching France by 1832, Belgium and Germany by 1835, Austria–Hungary by 1838, Italy and the Netherlands by 1839, and Switzerland by 1844. Albania was one of the last European nations to join the railroad age, constructing its first line in 1947.

By 1850 a railroad network had developed in Great Britain and Flanders, and significant beginnings had been made in the Paris Basin, Prussia, and Austria–Hungary (Figure 12.6). Elsewhere, only scattered fragments of future networks were to be seen. The great era of rail construction was completed by 1900, when the present network was intact. In most mainland countries of Europe, railroad building *preceded* major industrialization, unlike Britain, where railroads *followed* industrialization. For example, the first German steam railroad began operating in 1835, connecting the towns of Nürnberg and Fürth in Bayern, fully a quarter century before the great industrial rise of the Ruhr began. This antecedence allowed mainland industries somewhat greater choice of location, for they were not tied so closely to raw materials as were the earlier factories in Britain.

The advantage of railroads is their ability to carry a large volume of heavy items in a short time at a low cost. Higher terminal charges for loading and unloading place railroads at a disadvantage in competition with trucks for short-distance hauls—distances less than 56 to 80 kilometers (35 to 50 miles)—but the efficiency realized from larger loads gives railroads the competitive advantage for longer hauls. If the goods are to be transported more than 650 kilometers (400 miles), and time is not a major consideration, then waterways surpass railroads in efficiency.

Most railroads in Europe, in both Communist and non-Communist nations,

Figure 12.5 Railroad density, 1968. The figures shown are for miles of rail per hundred square miles of territory.

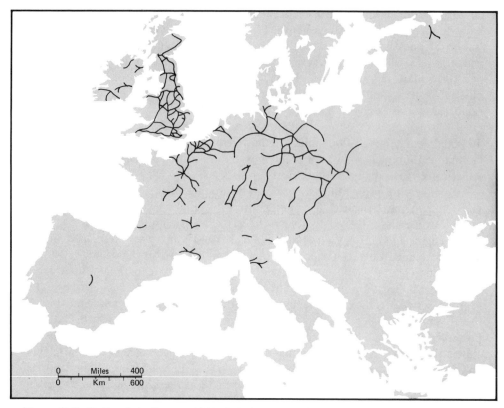

Figure 12.6   Railroads in Europe, 1850. Only in Great Britain and parts of the Low Country and Germany had a network been developed. (After Hoffman and Westermann.)

are owned by the state rather than private organizations. State ownership has avoided uneconomical competing lines which have plagued American railroads for many years. Another difference from American railroads is the greater reliance on electric power for locomotion. In some countries, including France, electric power is now dominant, and it is of increasing importance in others, such as West Germany (Figure 12.7). As recently as 1967, 37 percent of all locomotives in West Germany were still driven by steam power, as opposed to 31 percent electric and 32 percent diesel, but steam was in sharp decline.

Due to the later spread of the automobile in Europe, railroads have retained major importance as passenger carriers, not declining until the 1960s. Many workers still rely on trains to commute to their jobs, and almost all cities and towns of any significance have access to rail passenger service, though branch lines are being abandoned in some countries. The recent decline, which is confined mainly to western Europe, is reflected by the drop of passenger rail cars in West Germany from 22,610 in 1958 to 18,671 in 1967.

WATER TRANSPORT
Complementing the fine road and rail systems is an intricate network of waterways. It consists of Europe's peripheral seas and rivers, connected by a series of canals.

THE PERIPHERAL SEAS.   The interconnected oceans and seas which flank Europe on three sides have since antiquity provided a splendid opportunity for transportation. The outline of Europe shows deep indentations on all shorelines, with the result that no part of the culture area lies any great distance from the sea. In spite of the excessive political fragmentation, only five of the twenty-seven major independent countries are landlocked. It is small wonder that Europeans have long taken advantage of the pattern of peripheral seas to move their commodities from place to place.

The Mediterranean was the first to be used extensively. It was admirably suited to navigation for early peoples who had relatively few advanced marine skills, because ships could sail about its waters without ever losing sight of land. High, rocky coasts, whose promontories were made even more visible by the erection of temples and shrines, guided the sailors of ancient Phoenicia and Greece, as did the many mountainous islands. By "coasting" parallel to the shore or keeping island landfalls in sight, the sailors overcame much of the danger of sea transport. At a remarkably early date, Mediterranean seamen ventured out beyond Gibraltar as far as Cornwall, where tin mines were established. The braver and more competent mariners struck out across open seas, with no land in sight; thus the Phoenicians discovered Iceland a millennium before the Norse colonists arrived there.

Still, at the time of the Homeric epics, about 1200 B.C., the Greeks apparently were ignorant of even the western part of the Mediterranean. Presumably this lack of information was the heritage of a period of cultural decline after about 1400 B.C., during which Greek culture relapsed into illiteracy. Ulysses' relatively short voyage to lands around the Tyrrhenian Sea west of Italy placed him in unknown waters, where lack of familiarity caused his fear and imagination to people

Figure 12.7   An electric-powered passenger train, Le Mistral, races at high speed through the French countryside. It is named for the strong winds which blow down the Rhône–Saône valley. A large proportion of European railroad traffic relies on electric power. (Photo courtesy French National Railroads.)

the shores with one-eyed cannibalistic giants, sorceresses who changed men to swine, and the like. In later centuries the Greeks searched out every bay and cove around the Mediterranean and used the sea as the highway of their far-flung commercial empire. The Romans succeeded the Phoenicians and Greeks. They in turn gave way to other great Mediterranean maritime peoples, including the Byzantine Greeks and Venetians.

The use of the North and Baltic seas for trade increased gradually after the fall of the Roman Empire. By the eighth century a lively trade in furs, slaves, and amber was being carried on in the Baltic, while merchants in the North Sea handled cloth, wine, and wool. Disruption by Viking raids was followed in the Middle Ages by formation of the Hanseatic League, or Hansa, an economic union of many towns, mainly in countries around the shores of the North and Baltic seas.

With the Age of Discovery, the Atlantic assumed its present position as the major trade route of Europe. Beyond its waters the Europeans discovered and colonized much of the rest of the world, in particular the Americas. A major breakthrough in oceanic transport came in the nineteenth century when the British developed the first long-distance steamships made of steel.

INLAND WATERWAYS.   Complementing the well-situated peripheral seas are numerous navigable rivers, which man has improved through dredging, removing rapids, constructing locks, and digging connecting canals. The major use of rivers and canals for transportation began only in the Middle Ages, for the classical Mediterranean peoples did not have navigable rivers at their disposal. The rivers of southern Europe were generally too short and variable in flow to use for boats. Only after the commercial focus of Europe shifted north of the Alps did river traffic become important.

The North European Plain is drained by a series of parallel navigable rivers trending southeast to northwest in direction, most of which rise in the hills and mountains south of the plain. Those more favored by nature were already in major use by the 1100s and 1200s, and the feudal lords who resided along the banks of such streams as the Rhine made it a practice to collect tolls from ships passing beneath their strongholds. In modern times some rivers have been internationalized, and the countries through which they flow cannot charge unnecessary tolls or restrict traffic. The Rhine is now an international river.

The navigable rivers of Europe are bound together by canals, most of which date from recent times. Canal-building slightly antedated railroad construction, beginning in earnest in the late 1700s and reaching a peak in the first half of the nineteenth century. Most canals were designed to connect different rivers on the North European Plain, including those in the lowland section of Great Britain. The English were the leaders in canal-building as well as railroads, and by 1790 they had established a good network. Some 8000 kilometers (5000 miles) of canals were in use in the United Kingdom by the middle of the nineteenth century.

Mainland canal construction has continued into the present century. It is possible to move by river and canal across the North European Plain from France to Russia. The densest pattern of canals and navigable rivers found anywhere in the world lies between the Seine and Odra in France, the low countries, Germany, and western Poland. Perhaps most notable is the Mittelland Canal of Germany, which runs along the southern edge of the North German Plain, connecting the

Weser River and points further west with the city of Berlin. Other canals lead eastward to the Odra, Wisla, and Dnepr rivers and westward to the Rhine, Seine, Loire, and others. At the heart of this waterway network is the Rhine, which carries more traffic than any other river in the world.

Other canals were dug to connect adjacent seas. The Caledonia Canal, completed in 1822, leads across northern Scotland, while the Kiel Canal, also a product of the nineteenth century, connects the North and Baltic seas through the Schleswig–Holstein province of West Germany. In France, Atlantic–Mediterranean links were established by the Canal du Midi through the Gap of Carcassonne in the south and by canals linking the Rhône River to the Loire, Seine, and Rhine. In central and southeastern Europe, an improved Atlantic–Black Sea water route will be available by about 1980 as the Rhine–Main–Danube (Ludwig) canal is upgraded and locks at the difficult Iron Gate gorge on the lower Danube are constructed.

Inland waterways are used to a greater extent in Europe than in any other major industrial zone of the world. Rivers and canals carry fully 30 percent of all intercity freight traffic in Europe, as opposed to less than 10 percent in the United States. In some parts of Europe, however, the waterways have declined in importance, especially in Great Britain. In general, inland waterways can compete effectively with other forms of transportation only in cases where speed is unimportant and distance is great enough to allow the low movement costs to offset the high terminal charges. At distances less than about 560 to 650 kilometers (350 to 400 miles), highway and railroad transport is cheaper, and Great Britain is too small an island to offer the possibility or need for long-distance hauls. The British inland waterway system was built before competition from railroads and highways existed, and the development of these rival facilities rendered the rivers and canals obsolete. By 1948, some 6500 kilometers (4000 miles) of the original British waterway system had already been abandoned, and the decline has continued in recent decades. At present, with few exceptions the waterways of Great Britain perform a limited transport function, mostly on the canalized rivers. Another country where use of canals has declined is Sweden, where the Göta Canal built in the nineteenth century is now used mainly by private pleasure boats and small tourist ships. In Sweden the problems of winter freezing and railway and highway competition caused large-scale commercial abandonment of inland waterways. Moreover, many of the older European canals are of outmoded construction, too narrow or shallow for modern barges.

CANALIZATION OF THE MOSEL (MOSELLE) RIVER.   Representative of the recent and continuing expansion and improvement of inland waterways in the Seine–Odra core of mainland Europe is the canalization of the Mosel River. The highly successful project is centered in a 275-kilometer (170-mile) stretch between Koblenz, West Germany, where the Mosel flows into the Rhine, and Thionville in French Lorraine. The canalized river skirts the northern and western side of the Saar industrial area and also borders on Luxembourg for some distance. This project, completed in the 1960s, deepened the sinuous course of the Mosel by installing fourteen locks. Expense was minimal due to the absence of rapids, regularity of flow, and rarity of floods on the river.

Most Germans, including the Ruhr industrialists, opposed the project because of the boost it provided for metallurgical industries in the Lorraine province of France and in Luxembourg, but the West German government approved it as one concession to the French in exchange for the restoration of the Saar district. The canalization allows cheaper importation of Ruhr coking coal to the Lorraine and the Saar, but it also allows French ironmakers and steelmakers in Lorraine to import iron ore from foreign sources such as Sweden. The local iron-ore deposits of the Lorraine are of low quality and are not adequate for present or future needs.

THE PORTS OF EUROPE.   The elaborate network of seas, rivers, and canals focuses on Europe's numerous port facilities, most of which lie at the transshipment points between inland waterways and the open ocean. A string of major ports is found along the shores of the North and Baltic seas, at the mouths of the rivers of the North European Plain; these include, from west to east, Bordeaux (Garonne River), LeHavre (Seine), London (Thames), Antwerpen (Schelde), Rotterdam (Rhine), Bremerhaven (Weser), Hamburg (Elbe), Szczecin (Odra), and Gdańsk (Wisla). In contrast, the major ports of southern Europe, including Barcelona, Marseille, Genova, and Napoli, are generally not riverine. Instead, they are situated on coasts some distance removed from river mouths.

The greatest port of Europe is Rotterdam in the Netherlands, reflecting the huge volume of traffic carried by the Rhine and Maas rivers. Rotterdam began to grow rapidly in the last three decades of the nineteenth century, coincident with the rise of the Ruhr and other industrial areas along the Rhine. By 1938 the Dutch port was the largest in Europe in terms of tonnage handled; in 1962 it became number one tonnage port in the world, surpassing New York City. Rotterdam is primarily a transit port, serving to transship the raw materials entering the Rhine area and to export finished products and coking coal produced in Germany, eastern Belgium, and part of France and Switzerland. A rapidly increasing amount of industry is also located in Rotterdam, including the refining of imported petroleum.

The rapid expansion since the destruction of World War II has forced the Rotterdam port area to spread westward toward the North Sea, mainly on the island of Rozenburg, which forms the southern shore of the New Waterway (Nieuwe Waterweg), the main channel connecting Rotterdam to the sea. North of the New Waterway is an area of intensive market-garden agriculture which the Dutch did not wish to destroy by building new port facilities; thus mainly Rozenburg, laboriously won by reclamation in centuries past, is being sacrificed to Rotterdam's growth. However, some facilities are being constructed on the north bank of the New Waterway. Rozenburg is being developed in two separate projects, the Botlek Scheme and the Europoort Plan. The former project in eastern Rozenburg, begun in 1952, adds 1417 hectares (3500 acres) to the port area, including also new oilrefining facilities, chemical factories, and shipbuilding yards. Europoort in western Rozenburg, begun in 1958, is nearest the sea and handles the huge supertankers and other modern oversized vessels which cannot be accommodated at the older docks.

PIPELINES

Rudimental pipeline transport can be traced back to the aqueducts built widely in southern Europe to supply water for the Roman towns. Some Roman systems are still functional. Most pipelines date from World War II, when petroleum and natural gas began to displace coal as the primary fuels consumed in the major industrial centers of Europe.

The pattern of pipelines closely reflects the political division between East and West in Europe. In the Communist sector, excluding Yugoslavia, the Soviet Union is the major supplier, and the so-called friendship pipeline leads from the Volga–Urals oil field in the distant reaches of the East European Plain into Poland, East Germany, Czechoslovakia, and Hungary. Dependence on Soviet oil helps restrain any move on the part of these countries to escape Russian domination. Romania, which is self-sufficient in oil production, has been able to pursue a more independent foreign policy.

Western and southern Europe are supplied with oil mainly from the Middle East and North Africa. Several major pipelines lead northward from the Mediterranean, beginning at Trieste and Genova in Italy, Marseille in France, and Málaga in Spain. Two of these lines cross the Alps to the German city of Ingolstadt on the Danube River in the province of Bayern, where a major refining center is developing. The pipeline from Marseille passes north through the Rhône–Saône Corridor, Belfort Gate, and Upper Rhine Plain, reaching Karlsruhe in southwestern Germany and the Lorraine area of France. The Ruhr district is served by pipelines from both Rotterdam and Wilhelmshaven, the latter a port in northern Germany.

AIR TRANSPORT

The European transport system of roads, railroads, waterways, and pipelines has been supplemented in the twentieth century by ever-expanding use of air transport. Europe has a dense network of air routes and a large number of high-quality airlines, including Lufthansa (West Germany), Alitalia (Italy), Air France, Sabena (Belgium), KLM (Netherlands), British Overseas Airways, and many others. London's Heathrow Airport handles the world's largest volume of intercontinental traffic, and other major airports include Rhein-Main near Frankfurt, Orly south of Paris, Schiphol near Amsterdam, Tempelhof in West Berlin, and Kastrup at København.

As yet, the European air-transport system is an insignificant freight carrier, and freight charges remain high, here as elsewhere in the world. In both West Germany and Italy, two industrial giants of the Common Market, the leading airport is not located in the principal industrial core, indicating the unimportance of freight. Railroads are a major and successful competitor for the airlines in transporting businessmen between the various industrial centers.

Passenger traffic, especially the tourist trade, supports the various lines; consequently, catering to passengers has had a deciding influence in determining the location of the airfields which handle the largest volume. With several exceptions, the airports located in or near the capital cities of the various countries are the most important, suggesting that various types of business related to government also generate a great deal of traffic. One exception is West Germany, where the principal airport is Rhein-Main, near Frankfurt, rather than Bonn, which remains a small, nonindustrial city.

THE UNIQUE CHARACTER OF THE EUROPEAN TRANSPORT SYSTEM

The complex of roads, waterways, railroads, and other transport facilities found in Europe is not duplicated anywhere else in the world. Its uniqueness is based on a combination of traits. First, the great clustering of population in Europe, coupled with a high level of industrialization, has produced a transport network unequalled in density of routes. Hardly any areas are far removed from roads or railroads. Second, European countries, by American, Australian, or Soviet standards, are quite small, so all of Europe is built on a smaller scale, even the natural features. European visitors to America often feel overwhelmed by the dimensions of the land, just as German troops were bewildered by the seemingly endless Russian plains, which did not fit into their European concept of landform scale. Transport systems designed to serve small nations and small landform units can be expected to bear the imprint of miniaturization. For example, railroad rolling stock is smaller and trains make stops at shorter intervals than in the United States. Automobiles are smaller, a response both to greater crowding and to higher gasoline prices.

Also unique—at least from the American viewpoint—is the nationalization or seminationalization of transport facilities in Europe. Americans are accustomed to government control of highways and waterways, but European nations have also nationalized railroads, pipelines, and air transport. One result is fewer competing lines.

Another unique feature of European transport is the regional variety of systems. One country may emphasize railroads while its neighbor places greater investment in superhighways. The result is an assemblage of many different small-scale national transport systems in Europe, a contrast to the integration and grander scale of the American network.

INTEGRATION AND THE NEW MOBILITY

The regional variety of transport systems, coupled with inadequate connections across political borders, have caused major problems in recent decades as individual trade blocs in Europe moved toward economic integration. Since World War II, and especially since about 1960, international cooperation within Europe concerning the transport system has increased in an effort to improve the connections between countries.

Each nation had previously looked after its own transport facilities, with little or no regard to what its neighbors were doing; today much attention is focused on creating a network to serve all of Europe, a network designed to facilitate the movement of people and goods both within and between different countries. One example is the designation of European highways, selected international roads which will henceforth bear the same number in different countries. For example, Highway E (for Europe) -12 runs from Paris to Nürnberg, West Germany, and on beyond the Iron Curtain to Praha, Czechoslovakia, to Warszawá, Poland, and into the Soviet Union. Highway E-1 runs from Sicilia and southern Italy to Roma, Genova, Lyon, Paris, Le Havre, and from there by auto ferry to Southampton, England, and on to London.

The greatest progress toward integration of transport systems has been made in the area of the Common Market, which includes France, West Germany, Italy, the Netherlands, Belgium, and Luxembourg. The problems facing the Common Market countries as they work toward an integrated transport network are rooted in nationalism. Each country's system was built up prior to World War II to meet the particular needs of that country, in the light of strategic, economic, and physical environmental conditions. Almost every one of the Common Market member nations was unique in the particular pattern or emphasis of its transport system. The French government placed the greatest importance on railroads; even uneconomic lines were kept open as a public service. Both railroads and highways, however, concentrated on Paris, and interprovincial connections were ineffective.

Germany, on the other hand, had emphasized roads and pioneered superhighways with its· *Autobahn* system. The railroad network, built mainly before German unification in 1871, centered on different provincial capitals, while the *Autobahnen,* built after unification, linked the main industrial districts with Berlin. The highway system was severely disrupted by the partition of the country in 1945. In spite of the great importance of roads in Germany, however, the more efficient railroad system carried most of the freight.

Italy is also unique: It is the only Common Market member whose highways far exceed railroads and waterways as freight-carriers. In the Netherlands, on the other hand, 86 percent of all goods move by river and canal. The diversity is completed by Belgium, where an almost perfect balance between rail, highways, and inland water transport has been achieved.

Strategic motives prompted the individual countries to develop transport facilities which were not justified economically. Fearing to rely on the German Rhine River route, France built railroads and canals connecting the Alsace area with the French Atlantic coast, while the Germans, concerned with developing their own ports and rejecting total dependence on the Dutch port of Rotterdam as an outlet for the Rhineland, developed the port of Emden and tied it by canal to the Ruhr area.

Recognizing that full economic integration depends in part on a satisfactory overall transport network, the Common Market members have set about the task of converting the various national systems into a single international one. The development of a superhighway system caused the least problem, for the simple reason that relatively little mileage of such roads existed, except in West Germany, when the Common Market was founded. The great majority of superhighways have been built since the mid-1950s, their routes in part determined by international planning and cooperation to facilitate movement from country to country.

The railroad system has been improved by the double-tracking and electrification of select international routes such as Paris–Köln and Italy–West Germany via St. Gotthard and Brenner passes. Railroad reform also led to the establishment of the *Trans Europ Express,* serving the six Common Market countries plus Switzerland, the United Kingdom, and Austria. The Trans Europ Express is designed for businessmen moving between the major industrial centers of western Europe. It offers such attractions as (1) a guaranteed average speed of 140 kilometers (87 miles) per hour on level terrain, (2) a more than average amount of space per passenger, (3) border crossings free of delays, (4) high-quality food and service, (5) two lavatories per car, (6) a public address system to contact individual passengers, and (7) schedules designed to fit the needs of businessmen.

Since virtually all pipelines have been built since the origin of the Common Market, a functional international system exists today. Admirable cooperation led to the selection of south Germany as the oil-refining core of the Common Market, fed by pipelines originating in France and Italy.

The inland waterway system has been and is being altered to meet the needs of internationalism by such projects as the previously mentioned canalization of the Mosel River and the proposed construction of a new and better canal connection between the Rhône and Rhine rivers. A major north–south waterway route is emerging from Rotterdam to Marseille, via the Rhine, Rhône, and Saône, serving as a vital link in the Common Market area.

Internationalization has also permitted certain seaports to expand greatly and achieve their rightful economic status unhindered by the restrictive demands of nationalism. The remarkable rise of Rotterdam has already been mentioned. Other formerly national seaports have also become "Euroports," including Marseille, Antwerpen, Genova, and Le Havre. Marseille, formerly rather provincial, handled nearly six times as much tonnage in 1965 as in 1938 and is perhaps destined to become the second leading seaport in the Common Market. Much of its growth is due to the increased use of the Rhône–Rhine route between France and Germany and its location near North Africa and Middle Eastern oil supplies.

As a whole, the Common Market transport system is now dominated by north–south trunk lines. The Rhine–Rhône axis is the core of the system, and major highways, railroads, and pipelines parallel the waterways of this axis.

In addition to the integration of transport systems, there have been various international agreements on the movement of freight across borders, both within the Common Market and between different trade blocs. The agreements include moves toward standard freight rates, the awarding of special shipping privileges in both directions at many points along the Iron Curtain, and increased cooperation in scheduling of shipments. Europe is functioning increasingly as an economic unit, as the transport system is revised and expanded to better serve the newly developed unity.

12.2 TRADE

The essential purpose of the elaborate network of roads, waterways, railroads, pipelines, and air routes is to facilitate the exchange of goods. The peoples of Europe, more than those of most other parts of the world, depend on trade to perpetuate their way of life. The high European standard of living could not be maintained if the international and intercontinental trade ties which link the nations of Europe to each other and to the rest of the world were severed, for the culture area is poor in many resources.

INTRA-EUROPEAN TRADE

As described earlier, trade within Europe has been fundamentally altered by postwar developments, in particular the creation of the Common Market, European Free Trade Association, and COMECON. These, in turn, reflect changes in the political order, especially the East–West conflict. Few countries have failed to join one or another of the newly developed trade blocs. Exceptions are Spain, the Republic of Ireland, Greece, Yugoslavia, and Cyprus (Figure 10.4). Greece partially overcame the trade bloc isolation in 1963 by becoming an *Associated Country* of the Common Market, a temporary status presumably leading to full membership which allows many Greek products to enter the Common Market countries without tariff restrictions. Ireland will also soon become a member of the Common Market.

Most intra-European trade of the Common Market has been with members of the European Free Trade Association. The United Kingdom, Sweden, and Switzerland rank as the three leading European sources of import to the Common Market, while the major European consumers of Common Market exports are, in order, the United Kingdom, Switzerland, Spain, Denmark, and Austria. While trade with Communist Eastern Europe and the Soviet Union is increasing rapidly, it remains relatively unimportant at present for both the Common Market and the European Free Trade Association.

Within the European Free Trade Association, the most notable relationship was that which existed between the Scandinavian countries, especially Denmark and the United Kingdom. Denmark has long been an important supplier of food products to Britain, including dairy goods, meat, and eggs. The tie is so close that Denmark will probably join the Common Market when the United Kingdom does.

In Communist Europe, the Soviet Union attempted to establish a trade relationship in which the satellite countries would supply raw materials and consume Soviet-manufactured finished products. East Germany and western Czechoslovakia, areas where industrial development had long been established, were to be exceptions. Certain countries, in particular Romania, have rejected their position as economic colonies of the Soviet Union and sought trade ties with the West which might better allow them to develop industrially.

An important segment of the trade pattern within Europe, or at least within non-Communist Europe, can be described as a flow of raw materials and food from the less-industrialized peripheral countries inward to the manufacturing core (Figure 10.1). Finished products move in the opposite direction, from core to periphery. If those areas which export raw materials and import manufactured goods can be described as "colonial," then the periphery of Europe has colonial economic status.

EUROPE'S PLACE IN WORLD TRADE

While trade within Europe is vitally important, the exchange of goods between Europe and other parts of the world is of equal or even greater consequence. Much of the outside world functions as an extension of the colonial periphery of Europe, an area supplying raw materials for the industrial core of Europe and consuming a portion of its finished products. The manufacturers of the European core long ago found that adequate supplies of raw materials were not available within Europe itself. Their response was to reach out and annex the resources of Africa, the Middle East, and parts of the Orient and the Americas. Petroleum to fuel the factories and transport system reaches Europe from the oil-rich countries of the Middle East; cotton and wool for its textile mills arrive from India, Egypt, the United States, and Australia; meat, butter, tea, and wheat to feed its industrial population are imported from Argentina, Australia, New Zealand, India, and Canada; and so on. Europe lives far beyond its resource means.

To facilitate the movement of raw materials to Europe, and to guarantee their availability, many nations in the European culture area resorted traditionally to the practice of political colonialism or imperialism, and acquired political control over the areas supplying resources. To this end, the British, French, Dutch, and Belgians, mimicking the earlier success of the Spaniards and Portuguese, built huge overseas empires which areally far exceeded the size of the home countries. The Germans and Italians, though less successful, also acquired colonial empires; even tiny Denmark dabbled in colonialism.

Since World War II, Europeans have lost political control over nearly all the overseas empires they previously ruled. In some instances, as in the Dutch East Indies and Algeria, the Europeans were expelled by military force; in other cases they withdrew voluntarily.

The demise of imperialism had little effect on trade patterns. Underdeveloped lands which once supplied raw materials to Europe under the British or French flags today continue to supply them as independent countries. Economic colonialism has survived the death of political colonialism. The British Commonwealth preserves the trade patterns of the British Empire, though these are now endangered by the English move toward the Common Market, while the French Community links France to many of its former colonies. The Common Market offered a form of Associate Country membership to those countries in Africa which were once French, Belgian, or Italian colonies, and most of them accepted. Political colonialism itself has not totally vanished: Both the Netherlands and France retain small overseas territories which function as part of the Common Market. Over 80 percent of the value of Common Market exports is in manufactured goods, while the preponderance of imports are raw materials.

The United States is also a major trading partner of both the Common Market and the European Free Trade Association. Even here, however, the pattern of importing raw materials or partially processed goods and exporting manufactured goods persists, though many American-made industrial products do enter Europe. Japan has also risen to the position of a major trade partner of many European countries.

The greater part of western European overseas trade is with countries bordering on the Atlantic Ocean and those in the Middle East. Eastern Europe remains solidly in the Soviet economic sphere, and the Far East, an area in which Europeans once held colonies, appears to be almost entirely in the Japanese, American, and Chinese orbits.

*   *   *

THE HIGHLY DEVELOPED transport network and massive exchange of commodities are symptomatic of Europe's industrial, market-oriented economy. Much that is typically European is made possible by trade and the system of transportation. Without them, Europeans would not be among the healthiest, best fed, and richest peoples of the world.

SOURCES AND SUGGESTED READINGS

John W. Alexander. *Economic Geography*. Englewood Cliffs, N.J.: Prentice-Hall, 1963, chs. 26, 27.

J. H. Appleton. "Some Geographical Aspects of the Modernization of British Railways." *Geography*. Vol. 52 (1967), pp. 357–373.

J. H. Appleton. *The Geography of Communications in Great Britain*. London: Oxford University Press, 1962.

James Bird. *The Geography of the Port of London*. London: Hutchinson, 1957.

James Bird. "Seaports and the European Economic Community." *Geographical Journal*. Vol. 133 (1967), pp. 302–322.

R. Brunet. "Expansion et problèmes des canaux du Midi." *Revue Géographique des Pyrénées et du Sud-Ouest*. Vol. 35 (1964), pp. 207–213.

Albert S. Chapman. "Trans-Europ Express: Overall Travel Time in Competition for Passengers." *Economic Geography*. Vol. 44 (1968), pp. 283–295.

Robert E. Dickinson. "The Geography of Commuting in West Germany." *Annals, Association of American Geographers*. Vol. 49 (1959), pp. 443–456.

Robert E. Dickinson. "The Geography of Commuting: The Netherlands and Belgium." *Geographical Review*. Vol. 47 (1957), pp. 521–538.

Frans Dussart. "Les Transports en Belgique." *Zeitschrift für Verkehrssicherheit*. Vol. 4 (1958), pp. 1–16.

F. H. W. Green. "Bus Services in the British Isles." *Geographical Review*. Vol. 41 (1951), pp. 645–655.

Hartwig Haubrich. "Moselschiffahrt—Einst und Jetzt." *Geographische Rundschau*. Vol. 19 (1967), pp. 294–302.

George W. Hoffman. "The Iron Gate Project on the Danube River." *Professional Geographer*. Vol. 16 (1964), p. 45.

George W. Hoffman. "Thessaloniki: The Impact of a Changing Hinterland." *East European Quarterly*. Vol. 2 (1968), pp. 1–27.

Mark Jefferson. "The Civilizing Rails." *Economic Geography*. Vol. 4 (1928), pp. 217–231.

Llewellyn R. Jones. *The Geography of London River*. London: Methuen, 1931.

I. B. F. Kormoss (ed.). *Les chemins de fer et l'Europe*. Brugge, Belgium: De Tempel, 1969.

Hendrik Kuipers. "The Changing Landscape of the Island of Rozenburg (Rotterdam Port Area)." *Geographical Review*. Vol. 52 (1962), pp. 362–378.

J. Labadié. "Le grand Canal d'Alsace." *Géographia*. No. 27 (1953), pp. 28–31.

M. Laferrère. "Le projet de laison fluviale Rhine–Rhône." *Revue de Géographie de Lyon*. Vol. 37 (1962), pp. 113–129.

William R. Mead. "Three City Ports of Denmark." *Economic Geography*. Vol. 18 (1942), pp. 41–56.

Aloys A. Michel. "The Canalization of the Moselle and West European Integration." *Geographical Review*. Vol. 52 (1962), p. 475–491.

Francis J. Monkhouse. "Albert and Juliana: Two Great Waterways." *Scottish Geographical Magazine*. Vol. 72 (1956), pp. 163–176.

A. C. O'Dell. *Railways and Geography*. London: Hutchinson, 1956.

Erich Otremba. "Die Rhein–Main–Donau Linie im Rahmen des europäischen Wirtschaftraumes." *Geographische Rundschau*. Vol. 16 (1964), pp. 56–63.

Geoffrey Parker. *An Economic Geography of the Common Market*. London: Longmans, 1968.

J. Allan Patmore. "The British Railway Network in the Beeching Era." *Economic Geography*. Vol. 41 (1965), pp. 71–81.

J. Allan Patmore. "The Contraction of the Network of Railway Passenger Services in England and Wales, 1836–1962." *Institute of British Geographers, Transactions and Papers*. Vol. 38 (1966), pp. 105–118.

Roger Pilkington. "Joining the Rhine and the Rhône." *Geographical Magazine*. Vol. 39 (1966), pp. 214–228.

Norman J. G. Pounds. "Port and Outport in Northwest Europe." *Geographical Journal*. Vol. 109 (1947), pp. 216–228.

Allan L. Rodgers. "The Port of Genova: External and Internal Relations." *Annals, Association of American Geographers.* Vol. 48 (1958), pp. 319–351.

G. Schofield. "The Canalization of the Moselle." *Geography.* Vol. 50 (1965), pp. 161–163.

Kenneth R. Sealy. *The Geography of Air Transport.* London: Hutchinson, 1957.

Kenneth R. Sealy. "The Siting and Development of British Airports." *Geographical Journal.* Vol. 133 (1967), pp. 148–171.

Lawrence M. Sommers. "Distribution and Significance of the Foreign Trade Ports of Norway." *Economic Geography.* Vol. 36 (1960), pp. 306–312.

United Nations. *Statistical Yearbook. Annuaire Statistique.* New York: UN, various issues.

United Nations. *Yearbook of International Trade Statistics.* New York: UN, various issues.

H. D. Watts. "The Inland Waterways of the United Kingdom in the 1960's." *Economic Geography.* Vol. 43 (1967), pp. 303–313.

Guido G. Weigend. "Bordeaux: An Example of Changing Port Functions." *Geographical Review.* Vol. 45 (1955), pp. 217–243.

Westermanns Grosser Atlas zur Weltgeschichte. Braunschweig, West Germany: Georg Westermann, 1956.

H. P. White. "London's Rail Terminals and Their Suburban Traffic: A Geographical Appraisal." *Geographical Review.* Vol. 54 (1964), pp. 347–365.

CHAPTER THIRTEEN

Conclusion

Perhaps the major impressions gained from a geographical study of Europe are the deep-rooted internal diversity of this culture area and the propensity of its people for change and innovation. Change, a hallmark of the European way of life, is so important that an assessment of the direction of future geographical change seems an appropriate theme for this concluding chapter. Overall, the dominant direction of present and future changes appears to be toward integration, toward decreasing internal diversity.

13.1 THE EUROPEAN FUTURE

Almost every facet of the geography of Europe is now changing, in keeping with the dynamic character of this culture area which has long been a center of innovation. It is perhaps most convenient to view these changes and trends by topic.

THE PHYSICAL ENVIRONMENT

The environmental trend in Europe is depressing. Massive alteration of the natural surrounding, begun long ago by Neolithic farmers and Bronze Age axemen, has accelerated since the Industrial Revolution. The destruction of vegetation, accomplished by preindustrial Europeans, is now compounded by widespread pollution of water and air. Perhaps indicative of future conditions was the recent announcement by West German health officials that pollution has made swimming unsafe in the inland waterways of that country and in the adjacent Baltic Sea, North Sea, and Bodensee (Lake Konstanz). The only notable German reaction has been an increase in construction of swimming pools over the past decade.

Massive fish kills have occurred recently in the Rhine River, and there are few parts of Europe which have escaped the pollution problem. Even cities beyond the major industrial core are afflicted with air pollution, including Athínai, where a brownish haze often conceals the "glory that was Greece" from tourists arriving by airplane. The monuments and ruins of antiquity are steadily and rapidly disintegrating in the polluted air. Equally distressing is the litter problem. Many roadsides which were clean as recently as a decade ago are now covered with cans and broken bottles. The historic Pelopónnisian river Eurotas, in which ancient Spartans dipped their newborn children, is today littered with a variety of unsightly human refuse.

An ecological movement is already under way in the more advanced (and thus more polluted) countries of western Europe, but major progress is needed soon if the culture area is to remain a suitable habitat for man. Only in the United Kingdom has the movement led to notable reduction of air pollution, and even there the gains may well be temporary. Antipollution laws have been passed in a number of countries, but solution of the problem will be costly and slow. The more pessimistic ecologists suggest that abuse of the European environment will progress so far as to destroy the basis of present prosperity and way of life, bringing a period of cultural decline, a new Dark Age. It is more likely, however, that the Europeans will employ their vast technology and innovative abilities to solve the environmental problems which now face them.

POPULATION

Continued spread and acceptance of birth-control techniques should stabilize the European population within the next quarter-century or so. Rising literacy rates and improved health conditions in southern and eastern Europe will continue to lessen the contrast in living standard between different parts of the culture area. Average life expectancy and educational levels have already risen sharply in the peripheral regions of Europe during the last twenty-five years, and the trend seems likely to continue.

The improved standard of living in the south and east should diminish the migration of workers from those regions to the European Industrial core and induce others to return to their ancestral homes. Overseas emigration, the choice of many millions of economically oppressed Europeans in the past three or four centuries, will continue to decline, because of both widespread affluence in Europe and the stabilized population. Legal restrictions will diminish the immigration of peoples from former European colonies, such as Africa, the Indian subcontinent, and the West Indies.

LANGUAGE, RELIGION, AND RACE

The distribution of languages will increasingly duplicate the political pattern. The days are numbered for minority languages such as Gaelic, Welsh, Sorbian, Swedish (in Finland), Romansh, and Flemish (in France), as well as almost countless local dialects. Isolation was their refuge, and isolation is a rare phenomenon in Europe today. On the other hand, no movement toward a universal European language is evident, though increased bilingualism and even trilingualism seems likely.

The religious trend is definitely toward a decreased importance of organized churches and traditional Christian dogma, a disaffection now spreading even into the Mediterranean peninsular refuges of Eastern Orthodoxy and Roman Catholicism. Perhaps mainly as a result of this decline, the remnant churches will move increasingly toward union, an ecumenical mood well expressed by the ongoing efforts to reunite the Anglican and Methodist churches in the United Kingdom. Paradoxically, the hatred and conflict between Protestant and Catholic in Northern Ireland appears destined to continue, though the complex issue there concerns more than religious differences.

The trend toward greater uniformity can be seen even in the physical traits of Europeans. Average stature is becoming more uniform with the eradication of malnutrition, the brachycephalization of the population continues, and blondism is declining. Massive mixing of peoples, the result of forced and voluntary migrations, is partly responsible for the trend toward uniformity, as is a decrease in the influence of the physical environment.

POLITICAL GEOGRAPHY

The Soviet–American conflict, which has so profoundly shaped the political order in Europe since 1945, appears to be of lessening importance to the culture area. Over the next quarter-century, Europe will probably be increasingly neutralized, a trend aided by Soviet preoccupation with China and American concentration on serious internal problems.

The American and Soviet "withdrawal" from Europe could well lead to a revival of nationalism; it is already evident that the decreased threat of Soviet invasion has thwarted meaningful progress toward political union within the Common Market. The member nations of the Common Market still lack a uniform currency, a unified postal system, a federal capital city, and a design for the proposed federal government. No substantial progress toward union has been made in recent years outside the economic sphere. Meaningful unification without some outside threat or internal conquest does not fit the pattern exhibited in Europe's political past.

AGRICULTURE AND RURAL SETTLEMENT

Increased specialization and commercialization are unmistakably major trends in European agriculture. As a result of migration to the urban areas of non-Communist Europe, private farms will grow steadily larger and rural population will persist in its decline. The peasantry, that traditional agricultural society found throughout rural Europe as recently as two centuries ago, will disappear, replaced by a class of educated, entrepreneurial farmers. Indicative of these far-reaching changes is the presence of branch banks in most sizable agricultural villages in West Germany.

The fragmented landholding and farm village will give way in non-Communist Europe to unit-block farms and scattered residences, a duplication of the American or Australian pattern. In most of Communist Europe, the trend will be increased uniformity under the state-farm system, as the smaller collectives are joined and the remnant private farms eliminated. Increased mechanization will occur in all types of agriculture. The net result of these changes will be a much more efficient and productive agricultural system throughout Europe.

Traditional forms of rural architecture and building materials, already in sharp decline, will virtually disappear, depriving the European countryside of much of its charm. Already, half-timbering, mud-brick, and log construction are succumbing to the all-pervading concrete block, while traditional styles of folk-housing are giving way to the products of the professional architect's drawing board.

INDUSTRIES AND THE CITIES

The industrialization of Europe, now under way for over two centuries, will continue and spread markedly into the little-industrialized periphery. An increasing proportion of the European population will be concentrated in the cities and towns, and even poorly urbanized outlying areas such as the Balkans and Iberia will become dominated by cities. Much of the archaic will survive in the cities, but urban centers will increasingly bear the imprint of planning and modern steel and glass construction. Glass and steel skyscrapers already violate the serenity and dignity of London's traditional skyline, and the same development is occurring in many cities on the mainland. Particularly in Scandinavia and Finland, entirely new, modernistic satellite cities point the way of the well-planned European urban future. Many of the archaic urban relics of Europe's past may remain only as museum-piece cities, inhabited by people who earn their living from the tourist trade.

TRANSPORTATION

European use of the automobile will continue to rise until American levels are reached. Superhighway construction will be greatly expanded, but automobiles will be barred by law from access to the winding, narrow streets of many medieval or classical cores of Europe's cities. In response to the rise of the automobile, the use of passenger trains will probably become unimportant, and the compact structure of the cities could greatly loosen. Commuting, already on the rise, should continue to increase under the impetus provided by the automobile. Suburbs will become even more common as city-dwellers, using the automobile, flee the congestion and pollution of the central city.

EUROPEANIZATION OF THE WORLD

Another fundamental transition is occurring in Europe's ability to influence and shape the remainder of the world. Most of the Europeanization of alien cultures is now being carried on by peoples residing outside the Old World nucleus of Europe. Americans, Russians, and the strongly Europeanized Japanese are now the principal "missionaries" carrying the culture of Europe to foreign lands. The dynamic leadership long held by mother Europe has to a great degree passed to her overseas children. Indeed, currents of innovation more commonly flow from America to Europe today, reversing the traditional direction of movement. In a proper sense, however, "Americanization" is simply a continuation of Europeanization.

To some who know and love Europe, these geographical changes are offensive, because they lead to the destruction of ancient and beautiful traditions and landscapes. Europe has always changed, however, and change is basic to the entire European way of life. For better or worse, the future Europe will differ in many and diverse ways from the Europe of today, for to remain static would be to violate the essential principle of European culture.

13.2 DECLINING INTERNAL DIVERSITY

The human diversity of Europe, so pronounced as to partially conceal the more basic cultural unity of the area, was a major theme in the preceding discussions of linguistics, race, education, religion, politics, agriculture, industry, and transportation. It is appropriate now to reiterate the theme of unity proposed in the first chapter, particularly in view of declining internal diversity. Most of the changes just outlined are in the direction of greater uniformity. Europeans are perhaps more like each other today than at any time in the past, and the similarity increases with each decade.

Part of the trend toward decreased regional distinctiveness within Europe can be summarized as a continued spread outward of the traits found in the core of the European culture area (Figure 1.6). If the present trend continues, peripheral areas such as Iberia, the Balkans, and eastern Europe will in time come to share the high levels of industrialization, urbanization, education, transportation, and commercialization of agriculture which today typify the core.

Much decline of diversity can be attributed to the spread of the Industrial Revolution, that complex of innovations which is destroying myriad traditional agricultural subcultures in Europe and replacing them with a more uniform modern, industrial society. There is a certain sameness about tractors, steel mills, or hydroelectric plants regardless of where they are found. Another cause of declining diversity is the increased mingling of Europeans across international borders which is now taking place, producing an exchange of ideas. Southern Europeans have come by the millions to lands north of the Alps and Pyrenees as temporary laborers, and similar numbers of the northern Europeans have visited and experienced the southern lands as part of the rising tide of intra-European tourism. Such contacts tend to speed cultural diffusion and similarity. Mass communications, particularly television, have also strengthened interregional ties. The results of such contacts are as diverse and bizarre as beer-drinking Greeks, pizza-eating Germans, sauna-bathing Frenchmen, and rock-and-rolling Romanians.

*   *   *

TO THE GEOGRAPHER, the Europe of today and the future is of prime interest. Perhaps his most fundamental concern is in helping channel the flow of change and innovation in desirable directions. Urban and regional planning, traditional concerns of economic and cultural geographers, will place great demands on our academic discipline in the near future. Already European geographers have made lasting and significant contributions to planning, particularly in Britain, Scandinavia, West Germany, and the Netherlands, but much work lies ahead.

For well over a century, some geographers have directed attention to ecology, to man's role in changing the face of the earth. In coming decades physical geographers will be called upon to help solve the monumental environmental problems produced by the expanding technology of Europe's peoples. This may well be the greatest service that will be rendered by future geographers.

Concern with change will be complemented by the cultural-historical geographer's interest in preserving vestiges of Europe's past. Samples of traditional settlement patterns, folk architecture, peasant agricultural technology, household industry, and the like will be set aside for preservation, and the geographer will aid in this valuable work. In a culture so inclined to rapid change, contact with the physical vestiges of the past is desirable and perhaps even psychologically necessary.

Index

79 80 9 8 7 6 5 4